M000103872

Postsecular Cities

Continuum Resources in Religion and Political Culture
Series Editors: Graham Ward and Michael Hoelzl, The University of
Manchester, UK.

Aimed at undergraduates studying in this area, titles in this series look
specifically at the key topics involved in the relationship between religion and
politics, taking into account a broad range of religious perspectives, and
presenting clear, approachable texts for students grappling with often complex
concepts.

From Political Theory to Political Theology, edited Péter Losonczi and
Aakash Singh

The New Visibility of Religion, Graham Ward and Michael Hoelzl
Remoralizing Britain, edited by Peter Manly Scott, Christopher R. Baker
and Elaine L. Graham

Postsecular Cities

Space, Theory and Practice

Editors

Justin Beaumont
Christopher Baker

continuum

Continuum International Publishing Group

The Tower Building	80 Maiden Lane
11 York Road	Suite 704
London SE1 7NX	New York NY 10038

www.continuumbooks.com

© Justin Beaumont, Christopher Baker and Contributors 2011

All rights reserved. No part of this publication may be reproduced or transmitted in any form or by any means, electronic or mechanical, including photocopying, recording, or any information storage or retrieval system, without prior permission in writing from the publishers.

British Library Cataloguing-in-Publication Data
A catalogue record for this book is available from the British Library.

ISBN: PB: 978-1-4411-4425-6

Library of Congress Cataloging-in-Publication Data
A catalog record for this book is available from the Library of Congress.

Typeset by Newgen Imaging Systems Pvt Ltd, Chennai, India
Printed and bound in India

Contents

List of Contributors

About the Editors

Justin Beaumont is Assistant Professor at the Faculty of Spatial Sciences, University of Groningen in the Netherlands, and is the chief architect of the EU-7FP FACIT project. In the frame of new forms of urban politics, he has recently developed new enquires on the postsecular city, faith-based organizations and social justice in cities. His articles appear in *International Journal of Urban and Regional Research, Urban Studies, Environment and Planning A, Space and Polity, Area* and *TESG*. Justin is co-editor of *Spaces of Contention: Spatialities of Social Movements* (Aldershot: Ashgate, with Walter Nicholls and Byron Miller); *Exploring the Postsecular: The Religious, the Political and the Urban* (Leiden/Boston: Brill, with Arie Molendijk and Christoph Jedan); *Faith, Welfare and Exclusion in European Cities: The FBO Phenomenon* (Bristol: The Policy Press, with Paul Cloke and Jan Vranken) and *Faith That Works: Faith-based Organizations and Urban Social Justice* (Milton Keynes/Carlisle: Paternoster Press, with Paul Cloke).

Christopher Baker is Director of Research for the William Temple Foundation and Senior Lecturer in Public and Urban Theology at the University of Chester. He has written and researched extensively on the role of faith in urban regeneration, public policy and civil society in the United Kingdom and beyond. His book *The Hybrid Church in the City – Third Space Thinking* (Ashgate, 2007) was republished in 2009 by SCM Press. Other publications (jointly edited) include *Mapping the New Theological Space – Blurred Encounters in Faith, Politics and Community* (Ashgate, 2009) and *Remoralising Britain – Social, Ethical and Theological Perspectives on New Labour* (Continuum, 2009). His latest book, *Christianity and the New Social Order* (SCM Press), will be published in 2011.

About the Contributors

Gregory Ashworth is Professor of Heritage Management and Urban Tourism in the Department of Planning, Faculty of Spatial Sciences, University of Groningen, the Netherlands, and Visiting Professor at the Institute of Conservation, University of Gothenburg, Sweden. His research and publication interests have long focused upon heritage, tourism and place marketing/branding in urban contexts.

Rachael Chapman is Senior Lecturer at Northumbria University, Newcastle upon Tyne in the UK. Her research expertise and interests focus on governance and community participation, including faith and civil society engagement. She is currently leading a research project investigating effective engagement and partnership between local authorities and faith groups (funded by Local Government Improvement and Development), and has undertaken research on Hindu–Christian relations (funded by Department of Communities and Local Government) and the contribution of faith groups to social action and civil renewal (with Professor Vivien Lowndes, De Montfort University). She has published several articles and book chapters on faith representation and engagement in urban governance.

Paul Cloke is Professor of Geography at the University of Exeter, United Kingdom. His recent research has focused on geographies of ethics, with major projects on urban services for homeless people (with Jon May and Sarah Johnsen) and on campaigning for ethical consumption (with Clive Barnett, Nick Clarke and Alice Malpass) culminating in four books: *Swept Up Lives* (Wiley-Blackwell); *Consuming Ethics* (Wiley-Blackwell); *Governing Consumption* (Berg) and *Globalizing Responsibility* (Wiley-Blackwell). Paul has published over 20 books and 200 articles and chapters on aspects of social, cultural and political geography.

Andrew Davey is the National Adviser on Community and Urban Affairs for the Church of England. He has been a parish priest in inner London, and undertook doctoral research on liberation and narrative theologies from a parish perspective. He has written extensively on the impact of globalization within urban faith communities and the interaction of theology with critical urban theory. He is editor of the URBLOG website and an honorary lecturer at Manchester and Chester Universities. Andrew is author of *Urban Christianity and Global Order: Theological Resources for an Urban Future* (SPCK, 2001; Hendrickson, 2002), *The Urban Challenge* (Rikkyo University, 2005) and editor of *Crossover City: Resources for Urban Mission and Transformation* (Mowbray-Continuum, 2010).

John Eade is Professor of Sociology and Anthropology at Roehampton University, London, Executive Director of CRONEM (Centre for Research on Nationalism, Ethnicity and Multiculturalism) at the University of Surrey and Roehampton University and Visiting Professor at University College London. His research has focused on urban ethnicity, identity politics, the global city and pilgrimage. His publications include *Placing London* (2000) and *The Politics of Community* (1989), the single-edited *Living the Global City* (1997) and the co-edited *Accession and Migration* (2009), *Transnational Ties* (2008), *Global Ethics and Civil Society* (2005), *Reframing Pilgrimage* (2004), *Understanding the City* (2002), *Contesting the Sacred* (2000/1991) and *Divided Europeans* (1999). He is currently completing a co-authored book on Polish migrants in London.

Tovi Fenster is Professor of Geography at the Department of Geography and Human Environment, at the Tel Aviv University. She is the founder and Head of Planning for the Environment with Communities – PEC Lab (http://peclab.tau.

ac.il/) and previously Head of the Women and Gender Studies Program (2007–2009). She has had published articles and book chapters on ethnicity, citizenship and gender in planning and development. Tovi is the editor of *Gender, Planning and Human Rights* (1999, Routldege), the author of *The Global City and the Holy City: Narratives on Knowledge, Planning and Diversity* (Pearson, 2004) and editor (with Haim Yacobi) of *Remembering, Forgetting and City Builders* (Ashgate, 2010). She is also the founder and the first chair (2000–2003) of Bimkom – Planners for Planning Rights in Israel and has been on the board of directors of the Association for Civil Rights in Israel (1994–1999).

Robbie B. H. Goh is Associate Professor in the Department of English Language and Literature, National University of Singapore, Vice-Dean of the Faculty of Arts and Social Sciences, and Deputy Director of its Asia Research Institute. He works mainly on Asian Diasporic/Postcolonial Literatures and Cultures, and on Christianity in Asia. Recent publications include *Theorizing the Southeast Asian City as Text* (co-edited with Brenda S. A. Yeoh, 2003); *Asian Diasporas: Cultures, Identities, Representations* (co-edited with Shawn Wong, 2004), *Christianity in Southeast Asia* (2005), *Contours of Culture: Space and Social Difference in Singapore* (2005), and articles appearing in *Material Religion, Crossroads, Journal of Commonwealth Literature, Social Semiotics* and other journals.

Elaine Graham is Grosvenor Research Professor of Practical Theology at the University of Chester, UK, and was (until October 2009) Samuel Ferguson Professor of Social & Pastoral Theology) at the University of Manchester. Her publications include *Making the Difference: Gender, Personhood and Theology* (1995) and *Transforming Practice: Pastoral Theology in an Age of Uncertainty* (1996, 2nd ed., 2002), *Representations of the Post/ Human* (2002), *Words Made Flesh* (2009) and (with H. Walton and F. Ward) *Theological Reflection: Methods* (2005). Throughout her career, she has maintained an interest in the relationship between theology and social theory, through work on urban theology and the contribution of faith-based organizations to civil society. Between 2004 and 2006 she was a member of the multi-faith and ecumenical *Commission on Urban Life and Faith*, which was set up to examine the state of our cities and towns 20 years on from the report, *Faith in the City*. Its report was published as *Faithful Cities: A Call for Celebration, Vision and Justice* (Methodist Publishing House, 2006). She is currently working on a book on public theology in a postsecular society.

Clara Greed is Professor of Inclusive Urban Planning at the University of the West of England in Bristol. Her academic and professional work focuses on 'women and planning' issues, urban design, and planning for 'the city of everyday life' and the potential rapprochement between confessional faith-based discourses and other secular disciplines for the sake of a common planning agenda. She is also interested in evolving forms and patterns of church that are emerging to meet the complexities of the postsecular city.

Anni Greve is Associate Professor at Roskilde University, Denmark, with key competences in classical and modern sociology. Today most of her work concerns the implications of globalization for the analysis of the social world. Her specialist research interests are cities with success at a global level (Tokyo), and at the European level, new forms of social integration, religion, risk and security and bonds of civility. Her latest book *Sanctuaries of the City: Lessons from Tokyo*, is to be published in 2011 by Ashgate. Her work has been translated into English, French and Japanese. She is a founding member of Centre of Urban Studies at Roskilde University.

Leila Hamalainen (nee Thorp) is Lecturer in the Department of Public Policy, De Montfort University, Leicester. She has been active in researching the UK government's policy of Community Cohesion and has considered the position of faith groups in local governance. In particular, she is concerned with understanding changes to political interest representation and group recognition and identification within the public sphere. Her PhD assessed the changes to Polish civil society within this context, and in other work she has conducted an action research project on the UK policy of Preventing Violent Extremism and explored the citizenship of new migrants in relation to local governance. Related publications are Vivien Lowndes and Leila Thorp (2010) 'Preventing Violent Extremism – Why Local Context Matters, in *The New Extremism in 21st Century Britain* (Abingdon: Routledge); 'New Migrants, Citizenship and Local Governance: 'Poles' Apart? in *Changing Local Governance, Changing Citizens* (Bristol: The Policy Press).

David Ley is Canada Research Chair and Head of Geography at the University of British Columbia. His teaching and research focus is the social geography of large cities. Earlier research analysed gentrification and neighbourhood change; current work concerns immigration, including immigrant religion. Books include *The New Middle Class and the Re-making of the Central City, Neighbourhood Organizations and the Welfare State* (with Shlomo Hasson), and *A Social Geography of the City*. His new book, *Millionaire Migrants: Trans-Pacific Life Lines*, was published in 2010 by Wiley-Blackwell. David Ley is a Fellow of the Royal Society of Canada.

Gregor McLennan is Professor of Sociology and Director of the Institute for Advanced Studies at the University of Bristol. Author of *Marxism and the Methodologies of History*; *Marxism, Pluralism and Beyond*; *Pluralism*; *Exploring Society* and *Sociological Cultural Studies: Reflexivity and Positivity in the Human Sciences*, Gregor is also co-editor of a number of volumes of social and political theory. He is currently working on a book-length critical appraisal of postsecular social theory.

Angus Paddison is Lecturer in Theology in the Department of Theology and Religious Studies, University of Winchester, UK. His research has previously concentrated on the theological interpretation of Scripture, and he has published *Theological Hermeneutics and 1 Thessalonians* (2005) and *Scripture: A Very Theological Proposal* (2009), along with essays and contributions to edited volumes. His current research focuses on political theology and theological ethics, with an emphasis on the work of John Howard Yoder and Stanley Hauerwas. Angus

Paddison's next major book project is on political theology and radical democracy.

Leonie Sandercock is a Professor in the School of Community and Regional Planning at the University of British Columbia. Her recent books include *Towards Cosmopolis: Planning for Multicultural Cities* (1998); the edited collection *Making the Invisible Visible: a multicultural history of planning* (1998); and *Cosmopolis 2: Mongrel Cities of the 21st Century* (2003), which won the Davidoff Award of the American Collegiate Schools of Planning in 2005. Her research explores the potential of multimedia as a catalyst for community engagement, empowerment and policy dialogue. With Giovanni Attili, she made the award-winning documentary *Where Strangers Become Neighbours* (National Film Board of Canada, 2007). Sandercock and Attili's book plus DVD package, *Where Strangers Become Neighbours: The Integration of Immigrants in Vancouver*, was published by Springer in 2009. A second documentary with Giovanni Attili, *Finding our Way: Beyond Canada's Apartheid*, looks at relations between First Nations and non-Native Canadians in northern British Columbia (Moving Images, 2010; for more information, see www.facebook.com/FINDING.OUR.WAY.thefilm. Sandercock and Attili have also published an edited collection, *Multimedia Explorations in Urban Policy and Planning: Beyond the Flatlands* (Springer, 2010).

Maged Senbel is Assistant Professor of Urban Design at the School of Community and Regional Planning at the University of British Columbia. His research focuses on analytical methods for assessing the ecological performance of cities as well as the deliberative and participatory processes that contribute to implementing sustainable designs. He has given numerous keynote speeches on the relationship between spirituality and environmental ethics with an emphasis on Islamic epistemology. Maged is also a professional planner with expertise in community engagement in climate responsive urban design.

Nynke de Witte is a Researcher at the Dutch Court of Audit. She has an M.Phil in Political and Social Sciences from the University of Pompeu Fabra, Barcelona, and a Bachelor's and Master's degree in Human Geography from the Radboud University Nijmegen. From September 2008 to February 2010, she worked as a researcher for the EU seventh framework project FACIT (Faith-based Organisations and Exclusion in European Cities). From September 2006 to July 2008, she worked as a researcher for the EU sixth framework project EMILIE, A European Approach to Multicultural Citizenship.

Preface:
Towards the Postsecular City?

David Ley

A few years ago I returned, after a gap of two decades, to the site of my doctoral research in an Afro-American neighbourhood in inner-city Philadelphia. To be sure, visible changes had occurred. The neighbourhood had thinned out with the demolition of empty and abandoned structures, leaving eerie discontinuities in the built environment. The mainline church where I had met with local teenagers during my period of residence had disappeared to be replaced by a neat cluster of seniors' housing bearing the church's name *in memoriam*. Otherwise, there was limited new neighbourhood construction with one major exception. An independent Pentecostal church that had existed in an empty cinema during my fieldwork in the early 1970s had evidently prospered, for it had relocated to a new campus with an extensive parking lot and a substantial church structure accommodating five times as many worshippers as before. Here is persuasive evidence one might say for the existence of the postsecular city: the neighbourhood's largest single investment in the built environment over the past 30 years is a new Pentecostal complex, representing the growth sector of global Protestantism.

But on reflection, I wonder about that prefix 'post' in the putative postsecular city. In a recent essay on 'post-multiculturalism', I ruminated on the profusion of 'posts' in contemporary social science. Is the world indeed changing so rapidly across so many dimensions with such marked discontinuities that we can so confidently mark the end of one era and the start of another? Or are we miscalculating the degree of change that is taking place? Could it be that what has changed is the focus of our gaze rather than the things themselves? Let's return to inner city Philadelphia. When I conducted my fieldwork around 1970, I worked with a neighbourhood NGO that met in three different local churches. Ministers were members of the board, and a number of local volunteers were Christians. I made little of these overlapping identities in my text. Nearby – yet strangely unmentioned in my research – was the Zion Baptist Church, then headed by the 'Lion of Zion', the Rev. Leon Sullivan. At the time of my fieldwork Zion had close to 6,000 members. In addition to its spiritual and social ministries, the church launched a credit union, held a number of housing and industrial properties and built a retail mall

('Progress Plaza') as part of its economic development portfolio. It was arguably the major force for positive community development in a deindustrialized and asset-stripped setting. Yet my ethnography scarcely noticed it; my intellectual gaze was elsewhere. The constellation of religious settings, practices and community leadership was only of incidental interest in my research.

So from my own history of omissions, I would caution against too expansive a claim for novelty among the things themselves. What has changed in the postsecular city is our attention to them. In the global north, two important processes have contributed to this change of focus. The neoliberal turn and the stripping down of the welfare state have returned us to a condition where public charity once again is called upon, and charitable welfare has always been a calling of faith-based organizations. So religious institutions play a more public and more visible role in social service delivery. Second, 9/11, the War on Terror, and subsequent terrorist events in Europe and elsewhere have focused attention on militant mutations of world religions. But these events provide just the most spectacular version of a much broader engagement between the greater religious exuberance of the global south with a more somnolent spirituality in Europe and overseas regions of northern European settlement (with the important exception of the United States). Immigration from the developing world has been one of the forces bringing significant challenges to secularization theory in the old world. In his book, *God's Continent*, Philip Jenkins points to the role of immigration in re-invigorating religious membership in Europe. This is not simply a matter of the presence of the immigrant religion of Islam, for Jenkins notes that the pastors of four of the ten largest Protestant churches in England are now Africans.

These events have brought discussion of the place of religion in the public realm back into lively debate in modern societies whose secular elites had thought they had safely consigned faith-based discourse to personal practice and practical insignificance. Moreover, the pluralism of postmodern philosophies and multicultural societies make such dogmatic closures of the past no longer tenable. As the editors of this valuable collection state, it is this reconfigured discourse that gives substance to the idea of the postsecular city. Perhaps the clearest intellectual evidence of making space for religion is the reformulation of Jurgen Habermas, one of the most eloquent and thoughtful defenders of the Enlightenment project. In his 2006 essay in the *European Journal of Philosophy*, Habermas seeks to lay out the presuppositions for secular and faith-based *rapprochement* in the public sphere. Indeed, he had already gone further than this by opening public discussion with Joseph Cardinal Ratzinger on the mutual accommodation of secular and religious reason. A second line of evidence for the growing place of religion in the public sphere is the behaviour of a group whom Habermas calls 'militant secularists', those who attempt to batten down the hatches to keep the religious genie out of sight and out of mind. In the English-speaking world, Richard Dawkins and Christopher Hitchens would be among this group, together with their admirers who campaigned to post anti-theist advertisements on British buses. But many observers find such dogmatism grating. *The Guardian's* correspondent, Madeleine Bunting, astutely contrasted the middle class movement in 2009 to place anti-

Christian advertisements on public transport with the poor immigrant Bible readers she saw as passengers on her own London bus. The Habermas model would prefer reflexivity and mutual learning between the parties who claim the inside and the outside of the bus.

As is evident from the diversity of the chapters that follow, as yet, there is no consensus about approaches to studying the emerging consciousness, discourses and practices of religion in modern urban societies. Instead we find the vigour of individual creative insights. It is too early to force a consensus upon work that is vital and in its early stages of development. Authors in this book bring different theorists as travelling companions, and different interpretations of religion, or at least of spirituality. As Habermas has intimated, the tenor of the conversation between faith and social science requires reflexivity on both sides. The kind of transition that is needed is not satisfied with seeing the activism of faith-based organizations and their members as mere agents of a shadow state manipulated by impecunious but surveillant politicians, or as playing out roles prescribed by some grand theory. An older liberal or Marxist sociology of religion that saw religion in terms of a role-bearing function in a larger social system will make no progress in the more challenging world of hermeneutic discovery. But neither will a project that provocatively claims that only religion can examine religion be an adequate starting point. A much fuller intellectual project considers the actions of the caregivers, their definition of the situation and their extrapolation of a sacred text in everyday practice. Knowledge in this scenario requires not the colonization of religion by secular schematics but patient learning that pays tribute in its exposition to the language of faith and the categories of theology as well as the disciplines of the social sciences.

Introduction: The Rise of the Postsecular City

Justin Beaumont and Christopher Baker

This year (2010) marks the fortieth anniversary of the recording and release of *Bitches Brew*. This unconventional, radical and ground-breaking studio double album by Miles Davis revolutionized jazz history and became a progenitor of the jazz rock fusion genre of the 1970s and beyond. On this record, which brought to audiences Joe Zawinul's *Pharaoh's Dance*, Wayne Shorter's *Sanctuary,* as well as Miles's own *Spanish Key* and *Miles Runs the Voodoo Down*, Davis (for Duke Ellington the 'Picasso of Jazz') brought in electric piano and guitar into the more standard jazz repertoire, rejecting traditional jazz rhythms in favour of a darker, radicalized and looser rock-oriented and improvisational style. The fusion of African and Western influences as well as the incorporation of rock styles continues to inspire musicians across a variety of genres today, and the album remains one of the most important revelations in the history of music.

The notion of *fusion*, or the closely related but distinct 'rapprochement' for Paul Cloke (in this volume), similarly defines the spirit behind *Postsecular Cities*, which calls for radical new ways of thinking about cities at the interface between disciplines, theoretical orientations and philosophical perspectives. The book reflects the widespread belief that the twenty-first century is evolving in a significantly different way than that of the twentieth, which witnessed the advance of human rationality and technological progress, including urbanization, and called into question the public and cultural significance of religion. In this century, by contrast, religion, faith communities and spiritual values have returned to the centre of public life, especially public policy, governance, and social identity. Rapidly diversifying urban locations are the best places to witness the emergence of new spaces in which religions and spiritual traditions are creating both new alliances but also bifurcations with secular sectors. *Postsecular Cities* examines how the built environment reflects these trends.

The title of this essay collection equally draws attention to another landmark event which preceded *Bitches Brew* by just a few years. *The Secular City,* by American theologian Harvey Cox and first published in 1965, was a theological justification of the power of the modern city to radically reshape both human society and the church for the better. The secular city, for Cox, represented the urban–secular paradigm by which humankind was to attain the heights of autonomy, creativity and progress.

The *Technopolis*, as he called his secular city, best expressed for him the evidence (first suggested by his great mentor Dietrich Bonhoeffer over 20 years earlier) that humankind had 'come of age'. The truly radical theological premise at the heart of this positive reading of secularization in the mid-1960s (and thus just before the great disruptions of Paris in 1968, and the Vietnam protests in the United States and elsewhere) was that the secular city, and the human freedom and autonomy that it epitomized, was willed and ordained by God as an instrument of true human liberation. God, so Cox suggested, wills humankind to move beyond a religion that fosters dependency and promotes regressive superstition and authority, to a form of faith that encourages co-maturity; where in the words attributed to Jesus in St John's Gospel, we learn to worship God 'in Spirit and in Truth' (John 4:24). God wills this transformation by working within the processes of human history and development, rather than outside or against them.

This human-oriented view of salvation, history and development is located within a number of foundational events, as reflected in metanarratives of the Hebrew Scriptures. For example, the act of creation by God out of nothing (*ex nihilo*) in the first chapter of Genesis marks God's separation from nature. It marks the idea of human liberation from gods and local places and spaces, towards an understanding of God as covenant and universal presence. Meanwhile, the experience of God's chosen people wandering in the desert following their escape from slavery in Egypt, known as the Exodus, reflects the idea that God's will is achieved through historical events and political powers. Time is now linear, working towards a future dénouement, represented as a Heavenly City (a new Jerusalem – see later references in this volume), rather than cyclical. There is therefore no enchanted magic required to summon or placate the gods of nature. Rather, humankind has now advanced towards a disenchanted time where truth, liberation and salvation are to be found within the concrete and material processes and experiences of human endeavour and suffering. God is no longer controlled by magic or ritual.

The postsecular city, by contrast to the utopian liberal uplift of the secular city (in which the role of the church and theology is to act as force of social progressive change and a cultural exorciser against all oppressive practices which reinforce hierarchies of power and dependency), reflects a more contested space where hitherto distinct categories are increasingly converging within a postmetaphysical composite. In the postsecular city, the dividing lines (and hence) roles of religion and science, faith and reason, tradition and innovation are no longer rigidly enforced (or indeed enforcible), and new relations of possibility are emerging.

Recognizing that the 'turn to the postsecular' is indeed a contested and multifaceted trend, we offer a vigorous, open but structured dialogue between theory and practice, but even more excitingly, between the disciplines of human geography and theology. Both disciplines reflect on this powerful but enigmatic force shaping our urban humanity.

In this volume, we understand the term 'postsecular' as a continuation of the approach taken in the recent *Exploring the Postsecular* (Molendijk et al., 2010). In the first essay of that collection, one of us claims that the postsecular

> ...does not infer that we now live in a radically different age compared with half a century ago [rather, the term refers to] ... the limits of the secularization thesis and the ever-growing realization of radically plural societies in terms of religion, faith and belief within and between diverse urban societies. If we consider postsecular as the indication of diverse religious, humanist and secularist positionalities – and not merely an assumption of complete and total secularization – it is precisely the relations between these dimensions and not just the religious that are taken into account and [are] the focus of attention. (Beaumont, 2010: 6)

We use this important starting point to take the debate further via active dialogue between human geography (and social sciences more generally) with theology. While *Exploring the Postsecular* and the conference in Groningen that preceded it brought an exciting array of urbanists, geographers, sociologists, theologians and philosophers to the table, which generated a great deal of energy and enthusiasm, the event and subsequent publication were less able to overcome persistent disciplinary divides, epistemological and ontological positions (albeit largely implicit) and divergent word-views. Just as Rudyard Kipling lamented in his 1892 *Barack-Room Ballads* that '[Oh], East is East and West is West, and never the twain shall meet' (Kipling, 2010), similarly the degree of mutual dialogue and interaction, while nobly attempted, remained regrettably limited. *Postsecular Cities* makes an unprecedented and crucial step to overcome this deficiency.

Fortunately, we are now a million miles away, figuratively speaking, from Kipling's military ditties during the British imperial occupation of India. But nevertheless, questions about radically plural postmodern and postcolonial societies, mutual dialogue and progressive interaction between diverse social, cultural and political groups and identities, and the means for the reconciliation and unity in difference remain pressing (and largely unresolved) intellectual concerns. Without aligning too closely with the Situationist International, the new Babylonians and unitarist and psychogeographical interpretations of urbanism (in the vein of Guy Debord's *Society of the Spectacle* and others), we at any rate share a similar interest in new ways of thinking, seeing and understanding cities that pay attention to the flows of interaction between diverse groups, religious, humanist and secular; their relationships; and structures as well as emotions and the possibilities for emancipation they might entail. Let us be clear: by focusing on the changing role of religion in late capitalist societies for a better understanding of cities, we are not arguing for a new particularism nor yet another identity in multiplicity. Our approach aims towards greater interaction across and integration between disciplines in order to understand cities at the theoretical and epistemological nexus of the political economy of neoliberalism and religion.

Unsurprisingly, our approach does not come uncontested. Just as the initial reception to Miles's revolutionary masterpiece combined critical acclaim with what amounted to at times as downright aversion, nascent and developing debates on postsecularism and postsecular cities in particular have attracted a curious blend of sympathetic critics and more agnostic sceptics. We would place Lily Kong, the long-standing doyen and figurehead of the (new) geographies of religion at the National University of Singapore, in the first category. In a recent review of the literature, Kong notes the seductive appeal of the concept of the postsecular (Kong, 2010). She questions whether the contemporary situation actually reflects continuity or change; whether mutual engagements with the sacred and the secular reflect the arrival of something new or whether they are indicative of new expressions of what was and remains always there.

We seek to align ourselves with some of these important advances in the analysis of religion in cities and in human geography, more generally, in recent years. We wish to argue (critiques notwithstanding) that the concept of the postsecular presents a new, important and exciting conceptual apparatus in order to understand cities in ways that transcend the excesses of postmodern heterogeneity and nihilistic relativism with something fresh and new.

Marking the terrain

This volume will seek to achieve these aims in the context of seven specific areas of debate which the editors have identified as indicative of a shift from secular to postsecular discourses (see Beaumont, 2010 for more details). First, the re-emergence of the idea of the sacred as applied to the advancement of urban space and community development; second, the nature of the urban (postcolonial diversity/ plurality and global hub) as the locus in which the dynamics of religio-secular change are revealed and expressed with greatest intensity, if not always the greatest clarity; third, the return of the language of virtue in respect of public life/ civil society and the search for mutual understandings of the common good between religions and secularism; fourth, the ongoing commitment to social and urban justice on the part of religious organizations and traditions – for example, the Catholic social movement and its roots in such diverse movements as the worker priest movement in France, democratic movements in Eastern Europe and liberation theologies in Latin and South America and beyond; fifth, the connection between the growth of Pentecostal Christianity and neoliberal globalization, as well as evangelism and social justice within the most excluded and diasporic urban communities; sixth, the re-engagement of faith and politics, especially in the contentious areas of governance and public service delivery; and finally, the contested understanding of multiculturalism under the impact of recent high-profile cases of religious freedom of expression in relation to human rights legislation and the rise of Islamophobia.

Defining the meaning of postsecularism in the theory and practice of urban life stems from the key observation that it is in 'the urban' that the shift from secular to postsecular in terms of public space, building use, governance and civil society is most intensely observed and experienced. We believe therefore that it is imperative that hitherto somewhat abstract, episodic and multidisciplinary reflections are rooted in observation of and reflection upon highly concrete and specific urban case studies. This book therefore explores the changing dynamics between religion and postsecular cities in order to understand the growing resurgence of faith and spirituality in the urban and public realm since the start of the twenty-first century. Everywhere we look, questions of secularism and alleged postsecularism feature within academic, policy and media circles. However, very little work provides theoretical and empirical coherence on these issues across various disciplinary divides. The volume therefore provides an unprecedented collection of chapter contributions that offer a coherent reference source on postsecularism and how it impacts the urban realm.

The public resurgence of religion is clearly one of the defining features of this century (see Casanova, 1990), which has not continued the modernist and secularized trajectory assumed during the latter half of the twentieth century. Globalized societies on all continents find themselves caught in a series of contradictory dynamics, including simultaneous and dialectical processes of secularization alongside the growing deprivatization of faith and its re-emergence as a shaper of cultural, political, economic processes – for example, the growing significance of faith-based welfare/public service provision and social enterprise, the impact of new places of worship on urban and suburban spaces, the resurgence of Pentecostalism and its connection with neoliberal globalization and their joint impact on mega and global cities, especially in Southeast Asia, Africa and Latin America. This globalizing dynamic has led in recent times to the idea of the postsecular society, particularly within 'postsecular' sociology. For example, Peter Berger et al. (1999), in a reformulation of his original secularization thesis developed in the 1950s and 1960s, claims that it is now more accurate to talk about the processes of desecularization. By this concept, he refers to the exponential growth of those religious forms which could be labelled 'furious', 'supernaturalist', 'fundamentalist' or 'conservative' at the direct expense of those more liberal or mainstream forms of religion that are more comfortable within the currently perceived framework of modernity.

Meanwhile, Jürgen Habermas has recently sought to define and promote 'a postsecular self-understanding of society as a whole, in which the vigorous continuation of religion in a continually secularizing environment must be reckoned with' (Habermas, 2005: 26). To that end, therefore, postsecular culture must openly recognize religion not as a set of private beliefs but as an all-embracing source of energy, not only for the devout but for society in general as well (2006: 7–10). Alongside and of course mutually imbricated with these shifts in sociological perspectives are ongoing approaches to the spaces of religion reflected in the concept of new geographies of religion (Kong, 2010) and recent anthropological forays into spaces of modernity in relation to the urban (see Hancock and Srinivas, 2008 and the various contributions therein).

This book aims to reflect on the so-called rise of postsecular cities by offering different understandings of them from a variety of interdisciplinary perspectives. Although foregrounding the contributions of urban theory and praxis, other key voices contributing to a 360-degree view of this new space will be those from philosophy, sociology, political economy, contextual theology and cultural studies.

The contributions

Our multidisciplinary approach will be carried out with reference to four sections. The sections reflect a narrative structure that moves from an engagement with the current multidisciplinary understandings of the 'postsecular' and the postsecular city (Section 1: *Theoretical terrain* and 2: *Competing experiences of postsecular cities*), then addresses praxis emerging from the ground in this new geopolitical and cultural space between the secular and the religious/spiritual (Section 3: *Postsecular policies and practice*). Section 4: *Theologiocal and secular interpretations* reflects further on the nature of the postsecular city via case studies and theories presented from both religious/theological and secular-based perspectives, before a final chapter concludes with an identification of new trajectories and research agendas in respect of this important new area of praxis-based urban theory.

Section 1 consists of one chapter by Gregor McLennan that takes issue with the pioneering work of David Harvey and also Ash Amin in thinking about cities. He argues that Harvey's *Social Justice and the City* had three main components: realist epistemology, a priority of social justice over liberal rightness, and a sense of revolutionary transformation as a necessary consequence. Postsecular considerations, for McLennan, have overwhelmed, complicated, or put into question the straight secular(ist) basis of radical urban critique, thus allowing the conditions of 'faith' and 'faith groups', at least in principle, to come to dominate discussions of radical urban change. McLennan shows how critical realist epistemology has entered into debates around religion. He also shows how thinkers on the Left, like Eagleton and Dews, now view ethics from a quasi-religious standpoint and how Left political consciousness, as theorized by Badiou, Zizek and Unger, arguably take a spiritualized form. The chapter, moreover, takes issue with Ash Amin's (2006) theorization of the good city and draws conclusions about the sociological value of these contributions and their political motivations.

Section 2 begins with a chapter by Chris Baker and Justin Beaumont that maps and then analyses the impact of postcolonial religious identity and experience of the postsecular city, particularly with reference to UK-based research. Previous analyses have tended to be rather broad-brushed level and have generally ignored the closely grained and unique character of local spaces and spatialities. The authors attend to both the political and spatial dimensions of this interface between religion, spirituality and identity. They offer a brief review of ideas and theories regarding the postcolonial city, categorized into optimistic or pessimistic readings. Few readings of postcolonial urban space make reference to the role and significance of religion per se. The chapter presents a series of 'snapshots' of how religious faith and activity, especially that generated by immigrant communities, is creating different types of 'space' within the postsecular city. Three case studies (featuring different faith communities) will show how primarily religious identities interact with public norms and expectations generated by British society. The chapter concludes by correlating emerging evidence of this postcolonial religious experience with key thinking within political philosophy concerning the foundations of a new public space in the West.

Chapter 3, by Robbie Goh, examines the ways in which prominent city churches – including some of the so-called mega-churches – are increasingly positioning themselves as new church–market hubs. He argues that this process involves a kind of religious appropriation of the market, including a theological clarification of the relationship between religion and the market-wealth-numbers nexus. This relationship is, at the same time, market integration with the church – often in actual overlaps of physical space, otherwise in symbolic or connectional ways. The phenomenon is very much linked to the global city, both in terms of its ideological affinities (most evident in the transnational links of some of these churches) as well as in terms of religious capitalization on the branding, people movements and consumption ethos of the city.

In the following chapter, Tovi Fenster presents the visual representations of the Lefebvrian notion of the right to the city as it is expressed in the streets of Jerusalem. She claims that the emergence of the idea of the sacred in today's construction of public spaces, building use, governance and civil society is different in Jerusalem than in most cities in the world. While other papers in this volume report on the revival of religion as one of the explicit features of this century and a turning point from the modernist and secularized trajectory, Jerusalem, for Fenster, represents a case where religious-contested geographies are part of its history as well as its everyday life and a place where secularity and religiosity exist in constant tension. The chapter focuses on street signs and graffiti as visual representations of the struggle for the right to the city. Other elements such as the Sabbath songs, prayers from private homes (and not synagogues) and the appearance of Jewish rituals in the streets of the city during certain Jewish holidays represent different types of 'appropriation' of public spaces. These activities indicate intangible cultural boundaries between religiosity and secularity that should be looked at when investigating postsecular urban spaces.

Chapter 5, by Leonie Sandercock and Maged Senbel, explores the convergence of thinking across a number of fields, from environmental/ecological planning to landscape architecture, urban design and community economic development, around attachment to community and attachment to place. These attachments reflect love and deep knowledge of and reverence for one's bioregion, along with all forms of life therein, not only human. The authors argue that addressing this attachment goes back to basic questions of meaning and value and encourages the re-emergence of ideas of caring for each other and caring for the earth. Their approach is deeply spiritual and the values that are converging are doing so around the sacredness of places and their inhabitants. The chapter draws upon the authors' long-term experience with Neighbourhood House, one of the most culturally diverse, low income neighbourhoods in Vancouver, where a sense of welcome has been created that transcends preexisting expressions of xenophobia and other negativities.

Clara Greed in Chapter 6 argues that postsecular paradigms of urban theory (based on life 'truths' and the consideration of emotions and feelings) still offer little for the radical change in the position of women being taken seriously in the design and planning of cities. The chapter considers the growing role and influence of women in certain Pentecostal and charismatic groups, which often represent the most striking expression of a resurgent public religion, and reflects on the shifting geographies of religion that these new groups signify in terms of local social impact and global reach.

In Chapter 7, Elaine Graham and Andrew Davey argue that the churches and other faith groups in the United Kingdom have been significant players in urban policy and regeneration activities in the past two decades. The involvement of faith groups in policy formation and delivery has, according to the authors, diverted faith groups from developing a more grassroots critique of policy or a liberationist model for their own engagement with urban society. A developmentalist approach to poverty and social exclusion has meant that a discourse of *rights to the city* has failed to emerge in urban theological practice. Often, collusion in the name of partnership has meant that the church and other faith groups have not understood significant shifts in policy – such as the marginalization of neighbourhood renewal and the disappearance of a distinct urban policy focus both internationally and on the domestic agenda. The chapter considers the potential of a reformulation of a theological understanding of city making, provides a critique of faith engagement in urban politics and explores the importance of maintaining distinctive as well as overlapping perspectives on values and ethics from both religious and secular-based sectors.

Anni Greve in Chapter 8 explores the connection between ideas of sanctuary and liveability, reflecting on the significance and contribution to liveability played by religious but also quasi-religious sites in relation to the case study of Tokyo, Japan. She shows the crucial role of sanctuaries in constructing social trust relations between strangers. The overall hypothesis is that certain mega-cities are more robust than others because they offer spatial capacities that enable the development of a social etiquette for meeting strangers with confidence and trust. It is a leading idea that a source of Tokyo's success as 'liveable' is a heritage from the utopian early phase of modernism, namely, places of urban sociability. This chapter is based on a re-examination of the role of sanctuaries, ritual and theatre in promoting a social etiquette for meeting the stranger. The sanctuaries studied offer possibilities for acquiring a social etiquette, aesthetic skills and a social morality which point beyond the local community or the lodge formations, irregular intrigues and power plays of the national power elite.

The chapter by John Eade leads Section 3, which contextualizes the multiculturalism discourse through an analysis of the role of religion and minorities in contesting space (the applications in London to build mega mosques and churches, for example) and in the organization of people's religious lives through competing forms of religious provision (the tension between the Polish Catholic Mission and the English Catholic Church). These examples show that the multicultural discourse is shaped by abiding national traditions informed by the majority

Anglican Church so that one can talk about a certain degree of indigenization paralleled by drives to maintain distinctive modes of religious practice from the migrants' countries of origin. The chapter provides evidence of various forms of sacralization of urban space in London.

Chapter 10, by Greg Ashworth, argues that societies have always been to an extent plural, but the contemporary world is witnessing an increasing ethnic, social and cultural (including religious) diversity. The critical instrumental link between people, places and their governments is heritage, which is the principal instrument by which societies attempt to shape place identities in accordance with predetermined policy objectives. Thus, plural societies should create and be reflected in pluralized place identities: heterotopias in which social diversity, eclecticism, variety and often also ephemeralism and libertarianism are manifest. Heritage policy, however, was historically developed specifically to promote cohesive common values, purposes and interests. Societies may be pluralizing, but public heritage usually remains stubbornly in the singular. The chapter constructs a concordance of contemporary practice in heritage in the context of this pluralization of places and the societies that shape them. The use of heritage in public policies in the pursuit of five main types of social objective in the management of plural societies is described and exemplified. Conclusions are drawn about the limits to the effectiveness of such policies.

In Chapter 11, Rachael Chapman and Leila Hamalainen argue that debates about the role and place of faith in the public realm are re-emerging in light of contestation surrounding the decline of religion predicted by secularization theses. Indeed, there is evidence suggesting that the interface between faith communities and the state is changing and that faith groups are gaining increased influence in the public sphere within, what has been termed, the postsecular society. This chapter explores the changing interface between the state and faith groups in Britain, a country where the government is committed to working more closely with faith groups in the pursuit of strong, active and cohesive communities. The authors focus in particular on community cohesion; a policy area that sees faith communities as key players (alongside other groups) in promoting a common vision and sense of belonging, similar life opportunities and strong positive relationships between people of different backgrounds. The chapter argues there is a tendency within policy narratives towards an instrumental resource-based rationale, in which faith group resources are seen to contribute, and add value, to community cohesion goals. While the 'faithfulness' of faith communities is often acknowledged, evidence suggests that the role and place of 'spiritual' capital, including religious language, values, beliefs and reasoning is complex and contested in practice.

Chapter 12, by Nynke de Witte, builds on the latest EU 7th Framework Programme research on contributions of faith-based organizations in combating social exclusion in European cities. The chapter investigates empirically the theoretical claims that new geographies of religion redraw boundaries between the private and public sphere, contest established state–religion relations, and produce the need for postsecular politics with reference to the case of Amsterdam, the Netherlands. In an attempt to shed light on the meaning of the postsecular city from the perspective of the local state, the chapter discusses Amsterdam's recent policies and practices concerning subsidizing religious and faith-based organizations. The chapter introduces Dalferth's conceptualization of postsecular states, where de Witte uses an ideal type to evaluate Amsterdam's recent policy practices of state–religion cooperation, recently defended by the Board of Mayor and Alderman in the city, and recent (financial) support for religious communities and faith-based organizations in different policy areas. The chapter provides an assessment of Amsterdam's (postsecular) vision and policy practices, and draws some conclusions about postsecular state–religion relations.

Section 4 begins with a chapter by Angus Paddison who examines the theological and political questions raised by the work of faith-based organizations in urban settings, taking its rise from criticisms of public theology voiced by Stanley Hauerwas, John Milbank and William T. Cavanaugh. From the perspective advanced by these political theologians, the church's involvement in FBO initiatives risks the church being replaced by secular reason. The church risks being so placed when it is unable to see how the politics of its own life and convictions have the capacity to query the politics implicit in projects of the bureaucratic state. In pursuit of justice the church does not need to seek out models of public participation, but rather needs first to recognize its own life and worship as already a public enactment of justice. Paddison argues that the theological criticisms of public theology, which he tests in relation to some of the vocabulary used in support of FBOs, are an invitation to imagine political alternatives where religion is a truly public presence in urban projects. The chapter concludes with a discussion of radical democratic alternatives to the participation of religions in urban life, as suggested by Rowan Williams's call for a greater receptivity to people's 'multiple affiliations'.

Chapter 14, by Paul Cloke, shows that the recognition of emerging postsecular rapprochement in the contemporary city can surely learn much from important debates. For Cloke, the work of Klaus Eder provides insights into how the hushed-up voice of religion has been released back into the public sector, in order to make a ground-level contribution to public life. He asks in his chapter: what is it within faith-motivated communities that is leading to a re-emphasis of praxis rather than dogma, and to what degree is such praxis constrained by a perceived need to work within faith boundaries rather than in wider and potentially more risky partnerships. From Jurgen Habermas, the chapter argues, we can seek to learn more about how critiques of secularization reflect distinctions, for example, between secular and secularist, and about the degree to which mutualities are appearing between religious and secular discourses that permit broad-based alliances and a willingness to focus on ethical sympathies, even if that means setting moral differences aside. Cloke traces two currents that lie at the heart of emergent spaces of postsecular alliance in the city: the philosophical and political move beyond secularism, with attendant changes to public consciousness in areas of identity and difference; and the spiritual move towards religious praxis, with related possibilities for discursive crossover between faith-motivated and secular parties.

In the final chapter, Chris Baker and Justin Beaumont review the headline themes, concepts and experiences that have emerged in the course of the previous chapters and in doing so reflect on what has emerged in the course of this volume and what we have discovered about the nature of postsecular space. This reflection will then allow an assessment of the strengths and weaknesses of the concept of the postsecular city itself. The chapter concludes by identifying some areas of future research that the authors see as taking the areas of debate and discovery further.

References

Amin, A. (2006), 'The good city', *Urban Studies* 43(5–6), 1009–23.

Beaumont, J. R. (2010), 'Transcending the particular in postsecular cities'. In Molendijk, A. L., Beaumont, J. and C. Jedan (eds), *Exploring the Postsecular: the religious, the political and the urban*. Boston/Leiden: Brill, pp. 3–17.

Berger, P., Sacks, J., Martin, D., Weiming, T., Weigel, Davie, G. and Naim, A. A. A. (1999), *The Desecularisation of the World: Resurgent Religion and World Politics*. Grand Rapids, MI: Eerdmans Publishing.

Cassanova, J. (1990), *Public Religion in the Modern World*. Chicago, IL: University of Chicago.

Cox, H. (1990), *The Secular City: secularization and urbanization in theological perspective*, first published 1965, 25th anniversary edition. New York: Collier Books.

Debord, G. (2000), *Society of the Spectacle*, first published 1973. St. Petersburg, FL: Black & Red.

Habermas, J. (2005), 'Equal treatment of cultures and the limits of postmodern liberalism', *Journal of Political Philosophy* 13(1), 1–28.

— (2006), 'Religion in the public sphere', *European Journal of Philosophy* 14(1), 1–25.

Hancock, M. and Srinivas, S. (2008), 'Spaces of modernity: religion and the urban in Asia and Africa', *International Journal of Urban and Regional Research* 32(3), 617–30.

Harvey, D. (2009), *Social Justice and the City*, revised edition. Athens, GE: University of Georgia Press.

Kipling, R. (2010), *Barack-Room Ballads*, with a new introduction and annotations by Andrew Lycett, London/New York: A Signet Classic, a division of Penguin Books.

Kong, L. (2010), 'Global shifts, theoretical shifts: changing geographies of religion', *Progress in Human Geography*, published online 30 March.

Molendijk, A. L., Beaumont, J. and Jedan, C. (eds), *Exploring the Postsecular: The Religious, the Political and the Urban*. Boston/ Leiden: Brill.

Part I

Mapping the Theoretical Terrain

1 Postsecular Cities and Radical Critique: A Philosophical Sea Change?

Gregor McLennan

Introduction: paradigm lost

This chapter offers an analysis of some ways in which the 'problematic' of critical social theory has altered in the (purported) mood swing from secular to postsecular concerns. Since I am not an urbanist as such, the discussion is deliberately held at a general level. But equally, it can readily be seen that shifts of emphasis within radical approaches to the contemporary city have followed broader theoretical trends. And the key questions for current theorists, whether operating at the general philosophical or the specifically urbanist level, are whether a dramatic sea change in our metaphysical proclivities really is taking place, and whether this is a good and necessary thing for radical understanding and action. Now, these questions themselves can be addressed in two significantly different registers. According to one of these, the basic storyline of modernist self-comprehension, perhaps unexpectedly, is being sharply *reversed*. Whether viewed as a matter of historical reality or as the self-fulfilling mythology of atheistic intellectuals, the last two centuries in the West have constituted the epoch in which secular(ist) norms of enquiry, forms of political agency and social institutions replaced religious ones. But now things look, supposedly, very different again, because what Charles Taylor (2007) has called the 'malaise' of the modern social and moral imaginary has been fully exposed, resulting, if not in an all-round and uncritical 'revival of religion' exactly, then certainly in the kind of postsecularism that has no hesitation in being seriously *anti*-secularist in direction and intent.

The second take on the central questions is more 'continuist', certainly more 'agonistic', than it is straightforwardly 'reversalist'. According to this, crude secularism – whether couched in moral, sociological or methodological terms – is undoubtedly problematical and in need of (self)critical deconstruction. But postsecularism here is not a matter of turning back the clock or simply opening ourselves up anew to the all-embracing joys of the religious life and spiritually driven enquiry. Rather, it is a matter of applying to secularism the sort of probing and sceptical analysis previously meted out to religious apologetics whenever the latter was thought excessively to govern empirical or philosophical understanding. In that sense, postsecular questioning can be viewed more as reflexively *intra*-secular(ist) rather than *anti*-secular(ist) as such (see McLennan 2010a, 2010b). And in that light, one would be as disposed to note the *commonalities* as much as the disjunctures between secularist and religious outlooks with respect to certain values and procedures. For example, there is a manifest conjoint worry about the almost calculated superficiality of certain (ultra-pluralistic, modestly descriptiv-ist) styles of thinking that have developed in the wake of postmodernism and poststructuralism. Later, I cite Ash Amin's recent depiction of the city as prone to such accusations from both sides.

Meanwhile, let's remind ourselves of the impressive way that David Harvey's *Social Justice and the City* exemplified the theoretical genre that dominated radical urbanism through the 1970s and 1980s. Harvey sought to embed the cultural and spatial specificities of urban life within a totalizing framework of capital formation and historical transformation. A keen observer of empirical trends and proximate connections, Harvey's explanatory posture was unreservedly structuralist, insist-ing that the visible metropolis could only properly be comprehended by bringing the higher levels of abstraction into play, notably 'an ontological and epistemologi-cal position akin to that held by Marx' (Harvey, 1973: 301). Harvey articulated that benchmark in 'critical realist' terms, before that label had gained full currency within the radical philosophy movement of the time. Thus, the prescribed method was naturalistic, approaching all social phenomena in terms of their place in an open-textured but determinate totality of internal connections and emergent structures (Harvey, 1973: 288–90). Like the Althusserians, Harvey sought to analyse social life in its configuration of general relations, and relations *between* relations, so his approach was far from mechanical or reductionist. But equally it was taken for granted that the favoured philosophical conspectus pertained to an exclusively *material* world. And a certain scientism marked Harvey's insistence that when it came to transformative urban practice, only an epistemologically informed *politics* of justice would suffice, not a 'merely' ethical or spiritual motiva-tion, however well meant. While respecting the value commitments that people worked from, and noting the myriad forms of moral 'reciprocity' that sustained associations in the city, only 'socialist formulations' of redistribution would do (1973: Part Two), guided by a revolutionary 'synthesis' of structural theory and transformative practice (Part Three).

Harvey's general outlook is not only philosophically *realist*, but in some central way also clearly *secularist*. The index of *Social Justice in the City* lists no named reli-gion, and the word itself only appears under the (pejorative) subhead 'ideology'. In the course of his mode-of-productionist overview, Harvey explained the histori-cal specificity of 'theocracy' in terms of urban–countryside relations in past agrarian societies and revisited the affinities between various denominations and early regimes of capitalist accumulation. But otherwise, and despite the recentness, then, of debates around Harvey Cox's *The Secular City*, there was nothing at all on the role of faith in modern urban activism or on the status of religion in contemporary society more generally. Undoubtedly, the generic structuralism and anti-humanism of the early 1970s played its part in this 'silence'. Both Cox and the many Leftists who became interested in liberation theology and the like were absorbed by the sort of liaisons between humanism and existentialism that the Althusser generation then categorically denounced. But today, in turn, the excesses of hubristic scientism and the hypostatization of impersonal structural forces have themselves thoroughly been critiqued, making the absence of all reference in Harvey to religion and its resources – at least, given our increasingly postsecular sensibility – notable indeed. In order to trace how the secular problematic as represented by Harvey has come under pressure from (radical) postsecular thought, I engage with challenges mounted around three core concepts: *the real, the good* and (more briefly) *the radical.*

The real

Critical realism, especially as framed by Roy Bhaskar (1975, 1979), was pitched against an empiricist mainstream according to which knowledge is captured in universal generalizations derived from constantly conjoined observable events. Bhaskar's alternative ontology was stratified into three domains or levels: the real, the actual and the empirical. Of the three, the real is conceived as the deepest, comprising a large number of (sometimes cross-cutting) causal powers and generative tendencies that are only ever partially realized, if at all, at the level of the actual and only ever partially evidenced, if at all, at the level of the empirical (i.e. the one that involves direct human perception). This realist scenario not only yields a richer sense of the constitution of the world, it alone is thought to explain how the 'flat', 'thin' ontology of empiricism itself comes to be plausible. This is because, in some experimental scientific practices, the open and complex entities and interactions of nature can be artificially isolated, and exceptionless generalizations between factors produced. However, far from showing, as empiricists held, that exceptionless generality obtains in the world, and can be spotted as such, all it signifies is that closure can (sometimes) be scientifically produced and (some) real dispositions identified. The natural and social worlds themselves remain, as before, teeming, contradictory, moving processes that simply do not exist in that regularized way and cannot be held steady. The fallacy of empiricism, then, is to regard only one dimension of scientific practice as paradigmatic of the whole, and to elevate epistemology – the quest for universally valid, testable knowledge claims – above ontology.

The scientific realist perspective was quintessentially philosophical – metaphysical, even – in two main senses. First, the resort to ontology in order to overturn the dominant meta-theory of science started from a 'transcendental' argument in answer to the question, What must the world be like if it is to include and explain successful science? Second, within those many branches of natural and social science in which experimental closure was either unmanageable or unwanted, the power of conceptual *abstraction* had to take precedence over the data of observation, and retrospective explanation had to supplant the previous emphasis on prediction.

Many radical philosophers and sociologists subsequently took up the realist cause, so that by around 2007 the publisher Routledge alone had produced numerous 'studies' and 'interventions' in critical realism. Most of these volumes remained secular–Leftist in character, but they included three texts – *From East to West*, by Bhaskar (2000), *On Christian Belief*, by Andrew Collier (2003), and *Transcendence*, by Margaret Archer, Collier and Douglas Porpora (2004) – that signalled a dramatic 'religious turn' in critical realism, defined by the proposition that it was high time we became 'realist about God'. The central theme was that critical realism *not only* requires a 'transcendental' argument which allots priority to ontology over epistemology and enables the basic stratification of the domains of the real to be sketched; critical realism also confers legitimacy on the very *idea* of the transcendent, and indeed enables *insight* into transcendental reality. Moreover, the routine assumption that realism entails a thoroughgoing cosmic materialism, thus ruling out belief in God, is regarded as mistaken. To grasp this point, we must recall that, for most critical realists, a hefty degree of epistemological relativism is inescapable, even though we can legitimately reason to an 'intransitive' ontological realm beyond the particular construal of our current schemes of knowledge and evidence. Why then couldn't it be that our scientific and ideological commitment to materialism – which might well have 'local' epistemic advantages – is more relative than we think, and fails to capture the underlying nature of ultimate reality? For one thing, scientistic materialism systematically screens out or actively delegitimates types of evidential reasoning (those based on unique experiential testimony, for example) that may well be perfectly valid from a more encompassing perspective. For another, the 'integrative pluralism' that realism tends to advocate as an account of the world's complexity is responsive to the idea that the causal mechanisms characteristic of one order of being might turn out to be dependant upon, and interactive with, higher-level generative mechanisms of an altogether different sort. Overall, then, philosophical realism is necessarily metaphysical in certain respects, requiring a range of extra-scientific assumptions and possibilities, and ontological realism is in principle entirely compatible (if fallibly so) with belief in God, conceived in realist terms. Finally, none of this implies that realism about God is any less socially radical or any less committed to scientific rationality (in its place) than non-believing critical realism.

Roy Bhaskar's own pursuit of postsecular spirituality has been couched in such idiosyncratic and inflated terms (the 'Ultimatum', the 'Absolute Simpliciter' and suchlike), that friend and foe alike have felt it to be rather dubious as philosophical argumentation. The conjoined project of Archer et al. is more carefully wrought, so it is their version of religious realism that I will focus on for our purposes. However, it is worth noting that whether cogently sustained or not, Bhaskar's general stance is perhaps more fully aligned with postsecularism Take II than that of Archer et al. This is partly because Bhaskar has a more 'immanentist' notion of the 'ingredience' that higher levels of reality purportedly contribute to lower levels as a matter of ontological necessity. And it is also because he is ambivalent about whether it is God specifically that constitutes the 'categorial structure of the world' and the transcendent hope and healing that is central to a proper 'philosophy of Self-realisation', or whether, instead, 'God' is just a convenient shorthand for those self-sustaining generalities (see, e.g. Bhaskar, 2002: 150).

Archer, Collier and Porpora are convinced that, even if they seek to provide a more properly religious version of realism than Bhaskar, the original tenets of his realism are not being forsaken. They are also keen to stay identified, ethically and politically, with the Left, even if they want to challenge its unthinking secularism. For these reasons, Archer et al. limit themselves to establishing a 'level playing field' between atheistic realists and believer realists, the latter now 'coming out' in significant numbers (Archer et al., 2004: x, 6). Interestingly, these Christian realists have little time for traditional ontological/cosmological arguments for God or deductions of His existence from the marvels of nature – apologetics of that sort can only remain, they say, thoroughly inconclusive. Alternative defences of faith that highlight its principally emotional, moral or 'mythological' nature are unacceptable too; in effect, these concede to atheism by evading the fact that claims about God are *cognitive*, that is, adjudicable in principle and amenable to rational argument. Religious belief does not clash with science, but this is not because the game of faith is entirely separate from the game of truth. On the contrary, if religions cannot make good their truth claims in broadly realist terms, such that God is a being 'who pre-existed and is independent of all human minds and material things' (Collier, 2003: xv), then faith has no credible foundation at all. The task, therefore, is twofold: on the one hand, to strengthen believers' commitment to realist modes of understanding, and, on the other hand, to quell unbelieving realists' alarm at the notion that *revelation* (Collier), or at least *religious experience* (Archer), yields a legitimate and objective form of knowledge. The strategy used to achieve those twin goals is one that prioritizes the need for *symmetry* in the appraisal of secular and religious perspectives.

On the positive side of symmetry, so to speak, both secular and religious critical realism oppose Wittgensteinian, social constructionist, and postmodernist trends in social understanding. For any sort of realist, even if our grasp of objective reality is *filtered* through the norms and rules of our 'forms of life', even if it is generated in relation to social *functions* and ideologies, and even if its texture is necessarily *discursive*, questions of truth and objectivity are not exhausted by their contextual and expressive mediations. In fact, realism itself insists that, epistemically, our grasp of the real is always only partial and changing. Nevertheless, it is only by anticipating that changing views and differing perspectives are attempts to grasp an independent and common reality that we can make sense of enquiry at all and avoid a paralysing descent into subjectivism.

Second, secular and religious realism are thought to concur in that although we come through science and experience, to regard certain items of belief as 'alethic' in character – that is, so firmly based that we take them to be the incontrovertible truth of reality 'in itself' – knowledge of God is not exactly of that sort. Rather, reiterated episodes of 'judgmental rationality' are required to clarify God's being (Archer et al., 2004: 3). Taking these two positive points together, we get a third: realism about God has to be couched fallibly. Thus, 'God might be one of those things that exists independent of our knowledge of it', but it is 'something about which we might (always) be mistaken'. God's existence and nature do have objective ontological answers, but we might never be sure what they are (Archer et al., 2004: 1–3). Then again, most of what secular realists believe, including the *non*-existence of God, falls outside the realm of 'alethic' truth as well. So, atheistic and believing stances alike are not only equally subject to rational debate, but are equally rational, and in their different ways equally objective, too (2004: 3).

Third, science no less than faith takes on trust the words and actions of recognized authorities, accepting the validity of their conclusions in the round, and based on little more than hearsay. This is to diminish neither science nor hearsay, only to upgrade religious belief, since that too is based on the general – though never conclusive – reliability of testimony and expertise, and it also involves careful scrutiny of vital evidence. If that evidence seems thin to secularists, then the same applies to evidence for certain scientific hypotheses, and for many estimable beliefs about society (socialism, e.g. (2004: 15)). Secular realists may think that the systematic and public nature of scientific evidence differentiates it decisively from personal reports of revelation. But even here we might query whether scientific evidence, quite apart from its invariably partial nature, is precisely replicable as such, or 'public' in the sense of being entirely open to the presuppositionless and experience-free observation of all. Surely this notion of repeated, neutral, conclusive sensory witness is precisely what realism – and post-positivism generally – has exposed as an empiricist myth?

Re-placing objective accounts within the larger context of (variable) experience, Christian realists maintain that *lack* of belief in God constitutes as much an inclination derived from experience as its opposite. Atheists, on this basis, might reasonably be thought to have been trained/socialized into the experience of the 'transcendent absent' (2004: 12). The social and practical character of *experience* is critical here, as pressed effectively by Margaret Archer in particular. It is not just that our beliefs about something, or its absence for that matter, are social constructions – that's true; but to go too far down that track would give the realist game away altogether. It is rather that the nature of lived experience nurtures the kind of practical expertise in particular ways of being, the specific object and quality of which observing sociologists discount at their peril. So, when a great many people, even if not a majority, conclude through tried and tested routines and reflection that they have experienced the divine and the transcendent, and that they know what this means, it is illegitimate, and a secularist fallacy, not to grant that experienced level 'real' status. Otherwise, 'the world's contribution is thereby rendered illicit by an a priori methodological principle' (2004: 13). At the very least, the properly realist track is once again to follow the principle of symmetry. In mild form, in the absence of alethic truth, it is just as reasonable for believers to go by the lights of their experienced reality as it is for atheists to go by theirs. More emphatically, if sociologists rightly give the social and natural realms their relatively autonomous, yet interconnected, causal and cognitive status, they cannot withdraw that recognition from the spiritual realm.

These religious–realist arguments are strenuous, and perhaps the chief value of postsecularism is to blur the distinction between believers and non-believers simply by pushing all of us to listen carefully to those on the 'other side' and give them a fair run. But the authors I have been discussing would be the first to insist that if it is to be worthwhile, postsecular reflexivity needs to deliver something more than postmodern agonism or standard existential puzzlement. Further engagement with their case for symmetry is therefore required. The first thing to notice about this master trope is its derivation from the 1980s 'strong programme' in the sociology of scientific knowledge, motivation for which was almost diametrically opposed to that of Archer et al. The strong programmers challenged a traditional view that while adherence to *false* scientific notions might legitimately be sociologically explained (away), this could not be done for *true* or consistently successful scientific theories – because truth itself, and adherence to it, simply cannot be explained (away) in any extraneous terms. Against that mainstream view, sociologists of science bracketed out matters of truth, and social considerations were applied across the board. But Archer et al.'s realism is fully committed to the truth game, so that religious truths, just like those of science, are not only unavailable for reductionist treatment, they stand in serious competition with other truth claims. It is therefore slightly strange to frame this project in terms of merely achieving equal rights with sceptical alternatives.

In any event, symmetry in its purely formal aspect does not take the religious cause very far, because its register is necessarily *hypothetical*: *if* God exists, then He should be regarded in the same way that realists regard other fundamental generative mechanisms, with the proviso that God is *the* foundational generative mechanism, and the fount of unconditional love. In that light, debating the attributes and manifestations of God is then obviously not 'unreasonable' or 'irrational', because it is led by a respectable style of inference making. But it remains questionable whether anything of real consequence follows. Actual reasons given for or against God's existence are unlikely to be considered *equally* rational on all sides, and certainly not equally *objective*, as Archer et al. imply. They do not believe this themselves, and neither do atheists.

Slippage from symmetry continues with the point that, not being a matter of the alethic truth, all claims about God are subject to the due process of judgmental rationality. The thought seems to be that unlike, say, our ingrained assumption that the earth moves round the sun and not vice versa, which we all (now) take to hold absolutely about the nature of the world in itself, arguments about God are more elusive and controversial. Yet, leaving aside problems with the bizarre notion of alethic truth itself – Why should it differ from the plain truth? Are non-alethic truths supposed *not* to be true of reality in itself? – it soon becomes clear that, for these authors, nothing could be *more* alethic than their own 'minimal' conception of God. The phrasing itself is so essentialist and in principle so incontrovertible that anything more hesitant or open to empirical nuance is simply out of the question. Thus, 'God is the alpha and the omega, the beginning and the end. God is the origin of the universe and the telos towards which it returns. God not only creates the universe, establishing its ultimate, ontological properties, but also sustains the universe in each moment. God is the ultimate ground or deepest truth of all things, and hence of all beings' (2004: 24–25).

According to a final equalizing move, if religious beliefs are thoroughly *embedded* within practical experiences and habits, then the same must be said of scientific and atheist beliefs. Scientific attitudes are fostered in distinctive cultures of perception and training, and even atheism is governed by the habitual experience of not believing or of *absence*, specifically absence of the transcendent. But in this presentation, the valid experiential texture of both scientific and religious experience is considered to constitute their mode of truthful access to their respective ultimate realities; whereas the atheistic experience of absence is positioned exclusively as a *blockage* to ultimate reality, staged as the sort of deficiency or blindness that can only result in intense psychological denial. Here again, then, the ostensibly symmetry trope slips into one-sided manipulation. And it invites an effective 'tu quoque' response, albeit one that risks plunging the discussion into pantomime: if atheists, in their denial of the transcendent and the Lord, only reveal that they are experiencing Him in the form of absence, then perhaps religious believers, in their own denial of the real absence of their psychologically convenient deity, reveal that they are experiencing that absence in the form of contriving contrary absences for atheists who are not actually experiencing them. Of course, there is complexity here as well as comedy. There might well be absences (of legs, brothers, wealth) that are in some acceptable sense experienced, and reference to which can play an explanatory role in understanding beliefs and situations. But the postulation of specific absences does not necessarily license something as general as absence of the transcendent, nor does reference to absence constitute explanation without strong prior evidence or argument about the causal pathways through which it might be thought to operate. In any event, something like transcendence appears to be experienced by non-believers of numerous kinds, including killers, nature lovers, drug addicts, scientists, musicians, etc. So it is not clear that the reality of transcendence has any specific bearing on God's existence, or that it valorizes talk of an ontological level or realm called the Transcendent.

These objections, of course, are materialist in character, but the main point here is that, overall, the pursuit of symmetry looks rather contrived. Moreover, it is overridden by Archer et al.' s statement that while ontological realism about God may be consistent with critical realism, it is not after all required by the latter (2004: 5). This suggests that secular realists can safely continue to hold that we cannot be realist 'about God', partly because we cannot be realist about *anything* that particular – what exists, and in what relation to other things that exist, is the business of science and substantive enquiry. But the religious realist case has perhaps been cogent enough to throw doubt on whether such a spare and relatively scientistic formulation of realism either does justice to the metaphysical impulse within realism itself, or, relatedly, to the presumption among radicals that realism permits them to be more critical and more substantively informative than other philosophies. To that extent, the possibility of a postsecular realism might be worth further deliberation.

The good

If the first philosophical pillar of Harvey's secular urban theory – critical realism – has come under pressure from those 'coming out' for religion, with realists experiencing some degree of postsecular agonism as a result, what about the second pillar? This was the assumption that matters of social justice must be figured and tackled *politically*, where this means being driven from a hard-headed theoretical perspective rather than by intrinsic moral considerations. But that second pillar too, if not exactly crumbling, is under significant reconstruction, in the hands of Left theorists who have become unhappy with exclusively socio-naturalistic understandings of ethics and politics.

Thus, for Peter Dews in *The Idea of Evil* (2008), the complexity of ethics can only be grasped through revisiting the problem named in his title, such that 'issues once addressed by theodicy' must be reworked, not instead of, but alongside, 'our modern commitment to freedom and rational insight'. This necessary tension, Dews argues, was first strikingly formulated by Kant, whose inveterate progressiv-ism did not prevent him from thinking that our capacity to choose evil over good is fundamental and ineradicable. Dews seeks to show how in spite of all their efforts, the great modern thinkers have failed to get around the notion of evil as the consciously chosen enactment of something that is intrinsically *unjustifiable*, something that 'absolutely should not be'. Whether in relatively optimistic mode (Hegel, Adorno) or in one of sombre recognition (Schopenhauer, Levinas), the problem of evil has continued to haunt our project of making a better world. Paradoxically, perhaps, it is those, like Nietzsche, who by rationalist lights appear to be wantonly nihilistic, who either summon up or exemplify minimum resources of courage and, after a fashion, hope. Overall, the blunt message is that if we cannot forsake the secular trajectory of modernity, or socialistic goals, then materialist and sociological understanding must still be accepted as lacking moral density, because it does not face up to our endemic, troubled passion for undoing past wrongs, or our yearning for redemption.

The recent writings of Terry Eagleton sound similar notes. Eagleton's first instinct, let loose in *Reason, Faith, and Revolution* (2009a), is to mount a counter-polemic against what he sees as the thin-blooded rationalism of the likes of Richard Dawkins and Christopher Hitchens. 'Ditchkins' is lambasted for being ignorant about theology and for sneering, from the safe haven of their tedious middle-class *habitus*, at thoroughly well-intentioned, not-stupid religious people. As for their replay of the old contest between mystified religion and rational enlightenment, this is grotesquely overdrawn, because 'non-rational' elements cannot be elimi-nated from any of our evaluative schemes, and because 'many secular myths are degutted versions of sacred ones'. Finally, in relation to Ditchkins's bone-headed misunderstanding that believers imagine God to be a 'mega-manufacturer' and a pushy 'Nobodaddy', what the new atheists have to realize is that, in truth, God is an *artist* – gratuitously conjuring up the world for no particular purpose, sustaining all things in being with his love, demanding nothing from us other than that he should be allowed to love us in all our moral squalor. And all that, Eagleton feels, should be quite enough to put an end to the whole ridiculous 'God debate'.

A more exploratory vein is struck in *Trouble with Strangers* (2009b), in which Eagleton develops a perspective that combines Christianity and psychoanalysis. He works through the modern philosophical canon, plugging individual thinkers into one of three heuristic categories derived from Lacan – the Imaginary, the

Symbolic and the Real. He finds philosophers of the first stripe too gentrified and smug in their emphasis on *sociable benevolence* as the hallmark of ethical relations and experience. As in Lacan's theorization of the 'mirror phase', supposedly under-gone by all infants, the philosophers of the Imaginary remain trapped within 'the closed sphere of the ego', recognizing in the external world only some hazy, not-yet-separate double of their own dependent needy self. In the Symbolic order, by contrast, the 'addiction to desire' of the Imaginary is boldly left behind in an effort to systematize relations of self and society. Through the production of language, sign systems, theories, and rationally formulated goals for all, we construct definite (generalized) objects of attention and commitment. But, alas, these objectivizing moves are themselves conditional upon the repression of sentience, fantasy and dependency. The Symbolic thus entails a profound estrangement of self, a 'gash in our being', a mortal contradiction between settled projects and untrammelled desire-for-itself. Philosophers in that mode – and they will include atheists and Marxists – are considered by Eagleton to be too uptight and rule bound. Life in general, and morality in particular, are more inspired, unsettling and oriented around the impossible than these first two (necessary) aspects of ethics allow.

So an ethics of the Real is called for. The Real refers, supposedly, to 'the subject that is more than the subject'; that which 'is most permanently awry with us, and what is most truly of our essence'. The Real is the truth that cannot be totalized, the desire that cannot be satisfied, the drive that continues to desire despite our hard-won intuition that no particular object of desire will bring satisfaction. The Real therefore signals a convoluted, ardent longing that lies beyond any set of principles and all reasoned exchange. In such upturned terrain, the courage to confront and cope with the demands of the Real, for Eagleton – or at least the part of Eagleton that is trying to think with Lacan – constitutes the ethical *par excellence*. To act well in the shadow of dread and death; to grasp that no commitment to particular attrac-tions, however elevated, will ever be enough; yet to do what one can, in some unwavering way; this is morals beyond the reach of the merely good, and therefore something potentially redemptive. Unliveable in itself, the Real nevertheless 'releases an uncanny power to inaugurate a new human order' (Eagleton, 2009b: 195).

But the striking of the gavel of the Symbolic here – Order! – indicates that the ethics of the Real are not finally to be ratified. Whatever is valid in them, we are told, was already anticipated in Christianity itself. Moreover, Eagleton sharply exposes the conceptual contradictions and lacunae in lionized figures such as Levinas, and roundly condemns the elitist scorn for the mundane and common-place that is typically found among poststructuralists. In the end, it is a constructive *synthesis* between the three registers that Eagleton calls for, though to make this stand he needs to withdraw his own initial scorn of Imaginary and Symbolic think-ers. If the Real unflinchingly catches the 'tragic sense of life' with which sunny moralists cannot easily cope, Lacan's ethics of ironic heroism, in which we cleave to our (drive to) desire without any prospect of fulfilment, neglects the power of loving faith in its amelioration.

These Left-postsecular discourses on moral concepts and dire predicaments are bracing and at times profound. But they create further conundrums of their own, as well as overstating secular ethical impoverishment. For one thing, the strong logic of their positions leaves us precious little realistic hope; rather oddly, in fact, this seems to be partly their intention. In Dews's scenario, our evil propensities appear to be so ingrained, and non-elementalist contributions to their understanding so peripheral, that the ideals of the good society, or even the good person, seem nothing but foolish fantasies. Yet Dews's treatment of evil is too generic and static. Not only is he too dismissive of evolutionary perspectives on selfishness and altruism, he does not even bother to discuss them. As for sociological considerations, Michael Mann, for example, in *The Dark Side of Democracy* (2005), persuasively analyses murderous ethnic cleansing as a fundamentally *modern* phenomenon. He shows how this phenomenon has arisen in the messy anterior to democratization, in societies in which the *demos* and the *ethnos* become fused together at the expense of *class* identities. Additionally, Mann shows that perpetrators of radical evil emerge as different categories of actor – party–state elites, populist paramilitaries and some part of the mass of 'ordinary people' (though, importantly, never the *majority*) – each type coming on to the scene at a different stage, and committing increasingly vile deeds as the desperate sense that there is no alternative escalates. Even the rankest evildoers, therefore, are variously motivated – by ideology, bigotry, fearfulness, careerism, discipline, love of violence, comradeship and bureaucratic zeal (though Mann omits to mention misogyny). On inspection, radical evil turns out not to be *premeditated* in the normal sense, nor is it about sheer indulgence in gratuitous wickedness. Mann is not denying that some propensity for evil exists in all of us, or implying that what he is describing is less than fully grim. But thinking about evil in a timeless 'religious' way, he reasonably concludes, seriously exaggerates its inalterability and misrecognizes its concrete forms of existence.

More generally, Dews's 'central contention' amounts to a rather tame observation: that conflicts 'continue to arise' between the contrary pulls of 'freedom and autonomy' on the one hand, and 'due recognition of the intractability of moral evil' on the other (2008: 13–14.) The refrain is that on the swirling seas of the moral life, the good ship humanism persistently founders on the rocks of religion. But Dews and other postsecularists' assumption that the inextinguishable 'metaphysical desire' that appears to guarantee that recurrent outcome is essentially or uniquely *religious* in nature is unimaginative and contestable.

Eagleton's Christian–Lacan synthesis, for its part, is also ensnared in some unresolved difficulties. One theme is the 'banality of goodness', commitment to which, Eagleton affirms, is shared by Christianity and socialism. The quest for 'transformed humanity', in this frame, involves nothing much, necessarily, beyond vigorous prosecution of the struggles of 'actually existing men and women'. Morality is still demanding; it has to be militant; and it involves due reverence for exemplary sacrificial martyrdom – whether that of Christ or the 'guerilla fighters'. Yet we are not obliged, precisely, to become martyrs ourselves just for the sake of it, or to forsake our genuine nearside attachments. In the appropriate culture of the virtuous society, we can get progressively better at being human, to the point where goodness becomes almost spontaneous. These key aspects of *virtue ethics*, in terms of which allegiance to the prospect of reciprocal fulfilment and collective self-realization is the dictate of love and fellowship, develop Eagleton's sense that politics and ethics, love and justice are wholly inseparable (2009b: 301–307. But many atheists, of course, share that eudaemonic horizon: our own personal happiness is bound up with the human flourishing of all, the dutiful furtherance of which requires no extraneous source or further justification.

According to a significantly different, altogether higher-octane storyline in Eagleton, even egalitarian virtue ethics are too 'gentrified', because the ethics of love is decidedly surplus to all normal requirements. The move towards psychosocial replenishment can never be secure, because the 'disfiguring Real at the core of identity' cannot be extinguished. The Real, in fact, forms a duality, simultaneously cursed and sacred. The Christian mission is *part* of the Real, and not just its appreciative corrective, because God's intense personal love, which somehow carries the impersonal force of law, is both absolutely necessary and yet also impossible. The ethical ordeal is thus to pull the Good Real away from the brink of the Lacanian danger zone in the mad trust that 'love is stronger than death'; and everyone enlisted in that cause must be prepared to be done to death, because our relentless labour on behalf of the poor and the scapegoat can expect nothing less in this world.

These are two very different readings of the relationship between religion and ethics, by turns clashing and tangled. On Eagleton's first account, there is 'no conflict between immanence and transcendence, as there is for the Realists' (2009b: 292), but the cranked-up version says exactly the opposite. To relieve the pressure, Eagleton plays a rather astonishing get-out card: nothing in what he has put forward, he confides, depends upon the truth of *either* psychoanalysis *or* Christianity (2009b: 323). Having issued stern warnings about the inextinguishability of the Real within Christian ethical identity itself, and delivered homilies about the Creation 'as pure, unmotivated gift and grace', having 'absolutely no point beyond God's supreme self-delight' (2009b: 290), this coy withdrawal into 'for the sake of argument' mode appears to be simply self-defeating – as the Christian critical realists that we discussed in the previous section would be the first to point out.

The radical

The 'ethics of socialism' was intended to be Eagleton's third main tributary to an advanced moral synthesis, yet, remarkably, this discursive partner occupies only a handful of cursory sentences. Of course, Eagleton continues to see the immorality and rapaciousness of global capitalism as the main enemy, and his own way of belief hardly endorses religious revivalism as such. Concerning most things about religion, in fact, 'the bellicose ravings of Ditchkins are, if anything, too muted', he says (2009a: 57). But the energy for transformative politics now seems to come less from Marxist sources and more from the Christian preparedness for collective and subjective transfiguration. And it is notable that even where realism about God is categorically denied, some variants of contemporary postsecular radicalism find newly attractive the luminous *language and psychology* normally associated with it. Two snapshot examples of this 'continuist' – rather than 'reversalist' or 'agonistic' – current can be given.

Roberto Mangabeira Unger, in *The Self Awakened* (2007), disavows all quests to escape the reality of embodiment and temporality through ascent into some changeless, eternal space-beyond-space governed by the will of God. Instead, Unger endorses – 'to the hilt'– the utter historicity of things: ourselves as 'dying organisms', our societies and indeed nature itself. He therefore confirms key aspects of the time-worn Left critique of religion, placing it among the 'enslaving superstitions of the mind'. On the other hand, 'the naturalization of man will be his dehumanization', and we must not seek to construct a 'super-science' that will only 'place transformative will and imagination under a spell' (2007: 1, 35). For truly progressive social transformation to occur, profound personal renewal is required, something that must recognize our 'unstoppable longing' and enable us to 'demand the unconditional'. Consequently, 'we poison our relations to one another by denying to one another the acknowledgement of the infinity within', something best articulated in a 'theological vocabulary', though without the 'theological backdrop'. Our sense of societal *connection* pulls against our impulse towards *transcendence*, but both are vital for radical imagining. Unger envisages a projected first phase of self-awakening, involving respect, forbearance and fairness, leading to a higher plane of perception and agency, one in which compassion, self-sacrifice and mercy come to the fore. In this second awakening, we can only be ourselves by going *beyond* ourselves, by 'making good on the infinity within us', according to a certain (secular?) striving for divinity and the 'absolute'.

The infinite and the absolute play a central role in Alain Badiou's high-wired philosophy, too. For Badiou, to be radical is to follow, through thick and thin, the truth consequences of 'Events' – points of dramatic irruption which are contextually inexplicable, and which, for those whose subjectivity is formatively shaped in fidelity to them, totally alter the nature of our situations and value orientations. Developed at length in Badiou's earlier work, though subsequently toned down (Badiou, 2006, 2009), these tenets can readily be seen at work in his recent exchange on 'philosophy in the present' with Slavoj Zizek – another believer in *belief*, if not in God. Thus, for Badiou, the task of philosophy is 'to show that we must choose', and the transformation of life, not its tame continuity, is the proper goal of the radical. This involves philosophy inserting a difficult 'foreignness' into routine situations of thought and allegiance, and straining to theorize the universal, which 'is always an incalculable emergence, rather than a describable structure'. The universal, indeed, is a *singularity*, something that is 'subtracted from identitarian predicates', and possessed of the sort of univocal, exceptional valence that is 'not reducible to the human, which is to say something inhuman' (Badiou and Zizek, 2009: 5, 12, 24, 28–30, 74).

Now in Badiou and his followers (e.g. Meillassoux, 2009), the notion of the universal as embodying 'the infinite, the ontological law of being-multiple' ostensibly has *nothing* to do with religious spirituality, even if these writers are rather scathing about non-religious humanism too. But Badiou nevertheless grants that 'for a long time, the name for what surpasses humanity was "God"', and he has little patience for sophisticated hesitancy over whether or not God exists, despising the sort of vague, all-purpose type of spirituality that increasingly these days mediates the basic situation of choice (2009: 35, 73). It could also be maintained that fidelity to specifically *religious* Events forms a 'natural' addition to Badiou's favoured quartet of truth-driven, subject-binding practices: politics, love, science and art. Numerous criticisms could be levelled at Badiou's often merely declarative, and dangerously 'exceptionalist', stance on truth and ethics, some of which are in fact brilliantly rehearsed by Eagleton in *Trouble with Strangers*. But for our purposes, and following the second rather than the first of my two 'takes' on postsecularism as explained in the Introduction, what most matters is (a) that philosophical refigurings of the radical, just like reconsiderations of the real and the good, some-times bring secular and religious discourses into unexpectedly close connection; and therefore (b) it is misleading and unproductive to regard postsecularism *tout court* as an *anti*-secularist impulse.

Conclusion: paradigm regained?

The writers I have been discussing are not only reacting to perceived deficiencies of neo-Marxist and old-guard secularist conceptions of the real and the good; they are also downcast about the uncritical *pluralism* that has accompanied postmod-ern and liberal–multiculturalist approaches to theory and politics. Put simply, there is little *radical inspiration* to be drawn from such perspectives. In the context of theorizations of the city, a thin-secularist outlook of that sort is arguably at work in Ash Amin's (2006) considerations on 'The Good City'. For sure, Amin still recognizes the encompassing capitalist carapace of contemporary urban existence; and the damage done by persistent social inequality; and the need that even postmoderns might still have for a degree of 're-enchantment'. Yet the typically 'totalizing' and 'teleological' inclinations of socialist thinking and religious activism alike find little basic support here. Instead, Amin affirms the 'constitutive multiplicity of our times', something deemed sufficient to diffuse and defuse any overarching political notion of 'the human collectivity'. In the city of 'small gains and fragile truces', people find their own kind of hope and value within 'the myriad bolt-holes' that they occupy. It's not that a politics of care and respect cannot develop into an 'ever-widening habit of solidarity'; it's just more about enhancing heterotopic 'social vitality' in circumstances of fleeting connectivity, and more about 'sustaining a certain ease with unassimilated difference' than forging an insurgent subject of justice. The David Harvey of 1973 would, no doubt, have countered Amin with the contention that such local, transient means of bolstering 'the self-respect of people', however important in one dimension, are ultimately 'irrelevant to the basic economic structure of society' (Harvey, 1973: 281).

As it happens, today's Harvey might say something very similar, because he has recently returned in no uncertain terms to the thematic of his earlier work. In the wake of human rights discourse, Harvey thinks it is time to declare and specify 'another type of human right, that of the right to the city'. And this in turn requires attention to be given, yet again, to the basic issue of 'what kind of social ties, relationship to nature, lifestyles, technologies and aesthetic values we desire' (Harvey, 2008: 23). To launch into this new line of thought in any detail is not possible here. But two omissions are very curious, from the point of view of this chapter and given Harvey's sweeping canvas. First, *Social Justice in the City* gets not a single reference or bibliographical entry, even though several other works of Harvey's are checklisted. It is as if the author is articulating completely from scratch, for our global times, the role of urbanization and urbanism 'in absorbing the surplus product that capitalists perpetually produce in their search for profits (2008: 25). Second, as in that earlier (apparently forgotten) work, there is no mention whatsoever of religion or religious urban movements.

What do these silences mean for the postsecularism debate that we are concerned with in this volume? In terms of postsecularism Take I, we might regard Harvey as propelling a daring and unflinching case against it by way of a kind of 'double reversal' strategy. Thus, if it seemed for a moment that secularism in social comprehension had been punctured and superseded by postsecularism qua 'religious revival in thought', then the tables have been decisively turned once again, with normal (critical-materialist) service restored. In that vein, unapologetically and – to me – compellingly, Harvey portrays the contemporary global malaise as fundamentally a matter of profound and persistent structural divisions between rich and poor, the solution to which is to be found in the politics of . . . 'dare we call it class struggle?' (2008: 37). Little sign or possibility of any postsecular *rapprochement* here.

In terms of postsecularism Take II, though, the case is rather more perplexing. On the one hand, Harvey's new manifesto on the city might fairly be assumed by him or his readers to appeal to *anyone* passionate about advancing global social justice. The proposal would be that whatever else we may disagree about (Gods, for example), we can at least concur that the most pervasive source of inhumanity is the relentless logic and rule of capital, and correspondingly that the kind of human city we need is one that is substantially free from that dire hegemony. Such a message, if still somewhat reductive perhaps, could then be regarded as the condition of relevance of any serious postsecular urban paradigm, whether inflected towards religious belief or unbelief. On the other hand, as someone normally finely attuned to keynote changes in social mores and to the variety of styles of resistance, it is genuinely puzzling – and a deficit – that Harvey fails to include religious phenomena/activism in the multiple 'signs of rebellion' that he feels are arising 'everywhere' against 'the burgeoning processes of creative destruction that have dispossessed the masses of any right to the city whatsoever' (2008: 37). Equally, if the new universal right to the city can only be founded on serious debate about 'what kind of social ties, relationship to nature, lifestyles, technologies and aesthetic values we desire', it is hard to see, from any point of view, today, how that project could avoid explicit political and philosophical discussion concerning the place of religion in public life and personal identity.

References

Amin, A. (2006), 'The Good City', *Urban Studies* 43 (5/6), 1009–23.
Archer, M., Collier, A. and Porpora, D. (2004), *Transcendence: Critical Realism and God*. London: Routledge.

Badiou, A. (2006), *Being and Event*. London: Continuum.

—. (2009), *Logics of Worlds: Being and Event II*. London: Continuum.

Badiou, A., and Zizek, S. (2009), *Philosophy in the Present*. Cambridge: Polity.

Bhaskar, R. (1975), *A Realist Theory of Science*. Leeds: Leeds Books.

—. (1979), *The Possibility of Naturalism*. Brighton: Harvester Press.

—. (2000), *From East to West: Odyssey of a Soul*. London: Routledge.

—. (2002) *From Science to Emancipation: Journeys Towards Meta-Reality: a Philosophy for the Present: Alienation and the Actuality of Enlightenment*. London: Sage.

Collier, A. (2003), *On Christian Belief*. London: Routledge.

Dews, P. (2008), *The Idea of Evil*. Oxford: Blackwell.

Eagleton, T. (2009a), *Reason, Faith and Revolution: Reflections on the God Debate*. New Haven and London: Yale University Press.

—. (2009b), *Trouble With Strangers: A Study of Ethics*. Oxford: Wiley-Blackwell.

Harvey, D. (1973), *Social Justice and the City*. London: Edward Arnold.

—, 'The Right to the City', *New Left Review* series II 53, 23–40.

Mann, M. (2005), *The Dark Side of Democracy: Explaining Ethnic Cleansing*. Cambridge: Cambridge University Press.

McLennan, G. (2010a) 'Spaces of Post-secularism', in *Exploring the Postsecular: the religious, the political, the urban*, J. Beaumont, A. Molendijk and C. Jedan (eds). Leiden/Boston: Brill: 41–62.

—. (2010b), 'The Postsecular Turn', *Theory, Culture & Society* 27 (4), 3–20.

Meillassoux, Q. (2009), *After Finitude: An Essay on the Necessity of Contingency*. London: Continuum.

Taylor, C. (2007), *A Secular Age*. Cambridge, MA: Harvard University/Belknap Press.

Unger, R. (2007), *The Self Awakened: Pragmatism Unbound*. Cambridge, MA: Harvard University Press.

Part II

Competing Experiences of
Postsecular Cities

2 Postcolonialism and Religion: New Spaces of 'Belonging and Becoming' in the Postsecular City

Christopher Baker and Justin Beaumont

We have already acknowledged that the concept of the postsecular city is still a relatively recent and contested term. However, a working hypothesis currently informing our work is that the postsecular city is a public space which continues to be shaped by ongoing dynamics of secularization and secularism (as a political and cultural ideology) but that also has to negotiate and make space for the re-emergence of public expressions of religion and spirituality (see our Introduction). In the words of Habermas, we need 'a postsecular self-understanding of society as a whole in which the vigorous continuation of religion in a continually secularising environment must be reckoned with' (2005: 26).

In this chapter we shall be focusing on the new religious dynamics and energies brought to the public and political life of the Western 'secular' city by successive waves of global immigration from the South. Religious identity for the many carried along by these diasporic flows cannot be separated out into a private sphere of activity. As a core part of their whole identity, religion is primarily an integrating totality that influences and informs both private *and* public behaviour. This re-emergence of public religion in Western urban life, driven primarily by diasporic flows (although there are other dimensions to this debate such as the general re-enchantment of the West and the persistent and mutating presence of institutional Christian religion – often characterized as emerging or emergent church), is also therefore closely linked with ideas of the postcolonial city. These ideas coalesce around the notions of 'mongrel city' or 'cities of difference' in which narratives of fluid, hybridized and multiple identities (including religious or spiritual ones) disrupt colonial, modernist narratives based on static, stratified and essentialized hierarchies of value.

Previous analyses of the impact of religious identity on urban spaces have tended to be emblematic, and have generally ignored the closely grained and unique character of local spaces and spatialities. This chapter will therefore attempt to attend to both the political and spatial dimensions of this interface between

religion, spirituality, identity and local space in order to come to a fresh interpretation of this increasingly significant nexus of variables.

This overall aim will be achieved with reference to a three-stage argument.
The first stage offers a brief review of ideas and theories regarding the postcolonial
city (developed below) which will then be categorized into what might be
termed optimistic or pessimistic readings. It is clear that the majority of readings
concerning the potential of the postcolonial city are gloomy and dystopian. Most
commentators see the postcolonial city as an ongoing space of fragmented
and contested identities, whose attempts at the creation of an effective progressive
politics is hampered by continuing processes of neoliberal neocolonialism by the
global market (Massey, 2007; Harvey, 2006; Amin, Massey and Thrift, 2000).

The second stage addresses this deficit by offering a series of 'snapshots' of how
religious faith and activity, especially that generated by immigrant communities, is
creating different types of 'space' within the postsecular city (see also Ley, 2008).
Three case studies (drawn from some Leverhulme research featuring different faith
communities in the United Kingdom[1]) will show how primarily religious identities
interact with public norms and expectations generated by British society. These
spaces will be assessed for their capacity to reframe and influence urban life on a
daily, lived level. To help us understand this, the categories of spaces of 'belonging'
and 'becoming' will be used, which are in the process of being developed from the
Leverhulme research project mentioned above. For spaces of 'belonging', we will
refer to those emotionally supportive and nurturing benefits derived from belonging to religious or spiritual groups (such as Buddhist meditation classes). These
benefits are mediated through both social contact and connection, as well as through
practices associated with religious experiences, such as prayer, worship and meditation (see Baker, 2009b). These benefits are expressed in terms such as the following:

- Through my religious or spiritual group (RSG), I meet people who inspire me.
- I feel part of a wider family when I am in my RSG.
- I meet lots of different people through my RSG.
- I meet people who have the same beliefs as me through my RSG.
- I feel more secure and less anxious by taking part in RSG.
- Through my RSG, I can explore deeper questions.
- Through my RSG, I make connections with others who help me with life
  outside. (Leverhulme Research Project, 2010)[2]

The feelings of deep solidarity, trust and peacefulness engendered through
these technologies of belonging help provide a safe and supportive space by which
different identities – religious, cultural, ethnic (and with more difficulty, gendered)
– can be translated and negotiated into a functioning whole (see Bhabha, 1994).
Thus, religious participants move from spaces of belonging to spaces of 'becoming',
in ways (as we shall see) that allow them to become (or develop) a new identity
forged out of a number of different and sometimes competing and existing identities.
This new identity can be interpreted (again using Bhabha's conceptual and postcolonial framework) as emerging from a Thirdspace (Baker, 2009a). That is to say,

this new identity is a direct product of the competing pressures of the postsecular city, in which there is simultaneously both more acceptance of religious identities (for example, as part of government social policy), but equally more resistance against religious identity as certain secular institutions and public figures react negatively to the re-emergence of public religion.

The chapter concludes by correlating emerging evidence of this postcolonial religious experience with key thinking within political philosophy concerning the foundations of new public space in the West. More recently this rise of public religious expression has allowed religious identity to be foregrounded in relation to issues of human rights and equalities rather than subsumed within either issues of culture or ethnicity. The chapter suggests that current shifts towards recognizing the public validity of religious belief and expression are still too essentialized and static to reflect the fluid and complex experiences and needs of religious citizens. What is required is a bottom-up rather than top-down understanding of diversity which looks at how spaces of postcolonial religious interaction are formed and performed in the postsecular city. We conclude with a discussion of issues at stake when considering prospects for more progressive spaces of religious engagement in postcolonial spaces of cities.

The postcolonial city – space of opportunity or repression?

The history of the concept of postcolonialism, from the late 1950s onwards (see Fanon 1965; Said, 1978 and Blunt and McEwan, 2002) and its application to urban space has recently received a helpful and concise literature overview (King, 2009). As well as denoting historical processes of colonialism, the term has also been used as a critiquing concept, referring to the 'distinctive impact which colonialism has had on the economy, society, culture, spatial form and architecture of the city, but also in the way the city is understood and represented' (King, 2009: 1).

Relevant for this discussion is the caution that King advocates towards the use of the term, pointing out its Westerncentrism, and its privileging of certain dystopian neocolonial processes such as globalization and militarization which favour a 'global cities' type rhetoric and analysis (e.g. Harvey, 2001; Sassen, 1991; Castells, 1989, 1996). Under the terms of this discourse, cities are seen from the 'outside', as malleable receptacles for the processes of global capitalism to bend and distort local space as it wishes, for the sake of maximum return for the private sector.

Other examples of this 'dystopian' genre would be the influential volume on postcolonial urbanism from a South-East Asian context (Bishop et al., 2003) whose treatment of the destructive impact of war tourism on East Timor, Export Processing Zones (in the Philippines), as well as the demonization of Algerian youth in contemporary Paris, would be prime examples of this type of discourse. Meanwhile, additional melancholic readings of problematic postcolonial identity focus on a city region like Singapore. These readings reflect on the difficulties of locating an authentic Malaysian/Chinese literary voice in the context of British postcolonialism, and the unsettling 'haunting' of postcolonial cities by the restless spirits of those whose lives have been absorbed and recycled by the 'vampiric' city (see Pile, 2003).

In contrast (or at least running parallel) to this approach is the call from King to respect the 'insider' view of the postcolonial city, based on the lived experience of those who actually use urban space and wish to express their experience in their local dialects and idioms (King, 2009: 3). There is also a call to express more of the 'celebratory' memories of the postcolonial city, which of themselves point to a 'changing, vibrant future, a new kind of intellectual milieu created by new ethnicities, hybridised identities and diasporas that create new and distinctive cultures in each unique, geographically and culturally specific postcolonial city' (King, 2009: 5).

An example of this more 'celebratory' genre would be the work emerging in the mid- and late 1990s from primarily feminist critical geographers such as Massey (1994), Blunt and Rose (1994), Jacobs and Fincher (1998) and Sandercock (1998, 2003). Sandercock (whose latest work is featured in this volume) is particularly significant in that she explicitly links her positive vision of the postcolonial city based on difference and diversity (Cosmopolis) to the importance of creating spaces in which religion and spirituality can flourish (what she calls the City of Spirit). However, she is also under no illusions of the difficulties involved in creating sustainable political coalitions based on difference, and that community projects aimed at deep social or spatial transformation are often short lived. To some extent, these pragmatic and fluid coalitions simply reflect the ever-shifting spatial and cultural contexts in which local urban politics takes place, and she has no interest in creating monolithic utopias so characteristic of modernist planning and political economy.

These two approaches (namely, the insider and 'lived' view, and the celebratory vision of the plural and diverse city) help us move away from dualistic and abstract readings of postcolonial urban space into something that is more nuanced, textured and complex. It is in this spirit that this chapter now looks at the relationship between the British postcolonial urban experience and religious expression as a particular take on the postsecular city.

Religious spaces in the postcolonial city

This section begins to unpack the diversity of religious spaces in postcolonial urban contexts in the United Kingdom. This will constitute what we define as a textured mapping of space that looks not only at externalities with regard to how that 'religious' space is used, but also explores how these externalities reflect deeper and more hidden processes of identity formation and the expression of values and ethics. The three case studies, mainly emerging from recent research work for the Leverhulme Trust in the United Kingdom (see Note 1) have been deliberately selected to represent a wide diversity of spaces and religious traditions. The first religious space is a Hindu temple and community centre – a formal and demarcated space, but which nevertheless is used and interpreted in a surprising variety of ways. The second is a more political and fluid space – a homeless project run by the Salvation Army, a Christian denomination with a strong religious identity and evangelistic mission, but which nevertheless attracts a widely diverse range of volunteers. The third is an educational space – two Muslim study circles held in a mosque (one for men and one for women) which reveals the benefits of membership that such a group can offer. These include the motivation and confidence to participate in wider society but also a framework for a partially successful integration of religious, ethnic, gendered and political identities on a personal level.

The Hindu community centre

This 'flagship' space, located in a northern English city, combines a large temple, sports hall, kitchens and dining areas on the ground floor, as well as meeting rooms and seminar rooms on the upper floor. It runs several activities for the local Hindu community, including daily luncheon clubs, yoga classes, healthy eating classes, Indian harmonium classes, Indian dance and cookery classes, Gujarati and English classes (with GSCE accreditation). Its temple is the regional and often national centre for religious festivals and celebrations. Meanwhile, the centre also works in close partnership with secular agencies such as the National Health Service (NHS) for drop-in health clinics, the local social services, and the Local Authority who hire the space for its own meetings and initiatives. It also works closely with local schools and education authorities in providing hospitality and guided tours for those studying religion as part of the school curriculum. It is therefore both a building that reinforces Hindu religious and cultural identity for diasporic Indian communities (primarily from Africa) who have been settling in the area since the late 1940s, as well as being an open and welcoming place for those from the wider community who appreciate its resources and want to learn more about Hindu culture and religion.

What is particularly interesting about this religious space is not so much what it does, but the way in which it is viewed by different generations of the Indian community who live in the region. The elders of the community arrived in this part of the United Kingdom in the 1940s with little by way of resources. Although often better educated than those within the host community with whom they settled, this first generation was willing to take on low-paid jobs and poor housing (one member of a focus group for the Leverhulme project told us that they remembered 14 people living in a small terraced house). They also experienced initial racism, were deprived access to services such as banking, and so had little choice but to establish a strong community ethos, aimed at mutual support and service provision. Thus, they spent two or three decades establishing culturally appropriate support services for each other, including lending and saving facilities and slowly but surely taking over more properties for community use and saving hard as they went along. This self-sufficient strategy continued even when several first generation immigrants began to find better paid and more secure employment. During this period, they were also sending money back to India. As one research participant recalled, 'My wife used to work 48 hours for £2.50. I can't explain to people who get twenty to thirty pounds an hour, but this is how it started. People in India – they expected money from some of us and we used to send one pound'.

As the wealth and confidence of the first generation grew, there was a growing perception that a dedicated centre was required that combined a religious focus with cultural services, while also providing a showcase to the wider community concerning the vibrant nature of Hindu life and identity. The current centre was conceived and built over many years at a cost of £4 million, all of which was raised by local fundraising and effort. It therefore represents for this first generation of Hindu immigrants a powerful symbol of pride and cultural resilience. It is also clear that what they most value the building for is the temple space and the chance to pray and meditate in front of the deities. It is indeed a magnificent space, with craftsmen from India drafted to do authentic carvings and friezes. They also value the daily lunch club (co-funded by the local council) at which they all volunteer by shopping, cooking and washing up afterwards. It provides a focus for social activity and provides a sense of purpose and well-being, a view summed up by one focus group participant when they said; '... in my opinion ... we meet a lot of people here who we don't know. By meeting them we are getting to know them more and it is helping us healthwise too, because sitting at home you get sick and fed up'.

However, for all the efforts of this first generation to create an embedded sense of belonging and activity in the United Kingdom, there is still a sense of deep connection with their life back in Africa: 'Though we have come from East Africa our heart is still in East Africa – if we see something being done wrong there, we feel bad about it. We also keep our heart from where we come from' (as a reference to their Indian heritage). So feelings and ideas of belonging are still complex and perhaps unresolved for this group of immigrants who have doubly uprooted themselves across three continents. But how has this sense of identity within British society evolved in subsequent generations, and how are these younger identities reflected in attitudes towards the centre?

The main difference between the younger and older generations concerns the issue of religious practice. Many of the younger people in the research focus groups reflected that they were less religiously observant than their elders. This response was a typical one. 'I'm not very religious, but I will choose to do the things that I feel I believe in'. Another young person said, 'Most of the elderly are involved in the ritualistic form of worship, but the younger generation believe in God, but they are not into many rituals ... they would not want to come to the temple every day, but they would do it once in a week, once in a month. They would want to take part in the religious festivals which is a more fun activity to do where they sing, dance, meet friends ... but they are not into ritualistic activities'.

However, the cultural centre is still an important place for the younger generation. For a focus group member recently arrived in the United Kingdom from India, the sense of familiarity was important 'to have the support of your community members and [and environment] almost like the one you have come from ... It gives a feeling of confidence ... of security. There are a lot of social activities which helps you get ahead ... understanding what it is to be an Indian in the midst people of the UK and also being able to have a channel which will help you continue your culture, tradition and heritage'. Meanwhile, for those young Hindus born in Britain and for whom, in the words of one, 'it's very easy to become very Westernised and forget your culture', the temple and the centre and the many opportunities it offers fulfil an equally important function. 'Coming here [to the centre] does remind you of your culture so there is a nice feeling of security. The activities that go on here remind you of what being Indian is about'.

As well as a feeling of security, British-born Hindus also talk about the temple/ cultural centre and its activities in terms of the sense of 'confidence and teamwork' it gives them. As one of them remarks, 'all the activities that we learn here gives a lot of confidence to go out into the mainstream and work with them and mingle with them'. The joint religious and community activities represented by the building and its design seem to allow these younger Hindus to point both ways at the same time – a sense of being rooted in a tradition, but in an open and empow-ering way that allows them to integrate in mainstream society, and to feel confident as young British, Hindu, Guajarati citizens. As one young focus group members sums up, '. . . it's important to keep your identity as well as mix with other people and socialise with them'.

So for the younger generation, the temple and centre is not so important as a religious space, but a space of learning and participation that gives a sense of security, confidence and the importance of learning to be part of a team. It would seem that they are able to take advantage of the cultural capital built up by their forebears who sacrificed much to establish a stable and embedded presence in UK society. The role of this religious space is therefore more wide ranging and subtle than the simple remembering of rituals from a mother tongue within an alien culture. It would appear not to be a backward-looking space, but a dynamic and creative one, putting religious and cultural tradition at the service of the younger generation who, in turn, shape that religious and cultural capital to not only adapt but also shape the wider, pluralized culture in which they are located. This is represented by the hospitality that the temple and centre offer to those outside the worshipping community, offering important spaces of learning, well-being and political participation to those who live around it.

The Salvation Army homeless project

The Salvation Army has a long-established and proven track record of working in this area of social care, and this space represents a well-established research field in respect to showcasing an example of transformative faith-based urban praxis (Cloke et al., 2010). Most recent research in this area (Johnsen, 2009), while flag-ging up some interesting overlaps between faith-based and non-faith-based homeless service providers, is inconclusive with regard to possible 'added value' with respect to faith-based provision.

A new and embryonic approach to this research area is required: one that might suggest seeing this field as a volunteering space – a space which attracts an extraor-dinary variety of people into what is, on the surface at least, a faith-dominant environment. UK researcher Greg Smith has done some preliminary reflection on the nuanced complexity of this postsecular space based on his management experience of a Salvation Army homeless project which includes support of homeless people, the elderly, the unemployed and informal IT classes in the com-munity computer suite. He manages a team of approximately 25 external volunteers who facilitate at least one session per week. He reflects on the core mission of the Salvation Army to proclaim and build 'The Kingdom of God'. As a church, 'it remains an unashamedly evangelical and evangelising movement' while as a 'deliverer of public services it remains impressive as one of the largest charities in the UK with an annual budget of many billions and a workforce of thousands of paid employees' (Smith, 2010). This potential clash between spiritual and political agendas is to some extent resolved by the prohibition placed by external statutory authorities on any proselytization of clients. But neither is it the 'style of the Army in its community programmes to "Bible bash" or aggressively proclaim the importance of Christian faith and the need for salvation' (Smith, 2010).

The result of these dynamics is the creation of a space that one might characterize as 'implicitly religious and open access'. While the core identity and mission values of the Salvation Army couldn't be any more specifically Christian (including the importance of evangelization), its commitment to social justice as part of its core mission means it tempers this *explicit* identity in order to be able to provide public services to the widest possible groupings in society. Thus, a more *implicitly* religious identity is at work within these publically sponsored projects which also welcomes volunteers from a variety of faith backgrounds and those with none. The key to the success of this project is that this hybrid religious identity that strategically deploys both explicit and implicit religious/Christian identities (see Baker, 2008) not only attracts a diverse selection of volunteers, it also makes them feel comfortable and motivated to work in this challenging yet rewarding area of social care.

Simply put, the diversity of volunteers attracted to this project, in which both faith-based and secular social actors share the same voluntary space is fairly remarkable in a mundane sort of way. Smith (2010) records his initial of these social actors mapping in the following ways:

- three of four retired people who would probably call themselves Christian but are not actively practising but who want to keep active and connected with other people
- a Filipino woman recently arrived in the United Kingdom who is a practising Roman Catholic, but who was recommended to do voluntary work by employment advisors as a way of improving her skills and fluency in English while she is waiting for permission to work to be granted
- three well-qualified people of working age with no overt faith commitment who have become unemployed in the recent recession, who want to do something worthwhile while they seek work
- two well-qualified and 'hi-flying' working age men recuperating from ME/ Chronic fatigue syndrome who are testing out possibilities in the hope of being able to return to part-time work. Both are highly committed evangelical Christians who worship in other local churches
- half a dozen female students from the local university of further education (FE) college (some on social work courses) mostly with no strong faith commitment (though one is a Muslim), who are doing voluntary work to gain experience and improve their CVs and/or as a course requirement

- an unemployed IT professional who is a convinced atheist from a previous church background in which his father is an ordained minister;
- young, locally born Muslim woman who chooses always to wear Islamic dress, including a niqab face covering, but who wanted to offer service outside the confines of her own faith community
- a number of people with significant mental health issues or mild learning difficulties recommended to the project and often accompanied by their support workers who see volunteering as an element of therapy (Smith, 2010)

In order to understand its impact and potential, more research needs to be done in delving further into the motivations and benefits that such a wide variety of people are seeking to express and gain by engaging in this space. But the value of this case study offers three tantalizing insights into these emerging phenomenological spaces of postsecular engagement. First, it is perfectly possible to create a faith-oriented space in which both religious and secular people can collaborate in and contribute to common aims and express common values. Second, the array of motivations and different needs being met within this space: religious, vocational, humanist, professional, ethical, educational, even therapeutic, reminds us of the complexity and multi-levelled nature of outcomes such spaces now represent. These needs and motivations are perhaps part of a microcosm, a definition of the postsecular public space as a whole. A functionalist or instrumentalist reading of this space (based on binary codes such as voluntary vs. professional, religious vs. secular, fundamentalist vs. liberal, top-down vs. bottom-up, network vs. institution) will no longer suffice to explain or analyse these 'blurred encounters' (Reader and Baker, 2009). We need to develop new categories of analysis and theory to represent properly these extraordinary micro-public spaces of encounter (Amin, 2002). Third, it is a point of conjecture, but perhaps a significant one, that the explicitly faith-based framework of the Salvation Army project is more attractive to those of other faith traditions than a secular-based project (this certainly seems to have been a significant causal factor in the decision of one Muslim woman volunteer).

The Muslim study circles

Our final case study (from the Leverhulme research) reflects on the experience of two Muslim study circles which meet regularly at a Muslim centre, one for men only and the other for women. The study circle is a weekly meeting dedicated to discussing the application of the Koran to the problems and issues of everyday contemporary life, under the informed facilitation of an imam. These study circles thus present a snapshot into the way these young Muslims who are both British-born and more recent immigrants regard themselves as citizens in the United Kingdom and how their religious tradition and practice impacts on their sense of identity and well-being. I will analyse material from these focus groups under two headings: the resilience afforded by religious identity and religious spaces (such as mosques), including the dense social networks they create which span both local and global boundaries; and the strategies of citizenship generated by participation in these study circles.

There is little doubt that most mosques will represent some of the most diverse spaces to be found anywhere in the United Kingdom. As one of the women in our focus group reflected, 'Say like we are from different parts of the world, that's where we originate from, but the Islam that we are actually learning is just the basic fundamental principles of peace that apply to everyone from everywhere . . . [In our mosque] there's Bengali, there's English people, there's Bosnian people, there's Moroccan people, French people, Malaysian, Indonesian . . . also Somalians'. The sense of belonging to a global community is compared to that of a family, who come together in one symbolically significant space on a regular basis to share a common experience (be it of prayer, education and training, socializing or political awareness raising and charity work). There is thus a tremendous sense of solidarity to be derived from this experience, which appears to be mediated in the following ways. As one male contributor reflects, 'When you come on a Friday, you feel as though you are part of the sum . . . you notice across the whole [prayer] line there wouldn't be anyone who is the same race as you'. Another participant in our male study groups, a recent arrival in the United Kingdom, conveys some of this sense of solidarity: '. . . what everyone needs . . . we need to socialise with other people, we need to socialise in this type of city – it's very hard to get the right atmosphere, so I think this is the right place for me'. A fellow participant talks about the presence of 'a kind of atmosphere of togetherness' generated by the study group, in which everyone is treated the same. Another colleague talks in more concrete terms as to how certain types of religious practice generate this sense of 'togetherness': 'Islam has a lot of things in it about community-based living, like for fasting, you would break the fast together, you would pray together, it's more of a blessing if you pray together . . . you keep each other together in a stronger link'. There were clear references to the experiences of racism and discrimination faced by members of the study group, which at their most strongly felt, generate a palpable sense of fear and anxiety, and a sense of being corrupted by an alien and hostile culture. 'When we come to this place its like a way to escape, to keep you safe . . . then you can purify yourself and remember Allah again and you feel safe, even after you leave . . . and are in the middle of the dangerous area that is the city centre.'

So according to this experience, the mosque functions as a 'sanctuary' (as another male focus group participant referred to it), which, in certain cases, could function as a place of retreat from the wider community, and a space where differences based on religious (and cultural) identities and the rest of society are reinforced.

However, the Leverhulme research uncovers other perspectives that point in another direction. It suggests that the solidarity generated for diasporic communities by religious practices associated with their religious identity also generates strategies for practices of citizenship, and thus by implication, a more comfortable resolution of what can be experienced as conflicting identities based on religion, ethnic and national identities.

So, for example, there was much reference in both study groups to the ethical injunctions within Islam to be a good neighbour as part of the responsibility placed by the Koran on the believer to live out a virtuous life. There are clear distinctions made between the Muslim community (the Ummah) and the non-Muslim community. For example, the five pillars (prayer, pilgrimage, almsgiving, profession of faith in Allah and the Prophet, and fasting) are focused primarily on the well-being of Islam. However, virtuous behaviour within the Islamic community clearly spills out into compassion and concern for the whole created order, which several members of the male focus groups defined as 'being a role model for people around you ... be a good neighbour,' ' ... trying to create a better society ... hoping that [our] good morals will rub off on others,' ' ... somebody praying in the mosque will go outside and do something good, it will affect somebody else and so on ... it's a rebound effect'.

Meanwhile, it is perhaps within the women's focus group that a more nuanced and less 'instrumental' view of the link between religious faith and civic participation emerges. First, it is clear that the dense social support networks generated by the study circle and attendance at the mosque are vital to the well-being and emotional functioning of these women. The following responses are typical of sentiments expressed throughout the focus group discussions: 'It's like a big sisterhood, we all bond together'; 'It's about meeting different people's needs. If you want a bit of time to reflect on your own we just take over the childcare responsibilities'; 'You can listen to the speaker and chill out and calm down'; ' ... you know this place [study circle] is secure for someone who may be a little shaky about Islam or going through a bad time and just needs a secure environment where they can talk to someone or just come and sit and unload their head'. The religious dimension and purpose of the group are inextricably woven into these social benefits. Again, the following comment is a typical one, showing the clear links between religious practice and well-being. 'I found that a lot of my friends who are not religious don't understand praying. I tell them that it is my little moment with God ... you sit there and you talk to him and say everything that is going on in life ... it's a relief ... when you pray, you are unloading your problems'.

Second, the emotional security and solidarity created by these women who attend this particular study circle, and supported by the practice of prayer and worship and religious education within the mosque, generates significant numbers of specific outcomes that make a practical contribution to the well-being of others. For example:

- training in the use of computers and the internet
- Serenity Project (a group supporting mothers and young children within an Islamic environment).
- a Bosnia project
- raising money for earthquake victims in Kashmir.
- visits to Egypt to support an orphanage and other projects helping the visually impaired
- providing care support for an old woman recently out of hospital

The above evidence suggests that the main impact of this form of participation is primarily aimed at the well-being of the Islamic community (both locally and globally). However, there is also some evidence that this study circle is also equipping these women to participate with confidence in the wider community as good citizens, going about their daily business, but with an eye out for the wider implications for how their religious identity might be perceived and indeed received by others. Here are some typical responses: 'We respect that there are people who are our friends who have other religions'; 'My neighbours are non-Muslims so I don't see a difference really. They are all God's people, they are from Adam and that's how I see it'; 'One of my colleagues said, 'Why are you always so nice to people, as people do give you a hard time', but to me, [the person] who is giving me a hard time doesn't know me and when you know me, then you can judge me . . . There are a lot of people who don't know about Islam and if you get the right person to give that message I'm up for it'.

Conclusion

So let's recap. In this section we have looked at three contrasting religious spaces in what we are referring to in this chapter as the postcolonial and postsecular city.

The Hindu temple was a richly symbolic and beautiful space at the heart of a large modern complex of other well-appointed spaces for use by both the local Hindu and wider community (including local government and statutory providers). It represents a space of pride, self-sufficiency and embeddedness: physical proof that the Hindu community, present in its city for 60 years, has come of age. It is both rooted in traditional culture but open to the diverse, contemporary British setting in which it is located. As well as religious and cultural activities, the space provides for many educational, training and social support services. This allows the first generation of Hindu migrants to pass on, in relevant ways, traditions and language to the subsequent generations who speak of the confidence it gives them to forge new identities that are equally Gujarati, Hindu and British. With its pragmatic and flexible approach to meeting the needs of a wide variety of users, the building somehow epitomizes the rooted openness that seems to characterize the experience and philosophy of the Hindu community as a whole.

The Salvation Army homeless project was, at a cognitive level, a space that operated under the auspices of an explicitly Christian framework. However, at an ethical and pragmatic level, it was a space that was attractive to a wide range of volunteers: from different shades of theological opinion within the Christian denomination, those of other faith traditions and those who profess no faith. It is also possible to discern within this space, an implicit vision based on notions of the common good and working towards expression of a more just and inclusive society. To this extent, therefore, this sort of space possibly represents something of Sandercock's *cosmopolis* ideal, that is, a diverse and pluralized space in which people *do* express their sense of sharing an intertwined destiny. The fact that this is ostensibly a religious space, we argue, is likely to make it more appealing to diasporic communities for whom religion and faith are still explicit motivating drivers.

Finally, the Islamic study circles offer spaces of solidarity and sanctuary for both British-born and globally diasporic Muslim individuals. However, these are also safe spaces of engagement, in which religious and theological identities and questions can be brought into dialogue with other trends within UK society – namely, pluralization and secularization. Again, further research needs to be undertaken, but it would appear that there is a spectrum of engagement generated by these religious learning spaces. On one side of the spectrum, it could be that religious and cultural identity is reinforced within the study circle which leads to a hardening of Islamic identity over and against other identities. However, as the evidence suggests, there is also a dynamic that encourages a broader sense of confidence in participation that moves beyond a proactive care for the Muslim *ummah* into more generic forms of citizenship. This sense of citizenship is based on a clear commitment to living out a responsible life, based on religious injunctions contained within the Koran. It is expressed in being a good neighbour, a conscientious employee or employer and a positive role model to those beyond the Muslim community.

Coda – Religion in the public square in the postcolonial, postsecular city – a debate with Habermas

In concluding the arguments of this chapter, it is important that we frame the narratives emerging from these three protean spaces of postsecular, postcolonial engagement into a wider circulation of debate as to the future shape of the postsecular public space. As we have already seen in this volume, the last ten years have seen an accelerating interest in the re-emergence of religion in the public, urban sphere. Central to this debate has been the work of Jurgen Habermas, whose concerns for the creation and protection of an inclusive and robust public, democratic space, independent of the totalizing instincts of both the State and the Market, has been evident for the past 25 years or more (Habermas, 1987). Recently, he has turned his attention explicitly towards the role of religion in the cause of creating these robust and independent spaces, offering not only an analysis of the contribution (and the obstacles) religion brings to this debate, but also how the rest of the public sphere has to adapt in order to allow religion to play its fullest part. In two key articles written in 2005 and 2006, he develops some of his thinking about what a future civil society and public sphere with religion as an important component might look at.

The first, entitled *Equal Treatment of Cultures and the Limits of Postmodern Liberalism* (2005), begins with an overview of the historical bases of liberal philosophy and political economy (Locke, Kant, Rawls et al.), before updating these debates by addressing the key question of the moment, namely, how to safeguard the right of equality within increasingly diverse and plural societies with specific regard to freedom of religious expression within the public sphere, and including the issue of those social and cultural rights in which such expression is embedded (2005: 16).

Sometimes the cultural norms within religious communities can act across the rights of minorities within their ranks, such as children or women or members whose views are labelled as dissenting or dysfunctional (what Will Kymlica calls 'problematic rights' (quoted Habermas, 2005: 20) and what Habermas himself calls 'illiberal ways of life', 2005: 24). This cultural disenfranchisement is unacceptable within the norms generated by secular notions of equality (derived, as Habermas notes, from a Judeo-Christian 'genealogy' (2005: 24)). However, Habermas is aware of the pressure generated by secular power structures on religious traditions and cultures to 'modernise' (2005: 24). These pressures might be detrimental to the transmission of their cultural particularity or purity, and restrict their ability to participate authentically in the public sphere.

So the traditional secular model of the public sphere, whereby the role of 'community member' (for example, a religious community) is *differentiated* from 'member of society' is unsustainable (hence, the limits of postmodern liberalism which he alludes to in the title of his paper). This differentiation lies in the tension between a cognitive level of belief (i.e. the beliefs generated by the transcendental view of his or her religion) and the legal norms of the host community, whereby a secular society 'tells' the religious citizen that certain beliefs or practices are unacceptable or illegal. This therefore raises for Habermas the question of whether this differentiation (which is not required of secular citizens) and the cognitive dissonance it produces, creates an unfair and therefore unequal pressure (what he calls paying 'an unfair price') on religious citizens. These citizens, he argues, have to undergo an act of reflection or relativization whereby any cognitive dissonance is made bearable.

Habermas concludes these knotty arguments by saying that the guarantee of equal ethical liberties requires the secularization of state power, but it forbids 'the political overgeneralisation of the secularised world view'. He hints at the need for a 'dialectical understanding of cultural secularisation' (2005: 28) which reflects the limits of both religious and secular epistemologies, and requires a more mutual sharing of the cognitive tasks involved in attempting to understand each other's positions. '. . . secularised citizens may neither fundamentally deny truth potential to religious worldviews nor deny the right of believing citizens to make contributions to public discussion in religious language. A liberal political culture can even expect that secularised citizens take part in efforts to translate relevant contributions from religious language into a publically accessible language' (2005: 28).

Habermas's 2006 article, *Religion in the Public Sphere,* goes into greater detail as to what these shared cognitive tasks might be (and which there is not the scope to outline in this chapter). The overall tone is less prescriptive towards religious groups than his previous article, and more interested in outlining the changes that secularism must go through. For example, there is a more explicit critique of the 'naturalist background of secularism' (2006: 16) which in its more obvious mode, 'devalues all categories of statements that cannot be reduced to controlled observations, nomological propositions or causal explanations'. There is also more emphasis on not just a passive accommodation of religion, but an active 'learning' from religion (2006: 17) on the part of wider society. What is significant for the arguments in this chapter is that Habermas is far more explicit about the need for the secular state to recognize the significance of the *lived reality* of religious belief that makes the cognitive differentiation identified by Habermas in the previous article very difficult. Religion, he says, alluding to Augustinian concepts, is 'the seat of everyday life'. He continues, 'A devout person pursues her daily rounds by *drawing* on belief (original emphasis). Put differently, true belief is not only a doctrine ... but a source of energy that the person who has faith taps performatively and thus nurtures his or her entire life' (2006: 8).

This important recognition that religious belief is a fundamental component of both the practice and identity of a religious citizen's life moves our arguments into future areas of debate which we have begun to identify in respect of the case studies in this chapter. These are as follows:

- Religious spaces can be an indicative of both postsecular and postcolonial trends within our urban environment because of their highly performative nature.
- Despite the tendency to essentialize religious identity by even enlightened secularization theorists such as Habermas, the performative nature of religious practice and its impact means that it is both complex and fluid, and not easily analysable in terms of either/or categories.
- Indeed, some of these spaces operate more like a Third Space (see Bhabha, 1994, Baker, 2009) in which competing identities can be safely negotiated, and emergent and proactive rapprochements between people of different faiths, and none, can be performed and analysed.
- Again, the performative nature of religious engagement within the public space means that good practice in relation to equal rights in the public space is not likely to be theorized in ways that can lead to universal laws and principles. Indeed, we suggest that part of the new 'dialogical culturalism' implied by Habermas needs to be the realization that we may only be able to recognize good practice when it occurs and then apply any learning retrospectively.

It is with these four pointers to future research agendas that we conclude this chapter on the nature of the postcolonial encounter in the postsecular city. We hope to have shown the radically performative and complex nature of the interaction between religion, postcolonialism and postsecularism in the urban setting. This radical and flexible performativity so far resists embedded or static analysis – hence, the subtitle of this chapter. The emphasis on new spaces of belonging and becoming (in particular) hints at the emergence of new practices and strategies that, when they work well, are productive forms of activity for both religious and non-religious urban citizens alike.

Notes

1   Faith and Traditional Capitals: defining the public scope of religious capital (2007–2010) was a major research programme undertaken by the William Temple Foundation for the Leverhulme Trust. Building on WTF's previous work in urban regeneration, it is designed to test the concepts of religious and spiritual capital across the major religious and spiritual traditions in the United Kingdom. Over 150 participants contributed to 25 focus groups, and the

conversations were transcribed. These transcriptions were analysed using the thematic network method, and several of the emerging themes and statements that this generated were converted into a form suitable for use in a quantitative survey. Eight hundred respondents completed both paper and online versions of this survey. The research project, taken as a whole, represents a phenomenological account of the important connections between religious and spiritual capital and the spaces they create. These spaces (rooted and expressed in religious symbolism and practice) can represent a cumulative journey for many religious citizens which unfold from spaces of *belonging* to spaces to *becoming* to spaces of *participation* in an extending radius or dialogic movement of trust.

2   These are some of the 100 or so statements generated for the qualitative survey created for the Leverhulme/William Temple Foundation research project into religious and spiritual capital mentioned above, and which were completed by 800 respondents across faith communities in the United Kingdom.

References

Amin, A., Massey, D. and Thrift, N. (2000), *Cities for the Many, not the Few.* Bristol: Policy Press.

—. (2002), 'Ethnicity and the Multicultural City: Living with Diversity' *Environment and Planning A* 34, 959–80.

Baker, C. (2007) 'Entry to Enterprise: Constructing Local Political Economies in Manchester' in J. Atherton and H. Skinner (eds), *Through the Eye of a Needle – theological conversations over political economy.* Peterborough: Epworth Press.

—. (2009a), *The Hybrid Church in the City – Third Space Thinking* (2nd edn). London: SCM Press.

—. (2009b), 'Social, Religious and Spiritual capitals: A Psychological Perspective?' in M. de Souza, L.J. Francis, J. O'Higgins-Norman, and D. Scott (eds). *International Handbook of Education for Spirituality, Care and Wellbeing.* London: Springer.

Bhabha, H. (1994), *The Location of Culture.* London and New York: Routledge.

Bishop, R., Phillips, J., and Wei Wei, Y. (eds) (2003), *Postcolonial Urbanism – Southeast Asian Cities and Global Processes.* New York and London: Routledge.

Blunt, A., and Rose, G. (1994), *Writing Women and Space – Colonial and Post Colonial Geographies.* New York: Guilford Press.

Blunt, A., and McEwan, C. (2002), *Postcolonial Geographies.* New York and London: Continuum.

Castells, M. (1989), *The Informational City: Information, Technology, Economic Restructuring, and the Urban-Regional Process.* Oxford: Blackwell.

—. (1996), *The Rise of the Network Society.* Oxford and Cambridge, MA: Blackwell.

Cloke, P., May, J., and Johnsen, S. (2010), *Swept-Up Lives? Re-envisioning the Homeless City.* Chichester: Wiley-Blackwell.

Fanon, F. (1965), *A Dying Colonialism.* New York: Grove.

Fincher, R., and Jacobs, J. (1998), *Cities of Difference.* New York, GuilfordPress.

Habermas. J. (1987), *The Theory of Communicative Action Volume 2 – Lifeworld and System – a Critique of Functionalist Reason.* Boston: Beacon Press.

—. (2005), 'Equal Treatment of Cultures and the Limits of Postmodern Liberalism', *Journal of Political Philosophy* 13 (1), 1–28.

—. (2006), 'Religion in the Public Sphere', *European Journal of Philosophy* 14, 1–25.

Harvey, D. (2001), *Spaces of Capital – Towards a Critical Geography.* New York: Routledge.

—. (2006), *Spaces of Global Capitalism: A Theory of Uneven Geographical Development.* London: Verso.

Johnsen, S. (2009), 'The Difference that "aith' Makes: Faith-based Organisations and the Provision of Services for Homeless People." ESRC/AHRC Religion and Society, http://www.religionandsociety.org.uk/uploads/docs/2010_07/1278582059_Johnsen_Phase_1_Small_Grant_Project_Document.pdf (accessed 15 September 2010).

King, A. (2009), *Postcolonial cities* (Online paper), http://www.elsevierdirect.com/brochures/hugy/SampleContent/Postcolonial-Cities.pdf (Accessed 1 March 2010).

Ley, D. (2008), 'The Immigrant Church as an Urban Service Hub', *Urban Studies,* 45 (10), 2057–74.

Massey, D. (1994), *Space, Place and Gender.* Cambridge: Policy Press.

—. (2007), *World City.* Cambridge and Malden MA: Polity Press.

Pile, S. (2003), 'Perpetual Returns: Vampires and the Colonised City', in R. Bishop, J. Phillips and Y. Wei Wei (eds), *Postcolonial Urbanism: Southeast Asian Cities and Global Processes.* New York and London: Routledge.

Reader, J., and Baker, C. (2009), *Entering the New Theological Space: Blurred Encounters in Faith, Politics and Community.* Aldershot: Ashgate.

Said, E. (1979), *Orientalism.* New York: Vintage.

Sandercock, L. (1998), *Towards Cosmopolis: Planning for Multicultural Cities.* Chichester and New York: John Wiley.

—. (2003), *Cosmopolis II; Mongrel Cities in the 21st Century.* London and New York: Continuum.

Sassen, S. (1991), *The Global City: New York, London, Tokyo.* Princeton, NJ: Princeton University Press.

Smith, G. (2010), 'An Agenda for Researching Faith and Volunteering', unpublished paper at A Research Conference on Voluntary Action: Volunteering Counts, Manchester, March 2010.

3 Market Theory, Market Theology: The Business of the Church in the City

Robbie B. H. Goh

For the love of money is the root of all evil ...

(1 Timothy 6:10a)

No man can serve two masters. ... Ye cannot serve God and mammon

(Matthew 6:24)

They are not of the world, even as I am not of the world

(John 17:16)

Introduction: Protestant ethic, ministry ethos, and Christian businesses

The Protestant Church has (until quite recently) long been governed by an ethos which, based on a strict and uncompromising interpretation of biblical verses such as the above, frowned on any open rapprochement between church and market, individual believer and ostentatious wealth. This is notwithstanding Max Weber's famous thesis about the ideological link between the 'Protestant ethic' and the 'spirit of capitalism' which governed what might be termed the individual's business attitudes and aptitudes. Weber's account of the 'rationalization' of time and processes, the individual work ethic and the acquisitive capitalist spirit, which for him characterized the revolution from economic traditionalism to capitalist modernity, recognizes that these still went hand in hand with a 'hard frugality' and the desire not to 'consume but to earn' (Weber, 1958: 64–68). Weber goes so far as to say that the 'ideal type of the capitalist entrepreneur' is 'distinguished by a certain ascetic tendency' and 'avoids ostentation and unnecessary expenditure' (Weber, 1958: 71). The capitalism of the Protestant ethic was thus of such a nature as to reconcile acquisitiveness with frugality, materialism with the deliberate eschewal of ostentation, sublimating market ideology within church life and processes. One version of this sublimated capitalism is evinced by John Wesley, Methodism's founding father, with his famous aphorism: "'Earn all you can'. "Save all you can". "Give all you can"; only thus was the pursuit of money given moral and spiritual sanction, safeguarding the "spiritual health" of the individual believer' (Wesley, 1999: 7, 8).

Of course, this is not to say that sublimation was always successful, that all congregations (or for that matter, all individuals within a congregation) pursued this with the same zeal or efficacy, or that the balance between spiritual asceticism and commercial individualism was always well maintained. Tawney (1998: 220) argues that Calvin's legacy in Western Europe (a legacy that later travelled to and took deep root in America) was a two-stage evolving one, that moved from 'authoritarian regimentation' to an accelerating 'utilitarian individualism' that was increasingly open to commerce. Tawney observes that

> Puritanism in its later phases added a halo of ethical sanctification to the appeal of economic expediency, and offered a moral creed, in which the duties of religion and the calls of business ended their long estrangement in an unanticipated reconciliation. (1998: 239)

This reconciliatory process, although by no means unproblematic, was to gain momentum as Western Europe and North America progressively developed openly and even aggressively capitalist societies on the back of a historical legacy of Christian values.

It is difficult, however, to point to a specific moment as signalling the *fait accompli* of this reconciliation of church and market. Certainly it was under the banner of a sublimated, ascetic and selfless Protestant capitalism that Christian churches and para-church organizations spread the Gospel (and their own institutional blueprints) through many nations in the course of the nineteenth and much of the twentieth century, toeing the line of an unostentatious simplicity and a wariness towards the excesses of market society. Many mission hospitals, churches and schools in countries like India, China, Sri Lanka, Thailand and elsewhere operated by faith on shoestring budgets and with the most basic of facilities; indeed many of them continue to operate on such terms even today, with survival rather than ostentatious buildings and big-budget items foremost on their agendas (see Figures 3.1 and 3.2). While there is clearly a demarcation between churches in developed and developing countries, the transnational denominational, evangelical and other links mean that even first-world churches have to be mindful (to varying degrees) of the relative poverty of their third-world brethren, and often moderate their own expenditure and development in order to divert funds to the latter (and just out of a consciousness of and symbolic unity with the latter).[1] It is also true that the financial model of many churches, even in richer nations, remains a very traditional and communal one, relying on voluntary giving (regular tithes and offerings from the local congregation, financial support from government agencies, and other gifts) which are largely channelled to church and

Figure 3.1   Field station of a mission hospital in Bareilly, Uttar Pradesh, India

Figure 3.2   Mission school in Trinidad and Tobago

community expenditure, rather than on commercial enterprise and entrepreneurial projects which yield large incomes and amass large reserves.

This is not to say, of course, that striking examples of rich and ostentatious churches and church-related buildings, institutions and officials do not exist, in both developed nations (the norm) and (in some cases) developing ones. The rise of the televangelism industry, popular Christian media (including Christian recording artistes and best-selling Christian authors), and the so-called 'mega-churches' – all developments of the latter half of the twentieth century, and largely originating in (but by no means confined to) the United States – developed a model of Christian institutionalism that was unabashedly large scale, slickly rationalized in terms of processes, commercialized in its goals, and even ostentatious in terms of its accoutrements, finishes and facilities. Many of the famous televangelists – charismatic in personality as well as in theological doctrine, preaching the available impartation of spiritual gifts (including the financial gifts of the so-called 'prosperity gospel'), backed by often lavish studio sets, music and costumes – raised the soliciting of funds from their television audiences to a fine art, and ran large empires consisting not only of their own church and television programmes, but businesses based on other media products, merchandising, speaking engagements, artistes, properties and so on.

One of the biggest televangelists of the 1970s and 1980s was Jimmy Swaggart, who ran a huge empire comprising his popular television programme, a gospel music empire (he was himself a singer who sold more than 150 million records), a variety of charitable organizations, properties owned by Jimmy Swaggart Ministries, and other enterprises, and also owned a private jet (Kaufman, 1988). Swaggart was the subject of several investigations in the early 1980s, for misdirecting contributions intended for one of his children's charities to buildings and furnishings for his ministry, for preying on wealthy old supporters for their money, and other misdoings; although these allegations were covered up or otherwise dealt with. In 1988 he was suspended by the Assemblies of God for consorting with a prostitute (Kaufman, 1988). Swaggart's contemporary and fellow televangelist, Jim Bakker, operated a similarly extensive and high-finance business empire, which (in addition to his television show and media empire) included hotels and other properties, and the 'Heritage USA' theme park (Ostling and Kane, 1988). Like Swaggart, Bakker was indicted for financial misdeeds including scams on financial contributors, directing ministry monies into his own pockets, and tax evasion (Ostling and Kane, 1988).

Christian and charitable organizations often qualify for tax-exempt non-profit status, and often have reduced or no financial accountability and oversight. This is not only the case in the United States (where they are exempted from federal income tax under section 501 (c) (3) of the Internal Revenue Code), but also in countries like the United Kingdom, Australia, New Zealand, Singapore and elsewhere. Thus, large and financially successful churches and church-linked charitable organizations, and their leaders, are often prey to the temptation of financial gerrymandering and have also been on the receiving end of public scrutiny and calls for accountability (Blundell, 2008; Ferguson, 2005). Not all televangelists have succumbed to the lure of lavish lifestyles, of course, and some groups have been particularly careful about voluntarily coming under codes of transparency and accountability. In the 1970s, there were already calls for Christian churches and para-church organizations in America to submit to some form of financial over-sight, or else to face the possibility of government intervention in the public's interest. As a result, in 1979 the Evangelical Council for Financial Accountability (ECFA) was established (ECFA, 2009a). Membership in the ECFA is voluntary and only open to Christian ministries coming under section 501 (c) (3), whose annual revenues exceed US$100,000, and which submit audited accounts prepared by an independent CPA firm (ECFA, 2009b). ECFA members are entitled to use the ECFA seal which attests to their strict financial accountability, although they also have to continue complying with ECFA standards and best practices (ECFA, 2009c).

While most countries which grant tax-exempt status to churches and other religious organizations do not have oversight mechanisms (voluntary or other-wise) as extensive as those of the ECFA, there have been increasing concerns over churches-as-businesses and the lack of financial accountability over the often large amounts of money involved (Ferguson, 2005). In Singapore, a new Code of Governance for Charities, covering essential organizational principles such as managing conflicts of interest and the independence of Boards of Governors, was rolled out in 2007, as a proposed guideline for the operations of tax-exempt religious organizations (Tan, 2007a). However, measures such as the ECFA in the United States and Singapore's Code of Governance for Charities are by no means foolproof measures for ensuring financial accountability in Christian ministries and businesses: several prominent American evangelists (including Benny Hin, Kenneth and Gloria Copeland, and Paula and Randy White) have declined to join the ECFA and submit their extensive ministries to ECFA guidelines, while in Singapore some churches have expressed difficulty in complying with the Code of Governance (Tan, 2007a, 2007b; Kwon, 2008).

There thus remains considerable anxiety, both within Christian groups and watchdog organizations, as well as outside the church, about the financial dealings of church-related businesses, particularly the larger and more successful ones capable of bringing in tens of millions of dollars each year in tax-exempt revenues and donations. It is difficult to avoid the conclusion that 'many ministries now operate as corporations', and that 'Mega-church pastors run multi-million-dollar enterprises, selling not just Bibles, DVDs and paintings, but banquet facilities, gym memberships and nutritional classes. Some refer to themselves not just as pastors, but as CEOs' (Associated Press, 2007: 23).

While many churches and Christian ministries around the world continue to operate on balanced budgets drawn largely from donations, and to conform to principles of financial accountability, there is no doubt that principles of the market and the corporation have now firmly intruded into the Christian sphere. Some Christian pastors (or 'CEOs' as some may be styled) no longer necessarily exhibit the 'ascetic tendency' and the avoidance of 'ostentation and unnecessary expenditure' that Weber (1958: 71) observed in the Puritans. Such Christian ministry operations are no longer a strict repudiation of the principles of worldly mammon, but rather a slippery slope of negotiation and various combinations and admixtures. Naturally, this continues to breed anxieties and concerns about oversight and transparency not just in the public, but also among constituents of the Christian community.

Hub ideologies: urban flows and city ministries

If the ministry ethos and business principles converged much more strongly from the late twentieth century onwards, the business of Christian ministry really received a boost from the rise of global cities from the last few decades of the twentieth century. Indeed, it might be said that many of the factors that drive global cities – global capital flows, cosmopolitan cultures, people movements, tourism, rapid social change, a vibrant public sphere including in cyberspace, a sociocultural 'buzz' – are also the factors on which some churches and Christian ministries piggybacked to great growth in terms of financial and congregational numbers and the extension of their ministries. This is not to say that all 'mega-churches' – the term technically applies to churches with attendances of more than 2000 per week, although it more loosely applies to large and especially independent and Pentecostal churches (Connell, 2005; Thumma et al., 2005; Patterson, 2007) – are located in urban centres, although it is certainly true that many of the best-known ones are. Clearly some of the common principles underlying mega-church practices are those which also characterize the 'hub' ideology of global cities.

The systematic link between modern cities as hubs of human life and activity, and Christian missions focused on the city, can be seen as early as the 1820s and 1830s, in the urban Christian movements that sprouted in that period in response to the workers moving into cities like London, Glasgow, and later cities in other countries like New York, Boston and Paris, before spreading further afield in the late nineteenth and into the twentieth centuries. In England in the 1820s and 1830s, the 'non-Wesleyan Methodists' were busy with a social agenda to counteract social and political abuses while providing relief for the poor in London; while in Glasgow and surrounding areas, the work of Thomas Chalmers was highly influential in spurring an urban ministry programme to provide not just social welfare, but also literacy education and spiritual teaching for the working-class poor (Hempton, 1996: 35; Lewis, 1986: 35). In 1826, an evangelical Scotsman, David Naismith, established the Glasgow City Mission, organizing missionaries to comb the streets of the city looking to improve the daily lives of the urban poor in various ways; similar missions were established in Dublin in 1828 and London in 1835, and later in cities in North America as well (Orr, 1965: 45; Trainer n.d.: 2–3).

When George Williams established the 'society for improving the spiritual conditions of young men engaged in drapery and other trades' in London in 1844, the motive was clearly to minister to the urban tradesmen who were flocking to London in large numbers for work. That small group, which was subsequently to become a worldwide organization known as the Young Men's Christian Association (YMCA), was very much concerned with the 'spiritual welfare of [young men] in the various departments of commercial life' (YMCA 1857 frontispiece, cited in

Smith 1997). As the organization grew, and as its founder's fortunes improved, the YMCA developed a model of commercial networking and savvy which mobilized wealthy patrons and business leaders in the service of the organization's continuing mission of social and spiritual amelioration – a model which was subsequently applied to the other urban centres in which 'the Y' operated (Binfield, 1994: 13–14, 18). The YMCA was arguably the pioneering Christian urban–commercial enterprise, large-scale in its operations, drawing revenue in part from various commercial enterprises (most typically hotels, members' clubs, gyms and sporting facilities, shop rental), leveraging on business networks, and applying all this to a Christian mission of evangelism and social work (Lupkin, 1996: 42, 46).

However, despite its success in establishing Ys in many of the major cities around the world, the YMCA (like its sister organization, the YWCA) had difficulty reconciling its Christian calling with its social and commercial ones. In America, in the latter part of the twentieth century, YMCAs catered to an increasing 'religious diversity', and inevitably many of them began 'distancing [themselves] from the churches' (Putney, 1997: 232–35). The change in the spiritual character of many of these North American Ys was also accompanied by a process of suburbanization, so that even the original urban calling was lost. While many of the Ys around the world have remained true to the 'Paris Basis' – a resolution adopted by the delegates at the first World Conference in Paris in 1855, and which places 'Jesus Christ as . . . God and Saviour' firmly at the centre of the association's work – and have also remained very much urban organizations, others have become 'Christian' only by historical legacy and reflect a heterogeneity of activities ranging in locus from the urban to suburban, and along a continuum of secularity. Thus, while many Ys around the world continue to operate as Christian urban businesses, others are neither urban nor Christian in the sense of having a continuing evangelical calling and distinct Christian character.

The 1980s, however, saw a renewed focus on cities as the site for evangelism, and a slew of Christian urban enterprises which, if not all commercial in their sphere of influence and mode of operation, were nevertheless fully prepared to engage with the range of social phenomena and challenges (but also opportunities) that cities represented. In 1985, the *Faith in the City* report (commissioned by the Archbishop of Canterbury) exposed 'the realities of injustice and posited the role of faith actors in addressing social problems in UK inner cities' (Beaumont, 2008: 2012). The same decade saw a number of notable and influential publications on urban missions and ministries, including Ray Bakke's *The Urban Christian* (1987), Greenway and Monsma's *Cities: Missions' New Frontier* (1989) and John Dawson's *Taking our Cities for God* (1989), with later books of note including Robert C. Linthicum's *City of God, City of Satan* (1991) and Ray Bakke's *A Theology as Big as the City* (1997).

Most of these works, like the *Faith in the City* report, focused on the work of social engagement and social justice enterprises in the city, rather than on a Christian business model appropriate to urban operations. Indeed, the city was often seen as a necessary evil, an undeniably fallen zone: as Greenway and Monsma (1989: 27–28) sum it up:

Because of sin, cities today are human-centred, often violent, and rife with friction, greed and carnality. Sin runs freely through the streets and markets. Sin sits enthroned in high places of civic life. Cities are characterized by many broken covenants, most of all the broken covenant with God.

In this view, urban ministries have multiplied, not because of the particular excellences and virtues of the city which might sponsor greater evangelical outreach, but because of the dire need for Christian influence in such 'sinful' sites. Accordingly, the main work of urban ministries in this view is oppositional: 'By its solidarity with the economically, politically, and spiritually poor of the city, and by its confrontation of the powers that would seek to control and oppress rather than recognize their own poverty, the church would work for God's kingdom' (Linthicum, 1991: 105). While claiming that the city is 'God's creation', as modelled and prophetically fulfilled by the 'idealized Jerusalem', this position emphasizes the 'sinful' character of cities and the main work of social justice and relief that urban ministries must undertake (Linthicum, 1991: 24–25).

However, even within this view of the city as fallen, and in some ways working in a contrary direction, there is also the sense that the city is nevertheless a place of ministry opportunity because of the economic virtues of the city. The view of the city as a 'commercial hub' recognizes its positives, as a site of cultural diversity, the in-migration of many peoples, the site of jobs and economic opportunities, a hub of communications and networking, and so on. As urban missiologist Ray Bakke (1997: 12) puts it:

You see, there is no place to hide. The city is a media stage prop in this cybernetic era, and its presence will impact everyone eventually. So, even in places far from large cities, banks, businesses and families are linked up to urban centers. We must acknowledge, then, that not only do nearly three billion of the earth's nearly six billion persons live in cities, the other three billion are being urbanized as well. Sorry, you have an urban future, whether you like it or not.

Greenway and Monsma have a similar view, but emphasizing the human fluidity, diversity and economic opportunity of cities:

Cities are to be the target of mission penetration not only because most ethnic groups once living in rural areas now have representatives in cities; they are to be the target also because cities contain many social groups that have not yet been reached with the gospel. Furthermore, cities are centers of dominance and therefore are the pace-setters for a society. . . . No longer is the city mainly a geographical center for commerce, a market-place to expedite the flow of the earth's abundance and the products of humankind's cultural endeavours. Rather, the city has become an administrative center to provide welfare and relief to people in distress. (Greenway and Monsma, 1989: 20, 29)

While the notion of urban ministry as emphasizing social justice persists, there is also an acknowledgment of the city as a 'center for commerce, a marketplace to expedite the flow of the earth's abundance' (Greenway and Monsma, 1989: 29).

The city as a commercial hub in Christian ministry takes on several aspects:

1. As the site of 'abundance' creating the availability of funds that would not only sponsor new ministry initiatives, but even allow for a certain degree of independence from denominational 'paternalism' and control (Bakke, 1987: 48, 71). This also implies a corresponding scale in the financing of urban missions (Bakke, 1997: 14).
2. As the site of opportunity but also (mandate) for the church to engage in 'economic development': the 'creation of jobs, the organizing of people to create community industries and trades, job re-training, economic self-determination', and ultimately also the familiar social justice imperative of 'advocacy of the poor' (Linthicum, 1991: 168–69).
3. As the site of vocational and (especially) professional and business networks, recognizing that urban dwellers are 'identified by our jobs' (Bakke, 1987: 42–43, 116–17; Greenway and Monsma, 1989: 125).
4. As a place of intense competition, not only with the secular world over resources and the attention of urban dwellers, but even (lamentably) between different church groups and ministries for 'proselytes' (Bakke, 1987: 46–48).

While much of this thinking opens the door to urban ministries that leverage on urban business networks and capital flows, it will be evident that its main thrust is still on a kind of making do, a spiritual bricolage (as it were) in which Christian influence is to be forged out of discrete elements picked out of the business of urban life and flows, rather than being constituted in affinity with those very flows. For seminal urban missiologists like Bakke, Linthicum and others, cities (by virtue of their impact, size and needs) were too important to be ignored, but were also to be regarded with a continual suspicion and critical detachment. Greenway and Monsma perhaps best express this when they say that 'successful workers hurt for the city . . . for the sin and pain and suffering of the city are so intense that only the kind of person who can weep as Jesus wept over Jerusalem is going to accomplish any salvific good' (1989: 246). This salvific 'hurting' in urban ministry ensures that many urban churches and para-church organizations retain something of the 'ascetic' spiritual withdrawal from commerce exhibited in Wesley and the Puritan forebears, even as they respond wholeheartedly to the calling and opportunity of the city. Significantly, none of these urban missiologists envision or advocate an urban ministry organization which is profitably positioned in relation to urban commercial flows, and expansive in terms of properties, businesses and balance sheets.

Megaministries: The theo-deology of the global city-church

Then there are the ministries which are not only intensely aware of the many needs and opportunities of urban ministry, but have entirely rationalized their *modus operandi* in order to align themselves with the commercial and professional character of the city. These churches and ministries are often located in global cities (or contenders for global city status), have large congregations, and manage extensive enterprises ranging from the more familiar church ministries (multiple congregations in different languages and with different people groups, social out-reach, different evangelistic efforts) to highly successful brands of commercial products and activities (books and media products, property deals, clothing and other merchandising, and other businesses). Accordingly, these urban mega-ministries have diversified revenue streams – not merely the congregational tithes and other gifts that are the large part of most churches and Christian organi-zations, but also the income from their various business transactions – and presumably large revenue streams at that, as evident from the scale of their opera-tions and the financial outlays that these require. As these mega-ministries are usually based in countries under whose laws they operate as charities or nonprofit organizations, they have no obligation to make their accounts openly available to the public, which exacerbates the complexity of their financial structures and commercial enterprises.

The success – in terms of size, rapid growth and finances – of these mega-ministries, as much as the facility with which they position themselves within urban processes, distinguish them from other Christian urban ministries with a more "hurting salvific" attitude to the city. This is not to say that these mega-ministries do not also engage in social welfare activities (and even notable and successful ones), but that these activities are a part of a larger organizational logic which is distinct in its successful integration into the commercial ethos of the city. In large part, this theo-deology, as we might term it – this rapprochement between the organization's theological position and the commercial ideology of the global city – signifies a surmounting of the church's old suspicions regarding Babylon the commercial city, and mammon and this-worldliness. Theo-deology is marked, not merely by the crude 'prosperity gospel' which detractors are quick to attribute to many of these mega-ministries (Anderson, 2006; Leucke, 1997) – but which the latter themselves are quick to repudiate – but rather by a consistent justification of the business of the church through the salvific means to which the revenues from those businesses are put, and by a firm sense of the church's calling to claim a significant part of urban commercial life in order to represent and glorify God. Theo-deology is thus a complex re-interpretation of the church's position and calling within the essential processes and life of the global commercial city, bring-ing to bear arguments from urban spatial logic, social psychology, branding, professional networking and other discourses to scriptural teachings on evange-lism and the role of the church.

One of the biggest mega-ministries in Australia – and well known throughout the rest of the Christian world through its popular Christian music label – is Hillsong Church in Sydney (Connell, 2005). Hillsong, a very contemporary-styled, media-oriented church with roots in the Australian Assemblies of God and led by Pastor Brian Houston, sees average attendances of more than 20,000 across its different services in different 'campuses' in Sydney each weekend. Hillsong now also has a campus in Brisbane, Australia, and churches in London, Kiev, Stockholm, Cape Town and Paris (Hillsong Church, 2009d). Its reputation among churches outside of Australia was probably first based on its hugely popular Hillsong brand of Christian music, led by songwriters and worship leaders who became among the best-known names in contemporary Christian worship music: Geoff Bullock, Darlene Zschech and Reuben Morgan. Since the production of its first album in 1988, Hillsong Music has sold more than 11 million units and won more than 30 gold and platinum sales awards (Hillsong Music, 2009a). In addition to its music arm, Hillsong runs successful annual conferences with tens of thousands of international delegates, broadcasts television programmes and runs a performing arts academy and a leadership college, in addition to more traditional Christian social welfare ministries in the form of its 'I-Heart', 'CityCare' and other programmes (Hillsong Church, 2009e).

The business side of Hillsong has in recent years attracted considerable attention, both for its entrepreneurial drive and for its extensiveness and perceived lack of transparency (Ferguson, 2005; Connell, 2005: 325). The church itself has been very careful in recent years to articulate a Financial Charter and Corporate Governance statement, perhaps in response to scrutiny of its wealth and extensive business dealings. Questions about financial transparency and corporate governance aside, Hillsong is certainly remarkable for the way in which it has interwoven entrepreneurship into practically every aspect of its ministry. In its international reach and expansion, it resembles some aspects of the multinational corporation, if not in terms of the MNC's differentiation of operations (production, R&D, management) in different countries, then certainly in terms of its scope of operations and transnational networking, its desire to build a global brand represented by the now-familiar blue 'Hillsong' logo. Yet this global ambition is plausibly expressed in terms of the church's desire to 'influence the world with good' (Hillsong Church, 2009b), itself a humanized re-phrasing of biblical verses like Matthew 5: 16: 'Let your light so shine before men, that they may see your good works, and glorify your Father which is in heaven'. Hillsong's merchandising machinery is extremely sophisticated, from its glossy and extensive gift stores (the one in its main Baulkham Hills, Sydney, campus bears comparison with any upmarket retail store in a commercial mall – see Figure 3.3), to its highly effective online merchandising of countless products, its global network of 'sub-publishers', and its online administration and sale of licences for the use of Hillsong music. Yet of course, the merchandising of Hillsong's music and the Houstons' various books and other products is compatible with Hillsong Music's spiritual goal 'to build a strong and healthy local church, that resources the Body of Christ EVE-RYWHERE' (Hillsong Music, 2009a). Although the prices for many of its products and licences may be prohibitive for churches in some less wealthy countries, Hillsong permits its music to be used without fee in any church service, and its enforcement of copyrights protecting its own music is of course (as Hillsong Music points out) in conformity to standard copyright practices and laws (Hillsong Music, 2009b).

Beyond its diversified ministries and the management of its events and merchandise, Hillsong also has an extensive networking with the business community and has turned this into a significant source of influence and revenue.

Figure 3.3 Lobby and gift shop of Hillsong Church (Baulkham Hills campus), Sydney, Australia

The church publishes an influential Christian Business Directory (the 2007 New South Wales edition claimed a circulation of 65,000 and a readership of 250,000), profits from which 'go to social development work in local communities' (Coleman, 2007). The church's board of directors includes some of the foremost businessmen in Australia, including Nabi Saleh, co-owner of Gloria Jean's Coffee Australia (which is in a bid to buy over the parent company in America), who is on the church's audit and remuneration committees (Hillsong Church, 2009c; Ferguson, 2005: 41). Symbiotically, some of Gloria Jean's Coffee franchises are owned by Hillsong church members, and the coffee is sold at Hillsong conferences and at its church premises (Ferguson, 2005: 41). Hillsong's senior pastor, Brian Houston, owns several properties and is reportedly a silent partner in various property developments (Ferguson, 2005: 36).

This positioning of the church vis-a-vis the business community is not merely a matter of targeting and involving select persons, but is also written into Hillsong's spatial logic. Following the well-established principle of seeker-friendly American mega-church Willow Creek, Hillsong eschews prominent displays of the cross and traditional church architecture (steeples, towers, arches, columns, stained glass). Its buildings (almost none of which bear a cross, except for the chapel in one corner of the Baulkham Hills campus) all blend easily into the urban landscape – the city campus resembles a warehouse converted into a trendy club, while the sprawling Baulkham Hills campus fits right into its business park surroundings. In this spatial symbolism, the mega-ministry by choosing not to call attention to its difference vis-à-vis the urban environs, signals its priority to work within and alongside urban processes, rather than in the 'confrontational' way highlighted by many urban missiologists (Linthicum, 1991: 105).

The mega-ministry and the global city operate on similar and aligned terms, seeking to establish a global brand that will attract economies of scale in merchandising, travel, tourism, hospitality, property values and other commercial transactions – although clearly the city will be the major partner or category in this relationship, with the mega-ministry able to hitch onto various aspects of the global city's project. In this regard, it is interesting to note the ways in which Hillsong continually invokes Sydney's urban landscape, printing publicity and web pages which often feature backdrops comprising various views of the harbour bridge and opera house (Hillsong Church, 2009a,b). A major and heavily publicized Hillsong Music event of 2007 involved Darlene Zschech singing from an elevated position on the Sydney harbour bridge. Clearly, Hillsong's major events (such as the annual Hillsong conference), and even its regular stream of international visitors, benefit from and capitalize on Sydney's popularity as a tourist destination, while the mega-ministry for its part contributes to the tourism economy of the city. Indeed, by creating a global enterprise extending to other big cities like London and Paris, but with Sydney as the headquarters, Hillsong arguably advances Sydney's competitive standing as a global city in quite significant ways.

Hillsong, although an exemplar of the new mega-ministry-as-business, is by no means unique of course: Singapore's New Creation Church is similar to Hillsong in size (it has about 19,000 members), provenance (it was established in 1984, Hillsong in 1983, both growing from humble beginnings to their present massive statures), worship style and atmosphere (contemporary, media-savvy), and even affiliation (its pastor, Joseph Prince, regularly speaks at Hillsong events, and Hillsong's music team has visited New Creation on a number of occasions; New Creation Church, 2009b). Above all, it resembles Hillsong in its systematic and rationalized positioning of itself firmly within the commercial processes and landscape of the global city.

Although not nearly as extensive and transnational as Hillsong, New Creation's business ventures – managed by Rock Productions, the church's business arm – are by no means small. Like Hillsong, it markets its media products – mainly books and CDs by Pastor Prince, with some of its own musical CDs – in a sophisticated online store. It owns and operates a 232,000 square foot recreational centre and resort known as Marine Cove in Singapore's popular East Coast Parkway recreational area, which has food and beverage outlets, a bowling alley and sports facilities (Ong, 2002: P9). However, its landmark business venture is surely its plan to develop a S$660 million 'lifestyle hub' in partnership with listed property developer CapitaLand. Currently under development and expected to be completed in 2011, the hub will contain a 5,000-seat auditorium which the church will use for its services, thus saving on the $S784,000 monthly rental it pays to commercial mall Suntec City to rent the 1,400-seat auditorium where the church's services are currently being held (Suhaimi, 2007: 6; Tan, 2008: 8). It will also contain an amphitheatre, outdoor theatre, rooftop function area, two ballrooms, restaurants, wine bars, dance clubs and retail space (Suhaimi, 2007: 6). The church's share of the cost of the development, initially set at S$280 million, was later raised to $499.5 million; however, it had a ready $100 million to pay when it embarked on the project, and with its profitable businesses and a reported income of $55.4 million in 2008, the church's financial resources look to be entirely capable of handling this mega-project (Tan, 2008: 8).

Like Hillsong, New Creation's spatial strategy is thus to fit entirely into the land-scape of the commercial city – in the context of Singapore, this means the idiom of 'hub' lifestyle sites drawing large consumer crowds, mega-mall structures, and distinctive award-winning architecture. This comfortable fit is borne out by the 10 September 2007 newspaper coverage of the New Creation hub project, with a headline that emphasizes the cost of the 'lifestyle hub' and an artist's impression of the 'futuristic looking' building; it is easy to miss the fact that this is a church enterprise, since the New Creation name does not appear until the fourth para-graph of the story (Figure 3.4). The church's website, which features stylish renderings of the project, plays up (among other things) the attractive architec-ture of the building, announcing that the design 'has won the five-star award for Best Architecture in the Asia Pacific Commercial Property Awards 2009' (New Creation Church, 2009c).

New Creation's Lifestyle Hub – a first among churches in Singapore in terms of the size of the commercial investment and its partnership with a major listed company – embodies one of the church's 'core values', to be 'cutting edge' and to 'endeavour to be innovative and always at the forefront of all that we do' (New Creation Church, 2009d). 'Cutting edge' in terms of church operations in the Singapore context, it at the same time plugs perfectly into the vibrant 'lifestyle'

Figure 3.4 Coverage of New Creation's One-North Hub in *Straits Times*, 10 September 2007.

aspirations, multi-culturalism, internationally networked nature and financially buoyant character of Singapore as a global city. This is reinforced by some of the church's recent events, which are comfortably positioned within the large public festivities of Singapore's multi-cultural landscape, and in prominent landmarks such as the Singapore Expo Centre and tourist attraction Sentosa Island (New Creation Church, 2009a). As might be expected, there are voices from the public and also from the Christian fold that find New Creation's 'cutting edge' enterprises unsettling: in addition to the general wariness that is prompted by the church's size and financial clout, there have been a number of people who have left the church, citing unhappiness over its teachings of 'abundance and prosperity' (Ong, 2002: P9).

Conclusion: urban ministries, Trojan buildings and postsecular futures

It is unlikely that the split between 'ascetic' and commercially integrated urban ministries will disappear in the near future. If the reiterated biblical warnings against associating with 'mammon', being 'conformed to the world', and 'the love of money' were in any way to wane in potency, there would still be the stark example of the 'lowly' Jesus Christ riding into Jerusalem on a borrowed donkey (Zechariah 9: 9; Luke 19: 30–35) – the very image that U.S. Senator Charles Grassley invoked when calling for certain rich televangelists to submit their financial records to public scrutiny (Associated Press, 2007: 23). Not only members of the Christian community, but also the watchdogs of charities and non-profit organizations, and elements of the public in general, will continue to look askance at the big-budget commercial deals of highly successful and large mega-ministries. There is also the anomaly that these mega-ministries 'succeed' (so to speak) in entrepreneurial projects and commercial competition by virtue of a business model that is not exactly commercial: that is, their tax-exempt status, and their large pool of tithe- and offering-giving congregation members, the majority of whom (unlike shareholders in a publicly listed company) are not likely to challenge or even question the business decisions of the church's board or pastor. In that sense, the notion of a church 'business' in the city must only be a qualified and modified one.

Yet the success of mega-ministries like Hillsong, New Creation Church and many others in countries like the United States, Canada, Brazil, the United Kingdom, Nigeria, South Africa, Australia, New Zealand, Singapore, South Korea, the Philippines and elsewhere, suggests how much the tide of Christian urban ministry has turned, and how much more widespread the notion of the church-as-business has become than at any other earlier period. If the Swaggarts and Bakkers in their day invited that much more scrutiny (and ultimately, indictment) as much for their egregious stature as for their misdoings, the Hillsongs and New Creations of today (quite apart from adducing principles of their own financial transparency and good governance) are much more representative of a class of mega-ministries. It is, furthermore, a class whose boundaries are to a certain extent blurred by the very nature of the 'commercial city' and ministry therein: if New Creation's almost US$500 million-dollar partnership with a publicly listed company is a clear instance of church enterprise which puts it firmly in this class, the same qualitative (if not quantitative) argument might be made for the city YMCA which runs a small hotel, or even the urban ministry which organizes networks of businessmen and professionals in order to raise funds and expertise for small-scale social welfare projects. To adapt a phrase from Ray Bakke (1997: 12), there is 'no place to hide' from the fundamental commercial processes, once an urban ministry is established; it may still be possible to draw some kind of line, but the line will increasingly be a difficult quantitative one, rather than clear cut and absolute.

Therein lies the postsecular character of urban ministries, as of postsecular cities and postsecular societies in general: the older and more clear-cut distinction between the sacred and secular, the walled and spired church on the one hand and its fallen environs on the other, is elided within the city's incessant processes of social interweaving, networking, change and market relations. Cities are commercial and social hubs, and even agents of social justice which seek to align themselves with certain 'marginalized' groups in opposition to other 'privileged' ones, inevitably find their work enabled in various ways by the latter; these agents thus find themselves ironically to be part of the urban process of social mixing and market transaction, rather than apart from and in opposition to it. The pervasive nature of this process is likely to accelerate with the rise of global cities, mega-cities and urban sprawl, and with the increasing urbanization of the earth's population; Christian ministry, called to be in the city, will necessarily have to adapt to the city's nature and ways.

The crux of the postsecular urban ministry might thus be encapsulated in the ambivalence of the church-business building, such as Hillsong's business-park campus or New Creation's lifestyle hub: their seamless integration into their commercial environs is not simply or merely a selling-out of the distinct character of the church (as traditionalists might have it), but (from a spatial and symbolic logic) just as much the enfolding of the secular business of the city into the evangelical environs of the church. In the postsecular 'Trojan building', it will be increasingly difficult to say where one side ends and the other begins, nor to nicely ascertain the valence of each side; if this will pose a profound challenge to the transformative agenda of evangelism, it may pose no less a challenge to the secular resistance of the business world.

Notes

1   The views expressed in the articles and reports of *Harvest Force*, the newsletter of the Methodist Missions Society of the Methodist Church in Singapore, are representative. Written largely by Singaporean volunteers who have returned from mission trips to poor areas in surrounding countries, they often seek to raise consciousness among Christian communities in Singapore about the poor living conditions and great needs of these countries. One writer reports that 'the saddest part of this mission trip [to Thailand] was our visit to the two run down rickety slum buildings located one kilometre from the Youth Hostel . . . built of wood, it gets extremely cold in December and January'; while

another speaks of the 'hardships' faced by Thai tribal children forced to live in 'make-shift shelters' in order to get an education (Yuen, 2009: 24; Yeo, 2009: 20–21). This rhetoric of pathos is prevalent in the missions discourses of churches in developed countries, intended to direct attention and financial support to the needs of others in developing countries, and is thus in some ways a continuation of the sacrificial and temperate ethos that generally characterized the missions movements of the nineteenth century.

References

Anderson, M. (2006), "Big Box Religion." *Monterey County Weekly*, August 17.

Associated Press (2007), "Pastors Under Probe for Lavish Lifestyles." *Straits Times*, 15 November, 23.

Bakke, R., with Hart, J. (1987), *The Urban Christian: Effective Ministry in Today's Urban World*. Downer's Grove, IL: Intervarsity Press.

—. (1997), *A Theology as Big as The City*. Downer's Grove, IL: Intervarsity Press.

Beaumont, J. (2008), 'Introduction: Faith-based Organisations and Urban Social Issues'. *Urban Studies* 45, 2011–17.

Binfield, C. (1994), *George Williams in Context: A Portrait of the Founder of the YMCA*. Sheffield/London: Sheffield Academic Press in Association with YMCA England.

Blundell, S. (2008), 'The God Dividend', *New Zealand Listener* 2–8 February, www.listener.co.nz/issue/3534/features/10411/the_god_dividend.html (accessed 17 December 2009).

Coleman, (2007), 'Frequently Asked Questions', *Christian Business Directory 07*. Sydney: Hillsong Emerge.

Connell, J. (2005), 'Hillsong: A Megachurch in the Sydney Suburbs'. *Australian Geographer* 36 (3), 315–32.

ECFA Evangelical Council for Financial Accountability (2009a), 'History', www.ecfa.org/Content/GeneralBackground.aspx (accessed 17 December 2009).

—. (2009b), 'Membership Requirements', www.ecfa.org/Content.aspx?PageName=JoinIntro (accessed 24 December 2009).

—. (2009c), 'Standards and Best Practices', www.ecfa.org/Content/ECFABest-Practices.aspx (accessed 24 December 2009).

Ferguson, A. (2005), 'Prophet-Minded', *BRW* May 26–June 1, pp. 34–41.

Greenway, R. S., and Monsma, T. (1989), *Cities: Missions' New Frontier*. Grand Rapids, MI: Baker Books.

Hempton, D. (1996), *Religion and Political Culture in Britain and Ireland from the Glorious Revolution to the Decline of Empire*. Cambridge: Cambridge University Press.

Hillsong Church (2009a), 'About Hillsong', http://myhillsong.com/more-hillsong (accessed 29 December 2009).

—. (2009b), 'Brian and Bobbie', http://brianandbobbie.com/ (accessed 29 December 2009).

—. (2009c), 'Corporate Governance', http://myhillsong.com/corporate-goverance (accessed 29 December 2009).

—. (2009d), 'Home', http://hillsong.com/ (accessed 29 December 2009).

—. (2009e), 'My Hillsong Sydney', http://myhillsong.com/ (accessed 29 December 2009).

Hillsong Music. (2009a), 'About Us', http://www.hillsongmusic.com/help/about (accessed 29 December 2009).

—. (2009b), 'Copyright and Licensing FAQs', http://www.hillsongmusic.com/publishing/faq (accessed 29 December 2009).

Kaufman, J. (1988), 'The Fall of Jimmy Swaggart', *People.com* www.people.com/people/archive/article/0,,20098413,00.html (Accessed 15 December 2009).

Kwon, L. (2008), 'US Christians try to raise financial integrity amid money scandals', *Christian Today* 4 January, www.christiantoday.com/article/us.christians.try.to.raise.financial.integrity.amid.money.scandals/15979.htm (Accessed 24 December 2009).

Leucke, D. (1997), 'Is Willow Creek the Way of the Future?' *The Christian Century* May 1, 479–85.

Lewis, D. (1986), *Lighten Their Darkness: The Evangelical Mission to Working Class London, 1828–1860.* New York: Greenwood.

Linthicum, R. (1991), *City of God, City of Satan: A Biblical Theology of the Urban Church.* Grand Rapids, MI: Zondervan.

Lupkin, P. (1997), 'Manhood Factories: Architecture, Business, and the Evolving Urban Role of the YMCA, 1865–1925', in N. Mjagkij and M. Spratt (eds), *Men and Women Adrift: The YMCA and the YWCA in the City.* New York: New York University Press, pp. 40–64.

New Creation Church (2009a), 'Church Life-Events', http://www.newcreation.org.sg/church-life/photo-gallery/events/ (accessed 29 December 2009).

—. (2009b), 'History', http://www.newcreation.org.sg/about-us/history (accessed 29 December 2009).

—. (2009c), 'Integrated Hub @ One-North', http://www.rockproductions.com/one-north/project_updates/awards.htm (accessed 29 December 2009).

—. (2009d), 'Mission Statement and Core Values', http://www.newcreation.org.sg/about-us/mission-statement-core-values (accessed 29 December 2009).

Ong, S. (2002), 'Rise of New Churches', *Straits Times* 21 July, P8–P9.

Orr, J. (1965), *The Light of the Nations: Evangelical Renewal and Advance in the Nineteenth Century.* Exeter: Paternoster Press.

Ostling, R., and Kane, J. (1988), 'Jim Bakker's Crumbling World', *Time* 19 December, www.time.com/time/magazine/article/0,9171,956551,00.html (accessed 17 December 2009).

Patterson, B. (2007), 'Changing Face of Jesus', *Sunday Herald* May 6, www.news.com.au/heraldsun/story/0,21985,21676276–24909,00.html (accessed 17 August 2007).

Putney, C. (1997), 'From Character to Body Building: the YMCA and the Suburban Metropolis, 1950–1980', in N. Mjagkij and M. Spratt (eds), *Men and Women Adrift: The YMCA and the YWCA in the City.* New York: New York University Press, pp. 231–49.

Smith, M. (1997), 'George Williams and the YMCA', *Infed.* www.infed.org/walking/wa-ymca.htm (accessed 8 May 2006).

Suhaimi, N. (2007), 'Why Church Inked Buona Vista Mega-Property Deal', *Sunday Times* 16 September, 6.

Tan, D. (2008), 'Church Pastors Like None Other', *Sunday Times* 5 October, p. 8.

Tan, T. (2007a), 'Religious Group Takes Issue with Key Rule in Charity Code', *Straits Times* 21 July 2007, H9.

—. (2007b), 'No Separate Watchdog for Religious Charities', *Straits Times* 5 October, p. H3.

Tawney, R. H. (1998), *Religion and the Rise of Capitalism*. New Brunswick, NJ: Transaction Publishers.

Thumma, S., Travis D., and Bird, W. (2005), 'Megachurches Today'. Hartford Institute for Religion Research, www.hartfordinstitute.org/megachurch/megastoday2005_summaryreport.html (accessed 20 August 2007).

Trainer, P. (n.d.), *Mission to London: Tracing the Formation and Early Days of the London City Mission*. London City Mission, www.lcm.org.uk/Group/Group.aspx?id=8868 (accessed 5 May 2006).

Weber, M. (1958), *The Protestant Ethic and the Spirit of Capitalism*. New York: Charles Scribner's Sons.

Wesley, J. (1999), *The Right Way to Use Money*. Ilkeston: Morley's.

Yeo, H. (2009), 'The Children on the Hill', *Harvest Force* 3, 20–21.

Yuen, L. (2009), 'Plentiful Harvest But Few Labourers', *Harvest Forc*, 3, 24–25.

4 Non-Secular Cities? Visual and Sound Representations of the Religious–Secular Right to the City in Jerusalem

Tovi Fenster

This chapter presents the visual representations of the Lefebvrian notion of the right to the city as it is expressed in the streets of Jerusalem. It claims that the emergence of the idea of the sacred in today's construction of public spaces, building use, governance and civil society is different in Jerusalem than in most cities in the world. This chapter presents different perspectives than other chapters in this book in two ways: first, by using visual and sound representations of religious and secular practices of life. Second, the focus of the chapter on Jerusalem's secular religious[1] relations represents a case where religious-contested geographies are part of its history as well as its everyday life and a place where secularity and religiosity are in constant tension. Thus, while other chapters in this volume report on the revival of religion as one of the explicit features of this century and a turning point from the modernist and secularized trajectory, this one reports on historical relations between secular and religious groups rather than of their revival. These two different perspectives help to further illuminate the complicated nature of secularism, religiosity and postsecularism in current urban spaces by presenting new visual dimensions of these social and cultural trends.

After a contextual introduction which specifies the history of religious–secular relations in Jerusalem, the chapter presents a theoretical framework which links the notions of religiosity, secularity and the right to the city. The next three sections then discuss the visual and sound representations of religious–secular relations in Jerusalem. Section three focuses on street signs as modesty walls in the Mea Shearim ultra-orthodox neighbourhood in Jerusalem. Section four discusses the appearance of graffiti as markers of the religious–secular boundaries, and section five investigates the extent to which the sound of the Sabbath and other Jewish rituals become spatial markers of religious–secular boundaries. The chapter ends with a discussion on the right to the religious–secular city and its connection to urban governance in Jerusalem.

Historically, Jerusalem has been holy to Jews, Muslims and Christians originating from many centuries BC and continuing to this very day with constant battles around various holy sites like Al Aksa Mosque and the remains of the Jewish Temple which are literally located at the same site. These conflicts over religious sites effect the tensions between Jews and Palestinians' and their everyday life in the city, especially regarding the use of the holy sites. In addition to that, there are waves of increasing tension between secular and religious Jews caused by the disagreements about the meanings and expressions of the right to the city that each community relates to the other, both in daily life and especially in the Sabbath – the holy Jewish day. These tensions have increased recently because of the decision of the newly elected secular mayor to open up access to municipal public parking on the Sabbath. Some of the ultra-orthodox communities reacted fiercely by organizing demonstrations on the Sabbath itself with counter demonstrations by the secular residents against what they perceive as the religious enforcement in the city. These complicated and loaded relations are expressed in a variety of visual and sound elements that indicate the harsh feelings and the ambiguous emotions on both sides. In this chapter, I focus on the street signs and graffiti as visual representations of the fight for the right to the city. Other elements such as the Sabbath songs and prayers coming out of private homes (and not synagogues) and the appearance of Jewish rituals in the streets of the city during certain Jewish holidays represent different types of 'appropriation' of public spaces and of intangible cultural boundaries between religiosity and secularity that should be looked at when investigating postsecularism in urban spaces.

The discussion on religious–secular tensions in Jerusalem is incorporated within the wider context of Israel as a declared Jewish state, which faces constant conflicts in its social, cultural and political identity. Everyday life in Jerusalem contains many spatial expressions of these tensions between Jews and Palestinians and within the Jewish community between secular, religious and ultra-orthodox communities, which notably include disagreements on which public activities are allowed on the Sabbath. Legally, the Jewish law entails halting public transportation; the closure of shops, cinemas, theatres and other public activities on the Sabbath, but these laws are enforced differently in various cities in Israel. Thus, while the religious and ultra-orthodox perceive the Sabbath as a holy day and demand the prohibition of profane public activities in much more extreme ways than in other cities in Israel, the secular residents in Jerusalem in turn want to have the freedom to use public spaces and to have a variety of public and cultural activities available for them. To these demands, one can add the pressure of tourists visiting Jerusalem on Sabbath to have enough car parks in Jerusalem as the fulfilment of their right to the city. Such tensions are expressed in occasional violent fights and stone throwing at cars passing through ultra-orthodox neighbourhoods on the Sabbath, road blocking by ultra-orthodox men near their neighbourhoods, demonstrations against cultural activities on the Sabbath, and, lately, demonstrations against the opening of the municipal public car park on the Sabbath and the opening of a privately owned public car park on the Sabbath because of the ultra-orthodox claim that it is against the secular–religious status quo that has been hitherto agreed to in the city. Indeed, most of the literature dealing with secular–religious tensions in Jerusalem focuses on the physical and tangible expressions of the conflicts between the two communities. Thus, Hasson (1996); Hasson and Gonen (1996) and Shilav (1997) emphasize in their analysis the dynamics of 'spaces of conflicts' which were constructed between ultra-orthodox and secular Jewish people and the various strategies each side adopts to meet its goals. In addition to this important literature, I'd like to focus this chapter on the visual and sound representations of the conflict over the right to the city between religious and secular communities in Jerusalem. The discussion on street signs, graffiti, songs and prayers and Jewish rituals during holidays shows how these symbols become constant markers of the fight over 'whose city is it?' and 'whose right to the city?' (Fenster and Yacobi, 2005).

Religiosity, secularity and the right to the city

As Beaumont and Baker emphasize in their introduction to this volume book, the rationale behind the idea of the postsecular society is based on the impact of new places of worship on urban and suburban spaces, on the revival of Pentecostalism and its connection with neoliberal globalization and on their joint impact on mega and global cities, especially in Southern Asia, Africa and Latin America. This view echoes what Berger's (1999) analysis points to, as processes of desecularization expressed in the growth of religious forms that are labelled as fundamentalist or conservative which sometimes become more influential than the more liberal or mainstream forms of religion. Kong's (1990, 1993, 2001) work, developing the notion of spaces of religion reflected in the concept of new geographies of religion seems very relevant to the case of Jerusalem. She emphasizes that investigating the boundaries of religious–secular spaces in the city has been a prominent topic in the studies of geography of religion in the 1980s and 1990s, with the emphasis on mapping the distribution of religious groups over space at a particular point in time (Kong, 1990). With regard to Jerusalem, the research of Hershkowitz (1987) is of particular importance in examining the distribution of the religiously heterogeneous Jewish population and the conclusion that the residential pattern in Jerusalem is a function of religiousness or religiosity: the distribution of the ultra-orthodox is distinct from that of the non-extreme orthodox and the completely secular section of the population. Another body of research is the study of the impact of religion on the physical form of the landscape such as the study of cemeteries (Kong, 1990). Some of these works hint at a potential conflict between religious and secular groups in the demands of land or land use (Shilhav, 1983). As already noted, I wish to take the discussion of the conflicts of religious–secular urban spaces one step further and analyze their visual and sound expressions as related to the notion of the right to the city by connecting the religious–cultural constructions of urban spaces to the politics of urban governance (Kong, 2001).

The right to the city as Lefebvre defines it (1991a, 1991b) is a very relevant concept to discuss the articulation of religious–secular spaces in Jerusalem because it asserts a normative rather than a juridical right based on *inhabitance*. Those who inhabit the city have a right to the city. It is earned by living in the city, and it is shared between the urban dweller, the one that 'uses' the city without living in it and the city citizen, the one who lives in the city. This means that both those who live in the city permanently (such as residents) and those who use it temporarily (such as visitors and tourists) have the right to take part in the urban creation of everyday life in the city. This concept of the right to the city involves within it two main rights (Purcell, 2003), and these rights are crucial to understand the determination and re-determination of public spaces in Jerusalem: *The right to appropriate* urban space in the sense of the right to use, the right of inhabitants to 'full and complete use' of urban space in their everyday lives. It is the right to live in, play in, work in, represent, characterize, and occupy urban space in a particular city – the right to be an author of urban space. It is a creative product of and context for the everyday life of its inhabitants, visitors and tourists, a right that is not always fulfilled for the Jerusalem residents. The second component of the right to the city is *the right to participation*. It includes the rights of inhabitants to take a central role in decision making surrounding the production of urban space at any scale, within the state, capital or any other entity that takes part in the production of urban space. As Dikec (2001) points out, this entails the involvement of inhabitants in forms of institutionalized control over urban life which includes, among others, participation in political life and taking an active role in management and administration of the city (Dikec, 2001). In what follows, I analyse the visual and sound expressions of the Lefebvrian notion of the right to the city, and in doing so offer other perspectives to the analysis of this concept.

Street signs as modesty walls

The analysis of the way that street signs function as modesty walls is based on my previous work (Fenster, 2005, 2007) that explored women's mobility in the context of women's 'rights to the city', defined by Lefebvre (1991) and Mitchell (2003). There I focused on the Jerusalem neighbourhood of Mea Shearim[2] (see area 1 in map 4.1), because the interviews I carried out at that time indicated that it is a place whose occupants define 'rights to the city' in exclusionary and religiously orthodox ways.[3] Jewish orthodoxy, for example, requires women to dress modestly in public by covering their bodies and heads. Mea Shearim's occupants seek to apply these religious dress codes to all women who enter their neighbourhood, whether they are orthodox Jews or not. Mea Shearim was specifically established as a place where ultra-orthodox Jews could live in complete accordance with their religious regulations, making it a kind of sacred space. In my previous work (Fenster, 2005, 2007), I have analysed the gendered ghettoized character of this neighbourhood that has a clear visual and spatial expression. Large signs hang at the two main entrances to the neighbourhood on Mea Shearim Street – the main street of the neighbourhood – and also at the entrances to the small alleys and shops located within the neighbourhood. These signs pose a clear request in Hebrew and English. Sometimes the message in Hebrew and English is similar, sometimes it is slightly different (see Figure 4.1 taken in area 1, map 4.1): *Please do not pass our neighbourhood in immodest clothes.*

Figure 4.1 Street Signs in the main entrance to Mea Shearim (all photos are taken by the author)

Map 4.1 Jerusalem – Location Map of the Areas under Research

This request regarding modest clothing refers to women only as it is specified in the Hebrew language in the sign. Hebrew is a gendered language which uses feminine and masculine pronouns and verbs so that the gender of the object of a request or command is always clear. The signs also specify the exact meaning of modest clothing according to Jewish law and practice (Figures 4.1 and 4.2): *Modest clothes include: closed blouse, with long sleeves, long skirt, no trousers, no tight-fitting clothes.*

These specifications do not leave any room for individual interpretations as to what is the meaning of 'modest' as it is culturally constructed. It involves very detailed specifications related to the appropriate ways to cover all parts of women's bodies. At the bottom of this sign, there is a specific request using again the feminine gender in Hebrew. In English it says (figure 1): *Please do not disturb our children's education and our way of life as Jews committed to God and his Torah.*

The Hebrew version of this sign emphasizes the sacredness of the neighbourhood: *Please do not disrupt the sacredness of our neighbourhood and our way of life as Jews dedicated to God and his Torah.*

It is interesting to notice the different gendering in Hebrew and English, probably intended for the different target groups that these signs address – either Israeli women or tourists of either gender. The signs in Hebrew are more explicit about the sacredness of the place probably because the conflict is internal, that is, among Jewish groups, rather than with people from outside Israel such as tourists. The sign ends with mentioning 'the neighbourhood residents' as those who signed this request. Lately, similar signs in Hebrew only have begun to appear in shop entrances as well and again ask women (see Figure 4.2): *Please enter my shop with modest clothes only.*

This recent practice to install signs on shop entrances signifies the extremist tendencies to maintain modesty in the streets of Mea Shearim by people who live

Figure 4.2 Modesty Sign at the entrance to a small shop in Mea Shearim

in the neighbourhood, but also by shopkeepers who are not necessarily members of the community but who put up these signs to show the local residents that they follow the strict rules of modesty. They thus legitimate their space as appropriate for local residents.

The reasons for putting these signs in the streets and shop entrances reflect the sacredness of the Land of Israel as the promised biblical land in the eyes of the ultra-orthodox. This holiness necessitates practices of modesty and dress not only by ultra-orthodox women but by secular women as well because women's modesty is a very basic rule in the religious Jewish lifestyle (Shilav, 2004). These practices can be seen as symbolic 'border guards' which help to identify people as members or non-members of the community. However, these signs do not only appear in Mea Shearim. They are also placed in many other neighbourhoods where religious and ultra-orthodox people live, although with a lesser dominance than in Mea Shearim (see Figure 4.3 taken in area 5 on map 4.1). In map 4.1 we can see the spread of these street signs and how Mea Shearim represents the core of the visual emphasis of modesty walls and how this phenomenon spreads in the area in the vicinity of the neighbourhood marking visual boundaries between religious and secular areas in the city.

One interpretation of these signs is that they demonstrate the gated nature of the neighbourhood with 'modesty gates' or as its residents phrase it: 'modesty walls'. These walls construct the boundaries of the religious and cultural identities of its residents and transform its main streets into sacred spaces that exclude women of other beliefs who do not follow the strict rules of modest dress, along with mixed-gendered groups who disobey practices of gender segregation. However, such

Figure 4.3 Modesty Sign in area 5 nearby Mea Shearim

signs can also be interpreted as part of the politics of identity of the community, which struggles against 'intolerance of difference' in modernity (Kong, 2001). Moreover, these signs may express the 'right to difference' by ultra-orthodox women themselves who feel more comfortable in such a 'gated' space, in which their own modest dress is a norm rather than the exception as it would be in other secular public spaces in Jerusalem (Fenster, 2004).

As such, these signs serve as a defence against 'inappropriate' dress and lifestyle, which contradicts the group's norms and standards of behaviour. Such a construction of public spaces as sacred is contested in any case (Kong, 2001), mainly because sacred is a 'contested category' as it represents 'hierarchical power relations of domination and subordination, inclusion and exclusion, appropriation and dispossession' (Chidester and Linenthal, 1995: 17). A sacred place is constructed by appropriation of a property, through the politics of exclusion, by maintaining boundaries, and by distancing the inside from the outside (Kong, 2001). As Sibley mentions (1995, 1998), forms and norms of exclusion are not only the practices of the majority against the minority but also the practices of the minority against the majority as in the case of Mea Shearim. This practice of control and surveillance and the determination of clear boundaries of what is forbidden and permitted as a means of maintaining the sacredness of a space is not new. It is as old as ancient Judaism, and it goes back to the spatialized institution of the Second Temple and the structuring of private and public space at the individual day-to-day level (Valins, 2000).

The dominance of religious–secular spaces of conflict is so evident that secular women living in Jerusalem, regardless of their nationality, ethnicity, or religious identity, mentioned certain neighbourhoods, in particular Mea Shearim, as a cause for discomfort because of their dress (see Fenster, 2004 for details). Obviously, tensions within multi-religious communities exist in many other cities (Naylor and Ryan, 1998), and sometimes these tensions have effects on women's movement in urban spaces (Secor, 2002, 2004). However, Mea Shearim represents a more complicated situation: while such sacralization of space denies *individual* rights of secular women to the city, it might reflect the *group* right to difference claimed by the ultra-orthodox. It should be emphasized, however, that the right to the city, as Lefebvre interprets it, is never absolute. In many world cities, for example, corporate workplaces, hi-tech offices, and office buildings in general become 'privatized' and thus 'forbidden' beyond the reception desks, and entrances available to 'strangers' are always under surveillance and controlled with video cameras. This is especially so after the September 11 events in the United States when many 'public spaces' became 'privatized' or exclusionary through additional security measures. Similarly, the 'right to dress' in public spaces is also controlled to a certain extent. Women and men might be arrested if they walk in what is termed as 'improper' clothing in certain public spaces. There is also a large body of work which shows that women sometimes voluntarily limit their mobility and movement in public spaces because of fear of sexual harassment or assault (Madge, 1997; Pain, 1991, Valentine, 1989). Precisely because of these growing limitations of 'the right to the city' in the name of security, fear, religion and cultural norms, it becomes more and more important to analyse the visual expressions of such limitations which express the tensions between these powers (religious groups, hi-tech 'security' actors or patriarchal norms in general) and the *individual* right to the city. In the next section, I will detail the visual practices of the secular residents expressed in graffiti.

Graffiti as markers of the religious–secular boundaries and the right to appropriate urban space in Jerusalem

One of the latest visual representations of the religious–secular tensions in Jerusalem and a counter reaction to the street signs in Mea Shearim and in nearby neighbourhoods is the appearance of graffiti on religious–secular issues, especially in the areas which are known as the symbolic boundaries between religious and secular spaces in Jerusalem (see area 2 on map 4.1). The graffiti content indicates counter religious images and expresses protest against what is perceived as the growing dominance of religious influence in public spaces in Jerusalem with particular reference to the ultra-orthodox communities. This phenomenon started before the last municipal elections in Jerusalem with a graffiti titled '11.11 Jerusalem is theirs' (see Figures 4.4 and 4.5 taken in area 2, map 4.1). This expressed the fears and tensions of secular people before the municipal elections (on 11 November 2008) in which an ultra-orthodox candidate competed against a secular candidate who finally won the elections. Then other graffiti appeared with an illustration of an ultra-orthodox man (see Figure 4.6 taken in area 2 on map 4.1) and the sign 'not among us', meaning that the secular people do not want the ultra-orthodox people to live with them. Underneath, someone else wrote in handwriting: 'So where?' to express protest at *this* graffiti. In an article in Haaretz

Figure 4.4 Graffiti in area 2 marking the date of the municipal elections 11.11

Figure 4.5 Graffiti in area 2

Figure 4.6 Graffiti in area 2 saying: 'not among us'

(30/10/09), it was suggested that the graffiti in Jerusalem is different than that in Tel Aviv or in other cities in the world in that it contains political and social messages which express current conflicts. More recently, these images of ultra-orthodox people appear in other parts of the city, for example, near my home

Figure 4.7 Graffiti in area 4 saying: 'Iran is here'

located in a mixed neighbourhood relatively far from the core religious area in Jerusalem (Figure 4.7 in area 4, map 4.1). In this graffiti one can observe the same representation of the Jewish ultra-orthodox man with his beard with the sentence: 'Iran is here' to express the secular objection against the Jewish fundamentalism of some of the ultra-orthodox communities.

As has already been documented, the notion of graffiti has attracted the interest and attention of geographers, sociologists and scholars in cultural studies since the mid-1970s after its appearance in Northeastern U.S. cities such as New York and Philadelphia and its spread over the globe. The early sociological approaches of the late 1980s explained the appearance of graffiti as originating from social classes, with motives to form subcultural social groups and as a contra-hegemonic act of street gangs, which also involve professional artistic expressions in the mainstream scene of art galleries (Lachmann, 1988). Other perspectives emphasize the gender and age of the writers and present graffiti as an outgrowth of political radicalism and as an act of empowerment and identity construction (Macdonald, 2001). Another approach concentrates on the role of graffiti as a territorial marker of street gangs and social groups and explores the meaning of messages concerning their location in the territory of the group. Ley and Cybriwsky (1974), for example, showed how the content characteristic of graffiti messages changes throughout an urban territory of street gangs and social groups in Philadelphia, marking boundaries with aggressive and warning graffiti messages while the inner territory is marked with more dialogical messages. This perspective demonstrates how graffiti and the urban space function as a tool which social groups use in order to announce their presence and to define and claim their space, identity acknowledgement and authority. Graffiti also plays a significant role in constructing cultural and sociological notions of places through evoking reactive public discourse which then motivates further social constructions of the cultural and ideological urban landscape. Thus, graffiti discloses the 'urban other' and stimulates an ambivalent public discourse (transgression and disorder vs. creativity and art) within the readers, media, hegemonic groups and authorities. This public reaction towards graffiti contributes to the establishment of certain representations of urban space which is identified with cultural and moral values (Cresswell, 1992). This previous analysis of graffiti is very relevant to its later appearance in Jerusalem in streets and borderline areas (area 2 on map 4.1). In particular, it indicates protest against what is perceived as the religious hegemonic power which affects everyday life in the city. Graffiti in Jerusalem also indicates the territorial markers of secular spaces and the construction of secular notions of place through evoking public discourses. As Cresswell (1992) argues, the reaction of the public to graffiti contributes to the debate on moral or, in this case, on religious values in urban landscapes. Graffiti in Jerusalem is the visual expression of the fight for the right to the city and is part of the ongoing public debate taking place in local and national media and newspapers on whose city it is.

The sounds of the Sabbath and the Jewish rituals as markers of religious–secular boundaries

These two representations which are very dominant in the streets of Jerusalem are examples of anecdotal expressions of the right to the city. They take place at certain times (once a week in the case of Shabbat and once a year in the case of Hanukah) and in certain spaces (mixed religious–secular, religious and ultra-orthodox areas) and serve as other markers of the loose boundaries between the private and the public and as an indication of secular and religious areas in the city.

As is the case in many cities around the globe, Jerusalem is a city of constant religious sounds such as Christian church bells and the voices of the Muazin calling Muslims to pray. Those sounds that are aspatial in their nature sometimes cause conflicts, especially between Jews and Palestinians.[4] The Jewish prayers in synagogues are not loud or explicit, so here I refer mainly to the sounds of the Sabbath as the songs and prayers that are sung before and after the meals in religious people's homes and not synagogues. Walking in the streets at the time of Sabbath meals, one can identify the houses and flats from which such songs are heard and according to those where religious people live. It is this character of the sound and voice which transcends the private and the public space and makes them unique geographical markers of the loose boundaries between religiosity and secularism.

Another visual representation of these loose boundaries between religious and secular areas is the appearance of the Hanukah candlelights in the windows of the houses and in ultra-orthodox neighbourhoods in front of the houses (see Figure 4.8 of area 3 in map 4.1). During the Hanukah holiday, one can walk in the streets of Jerusalem and mark the areas where these candlelights appear as an indication of areas where religious people live and practice. As it is evident here, visualized and sound practices of 'using' or 'appropriating' spaces are important expressions of the battle for the right to the city from a religious–secular perspective.

Figure 4.8 Candle lights in Hanukah in area 3

Discussion – the right to the religious–secular city – urban governance in Jerusalem

This chapter has illustrated the visual and sound representations of the conflicts between the secular and religious Jews in Jerusalem. The first two representations, the street signs in Mea Shearim (and other neighbourhoods) and the graffiti, are markers of the fight for the right to the city, especially the right to use and the right to appropriate space within the two communities. The sounds and sights associated with domestic religious rituals are markers of the more anecdotal expressions of the right to the city and the fight for the right to appropriate and the right to use. Related to the first two examples, the question is: 'What is the role of the municipality in this conflict and how does the municipality perceive these street signs and graffiti which are considered illegal?'

In order to understand the municipality standpoint regarding the 'modesty signs', I talked to the chief of the City Enforcement Department at the Jerusalem Municipality, a department which deals with enforcing municipal bylaws, including those concerning licensing for street signs and businesses. I asked him about the legality of the signs in the streets of Mea Shearim and other streets in the city. He stated that, in general, the municipality is very rigid in enforcing municipal bylaws by imposing licensing for street signs and businesses. But in Mea Shearim, he said, it is different.

He explained that although the signs there are illegal as they were not approved and licensed by the municipality, the municipality's workers cannot enforce the law. The chief of the City Enforcement Department defined this area as 'outside the law and outside enforcing the law' (Interview, 20/07/03). He explains the difficulty of enforcing this bylaw in Mea Shearim and other neighbourhoods due to lack of enough labour power. He says: 'Even if we take down these signs they will put them up again'. This admission in fact reflects the struggle of the ultra-orthodox group to establish its politics of identity and community by challenging the sovereignty of the municipality and perhaps its 'intolerance to difference'. It also expresses the Mea Shearim's group's lack of recognition of the sovereignty of the municipality. But this is probably also an expression of the municipality's implicit politics (meaning policies that are not clear and public) not to interfere with Mea Shearim's practices because of local politics and power relations within the municipality's council. The chief of the City Enforcement Department admits that if such signs restricting movement appeared in secular neighbourhoods, the municipality would have reacted forcefully against this practice. Thus, in spite of their illegitimate status, these signs still hang in public spaces transforming the neighbourhood into a gated one. The same goes for the graffiti; despite its illegality, it seems that the municipality does not do much to clean the walls of these figures that might be offensive to the ultra-orthodox communities. It should be emphasized that this is not the only illegal 'bottom-up' initiation of the ultra-orthodox communities. In border neighbourhoods located between secular and religious areas, there are special roadblocks that are put on the streets on the Sabbath by the ultra-orthodox people themselves. These roadblocks do not have any sign of municipal, army or police identity. They are 'private' roadblocks which are in place to prevent cars from entering religious and ultra-orthodox neighbourhoods on the Sabbath (see Figures 4.9 and 4.10 taken in area 3 on map 4.1). This prompts us to raise the question of whether this 'bottom-up' initiation is part of what Dikec referred to as the right to participation that includes the involvement of inhabitants in forms of

Figure 4.9 Shabbat road block in area 3

Figure 4.10 Shabbat road block in area 3

institutionalized control over urban life. And if so, how does this involvement affect the right to participation of the secular people in the city?

To conclude, this chapter does not provide clear-cut answers to these complicated issues. Rather it presents the visual and aural expressions of the religious–secular fight over the right to the city, and the street signs which act as practices of sacredization of spaces and the graffiti which objects to these trends. In addition, this chapter has illustrated how the sound of songs and prayers represent more anecdotal and informal representations of the right to the city and of the loose boundaries between secular and religious areas in Jerusalem, this time projecting from the private to the public. Lastly, this chapter has emphasized how Jewish rituals of putting Hanukah candles in windows and outside the houses serve as an additional representation of these loose boundaries. The discussion on these visual and aural representations is designed to emphasize the fact that spaces of conflict in Jerusalem and in other cities around the world are not only tangible and clear cut as discussed in the current literature, but are also expressed in symbolic and intangible cultural representations, the analysis of which helps to further understand the complicated nature of secularism, religiosity and postsecularism in current urban spaces.

Notes

1   I use the terminology of 'religious' but in fact most of the chapter relates to the relationships between ultra-orthodox and secular Jewish communities in Jerusalem.
2   Mea Shearim's (Hebrew for 'one hundred gates') segregated character was determined in 1874 when the neighbourhood was established as one of the

first neighbourhoods built in west Jerusalem outside the walls of the old city. Its founders, members of the ultra-orthodox community, set up clear rules to maintain its religious identity and homogeneity. For example, they decided that residents would not sell or rent their flats to non-ultra-orthodox Jews, let alone to non-Jewish people (Ben Arie 1979). This means that the neighbourhood has been characterized from the outset as a 'ghettoized space', a reflection of the strong religious identities of its residents. Its site allocation, distant from what was then the city centre (in the old city) and distant from any means of public transportation, is another 'ghettoized expression' of the neighbourhood, meant to keep its religious identity and maintain its distinctive lifestyle (Ben Arie, 1979). It is important to emphasize this historical background as it highlights the distinctive character of this group within the ultra-orthodox community. The residents of Mea Shearim represent more conservative and extremist viewpoints than other ultra-orthodox communities, a viewpoint which perceives secular lifestyles, especially in the holy land of Israel, as illegitimate according to their interpretations of Jewish traditions and norms. Moreover, the ultra-orthodox community in Mea Shearim does not accept the sovereignty of the state of Israel and does not perceive itself as part of the citizenship discourse which entails specific duties to the state. (For example, men do not serve in the Israeli army although military duty is compulsory in Israel.) Moreover, within the framework of their religious way of life there is no room for individualism, let alone principles of democracy, equality and participation in civil 'secular' activities. It is a highly hierarchical and patriarchal society in which authority and power are determined according to family connections and degree of knowledge of the Jewish holy books (Fenster, 2007).

3   Most women I talked to in Jerusalem, either secular Jewish or Palestinians, mentioned the ultra-orthodox Mea Shearim neighbourhood as an area which they associated with discomfort; an area they avoid walking through because of the sense of threat there (see details in Fenster, 2004, 2007).

4   For example, there is a constant conflict these days between the Jewish neighbourhood of Pisgat Zeev which is located in the margins of the city and the Muazins from the nearby Palestinian village on the prayers of the Muazin in the loudspeakers at very early hours in the morning (Kol, Haair, 18/12/09).

References

Ben Arie, Y. (1979), *City as a Mirror of a Period – The New Jerusalem at its Beginning*. Yad Itzhak Ben Zvi Publications, Jerusalem (Hebrew).

Berger, P. et al. (1999), *The Desecularisation of the World: resurgent religion and world politics*. Grand Rapids, MI: Eerdmans Publishing.

Cresswell, T. (1992), 'The crucial "where" of graffiti: a geographical analysis of reactions to graffiti in New York', *Environment and Planning D: Society and Space* 10 (3), 329–44.

Chidester, D., and Linenthal, E. T. (1995), 'Introduction', In: D. Chidester and E. T. Linenthal (eds), *American Sacred Space.* Bloomington, IN: Indiana University Press, 1–42.

Dikec, M. (2001), 'Justice and the Spatial Imagination', *Environment and Planning A* 33, 1785–805.

Fenster, T. (2004), *The Global City and the Holy City – Narratives on Planning, Knowledge and Diversity.* London: Pearson.

—. (2005), 'The Right to the Gendered City: Different Formations of Belonging in Everyday Life', *The Journal of Gender Studies* 14 (3), 217–31.

—. (2007), 'Gender, Religion and Urban Management: Women's Everyday Life in the City', in K. Morin and J. K. Guelka (eds), *Women, Religion, Space.* University of Syracuse, 41–60.

Fenster, T. and Yacobi, H. (2005), 'Whose Right to the City?: Urban Planning and Local Knowledge in Globalizing Tel Aviv – Jaffa', *Planning, Theory and Practice* 6 (2), 191–211.

Hasson, Shlomo (1996), *The Struggle of the Cultural Character of Jerusalem.* Jerusalem: Floresheimer Institute (Hebrew).

Hasson, Shlomo, and Gonen, Amiram. (1996), *The Struggle for the Cultural Character of Jerusalem.* Jerusalem: Floresheimer Institute (Hebrew).

Hershkowitz, S. (1987), 'Residential Segragation by Religion: A Conceptual Framework', *Tijdschrift voor Economische en Sociale Geografie* 78, 44–52.

Kong, L. (1990), 'Geography and Religion: Trends and Prospects', *Progress in Human Geography* 14, 355–71.

—. (1993), 'Ideological Hegemony and the Political Symbolism of Religious Buildings in Singapore', *Environment and Planning D: Society and Space* 11, 23–45.

—. (2001), 'Mapping "New" Geographies of Religion: Politics and Poetics in Modernity' *Progress in Human Geography* 25 (2), 211–33.

Lachmann, R. (1988). 'Graffiti as Career and Ideology', *American Journal of Sociology* 94 (2), 229–50.

Lefebvre, H. (1991a), *Critique of Everyday Life.* London: Verso.

—. (1991b), *The Production of Space.* Oxford: Blackwell.

Ley, D., and Cybriwsky, R. (1974), 'Urban Graffiti as Territorial Markers', *Annals of the Association of American Geographers* 64 (4), 491–505.

Macdonald. N. (2001), *The Graffiti Sub Culture: Youth, Masculinity, and Identity in London and New York.* New York: Palgrave.

Madge, C. (1997), 'Public Parks and the Geography of Fear', *Tijdschrift Voor Economisch en Sociale Geografie* 88 (3), 237–50.

Mitchell, D. (2003), *The Right to the City: Social Justice and The Right for Public Space.* New York: The Guilford Press.

Naylor, S. K., and Ryan, J. R. (1998), 'Ethnicity and Cultural Landscapes: Mosques, Guradwaras, and Mandirs in England and Wales'. Paper presented at the Religion and Locality Conference', University of Leeds.

Purcell, M. (2003), 'Citizenship and the Right to the Global City: Reimagining the Capitalist World Order', *International Journal of Urban and Regional Studies* 27 (3), 564–90.

Secor, A. (2002), 'The Veil and Urban Space in Istanbul: Women's Dress, Mobility and Islamic Knowledge', *Gender, Place and Culture* 9 (1), 5–22.

Secor, A. (2004), '"There Is an Istanbul That Belongs to Me": Citizenship, Space and Identity in the City', *Annals of Association of American Geographers* 94 (2), 352–68.

Sibely, D. (1995), *Geographies of Exclusion*. London: Routledge.

—. (1998), 'Problemitizing Exclusion: Reflections on Space, Difference and Knowledge', *International Planning Studies* 3 (1), 93–100.

Shilav, Y. (1983), 'Principles for the Location of Synagougues: Symbolism and Functionalism in a Spatial Context', *Professional Geographer* 35, 324–29.

—. (1997), *Governance in an Ultra Orthodox City*. Jerusalem: Floresheimer Institute, (Hebrew).

—. (2004), personal communication.

Valins, O. (2000), 'Institutionalised Religion: Sacred Texts and Jewish Spatial Practice', *Geoforum* 31, 575–86.

5 Spirituality, Urban Life and the Urban Professions

Leonie Sandercock and Maged Senbel

> *What would it mean to live*
> *in a city whose people were changing*
> *each other's despair into hope? –*
> *You yourself must change it. –*
> *what would it feel like to know*
> *your country was changing? –*
> *You yourself must change it. –*
> *Though your life felt arduous*
> *new and unmapped and strange*
> *what would it mean to stand on the first*
> *page of the end of despair?*
>
> Adrienne Rich, from Dreams Before Waking (Rich, 1986: 46)

> *If I could make only one map for any community to use as the basis of decision making,*
> *I would opt for a map of sacred places. That information most enables community.*
>
> (Hester, 2006: 126)

> *The absence of a sustained focus on love in progressive circles arises from a collective failure*
> *to acknowledge the needs of the spirit and an overdetermined emphasis on material*
> *concerns. Without love, our efforts to liberate ourselves and our world community from*
> *oppression and exploitation are doomed.*
>
> (bell hooks, 1994: 243)

The paradox at the heart of planning

Planning is, at its core, an ethical enquiry: into how to live with each other in the shared spaces of multicultural cities and regions and how to live sustainably on the earth. But at the heart of the urban/land professions, there's an extraordinary paradox. The work of urban, social, community, environmental, and even land-use planning is fundamentally a work of hope, the work of organizing hope. And that in turn involves bringing people together to work through conflicts (about values and meaning as well as material things) and create new relationships of coexistence. And this work often takes place in the face of despair, as Adrienne Rich's poem tells us: the daily effort of overcoming despair. But where does this hope come from? Is secular humanism enough to inspire us? This chapter argues that something beyond secular humanism is essential if we are to tackle the social and ecological crises that are upon us. And that 'something', we will argue, is some kind of spirituality, which involves some sense of the sacred. Yet we have searched the planning literature in vain for any kind of recognition or exploration, let alone definition of this concept.

Given this vacuum within the planning field, we have looked beyond it for some guides to a working definition of spirituality. From Parker Palmer, a Quaker whose educational work we admire, we take the notion of spirituality as 'the diverse ways we answer the heart's longing to be connected with the largeness of life' (Palmer, 1998: 5). From bell hooks, a black feminist activist/scholar, we take the idea that a spiritual life is 'first and foremost about commitment to a way of thinking and behaving that honors principles of inter-being and connection' and also about mystery (hooks, 2001: 77).

Spirituality, then, in the context of urban life and the urban/land professions, we will interpret as a radical practice of connecting with awe: connecting to other people, and reconnecting to the natural world. The paradox at the heart of planning is that we do not discuss what makes that heart beat. We suggest that it is some sense of a relational politics, informed by love.

> Domination, oppression and injustice are the products of hatred and violence, not only of the maldistribution of rights and goods. This is often noticed in analyses that focus on oppression, domination and justice. Yet equally often those analyses fail to connect with our most obvious and powerful spiritual wellspring of hope and transformation in the face of that hatred and violence: love. (Porter, 2010: 238)

Libby Porter, a young planning academic and former planner who spent time working with indigenous people in Southeastern Australia, talks about love as a deep practice of connection: of selflessness, humility and compassion. It is not a 'model' of being or a set of rules, but an ethic towards others, a daily practice. Why would we be moved to action, she asks, 'if not from a deep ethical connection, beyond the realm of rational analysis, with others and their suffering' (Porter, ibid). And, we would add, with the suffering of non-human species, of the life force of the Earth itself (Naess, 1973).

At its best, modernist planning was imbued with a social justice mission, but its faith in the possibilities of a rational ordering of the city and a mechanistic design for living proved ultimately to be not only unsatisfying but also downright destructive. Destructive not only of the urban fabric, but also of the social fabric of neighbourhoods and communities. Reflecting on the evolution of planning thought and practice in the second half of the twentieth century, a possible (yet partial) explanation emerges for this void at the heart of planning. In its drive to emulate the social sciences, to conduct spatial and socio-economic analyses of cities and regions, as well as to develop regulatory systems governing land uses, planning was separated from its twin discipline, urban design. In many places, planning allied itself with the policy sciences or with the critical perspectives of geography and other social sciences and lost sight of an earlier part of its own tradition, that of place making. Urban designers have always been engaged with place making, asking about the qualities of great places, large and small, formal and informal. And within the urban design literature there has long been a search for the 'spirit of place', a quest for understanding of the magic and meaning in certain places (Eliade 1992; Norberg-Schulz 1980; Tuan 1974; Relph 1976; Seamon 1993; Hayden 1995). Landscape architect and educator Randolph Hester describes this as 'the pursuit of the sacred'.

> Sacred landscapes . . . are places that are endowed by a community with the power of highly revered convictions, values and virtues. These convictions, values, and virtues are experienced through the ritual use of those places. The qualities of these experiences range from the metaphysical (like transcendence, faith, and hope) to the practical (like empathy, serenity and charity) and to the earthly (like local wisdom, sense of community, and orientation). (Hester, 2006: 117)

Often associated with myth and religion, sacred places acknowledge the inexplicable and uncontrollable. And, in addition to traditionally sacred places such as churches and other religious sites, Hester argues that in today's world, 'prospect-refuge, biophilia, and ecological spiritualism serve contemporary needs for these expressions, often attempting to reconcile paradox and contradiction and reconnecting with primal forces' (Hester, ibid). Our project is very much congruent with Hester's in the pursuit of an expanded language of the sacred.

The past decade has seen a fascinating convergence of diverse literatures, from urban design and landscape architecture (Hester, 2006; Thayer, 2003) to economics, local economic development (Schumacher, 1999; Shuman, 2006) and community development (Sarkissian et al., 2009), ecological planning (Beatley, 2002), along with concerns about sustainability, climate change and 'peak oil' (Kunstler, 2005; Newman and Beatley, 2009): all converging on a central idea about what Thayer calls 'whole life place planning' (Thayer, 2003).

This convergence reflects a trend towards emphasis on preserving and enhancing natural, local conditions and a growing demand for ecosystemic social and physical planning. Implicit in the possibility of 'whole life place planning' is the gradual broadening of the ideas of 'the environment' and 'ecological planning' into domains formerly considered separately as cultural, social or political. As environmental issues rise to the surface of public concern, former contrasts between 'human' and 'natural' start to blur. The disproportionate number of toxic waste sites near low-income neighbourhoods, for example, has catalysed the environmental justice movement and illustrates the futility of separating environmental and social planning. The concerns of social planning have simultaneously expanded outwards to encompass reconnecting with nature, while ecosystem management and ecological planning have begun to incorporate issues of social capital, capacity building (community development) and human embeddedness in nature (Sarkissian, 1996).

This life place planning is both local and regional. Above all, it requires the re-establishment of a different sense of both time and place – two notions that have been undermined by the rise of globalization and electronic communication. Life place planning would restore an older concept of time: time for people to weigh and consider alternatives, time for renewable resources to regenerate, time for learning how land responds to change, and time for people to establish relations and build trust and common goals. And this different sense of time is focused on people's involvement in and collective affections for a place, the special place that is their life world, their life place.

The instinctive appeal of 'life place planning' is that it combines a gradual acknowledgement by local communities that limitations exist along with a recognition that less can be more, that joy and health come from connectedness, from being embedded in a web of interdependent relationships with all of life: with fellow humans as well as the rest of the natural world. In other words, it is driven by the kind of spirituality we have defined above.

While we have looked beyond the mainstream of planning literature to help us define spirituality, we will now look within the urban professions to find examples of such a praxis that are already transforming urban life in our own city of Vancouver: where planners as well as artists, community organizers and resident and student activists are embodying all of these dimensions of spirituality. In the next section we provide two stories from Vancouver, of movements that make manifest the lineaments of a spiritual practice in planning.

Spirituality at work in the city: two Vancouver stories

The Collingwood Neighbourhood House

They talk about this as a 'blessed place'. Pass through its hand-carved entrance gate and you enter a place where new Canadians and longtime citizens mix and mingle, sharing their food, their dreams, and their initiatives, in thirty six or so languages. The carving that frames the front door of the Collingwood Neighbourhood House (CNH) reflects the core values of this unique place: values of respect, inclusion, celebration, social justice. Carved by Gerry Sheena, (an Aboriginal Canadian and active community member) with the help of two apprentices, the gateway features a mother bear on one side, symbolizing family, and a wolf on the other, symbolizing community. Across the top of the carving, specific animals represent different cultures: an eagle, a lion, a dragon, a horse, an elephant and a jaguar. This is a contemporary adaptation of the traditional Aboriginal totem pole: the Multicultural Gateway sculpture.

Step into the lobby of this 26,000 square foot community facility and you will likely be greeted by Albert Battistoni, an 84 year-old volunteer who staffs the front desk seven days a week, alongside employees. Likely you will also pick up the scent of a coconut curry or whatever else is cooking that day in the kitchen adjacent to the reception area, and you will encounter groups of toddlers wandering through, a few seniors chatting in a corner, a group of youths bouncing up the stairs to their hang-out area, exuberantly greeting everyone else, and some homeless folks trying on shoes from one of the free clothing bins in the hallways. This bright and busy place is part community centre, part settlement house, part recreation club, part training facility: a place that literally buzzes with the kind of goodwill that makes daily life not only worth living but also imbued with meaning for some of this city's most marginalized citizens. What began over twenty years ago as a kitchen table community initiative is now a thriving gathering place, a place for everyone in this dense, multicultural urban neighbourhood of 45,000 people.

And yet, just 25 years ago, the Collingwood neighbourhood was experiencing rapid change from a predominantly Anglo-European demography to a much more culturally diverse population as a result of changes to immigration legislation. Oldtimers were becoming fearful and anxious and anti-immigrant sentiments and incidents were not uncommon. Collingwood, an old working class neighborhood on the eastern edge of the City of Vancouver[1], is now the most culturally diverse neighbourhood in the City. The Collingwood Neighbourhood House (CNH)[2] was established in 1985 just as the migration pattern into Vancouver was changing. By 2001, the residential population of the area was 51 per cent Chinese, 10 per cent English, with Filipino, Vietnamese and South Asian groups growing, alongside older Italian, Portuguese and German groups, and an even older Aboriginal presence. One-third of Collingwood's residents are low-income; the neighbourhood has the City's largest youth population (25 per cent under 19) and a growing aging population (16 per cent seniors)[3].

The CNH was established to provide much needed family and childcare services, but also to do community development work. Its founding members set out to diversify this work in terms of language and ethnicity. The CNH was the first institution in Vancouver – probably in Canada – to develop *an intercultural mission*, which is part of what makes its story significant. More important, though, are the details of how this was done.

What CNH does, literally, is to develop and provide services according to perceived local needs. But the organization's real purpose is to *build community*, so the services provided are not seen as merely services meeting a need (such as childcare) but also as providing *meeting places where people come together and connect through engaging in activities together*. One of the outstanding successes of the CNH has been their outreach through the arts, in the 'Building Community through Cultural Expression' program, and it is to one of those activities that we now turn. This is the story of the "Arts Pow Wow" and the rehabilitation of a neighbourhood park (Sandercock and Attili, 2009).

Since the 1970s neighbours had been complaining about youth gang activities in Slocan Park. There was vandalism, of cars, houses, and the park itself. Matters worsened in the 1980s with the opening of a new light rail line bringing crime, petty theft, assaults, prostitution, and intravenous drug use. In the late 1990s a group of residents led by environmental artist January Wolodarsky began a movement to reclaim the park, at the same time as Paula Carr, Community Development director at CNH, was bringing local leaders together to work in the surrounding area. A core group of four people was the initial catalyst: the environmental artist, a visual artist, a resident involved in a community newspaper, and an Aboriginal leader who wanted to work with Aboriginal youth and carving. Thus the four dimensions of the Arts Pow Wow were born: Aboriginal development; Neighbourhood physical and social development (Slocan Park); Community development (of artistic capacities and community resources); and Communication.

The Pow Wow practitioners used a great variety of tools in their work – from community mapping to murals, mosaics, puppetry, aboriginal carving, music, lantern making, gardening, physical recreation, video and information technology, the creation of sacred spaces; and a participatory action research approach. Six thousand residents were involved in the three years of the Arts Pow Wow's work in *community development planning and participatory design*. With the help of just one professional landscape architect, residents collectively designed and built this park, including all of the art, from the Guardian Spirit totem pole to the mosaics, lanterns, plantings, etc.

What the Slocan Park project demonstrates so well is that *an intercultural community can be created through a common project*. The range of people who became involved was extensive: Aboriginal youth and elders, the Chinese community through the Tai Chi group, primary and high school students, doing murals and plantings, African drummers. People started to see each other on a neighbour-to-neighbour basis, not as either strangers or as members of a group. *The park design is truly hybrid*, reflecting the multiple cultures that constitute this neighbourhood.

The larger lesson to be drawn from this story of the CNH and Slocan Park is an understanding of *the process through which strangers become neighbours*, transcending ethnic and other differences (see Attili and Sandercock, 2007; Sandercock and Attili, 2009; Sandercock and Attili, 2010). In Neighbourhood Houses, people from different cultural backgrounds are thrown together in new settings which disrupt familiar patterns and create the possibility of initiating new attachments. Through involvement in community gardens, child care facilities, youth projects, the regeneration of derelict spaces, recreational and training programs, what happens is the overcoming of feelings of strangeness in the simple process of sharing tasks and comparing ways of doing things. People shift from fear of the Other, to curiosity, to the possibility of connection and inclusion, to a growing sense of respect and awe.

There's an elderly Chinese man who joined a drumming group that plays in Slocan Park. He couldn't speak any English, so he couldn't participate with his neighbours, but every Friday he would come and drum with the African drummers. People formed friendships that way. The Tai Chi group, sixty or so Chinese folks using the park, were initially very reluctant to talk to strangers, but then the artists approached them and got them involved in the production of art, and the Tai Chi group is now a very strong supporter of what's happening in the park. They come out to help, they bring food for everyone, they helped to make mosaics, to raise the totem pole, they come to all the celebrations in the park, and they lobbied the Parks Board for improvements. So they became part of the community instead of separate from it.

What this account has not revealed are the wonderful human beings who have made all of this happen. Talk with any of the locals and any of the workers and volunteers at the House and they will quickly tell you that the CNH is the *heart* of this neighbourhood, and that the heart of CNH is Paula Carr, Executive Director and Director of Community Development. Just as quickly, Paula will explain that the mission of CNH has always been empowerment, and that it's really the local folks who've done all this themselves, with some enabling from 'professionals' like herself.

What has actually happened is something remarkable.[4] Collingwood was not always like this. But the vision of neighbourliness embodied in the staff, volunteers, and on the Board of CNH, has modeled an inclusionary rather than exclusionary way of being with strangers, a practice which has now become the norm. In the words of Terry Tayler, an 'oldtimer' who was part of the 'kitchen table initiative' and became the first President of the Board of CNH: 'I see a community that's got a heart, a feel of connectedness; the oldtimers are comfortable with the newcomers. There's give and take all the time. . . . It just shows what you can do if only you think big and if you open your heart'. Or in the words of Satinder Singh, who emigrated with her family from India twenty years ago: 'It's all about love and compassion. It's a blessed place. It has made an incredible difference in people's lives' (Attili and Sandercock, 2007).

If spirituality expresses a perennial human concern, often understood as the search for becoming fully human, which means recognizing the rights of others and striving for an equal dignity and respect for different races, sexes, ages and abilities, then the CNH is the embodiment of such a spirituality. If spirituality means seeking after something that makes us feel linked with a community of others, and awed by their humanity, and if it means linking with something larger than ourselves, then the CNH has made that tangible. It is spirit at work in urban life. Dialoguing and working with others is an act of trust and hope, an act capable of leaving both parties changed. At the heart of this kind of community development is the notion that we can make our lives better, that we can help each other and that we care about each other and the environment that nurtures us.

There is a magic in all this. And that is what we hear in the voices of the folks touched by CNH: reverence and celebration and gratitude for this magic of human community. As the CNH enters its second twenty years, it is worth recalling the words of Jane Addams, who started the first Settlement House in North America, in Chicago in 1889, precursor to today's Neighbourhood Houses: 'Our hope of social achievement . . . lies in a complete mobilization of the human spirit, using all our unrealized and unevoked capacity' (Addams, in Knight, 2005, frontispiece).

There is a larger context here in Vancouver of a changed planning culture ever since residents revolted against the pro-development City Council in the early 1970s and a new Director of Planning was hired, Ray Spaxman. Spaxman had a reputation as a planner who privileged neighbourhoods and neighbourliness and that has been a dominant civic value and virtue ever since. Spaxman's successor,

Larry Beasley, likes to talk about the importance of love in this work of place making. And younger members of the planning staff, like Nathan Edelson, who was the City's liaison with the Collingwood community in the 1980s when CNH was established, brings a similar devotion to community wellbeing to his work every day. Each of these planners brings the lineaments of spirituality to his professional work, without ever talking about religion as such. A similar spirit informs the community development approach at CNH. Terry Tayler, a resident leader, calls it 'opening the heart', while Paula Carr, the Executive Director for twenty years, thinks of it as a conscious practice of 'being in community'. And this in turn involves trust and respect, caring and connection, hope and healing. It is a practice of love that transforms a profession into a calling.

Spirituality, as it is practiced by planners, is a state of consciousness that permeates every aspect of their work. It is not adherence to a particular doctrine or scripture, but rather, as Paul Woodruff describes it, a condition of reverence. He argues, through an exploration of Greek mythology and Classic Confucianism, that reverence is a 'cardinal virtue ... able to team up with a wide range of practices and beliefs' (Woodruff, 2001: 136).

> Reverence begins in a deep understanding of human limitations; from this grows the capacity to be in awe of whatever we believe lies outside our control – God, truth, justice, nature, even death. The capacity for awe as it grows brings with it the capacity for respecting fellow human beings, flaws and all ... Simply put reverence is the virtue that keeps human beings from trying to act like gods. (Woodruff, 2001: 4)

There is no escaping the cacophony of protests that erupt at the mere mention of spirituality in planning discourse. Some professionals and academics genuinely fear the doctrinal or exclusionary politics that often come with organized religion. But spirituality in planning is not about arguing for or against God or for the superiority of a particular dogma. This is about upholding the values of awe and wonder and humility; values that we completely miss when we plan as though we are gods. As Woodruff reminds us, 'to forget that you are only human, to think you can act like a god – this is the opposite of reverence' (Woodruff, 2001: 4). The idea that we can cull, process, organize and redistribute populations of plants and animals to fulfill our plans, with no regard to consequences, is grasping at immortality. It presumes knowledge of the unknown. The idea has failed (Scott, 1998). We are no less mortal when we subdue natural systems. When our cities ascend into consumptive hyper-efficiency, our urban environments descend into vulnerability and soullessness.

Spirituality in planning is not a new type of planning but rather a layering of connectedness into the decisions and interactions that characterize our work. How might these layers change the outcome of planning decisions? Our second story captures one of the most enduring conflicts in city building. It involves the methodical appropriation of land by a powerful group from a less powerful group (in this instance, within the same institution).[5] In this case, an institution of higher learning plays the role of the feudal lord. This is the story of the farm at the University of British Columbia and how the land it inhabits is a contest between the sacred and the entrepreneurial.

Saving the last urban farm in Vancouver

On the surface the conflict is over land. The University of British Columbia (UBC) occupies 400 hectares on the western tip of a forested peninsula in Vancouver that juts out into the sea. It is lush land with views to majestic snow-capped mountains across the bay to the north and mountains on Vancouver Island across the sea to the west. The provincial government granted the University a 1200 hectare site stretching from the coast to include large swaths of forest adjacent to the City of Vancouver. The land was to serve as an endowment that could be logged, cleared and developed to generate capital for the university.

All of this land is part of the Musqueam First Nation traditional territory and the Musqueam sought to interrupt the transfer of land as it interfered with their aboriginal rights and title claims (Musqueam, 2010). In 2007 the Province reached an agreement with the Musqueam to transfer to them three parcels of land totalling 81 hectares. The legal battles between the provincial government and the Musqueam are a familiar struggle for autonomy, cultural legitimacy and for some measure of reparation for historical injustices. But for our story here, this is only the backdrop to a dispute internal to the university and it, too, is the struggle of a David against a Goliath. It is the struggle to save the farm.

When the campus was first established in 1925, agricultural lots were in the heart of campus and central to its mission. Over the years, as the campus grew to accommodate new disciplines and a growing population, agricultural activity moved further and further south and was eventually pushed into a forested area in the southern third of the campus (South Campus). Farming had become a sanitized, mechanized science. Land-based research and learning were seen as primitive pursuits that ought to be relegated to land-based universities in agricultural heartlands. UBC had aspirations to be a world-class university in a world-class city. A working farm was not a part of that vision. Instead, the university had built TRIUMF on South Campus, a facility that supports nuclear and particle physics, molecular and material science and nuclear medicine. Since opening in 1969, it has attracted more than a billion dollars in research. This facility was set to expand into the adjacent agricultural land in the early 1990s and agricultural scientists had stopped investing in that land.

In the meantime, faced with growing financial demands for the maintenance and upgrading of its academic facilities, the university administration put in motion a long-term plan for monetizing its land endowment by developing real estate in a number of areas within the campus boundaries. The University was also committed to increasing the resident population on campus to reduce automobile trips to and from campus. These forces culminated in the development of an Official Community Plan (OCP) that called for a new residential village in the south campus area that would displace the animal research facilities and approximately 13 hectares of forest. Both the neglected south campus agricultural field and another three hectares of farm plots close to the academic core of the campus were marked as future housing reserve. The university was essentially disinvesting from maintaining any agriculturally productive land on campus.

The convergence of a number of factors in the late 1990s gave rise to a new culture of valuing urban agriculture and urban ecology and of fighting to advance these values at the University. By the mid-1990s the Faculty of Agricultural Sciences had undergone considerable attrition and, after decades of declining enrollment, set about to reinvent itself. In 1997 a new Dean was hired to help make the faculty more relevant to contemporary societal priorities. Dean Moura Quayle hired a teaching professor, Alejandro Rojas, who developed a *Community of Learners* pedagogy that emphasized the collaborative production of knowledge (Rojas, 2009). Rojas touched countless students with his passion and commitment to facilitating a culture of citizenship and responsibility. Invigorated and empowered, students began to cast their critical gazes outwards onto the campus around them. They felt a growing responsibility to participate in the shaping of their surrounding environment. They were being taught to apply their passion, wisdom and critical insight to champion the cause of biodiversity, environmental security and ecosystem integrity. At the time there was talk of a special place at the southern end of campus, but no one knew much about it. Derek Masselink, a Masters of Landscape Architecture student, driven by a strong ethic of caring for the land, came across this "lost" field. He recognized it as a gem right away.

By this time, in the late 1990s, the university was holding a series of public open houses in which the university's official community plan and component neighbourhood plans were revealed. Derek and his classmates agitated in opposition to these plans but it was Derek who invited a local urban agriculture expert to the fallow field and asked him what to do about the impending development. Derek was told that without a clear champion (and there were none), saving the old farm would be up to him.

Today the farm is a hub of social, socio-economic, pedagogical, disciplinary and biological diversity (UBC Farm 2010). What was once a fallow field is now a thriving provider of fresh produce to numerous university food outlets and a weekly farmers market. It is surrounded by a tall coniferous forest and together they form the 24 hectare UBC Farm/Centre for Sustainable Food Systems. The farm serves as a model for urban agriculture, agro-forestry, interdisciplinary land based research and community service learning in sustainable food production.

The sights, sounds and scents of the farm are a refuge from the fast pace, noise and pollution of urban life. It is a majestic place that takes your breath away. Summer weekdays bring dozens of students, staff, volunteers, youth and children to work, learn and play on the farm. Different immigrant and refugee groups have their own plots where they are able to retain some modicum of tradition and connection to the cycles of life that every farm embodies. They are able to be grounded in the familiar practices of their home countries and their ancestors. They are able to connect to the earth's life nurturing qualities, to the sacredness of life.

Growing food in the city is about much more than sustaining ourselves. Instead, growing food cultivates attitudes of patience, tolerance, respect and forgiveness.

It slows us down and reminds us that the cycles of life, growth, death and decay take time. We can try to speed them up a little, but ultimately seasons dictate our cycles and the weather can wreak havoc on our most considered plans. We are not in control. We learn of the complex web of factors that need to coincide precisely to nurture life. Working directly with the soil and with compost, seeds, seedlings, the sun, water, drainage, rodents and disease is a constant reminder of the preciousness of life and of the profundity of nature's balance. It teaches reverence.

Urban agriculture also instills respect and admiration for others. We learn that cooperation is essential. As Derek puts it, "farming demands cooperation, it doesn't foster it, it demands it" (Masselink, 2009). Growing and preparing food is culturally specific and when farmers from ancient civilizations end up farming side by side, as happened on the UBC farm, their fascination with diverse practices turns into awe of the Other and of the unique circumstances that led to the evolution of their own culture. Kurdish refugees and Mayan immigrants from Guatemala grew similar crops on adjacent plots, but they did so differently. Where one would grow in irrigated troughs, the other would grow in ridges above the irrigation. The contrast was fascinating and was a clear demonstration of the richness of traditions in responding to specific climatic and historical needs and that, significantly, many paths can lead to fruition. Multiculturalism, pluralism and diversity were exemplified in ways that inspired mutual respect, admiration and even love.

Growing food builds bridges and a shared appreciation for diverse practices. At the mercy of powerful and immovable outside forces, farmers realize that working cooperatively is far more productive than being in competition. According to Derek,

> Understanding that you are at the mercy of larger forces pulls people together, you need support, and community and friendship . . . there are things in nature that are incredibly important to us from a physical or economic point of view, but also a spiritual point of view . . . we can continue to destroy nature or we can act in a way that protects these qualities and nurtures these qualities. (Masselink, 2009)

Surrounding the farm are significant wildlife corridors, which serve as integral habitat for frogs, eagles, hawks, owls and at least 60 other species of birds living in balance with an integrated farm ecosystem. That proximity is itself a teacher. The interface between non-human nature and human habitat is where we can appreciate our embeddedness in the web of life. The farm exemplifies the movement from a thriving ecosystem at the heart of which is rich biodiversity and little human influence, and as you move towards human activity the ecological relationships are stewarded to serve people. From food production to water purification to nutrient recycling, urban farms bring us closer to the natural cycles upon which we are dependent.

Derek may have been the catalyst for rebuilding the farm, but he did not do it alone. He developed a vision for the farm with the help of the Dean and many student volunteers. He became the first director of the farm and employed students and maintained a list of sympathetic citizens who were supportive of the farm.

Even though institutional pressure pushed Derek out by 2004, and even though all the animal research facilities and an avian centre were decommissioned, and almost 15 hectares of forest were razed, the farm has endured. The farm's subsequent director, Mark Bomford, has extended Derek's legacy and has been instrumental in building an ever-expanding network of contributors. Today the farm enjoys support from hundreds of students, faculty and staff at the university and dozens of volunteers belonging to a student led organization called Friends of the Farm.

Today there are competing visions for the future of the land. Even though UBC farm is a thriving institution with hundreds of active supporters, as far as the University's Campus Planning office is concerned, the site continues to be designated as a future housing reserve. The only concession by the University Administration has been to stipulate that there will be no market housing on the site and that the UBC farm will continue to exist. This does not preclude relocation. But dozens more people continue to visit the farm every day and are so enchanted by its vibrancy that they passionately apply their intellectual and emotional resources to help save it.

A stand for the farm is a stand for reverence, humility and connectedness, inclusion and hedging against a premature presumption of solutions. It is a stand against liquidating the asset of ecological integrity and agricultural productivity. The farm enriches our spirits when it helps demonetize the products of nature that give us physical and emotional sustenance. As Wendell Berry puts it:

> Most of us cannot imagine the wheat beyond the bread, or the farmer beyond the wheat, or the farm beyond the farmer, or the history beyond the farm. Most people cannot imagine the forest and the forest economy that produced their houses and furniture and paper; or the landscapes, the streams, and the weather that fill their pitchers and bathtubs and swimming pools with water. Most people appear to assume that when they have paid their money for these things they have entirely met their obligations. (Berry, 2001: 40)

The immense outpouring of emotion expressed in the campaign to save UBC Farm (Environmental Communications 2009, World News 2010) has tapped into a yearning that clearly goes beyond the desire for and appreciation of fresh food to the deeper 'ecological self' that craves connection with nature in the midst of the city. Arne Naess has coined the term the 'ecological self' in discussing the importance of identifying our self with all living beings, resulting in an expanded sense of self that goes beyond individual ego or consciousness to include society and relationships, as well as nonhuman nature (Naess, 1988). He argues that the larger 'Self' deserves the same care and respect that we afford our smaller individual selves and that this desire to care for nature emerges instinctively when we fully experience being in nature (Naess, 1973). Recent research builds on this reciprocity (Wilson, 1993; Kellert and Kahn, 2002) and demonstrates the many benefits of living in proximity to non-human nature and interacting with ecological systems (Kaplan and Kaplan, 1989; Kaplan, 1995; Maller et al., 2005 and Pedretti-Burls, 2007).

The deep caring and reverential regard of nature has led to what many have termed nature-based spirituality. Douglas Todd's edited collection canvassing the uniqueness of nature-inspired spiritual practice in the Pacific coastal rainforest of North America (which includes Vancouver) explores the distinction between conventional religion and nature-based spirituality (Todd, 2008). Todd brings together a range of perspectives that exemplify a movement that sees nature as a source of wisdom, values and meaning. For Gail Wells, nature based spiritualists consider themselves spiritual but not religious and focus their spiritual expression on nature.

> ... nature based spirituality includes a conviction that nature represents ultimate reality and as such, offers both a source of ethics and a framework of meaning for life. For its most passionate adherents, nature-based spirituality answers those two central questions that religion tries to answer: 'What is real?' and 'How shall we then live?' (Wells, 2008)

Nature is a place where we can both connect with our most reflective selves and also a place where our non-discreteness from other species and other people becomes powerfully obvious. Vibrant ecosystems in the city allow us to see each other with reverence as one organism, with each part dependent on the other. It invites us to care and to love and forego the primacy of our egos. Wells goes on to caution against the danger for nature-based spirituality to become distinctly private, 'offering comfort and solace at the risk of self-absorption and disconnection from the larger community' and warns against undermining the social justice activism that organized religion can mobilize (Wells, 2008: 255).

Pier Giorgio Di Cicco, the City of Toronto's Poet Laureate from 2004 to 2010, often speaks of the need for a spiritual revitalization of our cities. He bypasses the need to resolve the tension between conventional religion and idiosyncratic spirituality.

> The onus in the 21st century will not be 'diversity of culture', but 'diversity of spirituality'. As religion is increasingly privatized, for fear of feud, fanaticism and market irrelevance ... it will behoove the architect, the planner to design public space that mediates the spiritual instinct to communality and transcendence. The communing of streetscape, landscape, building, skyline enjoins the citizen to commune with projects and entities and reestablishes trust with others ... The effect of architecture and space on the entire person, in the advent and presence of other persons is universal. It gentles the civic creature. It can gently disparate cultures and peoples by the vocabulary of the sublime, bringing them to the point of awe, gratitude and mutuality by shared space, making such space sacred. (Di Cicco, 2008: 3)

We can therefore define spiritually enriching places in environments in which we understand our responsibilities to other living beings and to other humans. They are places where rights meet responsibilities in a union of humility and awe at our common humanity and collective destiny, despite our incredible diversity.

Conclusions

We began with a suggestion that the divorce between planning and urban design has orphaned the quest for place making both for community and for ecological integrity. Now we see the work of creating sacred and spiritually enriching spaces as a necessary antidote to the loss of meaning, inspiration and reverential connectedness that is the aftermath of the modern city.

The spirit at the heart of planning engages every day in a dance of faith and hope, engages in a struggle to moderate greed with generosity, to conjoin private ambition with civic ambition, to care for others as much as or more than we care about ourselves, to think as much or more about future generations as we do about our own, to mindfully weigh the importance of memory alongside the need for change.

Planning deals with people's visions for the future of their cities. What could be more precious, in terms of giving meaning to life beyond the here and now? Planning deals with land, with the memories and lifeways it carries, what it means to people in the present and what they want it to mean in the future. What could be more precious, in terms of our attachments to the earth, air and water, to family, home and place making? Planning deals with how people relate to each other within and between groups and communities. What could be more precious, in terms of our deep need for connection with others? And planning deals with how we as a community take care of one another. What could be more precious, in terms of our universal human fears of sickness, old age, poverty and death?

So why do we have all these sterile terms for describing what it is that we do, often making ourselves as a profession incomprehensible to those who live, love and struggle in cities? This chapter is about a different way of seeing planning, at the heart of which is the place of spirit and of the sacred in the everyday struggle to make meaning of our lives, make better places and create a better world. The intent here is to recognize that spirituality is embedded in planning work, whether we care to name it or not. But there may be some real purpose in naming it. It would mean a different way of seeing ourselves, representing ourselves to the world, and it would necessarily lead to different ways of teaching, which we might begin to think of as 'educating the heart'.

Notes

1   The City of Vancouver (population 600,000) is one of 21 municipalities in metropolitan Vancouver (population 2.3 million). It contains the original downtown core and the earliest neighbourhoods of European settlement.
2   The Neighbourhood House movement is a continuation of the Settlement House movement which began in the United Kingdom in the late nineteenth century and quickly spread to the United States. Jane Addams's Hull House on Chicago's poor and immigrant south side, founded in 1889, was the first Settlement House in the United States (see Sandercock and Attili, 2009 for more on this history).
3   The account that follows is drawn from Sandercock and Attili (2009).
4   The special 'spirit' of this place is revealed in the documentary by Attili and Sandercock (2007), 'Where strangers become neighbours'.
5   The history of the settlement of the province of British Columbia by Europeans is of course the story of the colonization of one group by another, in which

First Nations were removed from their lands and forced to live on tiny patches of marginalized land (see Attili and Sandercock, 2010).

References

Attili, G., and Sandercock, L. (2007), *Where Strangers Become Neighbours*. 50-minute documentary, Montreal: National Film Board of Canada.

—. (2010), *Finding Our Way*. 90-minute documentary, Vancouver: Moving Images.

Beatley, T. with Kristy Manning (2002), *The Ecology of Place: Planning for Environment, Economy, and Community*. Washington, DC: Island Press.

Berry, W. (2001), *In the Presence of Fear: Three Essays that Changed the World*. Barrington, MA: The Orion Society.

Di Cicco, P. G. (2008), 'Notes on Spirituality and Sacred Space' Retrieved August 30, 2009, from http://www.toronto.ca/culture/pdf/poet/2008/feb2008_notes_spirit.pdf.

Eliade, M. (1992), *Mystic Stories: The Sacred and the Profane*. New York: Columbia University Press.

Environmental Communications (2009), *UBC Farm on the map: is the farm finally saved?* Retrieved on August 9, 2010, from http://envirocommunications.wordpress.com/2009/12/21/ubc-farm-on-the-map-is-the-farm-finally-saved/

Hayden, D. (1995), *The Power of Place: Urban Landscapes as Public History*. Cambridge: MIT Press.

Hester, R. (2006), *Design for Ecological Democracy*. Cambridge: MIT Press.

hooks, bell. (1994), *Teaching to Transgress: Education as the Practice of Freedom*. New York: Routledge.

—. (2001). *All about Love. New Visions*. New York: Harper.

Kaplan, R., and Kaplan, S. (1989), *The Experience of Nature: A Psychological Perspective*. New York: Cambridge University Press.

Kaplan S. (1995), 'The restorative benefits of nature: Toward an integrative framework', *Journal of Environmental Psychology* 15, 169–82.

Kellert, S. (2005), *Building for Life*. Washington DC: Island Press.

Kellert, S., and P. Kahn (eds) (2002), *Children and Nature*. Cambridge, MA: MIT Press.

Knight, L.W. (2005), *Citizen: Jane Addams and the Struggle for Democracy*. Chicago: University of Chicago Press.

Lovelock, J. (1995), *The Ages of Gaia: A Biography of our Living Earth*. New York: Norton.

Maller, C., Townsend, M., Pryor, A., Brown, P., and St. Leger, L. (2005), 'Healthy Nature Healthy People: "Contact with Nature" as an Upstream Health Promotion Intervention for Populations', *Health Promotion International*, 21 (1).

Masselink, D. (2009), Personal Interview with Derek Masselink by Maged Senbel.

Muir, J. (1913), *The Story of My Boyhood and Youth*. Boston: Houghton Mifflin Company.

Musqueam (2010), Musqueam people's website retrieved on August 7, 2010, from http://www.musqueam.bc.ca/.

Naess, A. (1973), 'The Shallow and the Deep, Long-Range Ecology Movement: A Summary', *Inquiry: An Interdisciplinary Journal of Philosophy* 6, 95–100.

—. (1988), 'Self-realization: an ecological approach to being in the world'. In Seed, J., Macy, J., Fleming, P. and Naess, A., *Thinking Like a Mountain: Towards a Council of All Beings*. Gabriola Island, BC: New Society Publishers.

Newman, P. and Beatley, T. (2009), *Resilient Cities*. London: Earthscan.

Norberg-Schulz, C. (1980), *Genus Loci: Towards a Phenomenology of Architecture*. New York: Rizzoli.

Palmer, P. J. (1998), *The Courage to Teach: Exploring the Inner Landscape of a Teacher's Life*. San Francisco: Jossey Bass.

Pedretti-Burls, A. (2007), 'Ecotherapy: a therapeutic and educative model', *Journal of Mediterranean Ecology* 8, 19–25.

Porter, L. (2010), *Unlearning the Colonial Cultures of Planning*. Aldershot: Ashgate

Relph, E.C. (1976), *Place and Placelessness*. London: Pion.

Rich, A. (1986), *Your Native Land, Your Life*. New York: Norton.

Rojas, A. (2009), 'Towards Integration of Knowledge Through Sustainability Education and Its Potential Contribution to Environmental Security', in S. Allen-Gil, L. Stelljes & O. Borysova (eds), *Addressing Global Environmental Security Through Innovative Educational Curricula*. Dordrecht, the Netherlands: Springer.

Sandercock, L. and Attili.G. (2009), *Where Strangers Become Neighbours: Integrating Immigrants in Vancouver, Canada*. Dordrecht: Springer.

—. (2010), 'Digital Ethnography as Planning Praxis: an experiment with film as social research, community engagement and policy dialogue', *Planning Theory and Practice* 11 (1), 23–45.

Sarkissian, W. (1996), 'With a Whole Heart: Nurturing an Ethic of Caring for Nature in the Education of Australian Planners,' Unpublished PhD dissertation, Murdoch University, 1996.

Sarkissian, W., Hofer, N., Shore, Y., Vadja, S., and Wilkinson, C. (2009), *Kitchen Table Sustainability: Practical Recipes for Community Engagement with Sustainability*. London: Earthscan.

Schumacher, E. F. (1999), *Small is Beautiful: Economics as if People Mattered – Twenty-five years later . . . with Commentaries*. Vancouver: Hartley and Marks.

Scott, J. C. (1998), *Seeing Like a State: How Certain Schemes to Improve the Human Condition Have Failed*. New Haven, CT: Yale University Press.

Seamon, D. (ed) (1993), *Dwelling, Seeing and Designing: Toward a Phenomenological Ecology*. New York; State University of New York Press.

Shuman, M. (2006), *The Small Mart Revolution. How Local Businesses are Beating the Global Competition*. San Francisco: Berrett-Koehler Publishers.

Thayer, R. (2003), *Life Place: Bioregional Thought and Practice*. Berkeley: University of California Press.

Todd, D. (ed) (2008), *Cascadia: The Elusive Utopia: Exploring the Spirit of the Pacific Northwest*. Vancouver: Ronsdale Press.

Tuan, Y. (1974), *Topophilia: A Study of Environmental Perception, Attitudes, and Values*. Englewood Cliffs: Prentice-Hall.

UBC Farm (2010), offical website of the UBC farm, retrieved on August, 9, 2010, from http://www.landfood.ubc.ca/ubcfarm/.

Wells, G. (2008), 'Nature Based Spirituality in Cascadia: Prospects and Pitfalls', in D. Todd (ed), *Cascadia, The Elusive Utopia: Exploring the Spirit of the Pacific Northwest*. Vancouver: Ronsdale Press.

Wilson, E. O. (1992), *The Diversity of Life*. Penguin Books, London.

—. (1993), 'Biophilia and the Conservation Ethic'. In *The Biophilia Hypothesis* (ed. by Kellert, S. R., and Wilson, E. O.), pp. 31–41. Washington DC: Shearwater Books/Island Press.

Woodruff, P. (2001), *Reverence: Renewing a Forgotten Virtue*. New York: Oxford University Press.

World News (2010), Looking at UBC Farm Part I, viewed on August 9, 2010, from http://wn.com/Looking_at_the_UBC_Farm_Part_I.

6 A Feminist Critique of the Postsecular City: God and Gender

Clara Greed

Introduction: diversity or disparity

There has always been an uneasy relationship between religion and feminism because of the perceived patriarchal and misogynist nature of the Church and its apparent endorsement of women's oppression within society. Likewise the built environment professions have been male dominated and have historically provided little space for the consideration of women's needs or the demands of urban feminism within the city of man. Postsecularism provides an opportunity to take 'other' diverse issues into account, including feminism and religion, in conceptualizing what 'the city' should be like. But it is argued that physical change in the design and layout of cities is much harder to change because of the enduring influence of secular urban planning principles, which, paradoxically, are imbued with ancient sacred assumptions about the place of women in the city of man.

In this chapter, an initial discussion of the first and second wave of feminism reveals the underlying, ancient 'sacred' assumptions that have historically restricted women's place within the city of man, and which continue to influence modern secular urban policy makers' concepts of how cities should be planned. Then the dimensions of the postsecular urban phase, along with its unresolved dualisms, will be discussed as an introduction to the second half of the chapter which is concerned with the chances of either 'women' and/or 'faith groups' being accommodated within the public realm. These two strands will then be brought together in the penultimate section on 'Faithful women in the public realm [Gender and God]'. The chapter concludes that it should not be assumed that the development of postsecularism is going to be an improvement for either women, faith groups, or women of faith than in previous ideological phases, and therefore such groups need to find ways to rise above the constraints of the city to survive.

Definitions

The current postsecular phase is characterized by a re-emergence of faith in the public realm of civil society and the city (Baker, 2008), compared with twentieth-century attitudes (Cox, 1965). A new relativism is also a feature of postsecularism, allowing for the coexistence of a range of truths, with no one truth predominating; this is at odds with both secular scientific positivism and the absolutes of sacred dogma (Habermas and Ratzinger, 2007). Baines, following Habermas, argues that postsecularism is marked by a contest between religious lobbyists (which have grown in strength with the resurgence of fundamentalist religions) and secular pressure groups who promote diversity and equality (Baines, 2008). Although pluralism is a key characteristic of postsecularism, nevertheless, certain groups and issues become privileged above others (Du Toit, 1997: 5) with gender remaining low on the pecking order (Panelli, 1985; Baines, 2008). Tolerance towards religious groups has not been a characteristic of diversity policy either, in spite of the fact that religion is one of the valid 'minority categories' in UK equalities legislation, alongside race, disability, age, sexuality and gender (Coffey, 2003). Indeed, Bagilhole notes that the Racial and Religious Hatred Act of 2006 nearly made both the Bible and Qur'an illegal in their current form in the United Kingdom (Bagilhole, 2009: 107).

Feminism may be defined as a view of society and knowledge that is based upon the principle that men's views and interests dominate society and that unequal gender relations result in disadvantaging women (Panelli, 2004: 244). Gender refers to the cultural role ascribed to women in society. There are many different types of feminism ranging from radical to reformist, and, as with Christianity, from fundamentalist to liberal (Hakim, 2007). Feminists are not a unitary group, but a very broad church, and are concerned with a diverse range of issues, including, *inter alia*, 'the city' (Greed, 1994a; Booth et al., 1996; Panelli, 2004). There is no single generally accepted 'feminist critique' of postsecularism, but a variety of perspectives. I wrote this chapter from my own perspective – a broadly Christian feminist one – and as a town planner and urban feminist.

First-wave feminism and the sacred city

Feminism is a relatively recent phenomenon set against the span of history, with the first wave flowering at the turn of the twentieth century. Early feminists had to challenge ancient assumptions about 'the city' and its 'citizens' which were developed, during the sacred era, without including women; women were 'outsiders' to both church and city state. Women were either 'invisible' or 'other': deemed to be on the wrong side of the sacred/profane, spirit/body, rationality/emotions, clean/ unclean, good/evil divide (Douglas, 1966; Daly, 1991; Eliade, 1987). This mentality had a strong influence in shaping women's position in civil society. Because women were seen as the source of temptation, their existence had to be controlled, by restricting women's movement 'outside' in the public realm, and thus they were barred from religious or public office. If a woman stayed 'inside' within the private domestic realm of the house and 'accepted her role' as wife and mother, she was to be given honour and praise (Morgan, 1975; Boulding, 1992: 227). Subsequently this concept of 'separate spheres' was transmitted onto urban form and embodied in the layout and zoning of the modern city.

'Land-use zoning', which has been a cornerstone of modern town planning, may appear to be an innocuous process concerned with bringing order to urban chaos and improving the sanitation and functionality of cities. However, an investigation of the origins of the word 'zoning' reveals the murky roots of this apparently scientific planning principle, and its association with the control of women's place in urban space, chiefly by keeping women out of public life and civic space and within the domestic realm of house and home (Greed, 1994a: 70–81). Etymologically, 'zoning' has a loaded history. According to Boulding (1992, I: 227), in ancient Greek, the word *zona* conveys the idea of a belt, but also refers by inference, to the restriction of the 'loins' that is the control of sexuality and the production of children (the fruit of the loins), and thus is linked to the control of women's sexuality and related temptations and moral pollution. Likewise, Marilyn French points out (French, 1992: 76) the Hebrew word deployed for 'prostitute', 'zonah' (harlot), means 'she who goes out of doors' (outside the marital home); that is she is in the wrong place. In Latin, 'zonam solvere' means 'to loose the virgin zone', that is, to get married or lose one's virginity (or in medieval parlance to remove the chastity belt). So the roots of secular land use zoning derive from previous sacred periods of city organization, which prioritized the separation of women's spheres from the public realm of men. These beliefs were carried forward into modern secular town planning through zoning policy which separated home and work (residential and industrial zones), that is, perceived male and female spheres. In parallel, it is only a short etymological leap from *zona* to *zana,* and *sana* to sanitary, and thus to the obsession with sanitation and hygiene in the modern secular city. While infrastructural development of sewerage and drainage systems is vital, 'social hygiene' appeared to be more about controlling women than actual disease, especially the perceived dirtiness of working class women and men (dirtiness being as much a euphemism for unbri-dled sexuality as for lack of washing) (Greed, 1994a: 90–91).

By the late nineteenth century, the modern town planning movement was devel-oping, concerned with reform and accommodating the new proletariat that had flocked to the cities to participate in the Industrial Revolution (Tawney, 1922). While the principles of zoning and the related separation of public and domestic spheres were applied nationally to bring the new conurbations under control, greatly inconveniencing women in separating work from home, not all women were affected equally. Women's involvement and roles in these new industrial communities depended upon their class. Working class women's realm was limited inside the house to a minimal kitchen scullery in many model housing designs, thus rendering women's essential work in the home both marginal and invisible. While middle class women had servants to do the housework, unlike their husbands, they were unlikely to have special rooms allocated to their needs for study or recreation (Kerr, 1864; Pearson, 1988).

Women were not silent victims. Significant numbers of educated women actively campaigned to get women's needs and 'different' perspectives incorporated into housing design, model town development, urban planning, architecture and in welfare reform. Many first-wave feminists were involved in town planning, housing and architecture (Greed, 2004). In spite of the restrictions derived from a church-dominated society, many first-wave feminists were religiously inclined. Many had a strong moral agenda and were supporters of the temperance movement and Sunday observance. For example, a million women signed a petition in 1887 to make pubs close on Sundays (so the men did not drink their wages). The full rallying cry of the suffragette movement was 'votes for women and chastity for men'. Many feminist and suffrage groups were church based and saw feminism as being their God-given calling (Tickner, 1987: 223), and some marched under the banner (ibid.: 72) of the Church League for Women's Suffrage, emblazoned with the embroidered slogan 'the glorious liberty of the children of God'.

Second-wave feminism and the secular city

By contrast, the social construction and rationale of second-wave feminism has its roots in secular, humanistic academia, and so being both Christian and feminist has always been problematic (Storkey, 1985). Significantly, the founding mothers of the second wave of feminism included a number of women who had come from traditional Christian and Jewish religious family backgrounds (Daly, 1991; Friedan, 1963). Convent-educated authors, such as Greer (1973), Warner (1976) and Daly (1991), were among the most vociferous in their critique of religion and the perceived misogyny and patriarchal structure of the church.

During the twentieth century, town planning had become increasingly professionalized and male dominated and had distanced itself from its roots in utopianism, spiritualism, feminism and religion (Greed, 1994 (a)). It had become a local government bureaucratic function – a career – managed by male-dominated professionals who adopted a rationalistic, scientific approach to planning issues. 'Planning' of all sorts became the Zeitgeist of the post–World War II reconstruction period. The UK government sought to 'Build a Better Britain' firmly believing that 'the new Britain must be planned' (Greed, 2000: 245). Likewise, in American cities, zoning contributed to the development of mono-land-use residential suburbs, where 'bored middle-class, college-educated housewives' sat restlessly, being overwhelmed and depressed by 'the problem that has no name' awaiting the clarion call of second-wave feminism to set them free into the public realm of work and the city of man (Friedan, 1963).

What passed as common sense and 'science' in twentieth-century town planning was, in fact, replete with the earlier sacred overtones which disadvantage women. Patrick Geddes, one of the Fathers of Anglo-American town planning, clearly saw women as inferior and in need of control. Geddes was enamoured of Freud's association of the mother principle with 'stagnation' (*sic*) (Geddes and Thomson, 1889; Bologh, 1990: 14), and such attitudes shaped his approach to land-use zoning (Greed, 1994; Meller, 2007). Geddes's ideal rational city was divided into three zones: home, work and play. This model was based on a traditional male view of the world with no recognition given to the caring, family role of women, which also constituted work, and was undertaken in the home, not in some distant employment zone. Likewise, Le Corbusier, champion of the European planning movement, declared: 'a house is a machine for living in' and drew his inspiration from ancient occult and Masonic sources, in seeking to codify and control urban space and women's place within the city of man (Birkstead, 2009).

Nevertheless, a more 'scientific' and 'secular' view of the city did provide the setting for women's alternative views to be heard, without being fettered by the religious constraints of the past. The development of the second wave of feminism broadly coincides with the development of the secular city (Cox, 1965). Gradually, women architects and urban planners began to challenge and question the patriarchal assumptions implicit in urban theory and policy, resulting in a wave of feminist critique of the city of man, which both provided analysis of 'the problem' and contributed constructive policies as to how cities might be designed in a manner that recognized and planned for the needs of women as well as men. In spite of all this work, implementation of such policies has so far proved elusive, because to change policy, it is necessary to change the deeply ingrained 'worldview' of the policy makers (Greed, 2005a).

Dimensions of the postsecular city: opportunities or restrictions

In the past, women have been seen as 'other', as 'outsiders' to both church and state. They have generally been found on the wrong side of the divisions that structure society and the city, particularly in respect to the dualisms of sacred/profane, spirit/body, rationality/emotions and public/private. Therefore, their needs have been seen as secondary, unimportant or trivial when it comes to setting the agenda for town planning. While 'gender' issues have not fared well in the past, in contrast, 'God' fared much better; religion and the sacred were valued as extremely important considerations when designing cities. But by the twentieth century, sacred values had been supplanted by science, rationality and positivism as the basis for urban decision making. Subsequently, postsecularism has now created 'space' for the consideration of a variety of viewpoints and 'rights' within a relativistic, humanist agenda. A new moral code has developed, based upon the importance of promoting diversity and equality, in which gender is one significant consideration, along with ethnicity, age, disability, sexuality *inter alia*. Of course these differences do not exist in a vacuum but intersect in an individual's life (Bagilhole, 2009: 50–53), and therefore both race and gender must be taken into account when looking at the problems that the postsecular city presents for black Pentecostal Church members.

So can the postsecular city offer women greater hope? Many women have had difficulty identifying with the sacred/secular city shift, when their needs have neither been recognized nor met in the sacred and secular phases of city development. The current secular/postsecular city progression, purportedly, is being experienced by all of 'society'. But, it does not necessarily fit women's experiences of the built environment and its planners, because women are not really 'in the game'. They are still seen as 'other' and of little relevance in philosophical, political and theological debates, or to paradigm shifts within urban planning.

Nevertheless, postsecularism offers the opportunity more openly to discuss and expose the dualisms and disparities that have so hobbled women's lives, from a sociological, spatial and spiritual perspective (Keenan, 2003; CULAF, 2006; Sandercock, 2006; Hunt and Hamilton, 2007; McClure, 1995). Within postsecularism, intellectual space has also opened up for mainstream researchers to ask value-laden and 'subjective', even religious, questions as to whether the city is 'good' (Amin, 2006), and if so 'for whom' (Amin and Thrift, 2004; Baker, 2008). There is a new interest among academics, including some social geographers and feminists, in investigating the role of belief, religion and spiritual matters in shaping the city and urban society. The participation of the church in social welfare and the growth of faith-based communities are often presented as signs of the coming of the postsecular city (Beaumont, 2008).

But, this does not mean that the shape and form of cities is now being transformed by postsecularism, or that their planners and architects are now more responsive to the needs of women or other minorities or that they themselves 'understand' either 'feminism' or 'religion'. Rather than listening to, and acting upon, the issues that concern women, 'feminism' itself is being co-opted into and hailed as a positive product of postsecularism, presumably because feminists are also concerned with qualitative issues such as value judgements, moral debates, religion and environmentalism (Sandercock, 1997; Fenster, 2004). The new emancipatory city (Lees, 2004) arguably contains less space for women than its predecessors, in part as a result of a lack of adequate emphasis upon practical gender considerations within the equalities and diversity agenda (Greed, 2005a,b).

Likewise, postsecularism may 'allow' for a greater acknowledgement of the importance of religion in city life, but this is not yet manifested in the design of the built environment. The spiritual dimension remains sadly lacking in the urban planning agenda. There has been little connection between modern town planning and 'God' (Engtwich, 2007; Lyon, 1975; Sheppard, 1974) within the secular humanist academic world of which urban planning is a part (Arthur, 1991). But the postsecular paradigm shift is likely to take very much longer to be manifested in concrete changes in the shape and form of the city itself, one that might better meet women's needs. The archaeology of the past weighs heavily on the present nature of urban form and structure, and upon the subcultural values and attitudes of urban policy makers (Foucalt, 1972). Much depends upon the role of the gatekeepers and transmitters, that is, the politicians and decision makers, along with the built environment professionals, including the town planners, architects and developers, who determine what should be built where and for whom (Massey, 1984: 16; Greed, 1994a: 1–16).

The decisions made by the political and professional individuals responsible for planning the city are undoubtedly influenced by the dominant culture and belief systems of the time (Howe, 1990; Sandercock, 2000; Gorringe, 2002; Fewings, 2008). Unfortunately their ideal of what is 'right' and 'obvious' is likely to be based on their own limited life experience and therefore is out of touch with the realities of everyday life that women, working class people, people with disabilities, the elderly and ethnic minorities experience as they battle their way through the modern city. Like their predecessors, the kings and priests of sacred times, modern urban planners are unlikely to take gender considerations into account when putting their stamp on city development (Greed, 1994a: 11–13; Greed, 2000: 179–222; Hague et al., 2008). Nor are they likely to be *au fait* with philosophical and theological agendas concerning postsecularism.

Gender and city planning

Feminist planners who have spent many years arguing for the acknowledgement of, and action on, the 'different' needs of women in the city of man, initially welcomed the apparent freedom to put their case within the context of the new diversity agenda. But they were soon to find that 'gender' issues are low on the pecking order, thus reducing the chances of women's needs being taken fully into account in the design and planning of cities, especially in the world of town planning (Reeves, 2002). Gender has become just one minor factor among a list of other diversity considerations. But it is argued that gender overarches and intersects with all other personal characteristics, cross-cutting with other diversity components such as race, disability, sexuality, age, *inter alia* (Reeves, 2005). Therefore, women planners continue to contend that gender needs to be taken into account in all aspects of urban planning and development.

But what is the problem? A feminist critique of the city is always centred upon exploring the male/female dualism as to what is wrong with the city of man. It has been demonstrated by research and human experience that women suffer disadvantage within a built environment that is developed by men, primarily for other men (Greed, 1994a, 2005b). Women constitute 52 per cent of the UK population and 68 per cent of women (like 78 per cent of men) of working age are in employment (ONS, 2008). Thus, women constitute the majority of 'the public' for whom planning is intended, yet if the 'normal' average citizen is perceived to be male, then their needs are unlikely to be met by planning policy. But women use and experience the built environment differently from men and therefore have distinct needs and expectations in terms of the nature of urban structure and planning policy. As well as being workers, women are more likely to be the ones responsible for childcare, shopping and a range of other caring roles, all of which generate different usage of urban space. Fewer women than men have access to the use of a car, and they constitute the majority of public transport users in many areas. Their journey patterns reflect their attempts to combine their work and caring duties, so a woman's daily journeys might be as follows: from home to school to work – to shops to school and back home again. Thus, women tend to trip-chain their journeys as part of the multi-tasking they do every day to get everything done. If women's needs as workers and commuters were taken as seriously as men's in the planning policy-making process, this would have immense policy implications in reshaping citywide spatial policy.

A gender perspective would also affect detailed local planning decisions. For example, those enlightened local planning authorities that have specified that childcare provision should be a condition of granting planning permission for a new development find that on appeal, planning law will not support their efforts. Childcare provision is seen as 'ultra vires': that is, 'not a land use matter' because it is seen as being 'too social' and therefore outside the scope of planning law (Greed, 2005b). In contrast, planning proposals for playing fields mainly used for men's ball games are welcomed as valid spatial considerations, and not as merely a 'social' activity.

Attempts to increase the mixture of land uses in residential areas and thus reduce the inconvenience of zoning have met with little success, resulting in a continuation of the separation of work (employment areas) and home (housing estates) which many women find so impractical. Clearly the old sacred divisions and taboos regarding women's 'place' in the city, and the need for women to be separated and controlled continues. In contrast, many women planners would like to see 'the city of everyday life, the city of short distances, mixed land uses, good public transport and localised centres' (Greed, 2005b).

God and city planning

Church attendance has dramatically declined in the established Western historical denominations during the course of the increasingly secularized twentieth century. But globally, there has been an exponential growth among the new Pentecostal and charismatic churches, particularly in the developing, and non-Western world (Smith, 2007b: 116; Lyon, 2001). This is mirrored in the growth of predominantly black ethnic minority congregations in London and other large cities, and in enthusiasm/healing ministries and 'revival' services, especially in the United States (where, note, health insurance is not universal) (Bentley, 2008).

Many of these churches are desperately looking around the city for any type of building large enough to accommodate their congregations. There has been a steady growth in the numbers of planning applications for 'change of use' for a variety of types of buildings by such churches. But the planning law system has not kept up with the changing times, and is still firmly stuck in the secular era (CAG, 2008). Attempts to use large empty industrial units on the edge of the city are frequently thwarted by the local authority planners. For example, reasons given by the London Borough of Lewisham for enforcement proceedings against the use of one such industrial unit to a Pentecostal church included potential noise and disturbance, when no one is living nearby (Lewisham, 2008). Other reasons for refusal have included health and safety fears regarding the use of water for total immersion baptisms and failure to meet car parking requirements even when the congregation walks or arrives by minibus (Onuoha and Greed, 2002).

Black Pentecostal churches need large flexible premises to accommodate not just religious services but also the wide range of educational, welfare, catering and childcare activities. But such 'social' use of buildings and mixtures of property uses fall foul of planning law requirements, as they do not 'fit' into existing 'use class' zoning categories, and are deemed, like childcare facilities, ultra vires, 'not a land-use matter' or 'outside of [planning] law'. There is no specific 'worship' land use category under UK planning law, and so such buildings are 'judged' under laws created to deal with 'places of assembly, cinemas and dance halls' (D1 and D2) and found wanting. Yet, these new churches are zone-zappers, transcending the ancient dualisms of secular/sacred, mind/body, male/female, outside/inside, public/private, shrine/marketplace, and *gesellschaft/gemeinschaft*. They are motivated by the supplication in the Lord's Prayer 'Thy kingdom come on earth as it is in Heaven', and thus by a belief in miraculous intervention in the material world. Sheldrake

(2007) argues that one sign of postsecularism taking root is the transcendence of the old sacred/secular divide, while James Smith talks of the removal of the divide between sacred and secular altogether (Yong, 2007: 236; Smith, 2007a).

While for many white evangelicals and fundamentalists, political involvement seems to centre around campaigning against abortion and sexuality (Wallis, 2005), black Pentecostal women and men are generally more likely to have a wider political perspective on human rights issues, both at home and abroad. They are more likely to apply their belief in the miraculous to the political situation, and to intercede for the nations and their rulers, in the 'public realm', as an extension of their beliefs in physical healing, casting out of demons, and the operation of the gifts of the Holy Spirit in the 'personal realm', again challenging sacred/secular, spiritual/political divisions. Black women pastors are not necessarily consciously 'political' or 'feminist', but they are inevitably drawn into community politics and equality battles in dealing with specific local problems (Jamoul and Willis, 2008: 2048). They face opposition daily 'in the world' on the basis of race and gender, as they seek to carry out their leadership roles 'in the church' both in the United Kingdom and in linked Nigerian and Ghanaian churches (Soothill, 2007).

In spite of all this 'political' activity, there seems to be little connection with mainstream parties or links between New Labour's (and subsequent governments') apparent concern for 'faith communities' within the 'diversity and equality agenda', and the implications for high-level urban decision making and urban regeneration. Established ethnic–minority housing areas, along with their businesses, places of worship and community networks, are being demolished to make way for the London Olympics. For example, the Kingsway International Christian Community Church (KICC), a mega-church with over 12,000 members of 46 different nationalities, run by Pastor Matthew Ashimolowo and his co-pastor wife Yemishi, have now moved their mainly African congregation several miles out to a new location. Many years of 'good works' and locally relevant community activities are being spatially disrupted, including educational, youth, employment, welfare and housing programmes run by the church.

The planners appear to have little understanding of the spatial needs of such churches. Research shows that planning officers tend to treat planning applications by both Christian and Muslim faith groups with suspicion, as likely to be linked to 'fundamentalism' and therefore to be dismissed as socially divisive, when in reality, faith-based groups (and buildings) often provide inclusive social, economic and community facilities and contribute to urban regeneration (CAG, 2008). Many Christians argue that the current diversity agenda has reduced the freedom of Christians to express their faith in word and deed, and therefore in building construction, because a 'Balance of Rights' has not yet been developed adequately by UK case law and within EU legal directives (LCF, 2008; Bagilhole, 2009).

Faithful women in public space: bringing God and gender together

A characteristic of Pentecostal churches is that there are likely to be more women in positions of leadership and authority than found in traditional denominations

(Beckford, 2000: 49). In particular, there has been a long tradition of black women leaders, prophets, bishops and healers; many of the leaders of the original Azusa Street outpouring a century ago (that started the modern Pentecostal movement) were black women (Gee, 1967). There has always been a minority of white Pentecostal women leaders, evangelists, healers and prophets, too (Scotland, 1995: 314; Kay, 2000; Murray, 2008), especially in North America, such as Aimée Semple McPherson (1896–1944) and nowadays Joyce Meyer (1999). In Britain, across all denominations, women constitute less than 10 per cent of ministers, and much of this female leadership is found in Pentecostal and charismatic congregations, yet women constitute at least 60 per cent of all church members nationally (Buckeridge, 2008).

While for centuries European women were excluded from public office and therefore from public space, on the basis of Scripture (1 Timothy 2 v.11–15, and I Corinthians 11 v.5; Adams, 1973), nowadays low caste, working class and ethnic minority women are of such little importance that they have been left alone to preach and exert authority without condemnation (the double negative effect that breaks the mould). But, when black women church ministers have to deal with the outside world, their power and authority is not transferable or recognized. When undertaking research on racism in the planning system, it was found that churches headed by a woman pastor, particularly if she is black, are not given the same level of respect by planning officers, and their planning applications are more likely to be refused (Onuoha and Greed, 2003: 86–90).

In recent years, for completely different reasons, women have been 'allowed' to become ministers in some of the mainstream denominations. Increasingly women are being ordained in the Church of England, thus helping solve the 'man-power crisis', in these days of decline among the historic denominations. But women's faithfulness and willingness is often seen as a problem, not a cause for celebration. In fact, 'women' and their world are dismissed across a whole range of 'men's world' Christian literature, past and present. For example, Bishop David Sheppard in his otherwise groundbreaking urban theological study of the city concluded that the lack of men in the churches he visited was a sign of decline, not a sign of female power or renewal (Sheppard, 1974: 39), and this mentality is still to be found.

'Inside' the church there is still much suspicion regarding 'feminism' and ongoing theological discussion as to the 'role of women' (Storkey, 1985; Benvenuti, 2008). There is a backlash underway, particularly in the white evangelical churches. There has been a long-running debate in *Christianity*, a popular evangelical magazine, over the proposition that because women are the majority in most churches, it is their 'fault' that men are put off attending, because the church has become too feminized. Since the women seldom have a chance to speak and most of the ministers are still male, this is a strange condemnation. To 'solve' this problem some churches have started running 'men-only' gatherings in which 'special teaching' is given. To attract working class men, such churches have encouraged their male membership to become more 'blokey' by dressing more casually, going to the pub and football matches. This completely contradicts the old puritanical, evangelical commandments to be unworldly, pure and teetotal (Beech, 2007; Buckeridge, 2008;

Hastings, 2008). As a result, women are likely to feel even more unwanted, while few working class men are likely to be fooled or attracted by this latest attempt to bring them in. But surveys suggest there is a high level of belief in God in Britain, but many people have been put off over the years from actually going to church (Davie, 1994).

'Outside' the church, in public space, women are often the first to be picked on for their faith because they are more visible, being the ones that wear the scarves, veils and crosses; that is the outward signs of their inward beliefs. A feature of postsecularism is for new spiritualities and a greater sense of faith to emerge (McClure, 1995: 142), but many Christian women feel more vulnerable within the new diversity agenda because of 'what they look like'. For example, Nadia Eweida was fired for wearing a small cross while working as a member of the British Airways check-in staff at Heathrow Airport.[1] She argued that Muslim colleagues were allowed to wear head scarves, which could also be construed as outward religious symbols of inner faith. Muslim colleagues supported her and said they were not offended. Nevertheless, she was judged guilty and fired. Similar problems are encountered daily in the built environment professions, thus 'controlling' who is likely to get their voice heard when it comes to urban policy making (De Graft-Johnson et al., 2009: 14).

Conclusion

While the government now preaches the gospel of diversity and equality, and urban policy stresses the importance of social inclusion and equality for all, many have found that the postsecular city is unaccommodating to both gender and God. While postsecularism is purported to lead to a more diverse and less dogmatic society, not all sectors of society have benefited equally. Both women and non-traditional church groups have not yet experienced the benefits, because long-held patriarchal attitudes, dating from both the sacred and secular eras, are perpetuated through the operation of the diversity agenda and the spatial planning system. While the government might now stress the importance of respecting faith-based groups, this change of heart has not yet worked its way down into local authority planning departments when dealing with applications for multi-use church premises. Invisible, but powerful, barriers still restrict the nature and use of urban form so preventing congregations carrying out their functions of worship, evangelism and good works. It would seem that it is now acceptable for individuals to hold a variety of beliefs, but if they want to express these beliefs in their dress, nature of worship, building construction, or in 'good works', then they will soon come up against obstacles.

Because of the insurmountable spatial barriers encountered, and as a result of opportunities opening up because of developments in computer technology, many such churches are seeking ways to escape and rise above the constraints of the city and its planners. They are putting their efforts into webcasts, electronic virtual church development, and the development of satellite television channels. Why bother with battles over individual buildings or staying within the spatial confines of the city, when a church can reach an international audience of millions through satellite television and the internet? Both temporally and spatially church traditions are 'transgressed' as to when and where church takes place. Time-wise, an announcer on God TV asks, 'why wait till Sunday to go to Church, tune into God TV 24/7 where there is no need to wait to be blessed'. Space-wise, as prophesied in 1994 by a member of the KICC congregation, the congregation has become a 'church without walls'. Indeed God Himself has left the building (Frost, 2006) and escaped both the clutches of planners trapped in a secular time warp and the restrictions of the diversity and equality arm of postsecularism.

Note

1   The case was reported in October 2006 by the Lawyers Christian Fellowship website, www.lcf.org.

References

Adams, Q.M. (1973), *Neither Male nor Female: A Study of the Scriptures*. Ilfracombe: Stockwell, 212–19.

Amin, A. (2006), 'The Good City', *Urban Studies* 43 (5–6), 1009–232.

Amin, A., and Thrift, N. (2004), 'The "Emancipatory" City?', in L. Lees (ed).*The Emanicipatory City? Paradoxes and Possibilities*. London: Sage.

Arthur, C. (1991), 'Diversion around the God Slot: How Can the Humanities Ignore the Human Soul?' *The Times Higher* 8 November 1991. London: Times Newpaper Group.

Bagilhole, B. (2009), *Understanding Equal Opportunities and Diversity: the Social Differentiation and Intersections of Inequality*. Bristol: Policy Press.

Baines, B. (2009), 'Must Feminists Identify as Secular Citizens? Lessons from Ontario', in L. McCain and J. Grossman (eds), *Gender Equality: Dimensions of Women's Equal Citizenship*. Cambridge: Cambridge University Press.

Baker, C. (2008), 'Seeking Hope in the Indifferent City – Faith-based Contributions to Space of Production and Meaning-Making in the Postsecular City', Boston: Proceedings of the Association of American Geographers Annual Meeting.

Beaumont, J. (2008), 'Introduction: Faith-based Organisations and Urban Social Issues', *Urban Studies* 45 (10), 2019–34.

Beckford, R. (2000), *Dread and Pentecostal: A Political Theology for the Black Church in Britain*. London: SPCK.

Beech, C. (2007), *Spadework: Laying Foundations with 52 Men from the Bible*. London: Scripture Union.

Bentley, T. (2008), *The Reality of the Supernatural World*. Toronto: Toronto Destiny Press in association with FreshFire Ministries.

Benvenuti, S. (2008), 'Pentecostal Women in Ministry: Where Do We Go from Here?', *Cyberjournal for Pentecostal-Charismatic Research*, www.pctii.org/cyberj/cyberj1/ben.html (accessed February 2009).

Birkstead, J. (2009), *Le Corbusier and the Occult*. London: MIT Press.

Bologh, R. (1990), *Love or Greatness: Max Weber and Masculine Thinking: A Feminist Inquiry*. London: Unwin Hyman.

Booth, C., Darke, J., and Yeandle, S. (eds) (1996), *Changing Places: Women's Lives in the City*. London: Paul Chapman.

Boulding, E. (1992), *The Underside of History*, Volume I. London: Sage.

Buckeridge, J. (2008), 'No Man's Land: How Gender has Feminised the Church', *Christianity*, February, 38–40.

CAG (2008), *Responding to the Needs of Faith Communities: Places of Worship: Final Report*. London: CAG, Cooperative Advisory Group Planning Consultants.

Coffey, J. (2003), 'The Myth of Secular Tolerance', Cambridge Papers, www.jubilee-centre.org/documents/Themythofseculartolerance.htm   (accessed 31 July 2010).

Cox, H. (1965), *The Secular City: Secularisation and Urbanisation in Theological Retrospect*. Harmondsworth: Penguin.

CULF (Commission on Urban Life and Faith) (2006), *Faithful Cities: A Call for Celebration, Vision and Justice*. London: Methodist Publishing House.

Daly, M. (1991 [1973]), *Beyond God the Father: Towards a Philosophy of Women's Liberation*. London: Women's Press (1991 reprint).

Davie, G. (1994), *Believing without Belonging: Religion in Britain since 1945*. Oxford: Wiley-Blackwell.

Douglas, M. (1966), *Purity and Danger: An Analysis of the Concepts of Pollution and Taboo*. London: Ark.

Du Toit, C. (1997), 'Fin de Siécle and the Development of a Post-secular Religion: Intimations from the Truth and Reconciliation Commission', *Journal of Religion and Theology* 4 (1), 1–20.

Eliade, M. (1987), *The Sacred and Profane: The Nature of Religion*. New York: Harcourt.

Fenster, T. (2004), *The Global City and the Holy City: Narratives in Knowledge, Planning and Diversity*. Harlow, London: Pearson.

Fewings, P. (2008), *Ethics for the Built Environment*. London: Taylor and Francis.

Foucalt, M. (1972), *The Archaeology of Knowledge*. New York: Pantheon.

French, M. (1992), *The War against Women*. London: Hamish Hamilton.

Friedan, B. (1963*), The Feminine Mystique*. New York: Dell, 1982.

Frost, R. (2006), 'Ladies and Gentlemen: Pentecost: the Church Has Left the Building'. London: Share Jesus International.

Geddes, P., and Thomson, J. A. (1889), *The Evolution of Sex*. London: Scott.

Gee, D. (1967), *Wind and Flame: The Pentecostal Movement*, Croydon: Heath Press.

Gorringe, T. J. (2002), *A Theology of the Built Environment: Justice, Empowerment and Redemption*. Cambridge: Cambridge University Press.

Graft-Johnson, A., Sara, R., Gleed, F., and Brkljac, N. (2009), *Gathering and Reviewing Data on Diversity within the Construction Professions*. London: Construction Industry Council in association with University of the West of England.

Greed, C. (1994a), *Women and Planning: Creating Gendered Realities*. London: Routledge.

—. (1994b), 'The Place of Ethnography in Planning', *Planning Practice and Research* 9 (2), 119–27.

—. (2000), *Introducing Planning*. London: Continuum.

—. (2005a), 'Overcoming the Factors Inhibiting the Mainstreaming of Gender into Spatial Planning Policy in the United Kingdom', *Urban Studies* 42 (4), 1–31.

—. (2005b), 'An Investigation of the Effectiveness of Gender Mainstreaming as a Means of Integrating the Needs of Women and Men into Spatial Planning in the United Kingdom', *Progress in Planning* 64 (4), 239–321.

Greer, G. (1973), *The Female Eunuch*. London: Paladin.

Habermas, J., and Ratzinger, J. (2007), *The Dialectics of Secularisation: On Reason and Religion*. Rome: Ignatius Press.

Hague, C., Wakely, P., Crespin, J. and Jasko, C. (2008), *Making Planning Work: a Guide to Approaches and Skills*. Rugby: ITDG Publishing.

Hakim, C. (2007), 'Dancing with the Devil? Essentialism and other Feminist Heresies', *British Journal of Sociology* 58 (1), 123–32.

Hastings, J. (2008), 'Arthur White: Tough enough to follow Christ?', *Men Matters Magazine*, Autumn 2008, 8–10.

Howe, E. (1990), 'Normative Ethics in Planning', *Journal of the American Planning Association* 5 (2), 123–50.

Hunt, S., and Hamilton, M. (eds) (1997), *Charismatic Christianity: Sociological Perspectives*. London: Macmillan.

Jamoul, L., and Willis, J. (2008), 'Faith in Politics', *Urban Studies* 45 (10), 2035–56.

Kay, W. (2000), *Pentecostals in Britain*. Carlisle: Paternoster.

Keenan, W. (2003), 'Rediscovering the Theological in Sociology', *Theory, Culture and Society* 20 (1), 19–42.

Kerr, R. (1864), *The Gentleman's Home*. London: Nelson.

Lees, L. (2004), *The Emancipatory City? Paradoxes and Possibilities*. London: Sage.

Lewisham (2008), *Report from Planning Committee (A) on Elizabeth Industrial Estate Change of Use of Ground Floor*. London: London Borough of Lewisham, Case File DE/237/C/TP, DCS Number 100-054-444 (see www.planningresource.co.uk).

Lyon, D. (1975), *Christianity and Sociology*. London: Inter-Varsity Press.

—. (2001), 'Fundamentalisms: Paradoxical Products of Postmodernity', in Partridge, C (ed), *Fundamentalisms*. Carlisle and Waynesboro: PaterNoster Press.

Massey, D. (1984), *Spatial Divisions of Labour: Social Structures and the Geography of Production*. London: Macmillan.

McClure, J. (1995), 'Postmodern/Post-secular: Contemporary Fiction and Spirituality', *Modern Fiction Studies* 41 (1), 141–63.

McDowell, L. (1983), 'Towards an Understanding of the Gender Divisions of Urban Space', *Environment and Planning D: Society and Space* 1, 59–72.

Meller, H. (2007), 'Gender, Citizenship and the Making of the Modern Movement', in E. Darling and L. Whitworth (eds), *Women and the Making of the Built Environment*. Aldershot: Ashgate.

Meyers, J. (1999), *How to Succeed at Being Yourself*, Tulsa: Harrison House.

Morgan, E. (1975), *The Descent of Woman*. London: Souvenir Press.

Murray, M. (2008), 'This Isn't Just a Man's World: Ministry May be Seen as a Man's Game but We Talk to Two Women Who Disagree', *Joy Magazine* 170, 6–7.

Office of National Statistics (ONS) (2008), *Social Trends*. London: Office of National Statistics.

Onuoha, C., and Greed, C. (2003), 'A Retrospective Study of Racism in the Operation of the Planning System within the Inner City', University of the West of England, Occasional Paper 15, Section 6, pp. 86–90.

Panelli, R. (2004), *Social Geographies: From Difference to Action*. London: Sage.

Pearson, L. (1988), *The Architectural and Social History of Co-operative Living*. London: Macmillan.

Reeves, D. (2002), 'Mainstreaming Equality to Achieve Socially Sustainable Development: an Examination of the Gender Sensitivity of Strategic Plans in the UK with Implications for Theory and Practice', *Town Planning Review* 73 (2), 197–214.

—. (2005), *Planning for Diversity: Policy and Planning in a World of Difference*. London: Routledge.

Sandercock, L. (1997), *Towards Cosmopolis: Planning for Post-secular Cities*. Wiley: London

—. (2000), 'Cities of (In)difference and the Challenge for Planning', Dokumenten und Informationen zur Schweizerischen Orts-, Regional- und Landsplanung (Documents and Information on Swiss Local, Regional and State Planning), 140, 7–15.

—. (2006), 'Spirituality and the Urban Professions – the Paradox at the Heart of Urban Planning', *Planning Theory and Practice* 7 (1), 69–75.

Scotland, N. (1995), *Charismatics and the New Millennium: the Impact of Charismatic Christianity from 1960 Into the New Millennium*. Guildford: Eagle.

Sheldrake, P. (2007), 'Place the Sacred: Transcendence and the City', *Literature and Theology* 21 (3), 243–58.

Sheppard, D. (1974), *Built as a City: God and the Urban World Today*. London: Hodder and Stoughton.

Smith, J. (2007a), *Introducing Radical Orthodoxy: Mapping a Post-secular Theology*. Grand Rapids: Baker Academic Inc.

Smith, M. (2007b), *International Ties: Cities, Migration and Identities*. London: Palgrave.

Soothill, J. (2007), *Gender, Social Change and Spiritual Power: Charismatics in Ghana*. London: Brill.

Storkey, E. (1985), *What's Right with Feminism*. London: SPCK.

Tawney, R. (1966), *Religion and the Rise of Capitalism*. Harmondsworth: Penguin.

Tickner, L. (1987), *The Spectacle of Women: Imagery of the Suffrage Campaign (1907–14)*. London: Chatto and Windus.

Wallis, J. (2005), *God's Politics: Why the American Right Got It Wrong and the Left Doesn't Get It*. Oxford: Lion.

Warner, M. (1976), *Alone of All Her Sex: The Myth and the Cult of the Virgin Mary*. London: Quartet.

Yong, A. (2007), 'Radically Orthodox, Reformed, and Pentecostal, Rethinking the Intersection of Post Modernity and the Religions (sic) in Conversation with James KA Smith', *Journal of Pentecostal Theology* 15 (2), 233–50.

7 Inhabiting the Good City: The Politics of Hate and the Urbanisms of Hope

Andrew Davey and Elaine Graham

The voice of the church and other faith groups has become a significant contribution in the civic lives of our cities and the development of urban policy over the past 25 years. National government, regional development agencies, local authorities and neighbourhood renewal programmes all regularly engage with religious bodies as part of the planning and delivery of regeneration and services in urban communities. Of all the faith groups, it is the Church of England, through the ubiquity of its presence and experience, that has accompanied communities, previously designated as Urban Priority Areas, experiencing economic and physical regeneration, often from within broad-based partnerships which have brought about significant change (Graham and Lowe, 2009; Davey, 2000).

Beyond the revitalized city centres and metropolitan hum, the church has also been present within those communities which even government ministers have been willing to describe as 'disconnected', where

> Traditional, often semi-skilled, industrial jobs have continued to decline, while newly created higher paid jobs are open only to those with higher skill levels. In predominantly white areas, recent migration is sometimes perceived as changing communities in unpredictable ways. . . . creating new competition for jobs and social housing. . . . They think their area is changing – they say 'it's not my community anymore'. And feel helpless to do anything about it. 'No one speaks up for us'. (Denham, 2009)

Since the mid-eighties, the Church of England has produced significant documentation of urban conditions and has spoken of the Church's dilemma as it attempts to remain faithful within an urban parish structure which is increasingly overshadowed by suburban congregational agendas (ACUPA, 1985; CULF, 2006). While there have been calls for a greater awareness of contextual approaches where theological method might provide a common ground for different communities, predominant training and mission agendas have inclined towards suburban models and practice. It is apparent, however, that a distinct dimension within

British urban theological practice has been its tenacious interaction with liberation theology, a commitment to social justice and to 'keep faith' by maintaining a presence alongside marginalized communities in such places (CULF, 2006; Davey, 2008; Graham and Lowe, 2009).

Regenerated communities?

Urban regeneration has proved exacting and divisive for some communities. The experience of working in partnership has been mixed: some have found a vitality with many stakeholders around the table seeking to invigorate and rebuild neighbourhood; others have found partnerships to be uneven, and at times token, as concessions are made to a profit-led regeneration industry (Harvey, 2008; Steele, 2009). Despite their own transnationalism, however, faith communities have often seemed ill-equipped to tackle the global nature of the regeneration industry. Major inward investment has often come from interests with little regard for local impact, remodelling space and markets on a globalized template.

The fault is not entirely with the private sector. Often for the voluntary and faith sectors, regeneration activity has become a scramble for influence and status, or contracts and grants, with attendant risks of collusion in the name of partnership. At times this has meant that the church and other faith groups have missed or not understood significant shifts in policy, such as the marginalization of community-led neighbourhood renewal within what is now the Department for Communities and Local Government, and what Allan Cochrane (2007) identifies as the disappearance of a distinct urban policy focus from the political agenda. Justin Beaumont's analysis of the re-emergence of faith-based organizations in the wake of neoliberal retrenchment of the social democratic welfare state just as government is looking for partners from the community and voluntary sector to step into the breach neatly captures a further dimension of this greater prominence of faith-communities as political actors, not least some of the more contradictory and frustrating aspects. Certainly, as Beaumont argues, 'we need to conceptualise changing dynamics between religion, politics and postsecular society' (2008: 2019), but the realignments of capital, civil society and the nation–state as players in the regeneration game represent ambivalent opportunities for grass-roots activism. On the one hand, they offer new spaces for innovative forms of engagement, as with the enhanced public profile of faith-based organizations in policy matters. On the other, however, they engender alienation among those who find themselves receiving little benefit from urban regeneration strategies that regard cultural industries or prestigious property development as prime drivers of economic revival (see Graham and Lowe, 2009: 99–114; Harvey, 2008).

Theologians and faith-practitioners are only beginning to understand the consequences of asking 'Who is the city for?' as part of the 'What makes a good city?' debate. Yet questions of power, participation and the nature of citizenship are still crucial to any future patterns of regeneration, and the current disenchantment with local and national politics has a detrimental effect on the lives of our towns and cities. People are turning their backs on community and civic engagement as they see few prospects with the progress of the recession for the renewal of resources and infrastructure that might make a difference; or worse, they are turning to those who offer the alternative scenario of a nation that resists the changes brought on by globalization and immigration. This finds an outlet in the increasing hostility towards cosmopolitanism and multiculturalism perceived as a conspiracy against the white working class by the metropolitan (regenerated) elite.

Disorder, diversity and division

There has always been a strong theme within urban policy that urban places are disorderly, evidenced by riots and uprisings, as well as street-level crime attributable to the presence of minority ethnic communities (Cochrane, 2007: 71). While much early urban policy under New Labour shifted the emphasis of urban renewal to economic regeneration and the built environment, within the rhetoric of social exclusion there was a persistent fear of, in the words of Tony Blair, an 'underclass of people cut off from society's mainstream without any sense of shared purpose' (Blair, quoted in Lister, 2004: 108). The central efforts of New Labour's Social Exclusion Unit seemed aimed at the usual focuses of urban intervention, and the Unit was launched in 1997 by a prime ministerial visit to the multi-ethnic Aylesbury Estate in South London.

In parallel with this, much of the regeneration activity focused on the built environment has concentrated on appealing to a new metropolitan elite who demand 'defended spaces' within the urban core, gated and monitored by CCTV. While urban writers since Engels have celebrated the city as an encounter of strangers, urban restructuring has meant that those encounters with difference have become increasingly limited for those who can afford to 'opt out' from mixed neighbourhoods, community schools and other local interactions (Minton, 2009). An increasingly negative perception of ethnically diverse localities is part of this trend, along with the perceived threats to culture, faith and employment by mass immigration and the association of migrants with crime, disease and disorder.

After multiculturalism

Tariq Modood has defined multiculturalism as 'the recognition of group difference within the public sphere of laws, policies, democratic discourses and the terms of citizenship and national identity' (Modood, 2007: 2). Britain may be a multicultural society, therefore, but the adoption of policies of multiculturalism implies a 'normative response' (Parekh, 2006: 6) to the facts of ethnic and cultural difference. Diversity is upheld and celebrated, but in a way which adopts a highly pragmatic and non-prescriptive approach towards the implications of difference (Dinham, Furbey and Lowndes, 2009: 84–86).

Over the past 20 years, however, significant change has taken place within the interaction of immigrant communities in Britain as the post-immigration discourse of multiculturalism and 'political blackness' began to crack when faith entered the arena. For Tariq Modood, this was no better symbolized than in the battle over *The Satanic Verses* in the mid-1980s, when many Muslims were radicalized and organized, discovering a new community identity based on religion rather than colour. This shift had a significant impact on multicultural discourse in which religion was generally perceived as culturally interesting but waning in terms of political significance. Yet the emergence of Islam as a publicly articulated mark of identity was perceived as a threat by a secularized media establishment alongside the increasingly Islamophobic Right. What is noteworthy in terms of our concerns here is the significance that Modood attributes to the space created by cross-religious dialogue during the Rushdie affair.

> ... what was even more striking was that when the public rage against Muslims was at its most intense, Muslims neither sought nor were offered any special solidarity by any non-white minority. It was in fact, a group of white liberal Anglicans who tried to moderate hostility against angry Muslims, and it was in interfaith forum a rather than in political-black organizations that space was created for Muslims to state their case without being vilified. (Modood, 2002: 119)

It is not only the liberal elite or conservative media that struggled with the new postsecular public space, however. While much of the focus in community relations was concerned with 'multiculturalism' and the presence of Black and south Asian communities as an enrichment of British culture, such an emphasis did little to understand the impact of mass immigration upon white British (or English) identity. Indigenous white culture is often portrayed as eclipsed by a regime of 'steel-drums, samosas and saris' with few outlets other than football, 'chav' culture and the reoccupation of city centres through the night-time leisure economy (Collins, 2005; Garner, Cowles and Lung, 2009).

Some attempts have been made, however, to address this lack of attention. The Runnymede Trust, 'an independent policy research organization focusing on equality and justice through the promotion of a successful multi-ethnic society', recently published a document *Who cares about the white working class?* (Sveinsson, 2009). Exploring how issues of ethnicity and class play out in a constantly measured and monitored multicultural society, educationalist David Gillborn warns of the danger of creating 'white racial victimhood' and the myth of advantage given to minoritorized children in the education system, as well as the potentially negative effects that policy changes could have.

> By warning of the danger of inflaming support for racist parties, what actually happens is that politicians and commentators invoke the threat of racist violence as a means of disciplining calls for greater race equality. ... Official statistics reveal that most groups in poverty achieve relatively poor results *regardless* of ethnic background. (Gilborn, 2009)

Similarly, a recent report commissioned by the Department for Communities and Local Government argued that the successful integration of migrants into local communities is significantly conditioned by local, predominantly economic, factors:

> ... we found that in those [places] where social and environmental conditions were better, there was ... less apparent hostility to minorities ... By far the most frequent context for referring to ethnic minorities is that of perceived competition for resources – typically

housing, but also employment, benefits, territory and culture. (Garner, Cowles and Lung, 2009: 6)

Such resentment, while reprehensible, has to be seen as one response to economic pressures. Black and ethnic minorities and the forces of 'political correctness' are held up as scapegoats in a context of perceived unfairness of access to material benefits; and in a political climate in which the biggest threat to our way of life is often equated with so-called radical Islam, it is timely to consider how such attitudes feed into the activities of far-right political movements which represent, arguably, a far more tangible threat to democracy and social cohesion.

The 'postsecular' public space

As Modood comments, multiculturalism itself is, in many respects, a child of liberalism. It is founded, conceptually, on differences of ethnicity and 'race', reflecting the preoccupations of a relatively secular generation of social science which took little substantial account of religion as a marker of identity. This has led, increasingly, to criticisms of the public sector and local and national government, for example, for their lack of 'religious literacy' in taking account of the needs of different sections of the community. Many commentators (see especially Dinham et al., 2009) argue that the emergence of 'faith' into the multicultural pot has led to significant reappraisal not only of the liberal roots of multiculturalism but a recognition that questions of identity and allegiance across different communities in Britain are complex and fluid. As local and national government and other policy makers are rapidly discovering, religious affiliation and identity cannot be bracketed out of these contentions.

But the debate continues as to the appropriate kind of engagement by people of faith in the public domain. On the one hand, we have the greater public profile of faith-based groups as active participants in civil society; on the other, those who continue to believe that adherence to the demands of any kind of theology represents a denial of liberal values with an inevitable retreat into more pernicious forms of segregation and extremism. A recent contributor to the debate has been Alan Billings – priest, broadcaster and New Labour apologist. In *God and Community Cohesion: Help or Hindrance* (2009), Billings presents a pessimistic approach to attempts to establish common ground among faith communities and shared vision within diverse cities. He notes the precariousness of attempts to build cohesive communities at a time when the legitimacy of pluralism is barely acknowledged internally within religious traditions.

As a result, there has been growing attention to the question of the public role of religion in a multicultural society. Most prominently, and most controversially, of course, is the debate about social cohesion and the perceived 'threat' of radical Islam, and the implementation of policies such as The Prevent Strategy and 'Face-to-Face and Side-by-Side' (DCLG, 2007). There is criticism that the Preventing Violent Extremism (PVE) agenda fails to address issues of non-Islamic extremism and violence, not least that provoked by the presence of the British

National Party (BNP) and English Defence League (see Kundnani, 2009). There is also wide misgiving among faith communities themselves, especially within Islam, of the way in which faith-based organizations are being instrumentalized, almost as vehicles of social control, and that the predominant paradigm of faith and its public impact on the part of government is that of 'delivering' particular social outcomes. The bizarre reverse side is that Christian leaders find themselves having to explain to Muslims that they have no contact with or control over the BNP despite its claims of Christian identity.

More benignly, perhaps, is also the potential of faith groups to participate in programmes of social, cultural and economic renewal, and even, on the margins of mainstream political life, to take up certain aspects of welfare provision. So we have begun to see how so-called 'faith communities' are being brought into processes of governance and participation: as sources of capacity building in local communities and constructive agents in programmes of social cohesion, as well as in the prevention of religious and political extremism.

The problem of faith and 'whiteness' in a multicoloured society

But does this re-emergence of faith as part of a 'thick description' of modern citizenship actually disenfranchise some people? Ted Cantle, author of the Report into the Oldham riots of 2001, has remarked that 'the majority population have always felt unrepresented by the notion [of multiculturalism]' (Cantle in Lowndes, 2009: 93). He continues, 'if you ask white people, for example, if they have an ethnicity, they don't seem to appreciate that they have ... They also see "diversity" as something that is only relevant to minorities. Similarly, most [white] people see faith as another dimension which doesn't include them – the British tradition has been built upon the submerging of faith differences in the public sphere' (Cantle in Lowndes, 2009: 93). So there are ways in which 'multiculturalism', if not *failing* the indigenous white British population, has proved wanting in terms of white 'buy-in' which furnishes them with the means to construct an identity or self-understanding to match, and negotiate with, that of others. Stuart Hall is convinced, however, that while negotiation is critical over conflicts of 'outlook, belief and interest' they must not assume 'Eurocentric assimilation' as the starting or end point: 'The specific and particular "difference" of a group or community cannot be asserted absolutely, without regard to the wider context provided by all those "others" in relation to whom "particularity" acquires a relative value' (Hall, 2000: 234).

Assumptions are made about cultural homogeneity by those contesting a community, as well as by the media and commentators. It is apparent that white, African-Caribbean and Asian communities all contain elements of difference and hybridity that require internal negotiation, as well as challenges being made to an older leadership concerned with influence and stability, often in reaction to experiences of violence or indifference (Amin, 2002).

To what extent are Right-wing extremist groups exploiting that vacuum in white communities? The re-emergence of faith in terms of identity, rather than practice, gives rise to many tiny 'clashes of civilizations' which offer little space for greater and smaller narratives of interaction and negotiation between and within communities. There is certainly evidence to suggest that Right-wing extremist groups and movements are shifting their rhetoric increasingly towards Islamophobic statements and actions, as in, for example, the mobilization of the English Defence League to demonstrate against what it terms 'Islamic extremism' in places such as Luton, Rochdale, Birmingham and Manchester (*Searchlight*, August 2009: 8–9). Nick Griffin, leader of the BNP, has described Islam as a 'cancer' that needs 'chemotherapy ... to save civilization' (*Searchlight*, August 2009: 10).

What is intriguing is the attempt by many of these groups to hijack a 'Christian' identity around which they hope to rally indigenous White support that perceives itself as having been disenfranchised by the ideology of multiculturalism. So for example, the English Defence League reproduces images of Crusaders in its publicity, with a poem that includes the lines:

> The crusaders were once strong, now all but gone
> ... But im [sic] here sword out of sheath ...
> ... My thirst [f]or blood grows stronger
> The pain cant take no longer
> For foreign blood I hunger'. (Bartholomew, 2009)

In the campaign for the European elections in June 2009, the BNP produced an image of Jesus on a poster which was driven round northern cities on the back of the party's 'truth truck'. The post carried a quotation from John 15:20, reading, 'If they have persecuted me, they will also persecute you', and the commentary, 'What would *Jesus* Do? – Vote BNP'. The archbishops of Canterbury and York felt moved to issue a joint statement, together with a letter to be read in all parishes, repudiating these connections, saying:

> Christians have been deeply disturbed by the conscious adoption by the BNP of the language of our faith when the effect of those policies is not to promote those values but to foster fear and division within communities, especially between people of different faiths or racial background. (Joint Statement, 24 May 2009)

The BNP response was to issue a leaflet, distributed outside a number of churches and cathedrals, entitled *Judas Archbishops*:

> All over the UK pews are emptying; churches are closing down and turning into mosques/temples. Our distinctive Christian heritage is disappearing as whole regions of Britain become Islamified. .... The cowardly 'yes men', functionaries and time-servers leading the Church of England have consistently failed to lift a finger in defence of Britain against those who would destroy it. Cocooned in their ivory towers from any meaningful contact with the outside world, real life or ordinary people, they pass one surrender motion after another. (*Judas Archbishops* – BNP leaflet May 2009)

Such an association between whiteness and Christianity may appear irrelevant, particularly for anyone with any direct experience of the demographic profile of the twenty-first century urban church. It is remarkable to consider how far all the

Christian denominations, including the Church of England, depend increasingly for their continued viability on members whose personal or family backgrounds originate in Africa; the Caribbean and, increasingly, Eastern Europe or Latin America. The local is also the global; but it is emphatically not the racially pure English Church of BNP or EDL fantasy!

But this use of religion – or at least a discourse of a particular construal of religion – does seem to be a critical aspect of the rise of the far Right over the past couple of years. And this threat is not theoretical, since over 50 councillors are found in local authorities, and two BNP candidates, Nick Griffin and Andrew Brons, were elected to the European Parliament for the North-West and Yorkshire & Humberside regions respectively. The BNP's electoral strongholds seem to be in predominantly white working class communities with higher than average levels of unemployment and economic decline: post-industrial areas or large social housing developments. Admittedly, there were particular factors behind the success of the BNP in the local and European elections of May 2009, such as a slump in the traditional Labour vote, and widespread revulsion at the MPs' expenses scandal. Yet this may still be regarded as consistent with the opportunism of the far Right in exploiting people's disaffection with mainstream politics, including policies of multiculturalism and regeneration that are perceived as unfairly favouring ethnic minorities and metropolitan elites. It adds up to a serious problem of voter disengagement, a 'democratic deficit', that moves swiftly into the electoral vacuum of White British/English identity with dangerous consequences.

Alongside the democratic deficit comes the cultural deficit fed by a general religious illiteracy. Questions of identity are raised for the majority when the religious difference of 'the other' is perceived in public space: through civic celebrations of Eid or Diwali, the wearing of headscarves or turbans, the requests for prayer rooms or specially prepared food. The BNP's advocacy of Christian identity comes at a time when the reassertion of identity is encouraged by bishops and other leaders, whether it is the public wearing of crosses and crucifixes, the civic acknowledgement of Christmas as a Christian festival or the establishment of St George's Day as an English public holiday – all of which have found their place in the BNP's campaigns as tribal totems. The BNP continues to pedal its austere anti-abortion and anti-homosexuality policies as proof of its Christian credentials. A letter and leaflet sent to church leaders in February 2010 compared the 'integrity' of the BNP with other political groups.

> To support any of these parties would be unfaithfulness to Jesus Christ and would also incur God's displeasure. . . . The British National Party is committed to preserving our Christian heritage, culture and traditions, our Christian standards, morality and values, and our British civilisation, democracy and freedom of speech. If you are a Christian there is only one party for you. (BNP, 2010)

The right to the city

What are the tools and resources which might enable the church to rebuild its understanding of civic engagement in a culturally and religiously diverse society in the face of economic interests, disaffection with the political system and organized racism? The ability to mobilize across communities is critical to an urban rights discourse which has significant connections with a liberationist perspective, as well as the concerns of the emergent public theology movement (see Davey, 2008); but we have yet to develop an understanding and vocabulary that enables us to develop a theologically rooted progressive urbanism that overcomes alienation and celebrates the contribution of ordinary citizens through engaging outside the church's traditional comfort zones.

Influenced by the work of Henri Lefebvre, leading urbanists have identified the concept of 'the right to the city' *(le droit à la ville)* as a critical resource in the neoliberal postsecular city. Access and participation in urban life and spaces needs to be reasserted as cities restructure spatially, economically and socially. There can be no cities with 'elsewheres', communities that are left behind or marginalized. David Harvey argues that 'The freedom to make and remake our cities and ourselves is … one of the most precious yet neglected of our human rights' (Harvey, 2008). Ash Amin has written of the need to fashion a 'politics of well-being and emancipation out of multiplicity and difference and from the particularities of the urban experience' (Amin, 2006). It is a critical question for urbanists how a wider spectrum of interests can play a crucial part in reimagining the city and staking a claim to a common urban future. It is vital that the discourse and activities of urbanists (and theologians) are not another source of the alienation of the urban dispossessed. Patsy Healey's often quoted phrase about the common quest being 'how to manage our co-existence in shared space' is a starting point (Healey, 1997: 3). That shared space might be the neighbourhood, the municipality or the society. Finding commonality will move us to the edge of the concerns of funding and policy.

In recent years, church interventions have revealed a range of intersecting and opposing views of urban life, diversity, the power of urban structures, the meaning and pitfalls of living in close proximity to mainstream policy and solutions. Just as Alan Cochrane describes government urban interventions as a 'policy area presenting different forms of utopia' (Cochrane, 2007: 145), we need to consider the church's theology and work on the urban to be the construction of a vision or imaginary that needs earthing. Those utopias are imagined as part of a strategy for developing an understanding of the underlying values of the desired city (kingdom) and the activities (praxis or performance) needed for bringing it about. Decisions about how church property is used, how mission is carried out, how the church engages in the wider civic realm and identifies allies will all have implications for how the identity of the church forms among its members as well as within the local community. Who is the church there for? What will be the impact of those decisions on different faith or ethnic communities? Those performances are often matters of contestation as different imaginaries come into conflict: unambiguous evangelism among migrants or the pursuit of mutual action, the sale of a piece of land to fund new projects or social and affordable housing, a profitable lease to a private nursery or a volunteer playgroup, an academy school or a community college. Some of those choices may be counter cultural acts, or the creation of new 'habits' (as part of the imagination of utopias) that resist the often overwhelming cultural, theological and political pressure for caution and security to be found elsewhere in the church and our urban communities.

Ash Amin describes the good city

> . . . as an expanding habit of solidarity and as a practical but unsettled achievement, constantly building on experiments through which difference and multiplicity can be mobilised for common gain and against harm and want . . . A civic politics of getting the urban habit of living with diversity right is one way of thickening the ways in which an increasingly fragmented, disoriented and anxious society can regain some mechanism for the distribution of hopefulness . . . . (Amin, 2006: 1020–21)

In what ways might the church's action and theological interventions be expanding the 'habits of solidarity'? Three case studies follow, which illustrate possible ways in which the church within its community context has begun to articulate constructive forms of engagement with the political situation. We cannot pretend that by themselves they constitute decisive arguments in favour of maintaining the status quo, but maybe they start to indicate some of the principles for both church and society on which any civic role of religion might rest.

The first example shows how churches worked to build a positive political coalition in the fight against extremism. In advance of the June elections to the European Parliament, it was known that the BNP was statistically close to winning some seats, so a broad-based alliance called *HOPE not Hate* was founded, sponsored by trade unions, anti-fascist groups and the investigative anti-fascist journal *Searchlight* (www.hopenothate.org.uk/). Faith groups, including and especially Church of England leaders and staff, were also prominent. In northwest England, for example, the *HOPE not Hate* campaign was launched at Manchester Anglican Cathedral, and the resources of the staff of the diocesan Board for Ministry and Society kept up much of the momentum. Unfortunately, of course, the voting math only limited the scale of the BNP 'break through', but the campaign has continued to mobilize, for example, to ensure that there was a prominent Christian voice in the cross-community opposition to a rally organized by the EDL in Manchester in October 2009.

One framework for understanding the contribution of faith-based organizations to the public realm has been social capital theory. For Robert Putnam, a healthy civil society rests on people's capacity to be active citizens and to contribute to their communities, which is dependent on the skills, values and resources at their disposal that enable them to mobilize and to form relationships both within and between immediate communities of interest (Putnam, 2000). It has been further noted that religious people and organizations are particularly rich in sources of social capital, because they have strong values, a clear collective identity, possess buildings and physical resources that offer good facilities, and are well connected to local, national and global expressions of their faith (CULF, 2006; Baker and Skinner, 2005).

Nick Lowles, editor of *Searchlight*, writing in advance of the European elections, uses just such a model of faith groups as invaluable repositories of 'faithful capital' in reflecting on the *HOPE not Hate* campaign:

Faith groups will be crucial. They have a credibility and authority in many of the communities where local politicians have disengaged. In Greater Manchester alone, the Anglican Church has over 500 full-time employees and a similar number of part-time workers, and the church as a whole has the largest community outreach project in the country. Give these people the arguments and tools to take the message to their congregations and we are really beginning to motor. (Lowles, April 2009: 5)

The second example may be familiar from the BBC TV series, *The Choir: Unsung Town* (2009). This featured the community of South Oxhey, in Hertfordshire, a large post-war social housing estate, with many of the characteristics of high unemployment, low educational achievement and social problems: a community often considered out of place, or out of step, with the surrounding affluence of the Home Counties. The musician and conductor Gareth Malone established a community choir which has had notable success and continues to this day, despite initial problems of apathy and lack of confidence.

The invitation to the BBC to make the programme came originally from the local Anglican priest, Pam Wise. While much of the narrative of the subsequent series focused on the stories of individuals, the church was a constant source of support, providing an office base for Malone and a significant volunteer base. Once again, it is Lowles's evocation of the grass-roots activism both of *HOPE not Hate* and of the churches in general, that is probably the most critical role for the church in such areas where there are significant extremist threats. It is the church's localism and its capacity to mobilize a wealth of local social capital that potentially pays dividends in the shape of new and robust articulations of civic pride.

South Oxhey Community Choir is in many respects a classic case study in social capital, in that it illustrates how the revival of the instruments of local civil society helped to rejuvenate local community pride. Furthermore, a 'coda' to this story offers further suggestions that the choir has succeeded in fostering an alternative account of civic identity that is less prone to the resentments highlighted by the Runnymede Trust and DCLG. The BNP had earlier experienced some electoral gains in south Hertfordshire, including the election of a candidate to the county council. When the councillor concerned offered a portion of her discretionary 'community chest' budget to the choir, it was refused after much discussion on the grounds that the BNP did not share the vision of the community and the values which the choir project had tried to promote, a decision that drew considerable media coverage (*Watford Observer*, 2009; *Lancaster Unity*, 2009).

In Lancashire, the church's response to the 2001 riots and the subsequent report's assertion of spatial and cultural segregation has been focused on the *Building Bridges in Burnley* programme which seeks to 'achieve a shared sense of belonging amongst the people of Burnley' through a 'broad range of activities delivered to create opportunities for people from different faith, cultural, socio-economic contexts' (see http://bbburnley.co.uk/FaithFriends.aspx). The programme has had a major influence in communities where there had been little encounter or mutual understanding, particularly among young people. Activities have included inter-community encounters, the development of 'faith friends' – a shared chaplaincy programme in local schools, pilgrimages and participation in mainstream events such as Interfaith Week. The programme seeks to make faith visible as a uniting rather than excluding force in the community. A significant decision to base the programme in a mosque, rather than a church, provided a clear statement on the sharing of resources and access. On a recent visit the Archbishop of Canterbury commented:

> I think the depth of friendship there is between representatives of different faiths here is pretty impressive in itself, but also listening to a twelve year old talking about her part in building bridges between communities and the work that's done to keep children of different communities in touch with each other and sharing experiences, that is so precious and so unusual I think, in terms of the country as a whole, is something that ought to be bottled and exported from Burnley. (Radio Lancashire, 5 November 2009)

Building Bridges in Burnley has stood alongside similar programmes and interventions attempting to foster new links and confidence in the future across the town. An indication of the change experienced in Burnley since 2001 might be seen in the radical reduction in the BNP presence on the local council from 12 councillors to 3.

All these examples demonstrate the positive aspects of religious social capital and perhaps serve to confirm Robert Putnam's original diagnosis of its function in terms of bonding, bridging and linking (Putnam, 2000). For the community of South Oxhey, a shared activity not only brought people together but engendered a nascent sense of civic pride – a classic piece of 'bonding' social capital. Both *Hope not Hate* and *Building Bridges in Burnley* campaigns depend for their sustainability on creating common cause across diverse constituencies and demonstrate the continuing potential of faith-based organizations to mobilize human and physical resources at the local level. In addition, we see how the distinctive ability of faith-communities to combine a local presence with wider affiliations to national, sometimes international fellow-believers, represents an effective means of linking the concerns of neighbourhood campaigns to a wider political framework.

Conclusion

In the examples above and many others, we see the possibility of new forms of civil society emerging from the new postsecular contentions of religious identity and race. The reproduction of social capital is not always a natural outcome of the presence of faith in the public realm, which often enters that space out of the frustration and anger of groups which have been marginal to the economy of urban regeneration in the past decades. Violent competing claims are often local reactions to, or refractions of, wider structural forces played out on a global stage. The 'othering' of groups within our cities and towns, be it the racialized othering found in popular press portrayal of Muslims and other Asians, or the pseudo-sociological rhetoric of chavs and underclasses, find immediate scapegoats but fail to take into account issues of power, access to education and employment or the superficial appeal of pejorative media representation.

Urbanists often invoke the contested nature of urban space as a source of the city's dialectical creativity (see Merrifield, 2002). These points of friction and pain will need to be acknowledged and negotiated innovatively, rather than ignored or accommodated, if the urban is to be diverted from the dysfunctional and dystopian realities we have been describing. The church also needs to understand its own complicity in the demonic culture that it is now called into solidarity to confront, while celebrating the diversity and potential it undoubtedly has within itself. The church's engagement with the public realm of postsecular cities in the twenty-first century will need to shed its political naivety and class predisposition if it is to be alongside the struggles for social justice in cities that are increasingly diverse and may be in danger of being increasingly segregated.

References

Amin, A. (2002), 'Ethnicity and the Multicultural City: Living with Diversity', *Environment and Planning A* 34 (6), 959–80.

—. (2006), 'The Good City', *Urban Studies* 43 (5/6), 1009–23.

Archbishop's Commission on Urban Priority Areas (ACUPA) (1985), *Faith in the City: A Call for Action by Church and Nation*. London: Church House Publishing.

Archbishops' Commission on Urban Life and Faith (CULF) (2006), *Faithful Cities: A Call for Celebration, Vision and Justice*. Peterborough: Methodist Publishing House.

Baker, C., and Skinner, H. (2005), *Telling the Stories: How Churches are Contributing to Social Capital*. Manchester: William Temple Foundation.

Bartholomew, R. (2009), 'English Defence League Gets Medieval', *Bartholomew's Notes on Religion* online, 16 September 2009, http://barthsnotes.wordpress.com/2009/09/16/english-defence-league-gets-medieval/ (accessed 21 October 2009).

Beaumont, J. (2008), 'Faith Action on Urban Social Issues', *Urban Studies* 45 (10), 2019–34.

Billings, A. (2009), *God and Community Cohesion: Help or Hindrance?* London: SPCK.

BNP (2010), *Who Should Christians Vote For?* [sic] (Private circulation).

Cochrane, A. (2007), *Understanding Urban Policy: A Critical Approach*. Oxford: Blackwell.

Collins, M. (2005), *The Likes of Us: A Biography of the White Working Class*. London: Granta.

Davey, A. (2000), *Urban Christianity and Global Order*. London: SPCK.

—. (2008), 'Better Place: Performing the Urbanisms of Hope', *International Journal of Public Theology* 2 (1), 27–46.

Denham, J. (2009), 'Connecting Communities', Institute for Community Cohesion online, 14 October, www.communities.gov.uk/speeches/corporate/connectingcommunities (accessed 20 November 2009).

Department for Communities and Local Government (2007), *Face-to-Face and Side-by-Side: A Framework for Interfaith Dialogue and Social Action*, www.

communities.gov.uk/publications/communities/interfaithdialogue (accessed 21 October 2008).

Dinham, A., Furbey, R., and Lowndes, V. (eds) (2009), *Faith in the Public Realm: Controversies, Policies and Practices.* Bristol: Policy Press.

Garner, S., Cowles, J., Lung, B., and Stott, M. (2009), *Sources of Resentment and Perceptions of Ethnic Minorities among Poor White People in England.* London: Department for Communities and Local Government.

Gillborn, D. (2009), 'Education: The Numbers Game and the Construction of White Racial Victimhood', in K. Sveinssson (ed) *Who Cares about the White Working Class?* Runnymede Trust online, www.runnymedetrust.org/uploads/publications/pdfs/WhoCaresAboutTheWhiteWorkingClass-2009.pdf (accessed 11 November 2009).

Graham, E.L., and Lowe, S.R. (2009), *What Makes a Good City? Public Theology and the Urban Church.* London: DLT.

Green, L. (2009), *Let's Do Theology* (2nd edn). London: Continuum.

Hall, S. (2000), 'The Multi-Cultural Question', in B. Hesse (ed), *Un/settled Multiculturalisms: Diasporas, Entanglements, Transruptions.* London: Zed Books.

Harvey, D. (2008), 'The Right to the City', *New Left Review* 53: 23–40.

Healey, P. (1997), *Collaborative Planning. Shaping Places in Fragmented Societies* (2nd edn). London: Macmillan.

Kundnani, A. (2009), *Spooked: How Not To Prevent Violent Extremism.* IRR online, www.irr.org.uk/2009/october/ak000036.html (accessed 12 December 2009).

Lancaster Unity (2009), 'South Oxhey Community Choir Snubs British National Party Cash', October 16, http://lancasteruaf.blogspot.com/2009/10/south-oxhey-community-choir-snubs-bnp.html (accessed 21 October 2009).

Lister, R. (2004), *Poverty.* Cambridge: Polity Press.

Lowles, N. (2009), 'Editorial', *Searchlight,* April 2009, 4–5.

Merrifield, A. (2002), *Dialectical Urbanism.* London: Monthly Review Press.

Minton, A. (2009), *Ground Control.* Harmondsworth: Penguin.

Modood, T. (2002), 'The Place of Muslims in British Secular Multiculturalism', in N. Al-Sayyad and M. Castells (eds), *Muslim Europe or Euro-Islam: Politics, Culture, and Citizenship in the Age of Globalisation,* 113–30. Oxford: Lexington Books.

Northwest Regional Development Agency (2005), *Faith in England's Northwest: How Faith Communities Contribute to Social and Economic Wellbeing,* NWDA, online,*www.nwda.co.uk/media-library/publications/communities/faith-in-england-northwest-oct.aspx* (accessed 21 October 2008).

Parekh, B. (2006), *Rethinking Multiculturalism: Cultural Diversity and Political Theory* (2nd edn). Basingstoke: Palgrave Macmillan.

Putnam, R. (2000), *Bowling Alone: The Collapse and Revival of American Community.* New York: Simon and Schuster.

Steele, J. (2009), 'Social Justice, Social Control or the Pursuit of Happiness? The Goals and Values of the Regeneration Industry', in P. M. Scott, E. L. Graham and C. R. Baker (eds), *Remoralising Britain? Political, Ethical and Theological Perspectives on New Labour.* London and New York: Continuum.

Sveinssson, K. (ed) (2009), *Who Cares about the White Working Class?* Runnymede Trust online www.runnymedetrust.org/uploads/publications/ pdfs/WhoCaresAboutTheWhiteWorkingClass-2009.pdf (accessed 11 November 2009).

Watford Observer, 16 October 2009, 'South Oxhey Community Choir snubs BNP cash'.

Part III

Postsecular Policies and Praxis

8 Sanctuaries of Urban Virtues: Learning from Edo Tokyo

Anni Greve[1]

Introduction

The discourse of the 'postsecular city' has opened up a more general dispute about leading hegemonic concepts. The very concept of post-secularization suggests a shift away from secularization, with the implicit assumption that modernity has become secularized in terms of 'the disenchantment of the world'. Conversely, post-secularization has to do with the re-emergence of belief, faith and sacredness as collective phenomena, while the idea of the postsecular city suggests a return of the city as a scene 'in which the dynamics of religio–secular change are revealed and expressed with greatest intensity' (Baker and Beaumont, 2010). This discourse offers an opportunity for 'us' to go back in time and space. Is modernity really to be understood as disenchanted? Was Europe the only centre for this? What is the role, more precisely, of the city as a scene for religion, as well as for the phenomena of secularization? This chapter takes up the challenge by focusing on early modern Japan. It argues that there are more similarities than we might think between early modern Europe and early modern Japan. It offers an argument for cutting down Weber's historical thesis about secularization into a more moderate search for secularization phenomena, not in order to point to some kind of immaturity in Weber's thesis, as if there were only a single historical continuum, but rather to describe a more complex experience of 'similitude' between East and West. Secularization phenomena in the two hemispheres appeared to be the same but not completely comparable: they were counterparts.

The first part of the chapter offers an argument for secularization phenomena in early modern Japan. The idea that such phenomena are recent is questioned. In his work, Max Weber (1906, 1921) saw secularization as a phenomenon related to the industrial revolutions of the eighteenth and nineteenth centuries, and he offered an argument for a precise connection between religion, modernity and secularization. Those assumptions are not false, but they are insufficient. Secularization phenomena can be observed in many cultures as far back as the early modern era. In this chapter, I will join this debate with two leading hypotheses. The first concerns secularization understood as a rupture with the idea of the

divine legitimacy of the ruling powers. As in Europe, with the Westphalia separation of church and state in 1648, this separation took shape in Japan in the
seventeenth century. Not only did it pave the way for national unification and the
invention of a (spectacular) political theology, it also gave rise to the formation of
a proto-modern sphere of private life that lived in the *shadow* of secularization.

Another hypothesis concerns modernity understood as what has been called a
'transfert de sacralité' (transfer of sacred identity to new things; Ozouf in Greve
2006). The second part of the chapter presents an argument for studying people's
attachment to religious sanctuaries in this light. Today it is acknowledged that
citizens of late modernity attach themselves to religions in response to, and in
conditions of, social change and unrest. We are seeing a revival of religions in
modern urban societies, or the birth of 'the postsecular city'. Less attention has
been paid to similar mechanisms in the early modern era. The chapter therefore
offers an argument for studying people's attachment to religious sanctuaries in the
context of the enormous urban formations of the early modern era. The rise of
large-scale urban societies became a Pandora's Box in Japanese society, that is, a
metaphor for the unanticipated and irreversible consequences of horizontal networks of weak ties to the formation of 'sociation' (Simmel) or 'expressive solidarity'
(Durkheim). It is in this process that we see the attachment to religious sanctuaries, which thereby attain a new meaning for identity making.

Noting a counterpart

The Jesuits were among the first missionaries to travel to Japan, their missionary
activities beginning in earnest around 1549 with the arrival of Father Francis
Xavier, though all activities ended abruptly when, in the mid-1600s, all Christian
missionaries were banned from Japan. Xavier was excited about Japan: 'they are the
best race yet discovered, and I think among non-Christians their match will not
easily be found' (Lidin, 2002: 166). Also, a few decades later, the Italian Jesuit,
Alexandro Valignano,[2] reported meetings with an exotic, strange and yet strikingly
familiar culture: ' . . . Japan is a world the reverse of Europe; everything is so different and opposed that they are like us in practically nothing'. Yet he added, 'this
would not be surprising if they were like so many barbarians, but what astonishes
me is that they behave as very prudent and cultured people' (Shelton, 1999: 3). The
missionaries were stunned and probably felt insecure about where to start their
work of converting non-Christians into civilized people. Christians came with
precise ideas about the very idea of a 'religion' as a contradiction to the idea of a
'primitive' magic cult, and they believed that Christianity would offer the only true
path to civilization. However, in this strange Oriental culture, codes for civility
seemed to be a key order of social encountering.

During the Tokugawa era (1603–1867), visitors from abroad were rare. In *The
History of Japan Together with a Description of the Kingdom of Siam*, published in
1727, Engelbert Kaempfer described 'a valiant and virtuous people, enriched by a
mutual commerce among themselves, possessed of a country on which nature
hath lavish'd her most valuable treasures . . . "populous and wealthy Nipon"'

(Screech, 1996: 14). At the end of the eighteenth century, Carl Peter Thunberg, pupil and successor of Linnaeus, one of the great fathers of modern science, spent 18 months in Japan. He wrote (Screech, 1996: 210): 'their doctrine chiefly inculcates the following maxims: to lead a virtuous life, to do justice to every man, to behave at the same time to all persons with civility, to govern with equality, and to maintain an inviolate integrity of heart'.

How can an Oriental culture, which, following Max Weber, is of a completely different nature compared to Occidental culture, manifest such familiarity when it comes to universal codes for civility? This was the era of European colonialism, with its precise ideas about the relationship between Europe and other parts of the world as a relationship between 'modernity' and 'tradition'. In this historical period, 'the West never invaded Japan nor blockaded it, and it never had the writ to command. Japan, consequently remained fully independent' (Screech, 1996: 1). When the country finally opened its doors to foreign influences, it was more than well prepared for modernity. What had happened in the meantime?

In this chapter, I will use the gaze of the visitor and the experience of strangeness and familiarity as keys for methodology. The experience of both strangeness *and* familiarity is my point of departure. Following Michel Foucault (Foucault, 1970), I am not adopting this approach in order to point to some kind of immaturity as if there were only a single historical continuum, but rather invoking an experience of 'similitude'. Using a term of Walter Benjamin's, we are dealing with 'a non-synchronicity or incompatibility of personal experience' (Wiegel et al., 1996). The writing 'I' is situated within a countermovement of things and time, where things that appear here in the medium of a subjective now reappear in a number of different ritual settings elsewhere in the world.

My postulate is this: the experience of the writing I is one of familiarity *and* of estrangement – of familiarity because of the universal modus of meeting the stranger with hospitality, of estrangement because culture matters. Its *universal* dimension calls for broadening the research agenda by addressing a new set of questions concerning the skills required to meet the stranger with hospitality. Where were these skills acquired? From the literature on cosmopolitan virtues (Smith, 2007), we know that this is a disposition that is place bound to a realm in between the home and work; according to Hénaff and Strong (2001: 5), 'it is theatrical, associated with sight'. This chapter's concern is with its sanctuary qualities. I am interested in the specific ritual choreography for the meeting on equal terms, 'a kind of pantomime representation of spatiality' (Isozaki, 1963; Stewart, 2002: 226). Its *cultural* dimension, on the other hand, involves history, having to do with the site in its relationship to other sites in the city, and how the relationship between these sites changes over time. It is my contention that, during the years of self-imposed isolation, the sanctuaries were refined: 'it was a result of an organisational change that acted to make a new use of a potential that had long existed' (de Vries, 2002: 97). It appears as of the same but is not completely comparable. It is a counterpart to the sanctuaries of urban virtues to be found in early modern European cities, but situated within a distinct spatial configuration in contemporary Japanese cities.

Comparative historical sociology

In Max Weber's historical sociology, there is a leading idea about a single historical continuum: *first*, there is the period of traditional unity between politics and religious morality; *then*, in reaction to the religious civil wars that swept Europe in the centuries following the Reformation, there emerges secularization defined as a rupture with the idea of the ruling powers' divine legitimacy. This set up an autonomous rationale for government that refused to subordinate the ends of the state to divine command or to a particular faith. This in turn led to the privatization of religious convictions that, *finally*, went hand in hand with the spirit of capitalism. As Robert Fine (2003) argues, 'in this story, nothing *substantial* happened for around 350 years until in our own times everything happens at once'. And Peter Wagner remarks (2009: 253–55) that Weber restricts the concept of modernity to a single and unique experience: 'Modernity can be traced in space and time but tends to transcend historical time and cover all socio-cultural space'. Wagner points to the need to rethink the concept of modernity, which involves 'a spatio-temporally contextualised use of the concept'.

I agree with Wagner (2009: 255) that 'to take the modern commitment to autonomy seriously ... requires a more open conceptualisation of the contexts of modernity'. I will suggest approaching secularization by loosening the connections between 'religion', 'modernity' and 'secularization'. I am compelled to do this by the subject matter: since Japan was completely closed during the formative years of colonialism and capitalism, Western ideas about 'religion', 'modernity' and 'secularization' were only introduced later on. In Japan, the term 'religion' is recent, and in the main is the work of Christian scholars (Fitzgerald, 2000). It has caused trouble.[3] Shinto and Buddhism do not belong to the main monotheistic religions since neither of them have a unifying father figure, and yet certain of their rituals are comparable to the rituals of a 'real' religion. This has given rise to the distinction between 'religious ritual' and 'ritual' (Reader, 1991). Nevertheless, the Tokugawa era witnessed secularization phenomena in a double sense, defined as a rupture from the idea of the divine legitimacy of the ruling powers and as the emergence of a unique modern experience.

Edo versus Paris

Noting a counterpart is the first end result of comparative studies. With good reason, Japanese studies have come adrift from the idea of Japan as an exotic reflex, an example of a strange cultural Otherness in between 'East' and 'West' (Kurasawa, 2000), as well as from studies that dehistoricize Japanese national identity, as in the *Nihonjin ron* literature, which deals with what is uniquely Japanese. Increasingly, Japan has entered the field of comparative studies with themes that converge with those of the West, 'of knowledge and commitments, contract and practices' (Najita, 1996). One example is McClain's and Merriman's *Edo and Paris: Urban Life and the State in the Early Modern Era* (1994). The juxtaposition of the two cities, Edo (modern-day Tokyo) and Paris, suggests comparisons. For one thing, they shared resistance to the political regime, and a number of the articles offer documentation of 'the ways in which ordinary people made discontinuous claims – demands, attacks, petitions, expressions of support, and so forth – on other people – including authorities' (Ikegami and Tilly, 1994: 430).

However, the articles in that volume share an unresolved theoretical problem, namely, the conceptualization of the urban societal. Against the image of an urban population as docile bodies of the Tokugawa shogunate, a number of contributions argue for the completely opposite idea, namely, the urban societal understood negatively as what the public realm is deprived of, namely, a more authentic rebellious entity. In this article, I will suggest that the urban societal of Edo should be studied from the view of the shogunate reforms, while keeping in mind the twofold nature of urban governance relations as both *limiting* and *enabling*.

Secularization

As in Europe, Japan experienced a split between religion and political power as a late outcome of two dark centuries, in which the Tokugawa family assumed power after protracted and bloody civil wars and founded their shogunate (in 1603). The latter survived for 15 generations and 'stands as the world's classic case of state making through the monopolization of violence' (Ikegami and Tilly, 1991: 436). Before Tokugawa, the religious elites 'were often organised in distinct communities, monasteries, schools and the like, they were involved in many autonomous activities – artistic, intellectual, and even educational' (Eisenstadt, 1987: 251). During the Tokugawa era, their radius of action was severely restricted and religious life thoroughly reorganized. The sword-hunting edict of 1588 was of key importance: it banned the use of arms by the commoners and relegated that privilege to the warrior class. 'The Buddhist temples and Shinto shrines that formerly had military capacities were subdued and demilitarised by the rulers' (Ikegami, 2005: 129). This paved the way for a comprehensive reconfiguration of the religious realm in its relationship with political power. But, like absolute monarchies in Europe, it struggled with serious unresolved problems of divine legitimacy. For the sake of argument, I will make a brief comparison here.

In *The King's Two Bodies*, Ernst Kantorowicz (1957) traces the historical problem posed by the 'King's two bodies' – the body politic and the body natural – back to the late Middle Ages and demonstrates how

> The king's natural body has physical attributes, suffers, and dies, naturally, as do all humans; but the king's other body, the spiritual body, transcends the earthly and serves as a symbol of his office as majesty with the divine right to rule. The notion of the two bodies allowed for the continuity of monarchy even when the monarch died, as summed up in the formulation, 'The king is dead. Long live the king'. The spiritual king's legitimacy is unquestioned; he has divine rights to rule, his political power is sanctioned by sacred divinity. (Kantorowicz, 1957: 9)

During the Renaissance and the early modern era, a sort of confusion of genres followed alongside the birth of absolutism. It witnessed what Hénaff and Strong (2001: 22) have termed 'a profound change in the theatricality of the political realm: we pass from belief to make believe ... as soon as the context weakened and power became more a matter of acquired skill rather than a matter of authority conferred by tradition, the scene became blurry'. Hénaff and Strong continue,

> Progressively all aspects of the person of the king became public; everything about him concerns all his subjects. It is this tendency that Louis XIV takes to its heights when transforming the most ordinary of his private gestures (getting up, going to bed, dining, washing) into public ritual.... This means that the legitimacy of the monarchic power is no longer assured by religious evidence, as it was previously, but must be produced by an elaborate process of persuasion and seduction. Writers, historiographers, theologians and jurists work at persuasion; seduction is the staging work of architects, painters, engravers, musicians, decorators, landscape gardeners and other collaborators in princely splendour. (Hénaff and Strong, 2002: 15)

A political theology at its birth

Does it make sense to compare the Tokugawa shogunate with the absolute monarchies of Europe? Yes and no. Unlike the political theology of European monarchies, the Tokugawa regime was founded upon a literal split between the two bodies of the king: not only in bodies but also in geography. The spiritual body (the Emperor) was settled in Kyoto, whereas the natural body (the Shogun) had its headquarters in Edo. While the double body of the monarch in France drew directly from the doctrine of the double body of Christ, the divine origin of the Shogun was more doubtful. It was not at the centre of the divine mythologies, as was the case in European monarchies:

> In Japan, the emperor divinely descended from the gods, remained as the ultimate source of secular authority. The emperor delegated public powers to the Shogun with the expectation that authority was to be exercised not in the private interest of the Shogun and warrior estate but rather in a manner that contributed to the well-being of all of the people of the realm. (McClain and Merriman, 1994: 10)

It was a neo-feudal order which 'relied on sheer military might': 'neither Buddhist nor Confucian thought could provide a concept of natural or divine law to legitimate the public character of the rulers' domination' (Ikegami, 2005: 137). As a consequence, 'Tokugawa law resembles martial law, which is interested in order more than justice' (Esenbel, 2003: 44).

The shogunate evolved a pragmatic attitude to the main religions of Buddhism and Shinto: it picked and mixed in constructing a (spectacular) political theology. The regime was embodied in an extraordinary development of the 'theatre of the shogunate', involving the use of visual imagery to construct and maintain power (Screech, 2000). The Nikko mausoleum north of Edo is an example, built to the deification of the first Shogun, Tokugawa Ieyasu. However, unlike the holy sites of Kyoto, it lacks ethereal refinement and unintentionally perhaps confirms Edo's role as *de facto* the secular capital of Japan (Okawa, 1975; Isozaki, 2006).

In the shadow of secularization

How was power legitimized in society? In European absolute monarchies, the source of the state lay in the spiritual power of the Christian society. 'Its goal is to form, among baptized people a community based on faith and charity. Its model is not the city as it was in the city–state of the ancients but the family, that is, the private realm. Its linking principle is not a public one but an inter-individual one; it is not speech but charity' (Hénaff and Strong, 2001: 13). In Tokugawa Japan too, the model was not the city but the family. The ideal family was the *ie,* the stem-family household, which retained only one child as the heir in each generation. More than a biological unit, the *ie* was a corporate entity in the sense that it embraced non-kin such as servants, adopted heirs and the latter's unmarried children.

Edo, until 1500 a small fishing village, was selected for the headquarters and reconfigured accordingly. The governing of Edo was intended to keep this system in its place; therefore, too much freedom was feared. It might breed a mercantile independence that would put the social order at risk: 'particularly noticeable was the expansion of governmental involvement in the economic life of the townsmen' (Nobuhiku, 1994: 536). However, too much regulation would also threaten the system. To the shogunate, Edo was what Brussels is today to the European Union: 'Hegemony scarcely could be maintained if the cities were not well supplied. Fear too stirred the ruler's imaginations. If dearth were to render the social compact meaningless, disorder awaited' (McClain and Merriman, 1994: 29).

Increasingly the passions and interests of a growing merchant class had to be taken into account, and along with it the principle of meeting on equal terms in the marketplace. As in early modern Europe, it created a Pandora's Box with wide implications. Increasingly, Edo's citizens became caught between two worlds, one of status order and the increasingly limited environment of the home, the other of real-time relations at a distance. The rest of this article focuses on the type of real-time relations at a distance that urban sociability gave rise to.

Edo's explosive urbanization

In Edo during the seventeenth century, within a short period of time a great many rural inhabitants turned into city dwellers. They were forced to move into this big city and literally thrown into the maelstrom of strangers. They were deprived of access to political power and left in a cultural limbo and a moral vacuum. It is difficult to imagine the speed at which Edo became a large city by, as it were, importing population, even though this might have parallels in the planned economies of our time, such as the relocation of whole sections of the population in the Republic of China. I allow myself to assume that these are phenomena *of* the great city across time and space. The city is full of strangers and 'thus in this way a new form of activity was constituted' (Durkheim [1902b] 1984: xlvi).

What type of city was this? An anti-city is the dominant argument (Ashihara, 1989; Jinnai, 1995), that is, not a real city but a strictly segregated type of medieval castle town. At its centre was the castle of the shogun, while the upper classes (feudal lords and samurai) set up their mansions on the hills around the castle; the commoners (merchants and artisans) resided on the flat, reclaimed lands towards the east, in the 'city of water'. The commoners lived in small, close-knit communities with strong inward ties of commitment, were group-oriented and linked by the rules and rituals of traditional folk religions. Essentially, people remained immature. This argument, however, neglects the fact of Edo's explosive growth. The large influx of population affected not only the physical layout of the city, but also its everyday life. In early modern Japan, 'the creative centres of urban culture began in Kyoto and Osaka but soon moved to Edo as well'. This affected the city and the process of economic growth: 'urban growth was spectacular' (Hall, 1991: 26). Of early modern Japan's three great cities, Edo was the youngest and grew the fastest (Nobuhiko, 1994: 564). Until 1457 it was a small agricultural village. By 1720 it was one of the largest cities in the world, with 1.3 million inhabitants (Cybriwsky, 1998: 60).

I would like to refer to writers who wish to emphasize the importance of the explosive urbanization of the early modern era. Jan de Vries (1984: 3–4) writes, 'The urbanism of these centuries (the early modern) often seems lost between two well-mapped urban landscapes – those of the medieval city and the industrial city. Yet, "the post-medieval pre-industrial city" was a term too awkward to endure.' These writers have engaged in presenting 'early modern urbanization as a precondition for modern industrialization, challenging the view that it was industrialization that called modern urbanization into being'. On early modern Europe, Jan de Vries contends,

> The explosive urbanisation of the nineteenth century was, thus, not so much a result of a technological revolution lifting a ceiling that had long kept the lid on urban growth as it was a result of an organisational change that acted to make a new use of a potential that had long existed. (de Vries, 2002: 97)

In paraphrasing John A. Marino (2002: xvi), the following 'aims at restoring the unexpected strangeness of medieval and early modern imagery by decoupling it from anachronistic contemporary categories'. From this perspective, the large city is of specific interest – here people are thrown on one another. The shogunate wanted to keep things under control and made Edo its headquarters, but this policy also created explosive urban growth and with this, new modes of urban encountering. The commoners did live in tightly-knit close neighbourhoods, but in between the home and the ruling order of status hierarchies, specific kinds of spaces emerged that offered the opportunity to converse freely with people of a different social level whose company one might enjoy.

The remaining part of this article traces what the Germans call *Intensitätsinseln* or 'islands of intensity' (de Vries, 2002: 86) in time and space. It detects interstitial time in the city, with inspiration from Kevin Hetherington (2007), who invokes the Greek term *kairos*. The study therefore encircles and localizes 'the time of the moment' in the city. This is spatial and non-linear time, the time of the sanctuary.

Ambiguous sanctuaries

The sanctuary is a broad and yet quite delimited concept: broad in the sense that it includes more than a religious sanctuary in the orthodox meaning of the term, and delimited because it is defined with a point of departure from the religious sanctuary. It both shares qualities with, or can be deprived of, the orthodoxy of the religious sanctuary (Greve, 2006). Within religion, the sanctuary is a place of a completely different order to the profane, indefinite space that surrounds it. It has the quality of a 'vacuum' (Richot, in Desmarais, 1995). In following Michael May (1996, 2008), a place has the quality of a vacuum when it receives meaning from the ongoing meetings and exchanges and offers the specific kind of space which makes those meetings possible. It gives it a certain ambiguity or vagueness, and in principle it can be filled with what people bring with them (Albera, 2005).

In particular, I will claim that the commoners took advantage of the infrastructure provided by the authorities to appropriate the sanctuaries for their own desires. Edo was founded on sacred principles. At the time of its foundation, 'the three great protective temples of Edo – Sensoji in Asakusa, Toeisan Kanéiji in Ueno, and Zojoji in Shiba – were situated according to Taoist precepts. By then the city precinct did not yet reach as far as the temples themselves; the idea was to surround the city with religious spaces by placing the temples on distant uplands' (Jinnai, 1995: 15). The topography of the city was based on a spiral layout, which was realized through a system of canals and moats. The three temples were at the edge of the city and only reachable by boat in a pilgrimage through the city's canal system: 'within a divided city individuals moved across, through and over these divisions using "the watery way"' (Jinnai, 1995: 98–99). Thus, 'the conversion from ordinary living space was expressed both in the actual distribution of geographical setting and in people's consciousness', supporting the idea of the journey as a spiritual phase of separation from everyday life.

Such temples at the border of Edo entered into the category of ambiguous sanctuaries, being visited and claimed by various groups, and took on different meanings for those who attended them. In service to the ruling power of the shogunate, religious action 'took primarily the form of fulfilling one's obligations in the world. Ritual, prayer or meditation, all took second place to the primary ethical obligations'. But, 'there was also a tendency to make these moral obligations ends in themselves, that is, to endow them with ultimacy and make them "religious" in their own right' (Bellah, 1957: 79). This might be interpreted as a consequence of the very nature of the sanctuaries – if we agree to consider them as places of vacuum and vagueness which can be filled with what people bring with them – and of their location in the border area, which makes the issue of local groups' boundaries more sensitive. In this respect, sanctuaries were not only characterized by their religious ambiguity, they were also places of national ambiguity, places where the ambiguity of the border area is made visible to participants. The following section takes up two phenomena for discussion in order to illustrate this: the journey (disconnecting), and the sanctuary (the play and the theatre).

The journey

From its very beginning as the headquarters of the shogunate, Edo was associated with the journey: *first*, with the sudden large influx of people; *secondly*, as a consequence of intense commuting between Edo and the provinces; and *thirdly*, due to the needs of a service city that relied on other regions' deliverables. Thus, the post stations turned into a refuge for travellers and served as informal central gathering places to sip tea, relax and discuss whatever is on your mind. In her study of the Tôkaidô road travelling, Jill Traganou (2003: 147) writes that the post stations 'figured in the public imagination as places of informality and release, where one could come into contact with the extraordinary, the sacred and the marginal'.

Edo was not only associated with the journey to and from the city: within its borders too, a pantomime version of the journey and its 'stations' was born. Edo's formal structure of canal and moats supported this, functioning as a system of social segregation and of control from above. However, the deep anthropological structure of Edo as a place of informality and social non-attachment was, writes Hidenobu Jinnai (1995), concentrated along its river. The travel to the temples on the border of the city would turn into a pilgrimage, a rite of passage, leading to a realm of a completely different order: to what has been coined the Floating World (*ukiyo*). It influenced the placement of amusement centres, theatres and the like. The people possessed a unique 'bad' space on the edge of their city where many odd things could pass unnoticed by the order of the shogunate; 'effervescent locales created by a combination of the temporary playhouses and the energetic activity of the people within and around them, they created a sense of liberation' (Jinnai, 1995: 90).

Sakariba: the 'fascination of the crowd'

Sakariba is defined by a widely used Japanese dictionary as *hito no oku yoriatsumaru basho* or *hankagai*, 'a place where many people come together' or 'a busy street' (Shinmura, 1969: 871). *Ba* is 'place' and *sakaru* means 'to prosper' or 'flourish'. The noun for *sakari*, then, is 'height', 'peak', 'prime', 'bloom' (as well as 'heat' of animals) so that a direct translation would be 'a flourishing place', 'a prospering place', or simply 'a top place'. . . . One important characteristic of the *sakariba* is that such a place always has to be crowded and noisy . . . There is music in the air, there are the *'Irasshai'* yells of welcome from the boys – and the more polite *'Irasshaimase'* greetings from the girls . . . For the sociologist Ikei this overcrowding is the main characteristic of a *sakariba*, and he speaks of *zatto no miryoku*, 'fascination of the crowd'. (Linhart, 1986)

The *sakariba* offers an opportunity to escape into the masses of the many: it is the 'fascination of the crowd' which pulls many men to the amusement quarters at night. The sociologist Nozomu Ikai (Linhart, 1986) links the definition of a 'big city' to the existence of a *sakariba*. For him,

people who go to a *sakariba* enjoy an almost religious feeling among the crowd there, comparable a traditional festival, as one of the reasons for coming to a *sakariba* is, for many men, not only to get drunk with alcohol but to do so in the company of crowds of people. A *sakariba* is intense, vibrant, thick, even overloaded with experiences. It always has to be crowded and noisy, this overcrowding is the main characteristic of a *sakariba*.

Disconnected from moral purposes, a whole world of feelings, ideas and images emerge that follow their own laws. Caught up in flows, situations, rhythms, encounters and human forces produces effects beyond individual consciousness, 'the vision of social formations which are more than the people who occupy them at any one time' (Linhart, 1986).

An opportunity to converse freely

How should these zones at the peripheries be perceived? Linhart sees the *sakariba* as a response to the pressures of urban life, a zone of evaporation, a third zone in between work and home, 'a zone of liberty' (*kaiho kukan*):

> Whereas in most European cultures the conjugal family relationship fulfils the function of offering relief from the stress which has accumulated over the day at the workplace, in Japan there typically exist two separate worlds of men and women, with the effect that the *sakariba* institution functions to refresh and revitalise the male labour force for the next working day.... When a man is visiting a modern *sakariba*, he is on a journey, and for the Japanese on a journey shame can be thrown away! (Linhart, 1986)

An alternative idea is to fill these realms with subversive potential, studying these as 'alien territories' located in the margin, like Michel Foucault's *heterotopias* (Foucault, 1986), a void betwixt and between the sacred and the profane that offers a stage for unfaithful plays with truths and norms, the magic, the carnival, the transgressive, the dangerous. From this perspective, the zones at the peripheries have the potential for a suspension of the rules of law. Tranganou (2003) offers an argument for this: the *sakariba* challenged the existing social order. This fits well with an image of the urban societal understood negatively as what the public realm is deprived of: a more authentic rebellious entity.

A third option suggests focusing on the quality of *sakariba* as sanctuaries where, exempted from the necessity of domestic labour, men meet as equals. As well as being zones of evaporation, however, they were essential for meeting on equal terms, regardless of status order and class hierarchies. The Floating World offered the opportunity to converse freely with people. Timon Schreech (1996: 22) writes, 'at root they were brothel areas, but sex could be had more easily and cheaply elsewhere'. I quote him at length:

> The Floating World was really a space where the normal strictures of living dislodged or melted away. It was a profoundly important constituent of the mentality of the Edo-period urban classes – whether the disenfranchised merchants unable to buy into power, or the frustrated samurai brought up on a cult of arms but working as paper pushers. Far more of a forbidden fruit than sex was the opportunity to converse freely with people of another social level whose company one might enjoy, to float directives on

cut and quality of dress, or to over-spend in defiance of sumptuary laws. The Floating
World was where alternatives became, for a moment, possible. (ibid.)

How were skills for meeting the stranger with hospitality acquired? From the
literature on cosmopolitan virtues, we know that hospitality is a disposition that is
place-bound to a realm located in between the home and work. In Edo's Floating
World, people were able to enjoy a relatively unsupervised personal life at zones on
the peripheries with the possibility to perform as if in a sanctuary. They were eager
to come there out of free choice, they gathered as equals, and what counted were
the skills and merits performed when meeting. They did things differently there,
meeting as equals, and acted according to a social etiquette for equal men, as if in
a theatre. But although their ways of performing were not those of mainstream
culture, there were (universal) elements in the ritual: it is my point that these
elements were as of a religion.

The time of the sanctuary

*The fantastic can form the basis for a poetic understanding of the world so that it
makes sense.*

(Dorte Mandrup Ahnfeldt-Mollerup et al., 2009: 29)

Enormous crowds usually mark Japanese festivals and holidays. The Golden Week
at the beginning of May is 'vibrant, thick, even overloaded with experiences'. It is
against this 'liveliness' that the sanctuaries stand out as focuses of action, order,
calmness and ritual: you rinse your hands, take off your shoes and enter a different
world. You have to get down on your knees in the inner room of the sanctuary,
which is built in spatial sequences so as to stimulate a basic human desire to hide,
slip away or be secretive, having private places that no one else knows about.
Behind sliding doors, the priest can dress up to become another person; in the
sanctuary, the ritual is *sui generis*.

There is permeability between the Edo sense of play and the time of the sanctuary. Bognar (1997: 44) suggests that 'the techniques of ecstasy are not limited to the
new urban environment of Japan, but can be discovered in the rituals of the many
traditional Shinto and Buddhist festivals (*matsuri*) still celebrated today'. What is
going on in the Edo sense of play? Schreech writes:

> Beyond flight from life, or lucid re-enactment of it, the Edo sense of play (*asobi*) was a full
> re-scripting of experience. Ideas and manners not formulated by government dictate
> spun at the peripheries like orbs, but with gravitational pulls of their own. Neither revo-
> lutionary nor fully accepting, these lay athwart the division between contestation and
> compensation, unable to impinge on the centre, nor yet quite distant from it. (1996: 22)

In the discourse on the postsecular city, one important observation is that immigrants tend to be more religious than they were in their home country. In this
article, I suggest focused attention on to sanctuary life. When people on the move

become attached to religious sanctuaries, they tend to overdo the rituals. Thus, while refining these, the (universal) elements in ritual and ceremonies come to the fore.

> Case studies from different places and various cultures in Europe, South Africa, the Near East and India demonstrate noticeable parallels concerning the notions of embodiment and practice. Even though these upcoming perspectives share a rather redundant vocabulary they nevertheless seem to contribute to a common ground of a phenomenology of the body, of action and perception. (Holm et al., 2007)

Paradoxically, this rigidity creates opportunities for play. As Emile Durkheim pointed out in his late studies, when the ritual is serious it offers a solid choreography for 'free play'. It opens itself up to the time of the moment, the time of theatre. 'Indeed the life thus unleashed enjoys such great independence that it sometimes plays about in forms that have no aim or utility of any kind, but only for the pleasure of affirming itself' (Durkheim [1912a] 1995: 426).

What it involves is 'a way to think about, question, explore, express, create, recreate and affirm a whole human–divine relationship'. What they dramatize 'is not just an existing society itself, but its *mythology*' – a shared set of stories and beliefs that are 'how the society represents man and the world' (Watts Miller, 2004: 96).

Conclusion

The early modern era is a somewhat neglected period in Max Weber's historical sociology. As Robert Fine argues (2003) in a passage already quoted above, it is as if 'nothing substantial happened for around 350 years until in our times everything happens at once'. From this perspective, early modern Japan is a case in point. Having been completely closed for more than 250 years at this time, it offers a unique intellectual laboratory for studying this particular era. The article has therefore argued that Japan studies should be approached by emphasizing the striking similarity with early modern Europe rather than striking 'exotic' differences from it. *First,* as in Europe, early modern Japan experienced a split between religion and political power as a late outcome of two dark centuries of civil wars, which finally led to the country's unification. This paved the way for a comprehensive reconfiguration of the religious realm in its relationship with political power. As in European absolute monarchies, Japan's shogunate was confronted with the task of constructing a myth about its divine legitimacy: it picked and mixed from Shinto and Buddhism when constructing a political theology 'to make believe'. *Secondly,* the shogunate's choice of Edo for headquarters had unintended effects: within a few decades a large urban society had come into being. Taking its point of departure in writers who point out the importance of the explosive urbanization of the early modern era, the present article has suggested that Edo be studied from this angle. The city turned into a Pandora's Box, its citizens caught between two worlds: one of status order and the increasingly limited environment of the home, the other of real-time relations at a distance. The article has focused on the type of real-time relations at a distance that have arisen with urban sociability. *Thirdly,* the commoners in Edo took advantage of the urban infrastructure provided by the authorities to open up what Germans call *Intensitätsinseln*, 'islands of intensity' in time and space, the time of the sanctuary. It is my contention that the sanctuaries were refined during the years of self-imposed isolation. Paradoxically, this rigidity made possible the time of the moment, the time of theatre, a playground for teaching people how to make a life with those who are not like themselves.

Notes

1 Anni Greve is Associate Professor of Sociology, PhD, Department of Society and Globalisation, Roskilde University, Denmark.
2 Alessandro Valignano, February 15, 1539 – January 20, 1606. For further reading, see Moran, J. F., *The Japanese and the Jesuits: Alessandro Valignano in Sixteenth-Century Japan*. London: Routledge 1993.
3 The secularization hypothesis – that religion declines in industrial urban settings – was first developed out of studies in the West based largely on 'formal' religious behaviour, as seen, for example, in church attendance figures. Japan, as an industrialized, urban state with a non-Christian religious tradition, provides an important opportunity to test the applicability or otherwise of this idea in other settings. However, there is no clear equivalent to the formal religious community or 'church' in a Durkheimian sense except among some of the newer religious groups. Shinto shrines and Buddhist temples do bring people together for communal activities when organizing and performing certain festivals once or twice a year, but they hardly constitute the 'moral community' that Durkheim calls a 'church' (Lewis, 1986: 166).

References

Ahnfeldt-Mollerup, M., Rifbjerg, S., and Keiding, M. (eds) (2009), *Portræt: Dorte Mandrup Arkitekter*. København: Arkitektens Forlag.
Albera, D. (2005), 'Pèlerinages mixtes et sanctuaires 'ambigus' en Méditerranée', in S. Chiffoleau and A. Madoeuf (eds), *Les pèlerinages au Maghreb et au Moyen-Orient: éspaces publics, espaces du public*, Beyrouth: IFPO.
Ashihara, Y. (1989), *The Hidden Order: Tokyo through the Twentieth Century*. Tokyo: Kodansha International.
Bellah, R. N. (1957), *Tokugawa Religion: The Value of Pre-industrial Japan*. Glencoe, Illinois: The Falcon's Wing Press.
Bishop, R. et al. (eds) (2003), *Postcolonial Urbanism: Southeast Asian Cities and Global Processes*. London: Routledge.
Bognar, B (1997), *World Cities: Tokyo*. London: Academy Editions.
Cybriwsky, R. (1998), *Tokyo: The Shogun's City in the Twenty-first Century*. Chichester: John Wiley & Sons.

De Vries J. (1984), *European Urbanisation, 1500–1800*. London: Methuen.

—. (2002), 'Great Expectations: Early Modern History and the Social Sciences', in J A Marino (ed.), *Early Modern History and Social Sciences: Testing the Limits of Braudel's Mediterranean*. Missouri: Truman State University Press.

Desmarais, G. (1995), 'The Sacred Place: A Morphodynamic Hypothesis for the Foundation of Human Settlement', in *Nordisk Arkitekturforskning*, 8 (4), 31–50.

Durkheim, E. (1984 [1893b/1902b]), *The Division of Labour in Society*. London: Macmillan.

—. (1995 [1912a]), *The Elementary Forms of the Religious Life*. New York: The Free Press.

Eisenstadt, S. N., and Shachar, A. (1987), *Society, Culture and Urbanization*. London: Sage.

Esenbel, S. (2003), 'The People of Tokugawa Japan: The State of the Field in Early Modern Social/Economic History', in *Early Modern Japan*, Spring, 31–87.

Fine, R. (2003), 'Taking the 'ism' Out of Cosmopolitanism: An Essay in Reconstruction', *European Journal of Social Theory* 6, 4, 451–70.

Fitzgerald, T. (2000), *The Ideology of Religious Studies*. New York: Oxford University Press.

Foucault, M. (1970), *The Order of Things: An Archaeology of the Human Sciences*. London: Tavistock.

—. (1986), 'Of Other Spaces', *Diacritics* 16 (1), 22–27.

Greve, A. (2006), 'Civic Cohesion and Sanctuaries for Coming to Terms with Modernity', *Durkheimian Studies/Etudes durkheimiennes* n.s. 12. Oxford: The British Centre for Durkheimian Studies.

Hénaff, M., and Strong, T. (2001), 'The Conditions of Public Space: Vision, Speech and Theatricality', in M. Hénaff and T. Strong (eds), *Public Space and Democracy*. Minneapolis: University of Minnesota Press.

Hetherington, K. (2007), 'The Time of the Entrepreneurial City: Museum, Heritage and Kairos'. Paper presented at Ubiquitous Media: Asian Transformations Theory, Culture & Society 25th Anniversary Conference, University of Tokyo, 13–16 July.

Holm, B (2006), Forestillingens kraft: Omkring relationen Teater og Religion, in B. Holm (ed.), *Tro på teatret: Essays om religion og teater*. København: Multivers.

Ikegami, E. (2005), *Bonds of Civility: Aesthetic Networks and the Political Origins of Japanese Culture*. New York: Cambridge University Press.

Ikegami, E., and Charles, T. (1994), 'State Formation and Contention in Japan and France', in J. McClain and J. Merriman (eds), *Edo and Paris: Urban Life and the State in the Early Modern Era*. Ithaca, NY: Cornell University Press.

Isozaki, A. (2006), *Japan-ness in Architecture*. Cambridge, MA: MIT Press.

Jinnai, H. (1995), *Tokyo: A Spatial Anthropology*. Berkeley: University of California Press.

Kantorowicz, E. H. (1957), *The King's Two Bodies: A Study in Medieval Political Theology*. Princeton, NJ: Princeton University Press.

Kurasawa, F. (1999), 'The Exotic Effect: Foucault and the Question of Cultural Alterity', in *Journal of European Studies* 2 (2), 147–65.

Lidin, O. G. (2002), *Tanegashima: The Arrival of Europe in Japan*. Copenhagen: Nordic Institute of Asian Studies, NIAS Press.

Linhart, S. (1986), 'Sakariba: Zone of 'Evaporation' Between Work and Home?' in J. Hendry and J. Webber (eds), *Interpreting Japanese Society: Anthropological Approaches*. Curdridge, Southampton: Ashford Press.

Lewis, D. (1986), '"Years of calamity": Yakudoshi Observances in a City', in J. Hendry and J. Webber (eds), *Interpreting Japanese Society: Anthropological Approaches*. Curdridge, Southampton: Ashford Press.

Marino, J. A. (ed.) (2002), *Early Modern History and Social Sciences: Testing the Limits of Braudel's Mediterranean*. Missouri: Truman Sate University Press.

May, M. (1997), 'Rum, geometri, diagram: skematisk intuition af arkitektonisk rum', in *Laboratorium for Tid & Rum, Kunst, Arkitektur Og Det Offentlige Rum*. Odense: Kunsthallen Brandts Klædefabrik.

—. (2008), 'Measurement, Diagram, Art: Reflections on the Role of the Icon in Science and Aesthetics', in M. Søndergaard and P. Weibel (eds), *Magnet: Thorbjørn Lausten: Visual Systems*. Roskilde: Kehrer Verlag.

McClain, J., and Merriman, J. (1994), 'Edo and Paris: Cities and Power', in J. Merriman and J. McClain (eds), *Edo and Paris: Urban Life and the State in the Early Modern Era*. Ithaca, NY: Cornell University Press.

Moran, J. F. (1993), *The Japanese and the Jesuits: Alessandro Valignano in Sixteenth-Century Japan*. London: Routledge.

Najita, T. (1996), 'Traditional Co-operatives in Modern Japan: Rethinking Alternatives to Cosmopolitanism and Nativism', in Cynthia de Alcantara (ed.), *Social Futures, Global Visions*. Oxford: Blackwell.

Nobuhiku, N. (1994), 'Commercial Change and Urban Growth in Early Modern Japan', in Hall, John Whitney (ed.), *The Cambridge History of Japan, Volume 4: Early Modern Japan*. Cambridge: Cambridge University Press.

Okawa, N. (1975), *Edo Architecture: Katsura and Nikko*. New York: John Weatherhill.

Reader, I. (1991), *Religion in Contemporary Japan*. Basingstoke: Macmillan.

Screech, T. (1996), *The Western Scientific Gaze and Popular Imagery in Late Edo Japan: The Lens Within the Heart*. New York: Cambridge University Press.

—. (2000), *The Shogun's Painted Culture: Fear and Creativity in the Japanese State, 1760–1829*. London: Reaktion Books Ltd.

Shelton, B. (1999), *Learning from the Japanese City*. London: E&FN Spon.

Smith, W. (2007), 'Cosmopolitan Citizenship: Virtue, Irony and Worldliness', *European Journal of Social Theory* 10, 37–52.

Stewart, D. (2002), *The Making of a Modern Japanese Architecture: From the Founders to Shinohara and Isozaki*. New York: Kodunsha International.

Traganou J. (2003), *The Tôkaidô Road Travelling and Representation in Edo and Meiji Japan*. London: Routledge.

Wagner, P. (2009), 'Modernity as Experience and as Interpretation: Towards Something Like a Cultural Turn in the Sociology of "Modern Society"', in P. Hedström et al. (eds), *Frontiers of Sociology*. Leiden: Brill.

Watts Miller, W. (2004), 'Total Aesthetics. Art and *The Elemental Forms*', *Durkheimian Studies/Etudes durkheimiennes*, n.s.10: 88–118.

Weber, M. (2002 [1906]), *The Protestant Ethic and The Spirit of Capitalism*. London: Penguin.

Wiegel, S., et al. (1996), *Body and Image-Space: Re-Reading Walter Benjamin*. London: Routledge.

9 From Race to Religion: Multiculturalism and Contested Urban Space

John Eade

Introduction: the secular state and religious pluralism

There is a danger that the current debate about postsecularism in Britain and other Western European countries focuses on too short a historical perspective, *viz.* the period after the Second World War. Such a narrow focus encourages an overemphasis on the secular welfare states developed after 1945 and the ways in which secular welfarism became the dominant political and cultural narrative. Global migration has led to the rapid expansion of religious pluralism across Western Europe linked to the development of multicultural societies, despite the recent reaction against multicultural policies and talk of 'post-multiculturalism'. However, the emergence of religious pluralism precedes these global flows of people, ideas and images. Developments during the nineteenth and the first half of the twentieth century established public discourses and institutional practices, which have informed more recent changes highlighted by the postsecular debate. Since most of the global flows have involved Western cities, any discussion of the 'postsecular city' must look beyond the post-war secular welfare state to these earlier developments.

Although I have referred initially to Western Europe and Britain, this chapter will support my claim about the need to look beyond recent developments by focusing on the dominant nation within Britain's four nations – England – and the national capital, London. During the nineteenth century the key change was the government's transition from a defender of the established church's privileges to an increasingly neutral referee – at least in terms of law and formal practices – in the struggles between the Church of England and Nonconformist institutions. A religious pluralism was created where the Church of England became more and more one denomination among others rather than a dominant church (see Bruce, 1996). Yet the Church of England still acted as *primus inter pares* given its importance within national and monarchical rituals, institutional privileges such as episcopal representation in the House of Lords and close association with political, military and educational elites (see Hobsbawm and Ranger, 1992; Davie, 2000). Government also encouraged religious pluralism through the gradual elimination of historic discrimination against those beyond the bounds of Protestant traditions. Catholic and Jewish emancipation was pushed through Parliament in 1829 and 1835 respectively despite considerable opposition, and the Catholic hierarchy was formally recognized in the 1850s.

Jews and Catholics continued to encounter discrimination and prejudice in everyday life, and hostility was often most overtly expressed towards large settlements of Jews and Catholics in poor urban neighbourhoods. However, during the first half of the twentieth century, conflicts over religious issues weakened considerably. In terms of institutions and formal practice Jews and Catholics developed a denominational character similar to the Protestant churches where members of a central organization – the Board of Jewish Deputies and the Roman Catholic bishops – represented what they considered to be the interests of their particular 'community'. As local government expanded during the first half of the twentieth century, so the process of dealing with the interests of religious denominations, such as the building of churches, synagogues, schools and hospitals was devolved from central government to the local level. Local resistance to applications by religious 'outsiders' to alter the local landscape through the erection of prominent public buildings was channelled into the due process of formal planning procedures implemented by local officials, who were supposed to be free from religious bias.

The changing relationship between racial, secular and religious issues in post-1945 Britain

The arrival of labour migrants from the (former) colonies from the late 1940s moved debates concerning difference, discrimination and inequality away from religion towards race. This shift was reflected in the political and media debates which led to an emphasis on 'race relations' and the Race Relations Acts of 1965, 1968 and 1976, as well as the establishment of the Commission for Racial Equality. Academic research took up the theme in a vast outpouring of scholarship with such titles as *Race Relations* (Banton, 1967), *Race, Community and Conflict* (Rex and Moore, 1967), *The Empire Strikes Back: Race and Racism in 70s Britain* (CCCS, 1982), *The Local Politics of Race* (Ben Tovim et al., 1986) and so on.

This discussion of race focused primarily on secular issues – how was racial discrimination reflected in access to material resources such as jobs, housing, education, health and welfare services and amenities. Struggle was coordinated through an appeal to a 'black' community of resistance where ethnic differences based on religion, language or country of origin were acknowledged but secondary in terms of this particular struggle for equality.

Yet even during this period where 'race' was the prime consideration, the issue of religious solidarities and engagement found a voice. In 1985, *Faith in the City: A Call to Action by Church and Nation* highlighted the challenge faced by the

Church of England in 'inner city' areas and impoverished suburban council estates. Settled black and minority ethnic (BME) groups were also turning towards the issue of what permanent social and cultural institutions they should establish. A visible religious presence was established through the building of mosques, temples and churches or taking over redundant religious and secular buildings. Religious provision was also pursued in public sector arenas (schools and hospitals). This process was encouraged by transnational ties and the global flow of money, information and ideas. Religion as a contested field was also dramatically demonstrated in *The Satanic Verses* controversy of the late 1980s and Britain's involvement in the first 'Gulf war' of 1991.[1]

Religion and public space in British cities

As we have already seen, government extended its influence during the twentieth century through the growth of local government, whose impact was most visible in Britain's urban centres. Borough councils and metropolitan institutions were developed to administer the provision of public services, particularly housing, schools, welfare and amenities. In the poorer areas of Britain's cities, slum clearance programmes demonstrated most vividly the attempt by local government to improve the material conditions of its residents. A wide range of planning laws and procedures was generated, and planning departments at local government level acquired extensive powers, especially in the rebuilding of urban centres and the development of 'New Towns' after the Second World War.

The nineteenth- and twentieth-century expansion of Catholic churches and cathedrals, Nonconformist chapels and Jewish synagogues showed the ways in which religious denominations were able to publicly announce their presence. The appearance of these minority public places attracted considerable hostility during the eighteenth and nineteenth centuries – the Gordon Riots in 1780 were the most notorious instance of attacks on Catholic chapels in London. However, hostility became sporadic and highly localized during the nineteenth century. Furthermore, minority groups were not the only ones to attract hostility since evangelical Anglicans campaigned against High Church buildings in certain urban localities. As Nonconformists, Catholics and Jews began to spread out into the suburbs during the twentieth century, they built chapels, churches and synagogues without significant protest. By the end of the Second World War religious minorities were no longer associated primarily with poor, 'inner city' neighbourhoods.

The appearance of purpose-built mosques, madrassahs, temples and gurdwaras from the 1970s has followed, therefore, a well-trodden path. The usual pattern has been to move out from obscure beginnings in residential accommodation and community centres into larger buildings which were no longer in use, such as former churches, chapels, synagogues, cinemas, warehouses or pubs. Since these buildings had already been in public use planning, permission was relatively easy to obtain. Opposition usually emerged, however, when minority groups sought to redevelop a large site and erect a highly visible structure.

Sacralizing urban space and religious minorities:
disputes concerning mosques

The most extensive research on the emergence of minority places of worship
and the process of negotiating with local authorities has been undertaken by
Richard Gale (1999, 2004) and his collaborators (Gale and Naylor, 2002; Peach
and Gale, 2003).[2] While Gale has focused on cities outside London, particularly
Birmingham, this chapter will concentrate on the national capital and disputes
surrounding large-scale projects in particular. Furthermore, a comparison will be
undertaken across space and time by looking at different disputes involving large-
scale, purpose-built projects across London during the last 15 years.

London has long been Britain's largest city in terms of population and geographical spread. By mid-2007, London's population had grown to approximately
7.5 million[3] extending across 32 boroughs. The city's political structure was far
more complicated than other cities since although each borough plays a key role
in planning, the Greater London Council and, since 2000, the Greater London
Authority has been responsible for implementing an overall plan for the metropolis in the areas of economic development, transport and environmental and
social affairs. London has also enjoyed the status of a national capital and a major
international/global city. Furthermore, its economy has been far less reliant on
industrial production than other large cities such as Birmingham, Manchester and
Glasgow, and its historically large service sector has increased in importance
through the city's extensive global connections.

London has also been a prime destination for migrants and the 2001 Census
noted that the metropolis contained 'the highest proportion of people from minority ethnic groups' in the country[4], as well as 'the highest proportion of Muslims
(8.5 per cent), Hindus (4.1 per cent) Jews (2.1 per cent) Buddhists (0.8 per cent)
and people of other religions (0.5 per cent)'.[5] As migration has changed from
those coming – primarily former British colonies to asylum seekers, refugees and
migrant workers from central and Eastern Europe, so the ethnic composition of
London's boroughs has become even more diverse (see Vertovec, 2007).

To give some insight into the complex interweaving of political and cultural
processes that has shaped the development of new religious spaces across London,
four controversies during the last 15 years will be described here.

The first was located not far from London's largest airport, Heathrow. It involved
a very small group of Shias, Dawoodi Bohras[6], who had used a former youth
club in Southall in West London but decided to move after local protests about
parking, traffic congestion and noisy celebrations. After the Labour Party won the
local elections in 1986, the council offered to buy their current site in exchange for
a new site, and the Bohras decided to move to an industrial site a few miles north
in Northolt. Their application to build a large centre which included accommodation and prayer facilities met with the same protests about traffic congestion and
parking, as well as the change of use in an area designated for industry. After the
Bohras received planning permission to develop the site against fierce opposition
and rowdy public meetings, a sharper edge was given to the dispute. The local

newspaper reported that some local residents had opposed the development on
the grounds that

> Northolt is a 'garden suburb' and should not become another Southall. This is an alien
> development – an Islamic ghetto – and will lead to a racial imbalance. Integration, not
> separation, is required.[7]

Despite these objections the application was successful and like so many controversies involving new religious buildings over the centuries, the bitter feelings
swirling round this development have faded away. Those looking towards the
distant Dawoodi centre as they drove along the highway leading to and from the
M40 would have no inkling of the building's turbulent beginnings. Moreover, as in
Birmingham (see Gale, 2004), the local councillors and officials eventually adopted
a positive attitude towards the application. The development was also significant
economically since it showed that London boroughs were ready to welcome other
types of investment besides manufacturing.

The next three cases are located in London's 'East End'. The first of these cases
involved the building of the East London Mosque on a major thoroughfare in
Tower Hamlets. The mosque had been established in the 1940s and had occupied
two large buildings for decades. During the early 1980s planning permission was
secured from the Labour-led council to build an imposing mosque with a dome
and two minarets as well as facilities for a school and burials. The main point of
controversy was the application to increase the call to prayers from twice a day to
five. Opposition raised the usual issue of noise, but other factors were at play such
as hostility to 'alien' customs. The debate in the local newspaper led to comparisons
between Muslim and Christian calls to prayer with one contributor responding
thus to a mosque representative's reference to local church bells:

> What church bells? You hardly hear them these days. I would sooner listen to the
> tolling of church bells than someone screaming out words I cannot understand and don't
> want to.[8]

Local Anglican clergy, however, wrote in support of the *azan* – if not the increase
in its frequency:

> We have no complaint against their 'calls to prayer' and given all the other sounds of
> traffic, sirens, bells, people, trains and life in general [we] think that two short periods
> each day . . . are entirely reasonable.[9]

The mosque was successful in its application, and the special status it enjoyed was
further confirmed by its eventual acquisition of a neighbouring parking lot and
erection of the London Muslim Centre with flats and improved meeting facilities.
One of the members of the mosque's management committee, Dr Bari, also became
the chairman of the government-supported Muslim Council of Britain, and its
offices moved to new premises nearby. Unlike the Northolt development, the East

London Mosque was built in the heart of the Bangladeshi Muslim community, and the borough council was increasingly sensitive to Muslim needs despite factional disputes among Bangladeshi Labour councillors and local activists over this particular mosque's expansion and influence.

The third case proved to be far more complex.[10] It began in 2002 when a Muslim missionary group, the Tabligh Jamaat (hereafter referred to as TJ)[11] sought to develop its premises next to the 2012 Olympics site in Newham, a Labour Party stronghold and Tower Hamlets' eastern neighbour. Despite the apolitical stance the TJ formally adopted, the application ensured that they would become embroiled in the process of public meetings and negotiations with officials where they would be subject to the glare of political, media and residential opinion.

The initial proposal envisaged a large-scale development and was quickly dubbed by its opponents as the 'mega-mosque'. The plan was criticized for not only being far too large but also challenging the traditional hegemony which the Established Church had enjoyed:

> The scheme for the mosque, drawn up by the award-winning architects, MYAA, envisages a complex containing an Islamic garden, school and prayer space for as many as 70,000 worshippers — 23 times greater than the capacity of Liverpool cathedral, Britain's largest Christian place of worship.[12]

Local politicians were also quick to exploit fears aroused in the aftermath of 9/11 and 7/7 concerning the radicalization of young Muslims. A local councillor, who was a member of the Christian People's Alliance, used various media including the internet and the local newspaper to call for an independent enquiry by the government. He sought to link this local case to more global struggles by calling for a ban on the 'mega-mosque' in an email to the Center for Vigilant Freedom based in Washington. This group reported his objections in the following way:

> "Tablighi Jamaat radicalises and dehumanises Muslim young men," said Alan Craig. "They have a growing and ominous track record as further young men follow Tabligh teaching about Islam and then go on to plan horrendous atrocities . . . The dangerous truth about Tablighi Jamaat is coming out. We must watch the gap between what they say and what they do," said Cllr Craig, leader of the Christian Peoples Alliance group on Newham Council, who lives with his young family a mile from the mosque site. "It will be a horrendous security nightmare if they are allowed to build this large mosque so close to the Olympics." . . . Tablighi Jamaat is large, powerful, ambitious, secretive and apparently well-funded . . . They have deliberately stayed below the radar screen for too long. They must be now fully investigated by the government. And they must be banned from building their mega-mosque."[13]

The discourse concerning fundamentalism and exclusion had a direct impact on spatial practice, in other words. Yet, behind the public furore there existed another discourse and set of practices bound up with the planning process. Although political opposition to the mosque plan clearly impacted on the planning application, the Tabligh Jamaat could still achieve their aims as they learned how to play the game. An insight into the key considerations from a planning perspective was provided by a report produced for the local council by its Environmental Management Services department (made public, significantly, by a TJ website).

The report outlined the history of the site and the changes which had taken place since it was bought by the TJ. The focus was, not surprisingly, on the ways in which it had sought to comply not only with planning procedures, building regulations and local development plans but with such environmental issues as highway and pedestrian access, transport and parking and site contamination. However, it also revealed that the Tabligh's leaders had been very slow to learn the rules of the planning game. For example, a council document explained that when they submitted a planning application in 2001:

> Despite the earlier informatives, a Transport Assessment and a Contamination Report did not accompany the application. The agent was continually reminded of need to submit this additional information by both letters, emails and at the scheduled monthly meetings that occurred as part of the memorandum of Agreement. The Council's Transport Consultants offered their assistance by providing a scoping report of exactly what was required. Eventually, a traffic count was submitted but this failed to provide any analytical work, or provide information on existing traffic flows, junctions, parking levels, and also implications for the wider public transport network. As such, there was insufficient information for officers to fully consider the application.[14]

Even though the application was not approved, building works on the site still continued. When council officers met TJ representatives at the site, it was explained that 'certain younger members of the Trust [had become] impatient with the delays in dealing with the planning application, and had taken it upon themselves to proceed with the development'.[15] Although assurances were made that no more work would proceed, the officers returned a week later to find that 'further works had commenced and the extension had now almost been completed'.[16]

Clearly, the failure to abide by the rules of the planning game played into the hands of those who accused the TJ of not being open and trustworthy. However, council officers and political leaders continued to support the redevelopment as long as it complied with the formal procedures. As the planning report noted, if the site's owners 'make an application, do the opening work, and corrects (*sic*) any contraventions found there is nothing more that can be done under the Building Regulations. The Regulations are not designed to stop people building'.[17]

Furthermore, when in November 2008 Alan Craig asked the council to reclaim the site though a Compulsory Purchase Order, the leader of the council replied that

> The Trust have advised that they are currently preparing another application so that they can continue using the site for a further temporary period. . . . Development of the area will have to be resident-friendly and the facilities must serve everyone in the local community. There is currently no evidence that the Trust will not do [this] and therefore we are unable to CPO the site until they submit their masterplan for the site.[18]

Yet by September 2009 the TJ's attempt to develop the site was running out of steam. Newham and two other local authorities involved in redeveloping the Olympic area and its environs refused to let the dispute drag on and they had given the TJ the final deadline of January 2010 to come up with the Masterplan. A hostile website gleefully reported the council's response to a question raised by Alan Craig:

> The Trust maintained that the delays were largely due to funding problems coupled with a number of sweeping changes in their consultant team tasked with preparing the proposals.... Officers have sought to persuade the Trust to progress the Masterplan but to no avail and consequently my officers wrote to the Trust on the 20th July 2009, advising them that unless the Masterplan proposals are submitted by January 2010, the Council will consider enforcement proceedings to secure cessation of the current unauthorised use of the site.... The Trust also formally engaged with us, the LTGDC and ODA under our planning pre-application process in May 2009, to explore the possibility for applying for a new temporary planning consent for the existing use. All 3 Authorities have formally advised that any new application would unlikely to be successful because of conflict with longer term regeneration objectives.[19]

On 18 January 2010 *The Times* reported that the TJ faced eviction after the council had 'issued enforcement notices against the trust' since the Masterplan had still not been submitted.[20] According to the Islamophobia Watch website, the Muslim architect who had worked on the first proposal that had eventually been dropped by the TJ, claimed that '[a] lot of the people who are opposing the scheme have questionable motives ... There's Islamophobia'.[21] He was also reported as saying:

> I'm not surprised by what's happened . . . There was no one to manage the project. A sensitive and complex site requires quite a sophisticated approach. Tablighi Jamaat need to be a lot better organised. They need someone sophisticated to appreciate the design process and engage with the council and opponents.[22]

As with the two previous mosque developments, a Labour-led council had been largely supportive. The project reflected once more the economic and cultural changes taking place across London as a former industrial site provided the opportunity for a prestigious redevelopment by a religious minority. However, the application had been hampered by concerted external opposition, internal tensions and inexperience. The task was made even more difficult by its proximity to an Olympics site which was exposed to the full glare of metropolitan, national and global attention. The race to get ready for 2012 had raised the stakes even higher for the successful completion of the mosque development.

Sacralizing urban space and religious minorities: disputes concerning new churches

It must be borne in mind that controversy did not just surround plans involving mosques and madrassahs. Local resistance to large-scale projects proposed by other minorities – Hindus and Christian – also sometimes emerged and we turn now to an application to build a 'mega-church' by the Kingsway International Christian Centre (KICC). The KICC is the fastest growing Pentecostalist denomination supported predominantly by those with origins in Africa and the Caribbean. Its growing financial power linked to the increasing numbers of worshippers had already been noted in a *Daily Telegraph* report on the KICC's use of a former cinema in Walthamstow:

> [KICC] has assets of £22.9 million, which is three times the amount held by the foundation that maintains St Paul's Cathedral in central London. . . . Evangelical Pentecostalism is believed to be the only growing branch of Christianity in the UK with an estimated 300,000 worshippers . . . Four KICC directors also earn more than £80,000 a year, in contrast to a typical Church of England vicar who earns a salary of around £21,500.

Once again its fortunes had been affected by the Olympic site development since it was required to move from its Hackney premises in September 2008. *The Sunday Times* on 29 October 2006 ran a story on the plan to move to an industrial site further east in Havering borough under the headline – 'London to get £35m mega-church':

> Pastor Matthew Ashimolowo has commissioned architects to design Britain's first US-style "mega-church" with an amphitheatre and television studio. The 8,000-seat capacity of the £35m building, on a disused industrial site in Rainham, east London, will dwarf Liverpool Cathedral, the country's largest Anglican church, which can seat 3,000. . . . It is modelled on arena-style evangelical churches spreading across the American Bible Belt, which have a capacity for up to 18,000 worshippers.

Once more an implicitly invidious comparison was established between a new religious minority and the Established Church and Liverpool Cathedral was again brought into the picture. The article chose to emphasize the financial aspects of the development in ways that would further antagonize its readers:

> The building is partly funded by an estimated £13.5m windfall from taxpayers to compensate the church for having to make way from its present site, an East London factory, for the 2012 Olympics. The London Development Agency says it bought the site at the market price . . . Ashimolowo's Kingsway International Christian Centre (KICC) teaches a controversial "health and wealth" version of Christianity. It tells its followers, largely of African origin and living in deprived areas, that God wants people to be rich and healthy.[23]

The grandiose plans of this minority were being supported by the general taxpayer and more financially impoverished KICC members. The implication that the church's leaders were exploiting others was strengthened in the following paragraph where the financial improprieties of its pastor were rehearsed:

> In 2002 the charity which operated the KICC was found to have made payments of almost £1m "in breach of trust" to companies owned by Ashimolowo. The Charity Commission found "serious misconduct" and seized control after the church spent £120,000 celebrating

Ashimolowo's birthday, including the gift of an £80,000 car. It found Ashimolowo had used the church's Visa card to buy a £13,000 timeshare apartment in Florida and enjoyed free accommodation for him and his family, and that payments were made directly from congregational collections before they were banked.... After the inquiry, Ashimolowo was ordered to repay £200,000. A new charity with fresh trustees has since been established.

The proposal was turned down on familiar grounds:

Councillors unanimously objected to the [proposal] ... due to the inadequacy of local transport facilities and ... the development would conflict with the strategic employment policy for the area and that the site would be a poor location for a use of the scale and nature proposed.[24]

During the internet debate, which surrounded the report on the planning refusal on *The Guardian* website, other themes were rehearsed:

It's a bizarre turn of events. Britain is a Christian country and yet we allow Mosques to go up in the name of multi-culturalism, yet a church is denied permission.... Had it been a business park, a factory, a cinema or even a nightclub I imagine the outcome would have been somewhat different.[25]

The issue of jobs, which was raised in the councillors' objections to the proposal, was linked in another email to the issue of American grandiosity:

Contrary to some people's beliefs, had this been an application for a cinema or a night-club, it would also have been turned down! This land was bought with public money to create jobs. The KICC offered 75 jobs (all of which were already filled by people living in Hackney) so offered residents precisely nothing. ... Rainham residents adore our area, welcome regeneration, and believe we could be sitting in the future docklands! But no part of that involves a giant church of American proportions as we are not America! We are happy for the KICC to have small churches the way every other religion has. The giant church the KICC propose is a Want not a NEED.[26]

Conclusion

This chapter has sought to place the issue of postsecularism and the postsecular city in historical perspective. Postsecularism is not a recent phenomenon, and contemporary issues concerning the development of religious sites in London and other British cities bear uncanny resemblances to nineteenth-century disputes, even if the focus has shifted away from Catholic and Jewish newcomers towards Muslims, black Christians and others contributing to an increasing urban multi-cultural diversity. In both the past and the present, while disputes may be intense, the fears and hostilities have usually died away, and the new buildings have become accepted as part of the locality. As in Birmingham, local politicians and planners have gradually come to welcome new religious sites as a reflection of the changing economic and cultural environment of their localities.[27]

What is novel, however, is the way in which local disputes are now globalized through the rapid, virtual flow of information. The development of mosques, in particular, has become even more controversial since 9/11 so that local disputes have more easily become part of global controversies. Furthermore, London's position as both a large global city and a highly multicultural national capital makes disputes here more globally important than those in Birmingham and elsewhere. Winning the 2012 Olympics nomination has strengthened London's global position even more, of course, and this played a key role in the dispute over the Tabligh Jamaat's development plans. Yet, as the KICC case showed, proposals to build churches could also face concerted local opposition if they were on a grand scale and involved a racial minority. Here again the Olympics site complicated the KICC's plans since it forced them to move further east and into a more hostile locality.

The disputes outlined here reveal the usual secular issues bound up with state institutions – the need by the developers to learn the rules of the planning game and the concerns shared by politicians, planners and residents concerning traffic, noise, parking and jobs. However, what is more interesting is the symbolism on which opponents to the proposals drew. The symbols frequently established a link between local religious space and the Established Church. In other words, the Anglican Church still retains a dominant position symbolically in the public imagination and new religious groups are understood in relation to that church.

Although central and local governments have tried to act impartially through secular procedures, for some 'ordinary' members of the white majority at least, the real issue was the threat posed by religious, racialized minorities to traditional symbols. The grand schemes devised by Muslim groups in Northolt and Newham and by Pentecostalists in Havering were seen as out of place and out of scale. Both the TJ mosque and the KICC church threatened to eclipse the Anglican Church's largest cathedral, while the call to prayer from the East London Mosque symbolized the eclipse of church bells and the presence of an 'alien' religion.

The controversies discussed here also confirm the increasingly important role played by religious place making in the ethnic and racial dynamics of contemporary British cities noted by other scholars. However, if we set this place making within a wider historical perspective the debate about the postsecular city may actually reflect a growing awareness of the continuities with nineteenth- and early twentieth-century urban society as the hegemony of the post–Second World War secular welfare state declines.

Of course, state officials, such as planning officers, still play an important role in the process of religious place making. Yet they operate within a more crowded arena shaped, in part, by the wide range of new religious groups produced through global migration. Local authorities are eager to engage with these groups and the resources they generate through their global networks as local economies de-industrialize, the reliance on the service sector increases and welfare state functions are privatized. As we have seen, local resistance to the grand schemes proposed by minority religious organizations can be highly effective, but the rapid rise to prominence enjoyed by the East London Mosque shows how much can be achieved if the conditions are right – good internal organization, strong links with local politicians and planners and a large local religious constituency.

Notes

1 See the papers produced by the AHRC Writing British Asian Cities project, especially the paper by S. McLoughlin and J. Zavos, 'Writing religion in Br-Asian diasporas', www.leeds.ac.uk/writingbritishasiancities.

2 The political and cultural processes bound up with the development of mosques and other religious buildings by immigrant groups has attracted increasing attention among social scientists working across the world. For Britain see, for example, Hodgins (1981), Vertovec (1992), Metcalf (1996), Peach (2000), Nye (2001), Naylor and Ryan (2002, 2003), Nesbitt (2006), David (2009) and Garbin (2008, 2009); and in other countries, see Cesari and McLoughlin (2005), Kong (1993), Dunn (2001), Isin and Siemiatycki (2002) and Sunier (2005).

3 www.london.gov.uk/shaping-london/london-plan/docs/chapter1.pdf.

4 www.statistics.gov.uk/census2001/profiles/commentaries/ethnicity.asp (Accessed 12/8/2010).

5 Ibid.

6 The Bohras are a Shia sect with a long-established presence in India and their leader, Muhammad Burhanuddin, is based in Mumbai. They have also established an extensive global network, especially across the Middle East, the Gulf, W. Europe and N. America, through their traditional trading expertise and service sector skills.

7 *Ealing Gazette*, 25/11/1988, quoted in Eade (1996).

8 *East London Advertiser*, 25/4/1986, quoted in Eade (1996).

9 Ibid.

10 The discussion of this third case largely uses text from two papers I have written already for an edited volume on the 'fundamentalist city' and the *Journal for Town and City Management*, which will be published during 2010.

11 The TJ emerged in the N. India during the 1920s and focuses on undertaking a mission (*dawah*) among Sunni Muslims through spiritual renewal. Like the Dawoodi Bohras, the TJ has an extensive global network, and its British headquarters was established in Dewsbury in 1978. The TJ also took over a former synagogue in Tower Hamlets called the Markazi Masjid, where I attended a prayer meeting during the 1980s.

12 Sean O'Neill, 'Muslims oppose vast mosque plan', *The Times Online*, November 27, 2006, http://www.timesonline.co.uk/tol/news/uk/article651161.ece (Accessed 12/8/2010).

13 Alwaysonwatch, 9 July 2007, 'Olympics Mega-Mosque Linked To Recent UK Bomb Plots', http://alwaysonwatch2.blogspot.com/search?q=mega+mosque,(Accessed 12/8/2010).

14 Newham Borough Council, 5/7/2002, 'Retention and expansion of extensions to temporary mosque', Application No. P/01/1375, available at: http://megamosquenothanks.com/ (Accessed 12/8/2010).

15 Ibid.

16 Ibid.

17   Ibid.
18   T. Cohen, 'Application for London mega-mosque can go ahead', 2 November
     2008, *Religious Intelligence News*, www.religiousintelligence.com/tag/news/
     (accessed 27/6/2009).

References

Banton, M. (1967), *Race Relations*. London: Tavistock.

Ben Tovim, G. et al. (1986), *The Local Politics of Race*. Basingstoke: Macmillan.

Bruce, S. (1996). *Religion in the Modern World: From Cathedrals to Cults*. Oxford:
     Oxford University Press.

CCCS (1982), *The Empire Strikes Back: Race and Racism in 70s Britain*. London:
     Hutchinson.

Davie, G. (2000), *Religion in Modern Europe: A Memory Mutates*. Oxford: Oxford
     University Press.

Cesari, J. (2005), 'Mosque conflicts in European cities: Introduction', *Journal of
     Ethnic and Migration Studies*, 31 (6), 1015–24.

Cesari, J., and S. McLoughlin (eds) (2005), *European Muslims and the Secular State*.
     Aldershot: Ashgate.

David, A. (2009) 'Performing for the Gods? Dance and Embodied Ritual in British
     Hindu Temples', *Journal of South Asian Popular Culture*, 7 (3), 217–31.

Dunn, K. (2001), 'Representations of Islam in the Politics of Mosque Development
     in Sydney', *Tijdschrift voor Economische en Sociale Geografie* 92, 3, 291–308.

Eade, J. (1996), 'Nationalism, Community and the Islamization of Space in
     London', in B. Metcalf (ed), *Making Muslim Space in North America and Europe*.
     Berkeley: University of California Press.

—. (2010), 'Debating Fundamentalisms in the Global City: Christian and Muslim
     Migrants in London', in N. Alsayyad and M. Massoumi, *The Fundamentalist
     City*. New York: Routledge.

Isin, E. F., and Siemiatycki, M. (2002), 'Making Space for Mosques – Struggles for
     Urban Citizenship in Diasporic Toronto', in S. H. Razack (ed), *Race, Space and
     Law: Un-mapping and White Settler Society*. Toronto: Between the Lines Press.

Gale, R. (1999), 'Pride of Place and Places: South Asian Religious Groups and the
     City Planning Authority in Leicester', Papers in Planning Research, 172.
     Cardiff: Cardiff University Department of City and Regional Planning.

—. (2004), 'The Multicultural City and the Politics of Religious Architecture:
     Urban Planning, Mosques and Meaning-making in Birmingham, UK', *Built
     Environment* 30 (1), 18–32.

Gale, R., and Naylor, S. (2002), 'Religion, Planning and the City: The Spatial Politics
     of Ethnic Minority Expression in British Cities and Towns', *Ethnicities* 2 (3),
     387–409.

Garbin, D. (2009), 'Symbolic Geographies of the Sacred: Diasporic Territorialisa-
     tion and Charismatic Power in a Transnational Congolese Prophetic Church',
     in Hüwelmeier, G., and K. Krause (eds), *Travelling Spirits: Migrants, Markets
     and Moralities*. London: Routledge.

—. (2008), 'A Diasporic Sense of Place: Dynamics of Spatialization and Transnational Political Fields among Bangladeshi Muslims in Britain', in M. P. Smith and J. Eade (eds), *Transnational Ties: Cities, Identities, and Migrations.* New Brunswick and London: Transaction Publishers.

Hobsbawm, E., and Ranger, T. (eds) (1992), *The Invention of Tradition.* Cambridge: Cambridge University Press.

Hodgins, H. (1981), 'Planning Permission for Mosques: The Birmingham Experience', *Research Papers – Muslims in Europe* 9, 11–27.

Kong, L. (1993), 'Ideological Hegemony and the Political Symbolism of Religious Buildings in Singapore', *Environment and Planning D: Society and Space* 11, 23–45.

Metcalf, B. (ed) (1996), *Making Muslim Space in North America and Europe.* Berkeley: University of California Press.

Naylor, S., and Ryan, J. (2002), 'The Mosque in the Suburbs: Negotiating Religion and Ethnicity in South London', *Social and Cultural Geography Journal* 3, 39–59.

—. (2003), 'Mosques, Temples and Gurdwaras: New Sites of Religion in 20th Century Britain', in D. Gilbert, D. Matless and B. Short (eds) *Geographies of British Modernity: Space and Society in the Twentieth Century.* Oxford: Blackwell.

Nesbitt, E. (2006), 'Locating British Hindus' Sacred Space'. University of Warwick Institutional Repository, http://go.warwick.ac.uk/wrap (accessed December 18, 2010).

Nye, M. (2001), *Multiculturalism and Minority Religions in Britain – Krishna Consciousness, Religious Freedom and the Politics of Location.* Richmond, Surrey: Curzon Press.

Peach, C. (2000), 'The Cultural Landscape of South Asian Religion in English Cities', Oxford Conference on New Landscapes of Religion in the West, School of Geography, September.

Peach, C., and R. Gale (2003), 'Muslims, Hindus and Sikhs in the New Religious Landscape of England', *The Geographical Review* 93 (4), 469–90.

Rex, J., and R. Moore (1969), *Race, Community and Conflict.* London: OUP.

Sunier, T. (2005), 'Interests, Identities and the Public Sphere: Representing Islam in the Netherlands since the 1980s', in J. Cesari and S. McLoughlin (eds), *European Muslims and the Secular State.* Aldershot: Ashgate.

Vertovec, S. (1992), 'Community and Congregation in London Hindu Temples: Divergent Trends', *New Community,* 18 (2), 251–64.

—. (2007), 'Super-Diversity and Its Implications', *Ethnic and Racial Studies* 30 (6), 1024–54.

10 Public Pasts in Plural Societies: Models for Management in the Postsecular City

Greg Ashworth

The locus of this argument

This policy-oriented discussion explores one aspect of the way public pasts are used within public policy in pursuit of public goals. In this chapter, through the use of case studies, I will outline the role of religion, either implicitly or explicitly contained, within these models of public pasts in plural societies. The argument is based upon two propositions. First, public authorities have used public heritage as an instrument for the attainment of explicit or implicit contemporary policy objectives. Indeed, it can be argued that the involvement of governments in heritage, and cultural productivity in general, stems from a very specific requirement of national governments, since the mid-nineteenth century, to create, foster and demarcate the concept of nation which alone legitimates their existence and justifies their exercise of that government (Ashworth, 1991; Ashworth and Howard, 2000; Graham et al., 2000). There are of course many cases of heritage being conscripted to the service of non-national jurisdictions and ideologies, but the special dependence of nationalism upon the creation of and commitment to the mythical entity 'nation' explains these attempts at the 'nationalization of the past'. In short, it has been assumed that contemporary societies will use heritage as an instrument in the invention and management of collective identity, most especially as expressed through the shaping of place identities because the existence of such entities underpins nationalist ideology.

Second, society has always been plural in some senses. The unity of character or purpose implied by the imagined entity 'nation' was always a chimera, uneasily sustained by a complicity between governors and governed, for so long as it was in the interest of both. However, for various reasons, this conspiracy of suspended disbelief is increasingly less tenable. For example, there has been a diffusion through space of economic production, consumption, cultures, ways of life, belief systems and people themselves in a process we so inadequately label as globalization. This may not be an exclusively twenty-first century phenomenon; in many respects it is as much a consequence of the largely nineteenth century European imperial project. In seeming contradiction many have commented upon a fragmentation, indeed atomization of society, and shift from the collective towards the individual. In any event the only agreement discernable in this heap of diffuse and varied ideas is that society has become more plural and that these pluralities are increasing and likely to continue to increase.

The tensions inherent in the two propositions are obvious. The first requires clarity, homogeneity and sharp demarcation, while the second provides opaqueness, heterogeneity and a bounding fuzziness. The aim of this chapter is neither to critique the present situation of mismatch and anomaly between political goal and social reality nor to reconstruct the relationship between public heritage and the societies it serves. It is rather to construct a concordance of contemporary practice as it can be observed, through an array of models for the government of plural societies. These models are neither predictive nor prescriptive: they are graphical summaries of a variety of quite different ways that public heritage can serve as an instrument for the attainment of different social outcomes within plural societies. This is a necessarily speculative and a reconnaissance of a field that is currently receiving more political than academic attention (Ashworth, 2007).

The place of religion in the discussion

The diversity of religious practice is one aspect of this pluralization of society and may be attributed to two quite separate consequences of the global success of Western secular liberalism. First, the stress on the individual and on personal responsibility has led to a retreat from collective allegiances and if not a fragmentation of the large monolithic religious organizations, at least a crumbling at the edges and an increasing diversity of belief and practice. Secondly, the creation of global labour markets encouraged a global migration that has intruded previously alien and often exotic religions into the mainstream of previously relatively religiously homogeneous societies. Religious practice and associated symbolisms have returned to the political agenda in Western countries after an absence of some 300 years. In that sense religion has become again a political matter, although religious belief or even public practice is rarely an issue in itself. It is more usually related to other linguistic, ethnic or even political programmes and aspirations. Religious adherence becomes just a simple means of labelling groups whose actions and objectives have little or nothing to do with religion (Northern Ireland's Catholics and Protestants being the most obvious example).

The introduction of the city into the discussion

Much of the discussion so far has been at the national or international level, but it is at the local, especially urban scale, that the issues become evident not least through the visibility of symbols, and both the conflicts and their resolution in policy become embedded in quite routine mundane town planning and urban management matters. In particular, the management of public space as a public good has implications, implicit or explicit, for the public expression of collective values.

The so-called minaret issue, for example, is a common ingredient in heated debate in numerous Western cities, where the skyline becomes a public visible expression of the presence of a religious group. Sweden, France, Italy, Austria, Greece, Germany and Slovenia have all discussed the possibility of legislation to restrict or even prevent the building of new mosques with minarets, and in Switzerland the issue has been raised in a referendum and approved despite the small number of Muslims in the country and the very small number of planning applications for new mosque building. It remains uncertain what the implications of this result may be at the level of local planning decision making or its impact in other countries. In no case, it should be noted, has any such national legislation yet been enacted, and at a local scale decisions are couched, at least ostensibly, not in religious or ethnic terms but in aesthetic and functional planning considerations. The issue threatens to raise issues of local versus national decision making. Political parties representing voters with Islamophobic concerns tend in many jurisdictions to be locally concentrated. This may give rise to curious and legally untenable discrepancies between national and local policies. In the Netherlands, for example, recent (2010) local elections returned the Party for Freedom (PVV) as the largest party in the city of Almere (the fourth largest city in the Netherlands) and almost the largest in The Hague (the seat of government). The stated local policies of this party include a ban on new mosque building and ordinances forbidding the wearing of headscarves in public buildings and veils in public space, thus threatening to impose regulations locally that have no national legal sanction.

The case of the Barnet *eruv* (hearth) illustrates the much wider point in which the attempt to create an exclusive heritage at the local level may cause controversy from those excluded or even some of those arbitrarily included. Some Orthodox Jewish communities require an extensive area around their residential areas to be visibly marked as their *eruv*. This marked area is by religious law considered to be inside, rather than outside, the extended home and therefore traversable by Orthodox Jews on the Sabbath. In the Barnet area of North London, home to a number of different communities of Jews, a request was made in 1992 to the planning authority for permission to erect a series of poles joined by wire in order to mark such an *eruv* with a perimeter of some 15 kilometres. This provoked considerable controversy from both non-Jewish residents, who felt estranged and even repelled by the idea of a visible change in their residential environment, and also by some more secular Jews who felt the idea held them up to public ridicule as legalistic pedants. The local authority was compelled to choose between the heritage requirements of one exclusive religious group and the opposition of other groups who resented being excluded as well as fearing the effect upon property values. Such marking of *eruvin* had previously occurred in more than a dozen U.S. cities, as well as in Toronto, Melbourne, Sydney and Johannesburg, with considerable local controversy in some cases (Ashworth et al., 2007). Permission was finally granted in Barnet in 2001 and has had few noticeable deleterious effects on the neighbourhood.

The deliberate creation of an unashamedly secular city designed to contrast with, and demonstrate its superiority to, the religious city reached its apogee in the *Sovgorod*. These socialist New Towns were intended to be a clear rejection of the historic cities of Europe, with their legacies of the now superseded and discarded pasts, and to be uncontaminated by the religious and political ideological baggage of the past. They nurtured and promulgated the secular socialist values of the present and future through the 'socialist realism', formulated in 1934 by the First All Union Conference of Soviet Writers as the only acceptable approach to art and design.

Poland's Nowa Huta is perhaps the most impressive of these towns in its magnificent, monumental building structures and renaissance radial town plan. It was deliberately located close to Kraków, which had functioned as the religious, political and cultural centre of fifteenth-century Jagiellonian Poland and particularly as the centre of the revived bourgeois nationalism of the nineteenth century. The economic raison d'être of Nowa Huta was the Lenin Steelworks, employing 43,000 workers at its peak in the 1970s, which represented the new industrial Poland peopled by the new industrial secular proletariat. The social and economic contrast with Catholic, intellectual Kraków was underlined by the physical manifestations of the contrasting skylines, industrial building and dense apartments as against medieval church spires and a castle; driven home by the pall of polluting smoke blowing from one onto the other.

Churches represented for the communist regime the worst aspects of the nationalist, class-ridden, superstitious old Poland and thus had no place in the new Nowa Huta. However the labour force for the steelworks was largely recruited from the surrounding rural areas and tended to be actively Catholic. A struggle ensued between the authorities and the residents over the provision of a church to service the religious needs of some 220,000 practising Catholics in the new town. Open air masses were held in defiance of the disapproval of the authorities from 1957 but only in 1977 was the Ark of Our Lady built, the church rapidly becoming a symbol and focus of opposition. The irony was that, in reality, a town intended as the vanguard of secularism became the centre of resistance to it, encouraged by the same economic and design features that were intended to foster support. The close camaraderie of the steel workers allowed the development of the unofficial trade union, 'Solidarity', and even the neighbourhood units and communal facilities, designed to increase social interaction among residents, served to spread and reinforce their dissent. The dominating statue of Lenin in Central Square was regularly vandalized and eventually removed in 1989, when Lenin Street was renamed Pope John Paul II Street in a clear assertion of the victory of postsecularism (Ashworth et al., 2007). Similar events have been replicated throughout post-Soviet Europe in which the symbols of a secular communism have been replaced by those of a resurgent religious, often nationalist, ideology as Alisauskiena (2005) exemplified mainly in respect to Lithuania.

Some pluralities

This argument focuses upon the social consequences of religious pluralism, but any exploration of the relationship must first be aware of the existence of a number of overlapping pluralities. The core of the argument underpinning public policy for plural societies is that there is a relationship between identity as a collective social attribute and public heritage policy as instrument for its attainment. The assumption is that people will identify with specific places, and that this identification by individuals can be aggregated into a collective identity and that much of the link between the two is through the idea of place identity.

Plurality of place identities

People identify with other people. 'I am one of them' or equally possible, 'I am not one of them'. Most of this identification has little to do with places but relates to associations of kin, culture, biogenetics, ideology, class or lifestyle (Bhabha, 1994). Some such identification, however, is linked to places, which become more than just spaces within which identified groups exist and interact: they are endowed with meanings and used as transmitters of such meanings. This is assumed to be axiomatic, but when using such common expressions as 'genius loci' or 'sense of place', it must always be remembered that a locus has no genius and places cannot sense anything. There is no *lieux de memoire*. The point here is just that place identity that dominates much of the thinking, especially of geographers and place planners and managers, is only one type of identity and generally not the most significant for most people most of the time. Secondly, the increasing diversity and fragmentation of societies, argued above, leads inevitably to a pluralization of identities, both between but also within individuals. The relevance of this to heritage, and specifically policies for public heritage, is that diverse pasts become transformed through diverse heritages into diverse identities. Historians may point out that this social diversity is no novelty of our age but a condition of humanity once more than one person existed. This may well be so, in which case the contemporary novelty lies in the consciousness of a previously concealed situation and the will to act upon it.

Plurality of public goals

The roles that public heritage are expected to fulfil in public spaces are also plural and not confined to collective place identities, social cohesion or social inclusion/exclusion. Heritage is being loaded with expectations that go far beyond only social solidarity and inclusiveness. These expectations include political and philosophical legitimation, the enhancement of a perceived quality of life through environmental amenity and the commodification and marketing of place products, especially for tourism. Issues arise from the very diversity of the expectations that public agencies place upon the increasing uses of heritage in policy. These are revealed in a number of inherent, although not always apparent, tensions.

Place identities are deliberately and consciously invented, fostered and promoted through a series of dichotomies, including:

- to promote generic places within global markets and to reinforce a countervailing localism;
- to express universal cultural values and to differentiate between localities through enhancing the distinctiveness of places;
- to reflect and celebrate social and cultural heterogeneity while enhancing social cohesion and homogeneity;
- as an expression of unique individuality and an instrument of official policies for collective goals; and
- to brand economic place products for export, especially through tourism and to satisfy the local social and cultural objectives of residents.

Thus, heritage is certainly used as an instrument of policy, but there are many different instruments that can be forged from it in pursuit of different and sometimes contradictory goals. Thus, the many producers of public heritage, who may themselves be both public and private, official and non-official, have varied and multiple objectives for its creation and management.

Plurality in public consumption

There has long been a series of axioms stemming from a vision of public heritage from a producer standpoint that postulates the existence of a simple causal relationship between governments and citizens. This has been used both to justify and to dispute the deliberate use of heritage as an instrument of political policy as described here. In retrospect it is difficult to understand how such simplistic automatism, assumed in the widely accepted notions of state legitimation (Habermas, 1973) 'cultural capital' (Bourdieu, 1977) and 'dominant ideology' (Abercrombie, 1982) was accepted without serious challenge for a generation. At its least, the efficacy of the messages of the 'dominant class' have been overestimated, while the strength of resistance of the 'subordinate class' has been underestimated. It may be that much official heritage is actually created and managed by and for a relatively small social elite who are effectively conversing with themselves in an exercise of self-justification rather than engaging in the propagation of any specific dominant ideology to the majority. Equally it may be that such a simple dichotomy of dominant and subordinate is compounded by the multiplicity and variety of such groups who consequently express conflicting or confusing messages; or they may not actually exist at all.

When viewed from the standpoint of the consumer rather than producer of heritage, then the individual experience of heritage is necessarily plural because not only is it consumed for diverse purposes, it also contains two obvious dichotomies. The first stems from the contrast between public and private heritages. The focus in this and most other discussions is on the former, while the latter has a far deeper significance for most people. Secondly, and additionally, heritage can be consumed for collective or individual goals. The tensions or at least contrasts resulting from this inherent condition are compounded in place-bound identification by the factor of spatial scale. Individuals have always been capable of identifying with different spatial jurisdictional or imaginable scales. This has been graphically and usefully labelled the Russian Doll model (Ashworth and Howard, 2000), as long as the use of the analogy does not assume any predetermined or stable hierarchy in the packing of the components.

Plurality in public communication

Finally in this catalogue of pluralizations, the question of how can also be answered by lists of multiple media of public communication in public spaces. The point raised here is that there is a multiplicity of instruments available, which are under the control of various agencies and individuals. Governments and their agencies at various jurisdictional levels may use public statuary, memorialization marking, public design and even attempt to prescribe the public landscape of public language and signage (as in Quebec's notorious Bill 101, for instance, which imposed French as the only visible language permitted in public signage). Governments may adopt the techniques of marketing using both diverse advertising media but also public-built environmental architecture and design to communicate their heritage messages. Strategic place branding may be executed through 'hallmarking', 'flagship' construction and 'signature' designing as a means of communicating the brand image (Kavaratzis and Ashworth, 2005). Governments also have at their disposal, either directly or indirectly through their control of subsidies, a wide range of cultural facilities and performances, which can be used to communicate their messages.

However, almost all of the above media also operate outside the control of governments. Commercial enterprises, voluntary associations, political and social pressure groups and even individuals also have access to many of these media channels and frequently can operate them more effectively. Even similar facilities may be managed quite differently. For instance, a number of museums in South Africa, which were part of the official system and communicated the officially accepted ideological message of apartheid are now privately owned in order to safeguard that message from change (e.g. the Voortrekker monument and museum outside Pretoria and Taal Monument at Paarl). Whereas museums which were private and discordant in their message (e.g. 'District 6' or Bo Kaap museums, Cape Town) are now official in both their message and their management (Ashworth, 2004).

The very multiplicity of channels is likely to lead to a multiplicity of messages even if these emanate initially from the same source and are intended to attain the same general result. Many, however, emanate from quite different sources and are intended to achieve quite different results. The simple point is just that not only are the producers and consumers of heritage plural, so also are the media of heritage communication.

Management models of plural societies and the roles of heritage

The above description of the inherent pluralization of goals, instruments and societies is given here as an introduction to the investigation of a range of models of plural society as expressed in public policies. This list is not necessarily complete, exclusive or comprehensive, and the application in particular places is also rarely clear cut: variants of more than one model can coexist at the same place. Similarly policies may vary though time: the same place may experience the application of successive models. The objective is not only to demonstrate that there are many quite different policy reactions to the pluralization of society encapsulated in particular social models, but to illustrate that heritage, which is often reflected in religious identity, plays a critical but different role in each.

There are five main models presented here (assimilation, melting pot, pillar, core+ and salad bowl). Each of these models admits of variants, some of which are prevalent enough to be included (Figure 10.1). These models can be arrayed along two main axes. Those striving to produce a singular outcome, a homogeneous social product, however imperfectly (notably the assimilation and melting pot models) are at one extreme while those self-consciously embracing a culturally plural society (pillar and salad bowl models) are at the other. Similarly there is a spectrum of assumed stability. The assimilation and pillar models are at one extreme, having an intrinsic assumed stability, while the melting pot, salad bowl and core+ models are assumed to be intrinsically unstable, not least because they are supposed to be capable of treating changeable ingredients within the mix and producing different outcomes. There are in addition two quite common variants: the two-directional model in which a single core is in effect projected differently for internal and external consumption, and the third-party imported core model, in which a diverse society imports a core acceptable to all, best exemplified by culturally plural postcolonial states using the heritage of the colonial experience, especially language, as a binding element. There are no lines connecting different models within the diagram. This is because there is no anticipated or inevitable sequence of change or evolution between the models. No timeline is to be inferred.

It would be difficult to argue that any of these models was inherently either secular or religious. Religion has played a major role in all of them at different times. Religion has been used as the most important defining characteristic of both assimilation and melting-pot models and indeed was the original justification for pillar models in particular. However both secularist and religious agendas can and have been pursued using each the models examined in specific cases.

Assigning cases to particular models has its hazards. It is quite possible for more than one model to be pursued simultaneously by different agencies or hierarchical levels within the same jurisdiction. Equally, policies change through time so that elements of quite different policy models can be detected at various stages of their implementation in the same place. Each model will now be briefly introduced through the three successive questions: What is it?, Where is it, or was it, to be found? and How is heritage used as an instrument of its application?

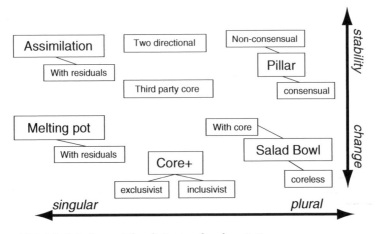

Figure 10.1 Models for social policies in plural societies

The assimilation model

These models, also referred to as 'integrationist' or 'single-core' models, are where society accepts only one legitimate set of collective common values, social norms and practices and ethnic cultural characteristics. Deviance from this single core is tolerated only if it is either so minor as to be an acceptable non-threatening subsidiary variant, or just a temporary phenomenon in process of adaptation to the core. Crucially, the core is expected to remain unaffected by subsequent additions to it.

Geographically and historically, this has been probably the most widespread model. Its origins are in religious difference and stem from the post-reformation European principle of *cuius regio, eius religio*. It has been a deep-seated touchstone of attachment to the idea of insiders/outsiders, greatly exacerbated by the rise of nineteenth-century romantic nationalism with its concepts of the desirable unity of folk, nation and state. The unexpected re-emergence of European ethnocentrist popularism, amounting at times to an ethnic and racial nationalism in the United Kingdom in the 1970s, Germany, Austria, France and Belgium in the 1980s/1990s, and least expected in Denmark and the Netherlands since 2000 was a response to a relatively small number of migrants with racial, religious or other cultural traits that diverged sharply from those of the majority society. The result was the emergence of a racist and xenophobic minority drawn mainly from the dispossessed indigenous white underclass, cynically exploited by opportunist politicians. The result has been an atavistic attempt to reject cultural pluralism and replace it by a xenophobia concealed under a cloak of functional pragmatism or even, as in the Netherlands, a defence of individual freedom of expression.

Assimilatory polices are actively pursued through discriminatory immigration legislation, selective deportation, 'citizenship' propaganda and the like. A switch from race to religion as the denominator of group distinction is notable in a number of Western European countries. In the Netherlands the first wave of immigration came from the Moluccas, Suriname and the Antilles, with race rather than religion being the divisive characteristic. After all, the majority of these immigrants were Christian. The second wave, however, from the 1970s onwards was increasingly non-Christian and religion became the divisive characteristic, although maybe sometimes used as a more acceptable surrogate. A similar switch occurred in Britain from the Christian West Indies to the non-Christian Indian sub-continent.

The function of heritage in this model is to act as an instrument of assimilation of outsiders into the core while constantly reaffirming and strengthening it to insiders. The vehicles of transmission include educational curricula (history and geography are usually favoured subjects when used as *vaterlandse geschischte* and *heimatkunde*), museum interpretations, public statuary, commemorative events and public place nomenclature. The major practical problem with the model is the management of the heritage of non-conforming groups. Here there are three policy options. The first is digestion of the heritage of dissonant groups into the core through reinterpretation. The second is marginalization of such heritage through the museumification or vernacularization of deviant cultures as a means of rendering them irrelevant and thus harmless (Tunbridge and Ashworth, 1996). A third heritage policy option is simply denial, which may take the form of ignoring, concealing or even destroying non-conforming heritage (as illustrated by the claim and counterclaim in Palestine/Israel that archaeology deliberately promotes or destroys artefacts in order to support or deny conflicting land claims) (Ashworth et al., 2007).

Melting pot model

The idea of the melting pot is simple. The analogy from the steel industry was coined (in 1913 in the United States) and developed as a conscious policy especially in settler societies in which ethnically diverse immigrant streams were 'smelted' into a new creation with a new homogeneous identity. The diverse ingredients produced not a composite or an amalgam of the ingredients but a new and unique product. The new citizen abandons the cultural baggage that may have accompanied the migration and adopts an identification with the new place, its society and its values. The reality was always somewhat more complex. The mix of ingredients could vary through time, few settler societies created their identities on a tabula rasa, and above all there always remained residues of the unsmeltable, that is, social groups that for one reason or another were incompletely absorbed into the whole or even rejected completely by it.

Settler societies of Europeans overseas have always maintained an uneasy balance between melting pot and salad bowl models. As long as the immigrant streams were not too racially or culturally heterogeneous, then the melting pot model seemed to operate smoothly, aided by ethnic and racial quota systems intended to guarantee that the ingredients in the pot would be not so varied as to threaten its capacity to assimilate them into the new product. Although this model was derived in, and normally associated with, Western colonies of settlement, it has a wider application not least in nation-building in postcolonial states, which face the task of constructing new nations from culturally diverse populations within non-nationally demarcated colonial boundaries. Also, Soviet society had a similar need and from time to time devised similar policies. The concept of year zero was strong in the communist, as in many previous, revolutions. This denial of heritage and deliberate rejection of the baggage of an equally rejected past always coexisted uneasily with cultural nationalism.

It is sometimes argued that settler societies have inevitably had a shorter history than the old world origins of their populations and that they must therefore have less heritage. The reverse is, of course, the case, as heritage is not defined by pasts but by contemporary need for it and new nation building would seem an obvious pressing need in such societies. This need is expressed through the assertive use of the symbolisms of the new society and rejection or concealment of the old. The treatment of what could be termed heritage residues has always posed difficulties and is a matter of continuing controversy in most settler societies. There are three main types of policy: ignore, marginalize or engage in cultural hyphenation. Most aboriginal populations were variously subject to the first two policies: Australian aborigines, U.S. 'Indians' and Canadian Inuit and 'Indians' were until quite recently deliberately excluded from the melting pot as being both undesirable and unsmeltable ingredients. Black and, more recently, Hispanic groups were not only racially separate from the mainstream but also economically and politically marginalized through slavery in the one case and conquest and peonage in the second. Current resolution of the unsmeltable ingredients of the melting pot is hyphenation. However it remains unclear whether such hyphenated individuals are a new hybrid breed or a minor variant of the core. The rise of hyphen-specific heritage in the form of educational programmes, heritage trails, museums, exhibitions and statuary raises similar ambiguities about whether the intention is internal group cohesion and separation from the mainstream or a wider inclusion of such groups in a more nuanced core product.

The pillar model

This model was in many ways a defensive reaction in societies sharply separated by originally religious division. An overall unity is maintained while satisfying the fissiparous tendencies of the constituent groups. Society is conceived as being a set of pillars, each self-contained and having little interaction with the others. Each has sovereignty within its own group, is not required to interact with the others but only to accept the right of others to exist. Collectively, however, all the pillars support the superstructure of the unified state which imposes a minimal uniformity in a parity of esteem and resources, allowing each group to manage its own cultural, social, educational, political and even economic institutions. It depends upon the idea of maintaining separation and minimal contact between the groups without privileging any particular group.

Although not dissimilar in some respects to the Ottoman 'millet system', in which each non-Muslim religious group was separately tolerated, governed and taxed, the idea as currently applied originated in the Netherlands (where it is known as *verzuiling* or pillarization) as a pragmatic solution to the problem of the post-reformation religious divisions that plunged much of the rest of Europe into civil war (Lijphart, 1968). The simple two-fold division of Protestant and Catholic pillars (*zuilen*) was later supplemented by others, based on socio-economic ideologies and even a non-sectarian pillar for those rejecting all the others. Paradoxically perhaps, although the pillar model was developed quite specifically to manage religious difference, it also allows the important secular requirement of the separation of religion from the state to occur. The survival of the model has been threatened by a secularization and individualization of society, which has weakened the solidarity of the pillar groups but also by the rise of Islam, which, reasonably enough, increasingly demands its own pillar and appropriate institutional recognition and support. There is a tempting parallel to be traced between the Dutch separate but equal pillarization and the ideology of apartheid developed by Afrikaner, Dutch and German ideologues in the 1930s. However, physical separation based exclusively on race, not culture, was incomplete due to the economic dependence of the white pillar on non-white labour and by no means reflected an equality of provision or esteem within the state as a whole. Speculation about other potential applications of pillar models as a solution, or at least accommodation, of intractable division in, for example Palestine/Israel, Cyprus, Lebanon or even Ireland/Northern Ireland, remain, however intriguing, as speculation.

The roles of heritage are quite self-evident. Each group creates, manages and consumes its own heritage for its own exclusive consumption, often financed equally by the central state. An archetypical case would be the Castle museum in Londonderry/Derry, in which the visitor may choose to follow an orange (Unionist/Protestant) or a green (Nationalist/Catholic) path through separate exhibits and heritage interpretations. South Africa, as in the apartheid regime, exhibits incomplete and officially unsanctioned, echoes of this with separate 'white' (specifically Afrikaner, 'the survival of the volk') and 'black' (specifically 'freedom struggle') heritages (Ashworth, 2004).

The core+ model

This is in many ways the least stable, or the most flexible, of the models which may emerge through a failure of either the assimilatory or melting pot models to produce a singular acceptable homogeneity or a breakdown in the 'separate but equal' character of the pillars in the pillar model. The result is a core+ variants model in which a substantial core remains functioning as what has been called a *leitkultur* but to it is added such other social groups as are seen to be unthreatening to the existence of the core and even contributing a useful addition to its variety. Core enhancement takes place through add-ons which can be scalar (e.g. regional variants) or ethnic in a hyphenation, without the ambiguity as to which element takes precedence.

Many Northern European societies have adopted, more incrementally than consciously, such core+ models in reaction to either the continued existence of relict or incomplete 'semi-nations' (Fries, Scots, Bretons, Catalans etc.) or to more recent immigration of groups with sharply different and, at least in the short term, not assimilable racial or ethnic characteristics. Core+ models are also prevalent in many postcolonial states engaged in nation building from ethnic diversity where an accepted majority culture is supplemented by other ethnic cultural groups.

Heritage may be employed either defensively, to create and sustain the essential character of the core, or, more positively, as deliberately enhancing of the core through add-ons. These may consist of inclusivist add-ons where ethnic cultural variety receives general public recognition and support as contributing to society as a whole and is open to general participation from society. The Notting Hill carnival, although originally West Indian, now attracts much wider participation and acceptance than would be an archetypical case on the inclusivist cultural add-on. Conversely add-ons can be exclusivist, where divergent ethnic groups are tolerated as closed entities, which are non-threatening but equally non-participatory and generally unsupported by public heritage actions. Chinese communities in many Western cities would be an example. The Northern and Midland post-industrial cities of the United Kingdom provide numerous cases of the emergence of core+ models. An important aspect of the general topic of multicultural heritage receiving attention within heritage policy agencies is the question of social inclusion. Throughout this literature the unproven assumption is made that such social inclusion operates within an inclusivist core+ social model where the ethnic or cultural add-on has become something of a cliché in urban heritage planning as well as in tourism product-line development. However, currently it is proving difficult to accommodate Islam within such models. There is little difficulty in treating, for example, London's Brick Lane Bangladeshi community as an add-on, which is in part as an inclusivist curry-rich Bangaltown and in part as an exclusivist linguistically and religious group. However, an essential characteristic of core+ models is that the add-ons are non-threatening to a core that is accepted by all as providing certain common values. The debate on the role of Islamic groups in Western societies focuses precisely upon whether this is, or could be, the case (as witness the reaction to the Anglican Primate's 2008 remarks on the possible acceptability of Sharia law alongside Common Law in England (Williams, 2008)).

Third-party core variant

There is a variant of the core+ model in which the core is provided not by an existing cultural group but is imported. A deep social diversity is overarched by some imported third-party culture, which provides a neutral, and thus acceptable, integrating element. The most evident case is Singapore. Here, Chinese cultural groups (or rather a number of quite distinctively different Chinese cultures ranging from the 'Straits Chinese' to more recent migrants from different regions of China and elsewhere in South East Asia), Indian and Malayan groups combine in a small but populous island state. The English language provides the official and unofficial lingua franca and British colonial history provides the unifying heritage. In that sense all Singaporeans regard themselves as not only members of their own ethnic group but also as the collective heirs of Raffles. Many other postcolonial states also spring to mind such as Suriname and much of West Africa using the Dutch and French colonial linguistic and cultural heritage respectively. The roles of heritage are to interpret and promote both the heritage of the various groups exclusively to them but also the imported core heritage to all.

The salad bowl model

Diverse ingredients are brought together and collectively create a whole without losing their distinctive characteristics. The result is the salad bowl. More recent analogy variants are the rainbow, in which different and contrasting colours merge seamlessly but without loss of pigment, or the mosaic, in which individual tesserae create a pattern through their combination but remain individually identifiable.

The self-designated archetype of the salad bowl model is Canada, where the phrase originated. If the United States was born in a revolution that demanded a new citizen for a new nation, then Canada was born in opposition to that revolution and therefore clearly did not require the melting pot. Loyalty to the crown, and thus the established order, was required – not homogeneity of language, religion or social custom. It became therefore a necessity, if the confederation was to survive, to discover and strongly propagate a workable model to accommodate an inherent diversity, which has come close to fragmenting the state.

The other well-known case is post-apartheid South Africa, where the successor regime faces quite profound racial, social, ethnic and economic divisions, compounded by a recent history of hostility between them. The alternative model of social diversity to apartheid is the officially proclaimed 'rainbow nation'. It is of course far too early to judge the success of this most far-reaching racial and social experiment. If it works it will provide a unique model for many other parts of the world: if it fails it will discourage similar experimentation.

There are two main difficulties with this model. First there is the question of scale. At what scale does a combination of distinctive elements occur? In Canada this is clearly at the federal scale. The provinces, and, even more pronounced, the localities within them, remain for the most part distinctively mono-cultural. Secondly, there is the question of whether there is a necessity for some binding element: a dressing on the salad, regular structure to the rainbow or pattern in the mosaic. In Canada this was provided by the loyalist myth (Grant, 1965) and in Australia by a strong numerical and political dominance of a single cultural origin. The issue now arises in both countries as to the possible sustainable existence of a coreless diversity.

There are two main sets of policy instruments that can be labelled inclusivist and exclusivist. Inclusivist policies not only endeavour to include every possible social group but equally invite everyone to be part of all such heritages. Such policies have two main problems. First, there is an absence of weighting within the selection: all make a contribution presumably equally. Secondly, inclusivist policies may be resisted as tending to dilute and distort group heritages.

Conversely exclusivist heritage recognizes, but also empowers, each distinctive group with its own heritage. The assumption often made that social inclusion through heritage is a self-evident social benefit, is challenged by exclusivist heritages that are non-threatening to the rest. Similarly the rise of the idea of cultural empowerment whereby groups are encouraged to re-establish ownership and control of their own heritage can be highly exclusivist. Not only may group outsiders be afforded a lower priority in experiencing such heritage. In extreme cases, which have occurred, it can become not just 'theirs to preserve but also theirs to destroy'.

Conclusion – limits of heritage policies

Having stated that heritage is the principal instrument for the implementation of public policy models (especially through the management of public space, as a public good), in cultural pluralist societies, it is necessary to re-emphasize some cautionary caveats. The significance of public heritage in its official instrument role is likely to be overestimated for three reasons. First, it is too easy, especially for geographers, to raise the idea of place to the status of an article of faith as self-evident truth. The bland assumption that people identify with places can be challenged. The link between religion and place is complex and often weak. There are many individuals and groups that have no particular place associations. There are diasporic nations (such as Roma or non-zionist Jews) and many social and cultural identities that need no relation to specific places. Further, it can be asserted that the concept of community has a decreasing place-bounded dependence. Places matter less than we think, and therefore place-bound policy is likely to be less effective than official agencies might hope or expect. Secondly, the influence of public heritage policy is reduced by the multiplicity of official agencies operating in this field and the absence of coherence or consistency in the messages they attempt to project. Thirdly, most public heritage producers and promoters under-estimate or fail to understand the reactions of their targeted consumers. Most public heritage is not noticed or if noticed is ignored. While marvelling at the large numbers of museum visitors, heritage guide purchasers or viewers of television heritage programming, we should not be blind to the even larger number who eschew all of these activities. Even if noticed and experienced, it is highly unlikely that public heritage will be understood in the way the producers of it intended. Such evidence as does exist suggests that consumers have conscious or unconscious strategies of resistance to the messages intentionally conveyed by public heritage. They change and adapt public heritage to conform to their more significant private heritages, even to the extent of creating a counter-culture supported by a counter-heritage which, because it is being unexpressed publicly is unknown to the public authorities. Whether a particular city can be labelled 'secular' or 'postsecular' as a consequence of the content and tone of its public policies is probably less important than how it is experienced by its citizens. In short, in the field of public response to plural cultures, while public heritage is important, it is less important than its producers believe, which is, perhaps, the most optimistic message of this argument.

References

Abercrombie, N., Hill, S., and Turner, B. (1980), *The Dominant Ideology Thesis.* London: Allen & Unwin.

Alisauskiena, M. (2005), *Religious Life in Post-secular Space: The Case of Visaginas City in Lithuania.* Habitus, http://habitusnetwork.org.

Ashworth, G. J. (1991), *Heritage Planning.* Groningen: Geopers.

—. (2004), 'Tourism and the Heritage of Atrocity: Managing the Heritage of South African Apartheid', in T. V. Singh (ed.) *New Horizons in Tourism: Strange Experiences and Even Stranger Practices.* Wallingford: CABI Publishing.

—. (2007), 'Plural Pasts for Plural Publics in Plural Places: A Taxonomy of Heritage Policies for Plural Societies', in G. J. Ashworth, P. Groote and T. Haartsen (eds), *Public Places: Public Pasts.* Utrecht/Groningen: Netherlands Geographical Studies 348, 13–26.

Ashworth, G. J., and Howard, P. (2000), *European Heritage Planning and Management.* Bristol: Intellect.

Ashworth, G .J., Graham, B., and Tunbridge, J. (2007), *Pluralising Pasts: Heritage, Identity and Place in Multicultural Societies.* London: Pluto.

Bhabha, H. K. (1994), *The Location of Culture.* London: Routledge.

Bourdieu, P. (1977), *Outline of a Theory of Practice.* Cambridge: Cambridge University Press.

Graham, B., Ashworth, G. J., and Tunbridge, J. (2000), *A Geography of Heritage.* London: Arnold.

Grant, G. (1965), *Lament for a Nation: The Defeat of Canadian Nationalism.* Ottawa: Carleton University Press.

Habermas, J. (1973), *Legimationenprobleme in Spätkapitalismus.* Frankfurt am Main: Suhrkamp.

Kavaratzis, M., and Ashworth, G. J. (2005), 'City Branding: An Effective Assertion of Place Identity or a Transitory Marketing Trick', *Tijdschrift voor Economische en Sociale Geografie* 96, 5, 506–14.

Lijphart, A. (1968), *The Politics of Accommodation: Pluralism and Democracy in The Netherlands.* Berkeley: University of California Press.

Tunbridge, J., and Ashworth, G. (1996), *Dissonant Heritage: The Management of the Past as a Resource in Conflict.* Chichester: Wiley.

Williams, R. (2008), Interview BBC radio 4 2 July 2008, http://news.bbc.co.uk/2/uk_news/7232661.stm (accessed 17 March 2010).

11 Understanding Faith-Based Engagement and Volunteering in the Postsecular Society: Motivations, Rationales and Translation

Rachael Chapman and Leila Hamalainen

Introduction

Debates about the role and place of faith in the British public realm are re-emerging in light of the increasing prominence of faith engagement in co-governance with the state. Faith engagement is linked to policies of social inclusion, community cohesion and the prevention of violent extremism, together with the provision by faith-based organizations (FBOs) of state-funded welfare programmes and initiatives. Much of the associated literature has so far examined the potential contribution of FBOs to the policy domain, together with related challenges and controversies. This has highlighted a clash between competing rationalities of a more 'secular' and instrumental state on the one hand, and a more spiritual and religious faith sector on the other. Normative debates have also arisen about how 'religious' and 'secular' partners and citizens should treat each other, and how, and to what extent religious motivations and reasoning should be accommodated within a more secular policy context. However, little empirical analysis has been undertaken to determine how this plays out in practice, and few studies have provided an in-depth analysis of the motivations of FBOs and volunteers for engaging in co-governance, either through state-funded social action and/or through participation in public policy decision making.

Drawing upon primary research, this chapter explores the rationale and motivations behind volunteering and engagement in co-governance through FBOs with a view to contributing to the above debates.[1] The next section outlines key developments and debates associated with faith and faith-based volunteering and engagement in the public realm. We then present empirical analysis of the motivations of FBOs and volunteers for engaging in social action and co-governance[2] and an initial examination as to how and to what extent religious motivations and reasoning are being presented and accommodated within a more secular policy context. We argue that a labelling of 'faith' or 'secular' organizations and citizens can obscure more than it illuminates by downplaying overlapping boundaries, motivations, beliefs and identities between the two. It also suggests a greater onus appears to be placed on FBOs and citizens to translate religious reasoning, approach and language into more 'secular' forms.

Faith and faith-based volunteering in the public realm

The relationship between faith and politics in Britain is complex, and notions of secularization are contested. As Dinham and Lowndes (2009: 3) suggest, "the data show patterns which contradict those predicted by the secularisation thesis" of the end of religion. They point out that although church attendance is in decline in the United Kingdom, reported levels of religious affiliation remain at about three quarters of the population, reflecting what has been described as the phenomenon of 'believing without belonging' (Davie, 1994). Christianity is the predominant religion, with Muslims forming the next largest religious group. There are also relatively large groupings of Hindus, Sikhs and Jews, together with smaller numbers of Buddhists, Bahá'ís, Jains and Zorastrians (Weller, 2007: 21). The UK constitutional arrangements add further complexity to the issue of secularization, with the established Church of England having a special relationship with the state. The monarch acts both as head of the state and head of the Church of England, and 24 of the Church of England's bishops and two archbishops sit in the House of Lords as a right of privilege.

Added to this is the government's commitment to work more closely with faith communities in order to build strong, active and cohesive communities. This has opened up new opportunities for faith organizations and citizens to engage in the policy process from the early 1990s onwards: for example, through representation on partnership bodies (such as local strategic partnerships), consultations and the provision by FBOs of state-funded welfare services and programmes aimed at facilitating community cohesion.[3] Such opportunities have emerged in the context of broader UK government agendas towards partnership, democratic renewal, community empowerment and cohesion, together with concerns over polarization and religious extremism.

Religion also remains an important arena for civic participation and volunteering in Britain, although the relationship between them is far from straightforward (Dinham and Lowndes, 2009: 3). Based on Home Office Citizenship Survey findings, religious practice has a bigger impact on volunteering than affiliation, which makes little difference, and further analysis suggests that social class related factors such as education or housing tenure 'have an equal or bigger impact on formal volunteering than actively practicing religion and that this is true for all religions' (NCVO, 2007: 11, 13). The faith sector encompasses many charitable organizations that are shaped by faith, but which do not necessarily involve any religious activities. Some FBOs work in partnership with the state through the delivery of state-funded initiatives. Although many FBOs remain self-financing, survey research in North West England (NWRDA, 2003) indicates that 27 per cent received public funding. Further research by Ravat (2004) reported that 11 per cent of faith-based projects received funding by the local authority in Leicester.

The increased engagement of faith in the public realm has prompted a growing body of literature on the role of faith in politics and civil society in Britain. Much of this has focused on the contribution and experience of faith engagement in the policy process or society more broadly, for example, in relation to urban regeneration (Farnell et al., 2003), social capital (e.g. Furbey et al., 2006; Baker and Skinner, 2005), civil renewal (Lowndes and Chapman 2005 and 2007) and rural communities (Grieve et al., 2007; Farnell et al., 2006). This research suggests faith-based organizations make significant contributions to the public domain through their spiritual and religious capital, resources, leadership and potential for representing and engaging particular communities (see NCVO, 2007; Berkeley et al., 2006; Furbey et al., 2006; Lowndes and Chapman, 2005; Baker and Skinner, 2005).

The research also highlights various tensions associated with faith engagement in the public realm. Lowndes and Chapman (2005 and 2007), for example, reveal cynicism among faith groups of perceived attempts by policy makers and practitioners to 'hijack the normative agenda' by claiming grass-roots legitimacy on the basis of faith group involvement without actually engaging with the values and beliefs of those groups. They go on to suggest that policy makers and practitioners may be uncomfortable with discussing some values explicitly, especially where reference is made to religion. Furbey (2007: 36) similarly points out that 'religious beliefs (as opposed to 'values') are usually kept firmly in the background in public policy debate yet, explicitly or implicitly, beliefs or understandings are, for most people of faith, an essential source of motivation and direction' (see also Smith, 2004). A survey of faith representation on local public partnerships (Berkeley et al., 2006) also revealed 44 per cent of over 100 faith representatives felt their main partnership was not open to discussing faith issues. Cases of misunderstanding and overt hostility towards faith partners are also reported (see Baker, 2009). There is also a perception among faith communities that they are discriminated against in the allocation of public funding. This is linked to perceptions around the lack of understanding of faith groups or acceptance that funding would be used for non-religious activities, together with concerns among funders of proselytization or that certain sections of the community would be marginalized or excluded in their activities (see Reith, 2003).

Many of these tensions have been linked to a lack of understanding and ignorance on both sides – by statutory partners about the nature of different faith group beliefs, motivations and activities; and by faith communities about government and policy agendas and processes. Other tensions, particularly those associated with differences in beliefs, motivation and approach, have been linked to underlying policy rationales for faith engagement. Dinham and Lowndes (2008: 13), for example, identify an instrumentalist rationale of faith engagement among policy makers that sees 'Faith communities as "repositories" (Home Office, 2004) of resources for addressing issues of public significance, including urban governance in general and the more specific issues of community cohesion and the prevention of religious extremism'.

This rationale has been criticized for ignoring or downplaying the importance of 'faith' and 'faithfulness' in understanding the motivations of faith groups for engaging in the public domain. In this way 'instrumental engagement' is said to obscure the realities of faith communities' own aspirations and motivations by assuming a model of engagement not reflected in practice (Dinham and Lowndes, 2008). Dinham (forthcoming) defines this assumed model further in relation to faith groups' engagement in social enterprise activities. He suggests that there are specific tensions between FBOs and policy makers around which activities are supported (at the expense of others); the way in which FBOs are asked to engage in agendas (bureaucratic systematization of working practices) and the way in which the quality of such engagement is assessed (marketized assessment criteria).

Linked to such tensions are normative debates about how 'religious' and 'secular' partners and citizens should treat each other, and how, and to what extent religious motivations and reasoning should be accommodated within a more secular policy context. In relation to this, Habermas (2006) raises concerns of an asymmetrical burden on faith groups to translate religious reasoning and language into more secular forms; a concern that, given the tensions outlined above, could have some bearing in the British policy context. More specifically, he argues that:

> When secularised citizens act in their role as citizens of the state, they must not deny in principle that religious images of the world have the potential to express truth. Nor must they refuse their believing fellow citizens the right to make contributions in a religious language to public debates. Indeed, a liberal political culture can expect that the secularised citizens play their part in the endeavours to translate relevant contributions from the religious language into a language that is accessible to the public as a whole. (Habermas, 2006: 51–52)

Rawls, on the other hand, suggests that although an individual may have religious motivations for acting, 'ultimately these must be justified by public reasons (as Rawls defines them) for the positions it holds in relation to decisions about public policy' (Bretherton, 2010: 46).

To date, much of the literature has focused on the policy rationales and associated opportunities, tensions and controversies for faith engagement. Fewer studies have explored in any depth the motivations for engagement in social action and co-governance by and through FBOs, and there has been little empirical exploration as to the potential for an asymmetric burden on faith groups to translate religious reasoning and language into more secular forms. Drawing upon primary data, this chapter explores these aspects as they take place between individuals and what can loosely be referred to as FBOs, and between FBOs and the state. The analysis draws across six projects in which a total of 81 interviews and 12 focus groups were conducted with: faith leaders, activists, representatives and volunteers of faith-based organizations from Christian, Muslim, Hindu, Sikh, Jain, Jewish, Pagan, Quaker and Baháʼí communities; and individuals from the wider voluntary and community sector, the Home Office, the Department for Communities and Local Government and statutory bodies (including local authorities, fire and rescue services and the police).

Motivations for engagement through FBOs

The research highlights a number of complex and overlapping motivations/rationales for engagement in social action and co-governance. These can be categorized as follows: 'helping others', as a way of expressing identities, values and beliefs; 'giving something back' as a way of serving the community; 'getting on': acting out of self or organizational interests and seeking transformation.

Helping others as a way of expressing identities, values and beliefs

Helping others can be expressed as a motivation that logically pours from a number of different faiths' beliefs, values and identities, which Baker (2009) terms spiritual capital. These include sub-kajaria, both giving and a reward that continues, even after death (Muslim), love thy neighbour as yourself (Christian), caring for the environment and other people in general (Pagan), service to the community (Bahá'í) and well-being of others (Sikh). Wolfe (1998, cited in Lukka and Locke 2000) refers to this as 'environmental altruism', whereby religious beliefs, values and institutions form part of a larger social structure that is both shaped by and influences individual conduct. Wolfe argues that religious parables, such as the Good Samaritan in Christianity, form part of a cultural repertoire which can inform practice; in the case of the Good Samaritan, by encouraging human kindness and fellow feeling towards strangers (see Lukka and Locke 2000). Our research found that 'living out' values and principles associated with religion are an important motivating factor behind the involvement and conduct of some faith 'representatives' and volunteers who seek to protect and further the interests of others, including those perceived to be less fortunate, marginalized and excluded. A bishop of the Pentecostal Church, who sits on various partnerships, for example, explained that he feels a responsibility to lobby and argue with the people who hold power to help ensure all people can access services appropriately. He pointed out that:

> [when you are delivering services] you have to stop and check to see whether you are actually delivering equitably across the patch. And where you're not delivering, you still have a responsibility to help people to ensure that they can access services and you have a responsibility to lobby and to argue and to agitate with the people who hold the power, even though they may not share my values. My values drive me to hold them to account.

Values, such as equity, equality and justice, are also likely to motivate people of no religion to engage in social action and co-governance whether through faith-based or more secular organizations (see Taylor and Warburton, 2003). As a faith regeneration officer of Christian faith stated, secular and humanist societies have a belief structure and values which can inform their actions. It is also clear that religion is not the only influencing factor and that wider social, political and cultural principles shared with non-religious people can also be important (see Farnell et al. 2003 and Lukka et al. 2003). In several cases, it is difficult to separate such factors. As one Muslim volunteer remarked:

A lot of people in our family volunteer because part of volunteering is part of your faith. Certainly Islam encourages it, it's part of giving charity so it's incorporated in that. I do find a lot of people do volunteering because it is their faith but obviously because they want to as well.

Another Jewish volunteer stated their involvement was 'something they grew up with' and was so natural to their way of life they questioned why you wouldn't do it. This kind of motivation was expressed as a logical part of an individual's life story. In many ways it seemed to define who they were at a particular time and what their purpose in life was according to them.

What is perhaps distinctive in terms of engagement and volunteering in a faith-based context is the religious basis on which some values, beliefs, identities and actions are founded (Chapman, 2009). For some this is associated with a belief in and commitment to God. As a faith regeneration officer of Christian faith commented:

I guess at the heart of it, the difference between other voluntary organisations and faith groups is a sense of otherness ... people of faith believe that there is something else, something higher and greater than they are ... you are not just serving others because you think it's right to serve others, you're serving others because you're commanded to do so or that it's the right thing or somehow it enhances your relationship with God ... It's that serving of others, being of service to God, that differs and that commitment to God provides you with that sense of commitment to others.

In some cases, motivation for social action and engagement in co-governance may stem from a specific need or issue associated with religion. This is the case for one faith-based charitable organization that works with the local authority to provide 24/7 burial services to help meet religious requirements for Muslim burials to take place as soon as possible after death.

Religious leadership and active participation in religious activities and community life can also help support, inspire and provide opportunities for individuals to 'live out' their values and beliefs, which for some offer a distinctive aspect of faith-based civic engagement and social action. As one interviewee commented:

What they [FBOs] have that secular organisations don't have are priests, kind of teachers, who are key figures, who are authoritative exponents of the culture. So, you know, there's an explicit mission or message from those people to anybody who's involved in the group about the culture, about the values, about the basis of it, which you won't find in many secular groups except in the early days of those which have charismatic founders." (academic and former VCS employee)

Similarly, the bishop of the Pentecostal Church remarked that living in the faith community:

re-energises me and reminds me of why I'm doing this because we all probably forget because of the pressures. . . . I hope what happens to a faith-based group is what I described a while ago; that we would be somewhat more zealous about ensuring that those God-given and God-directed values that we hold dear are lived out.

As for providing opportunities, one Evangelical Christian volunteer commented that:

> For me I was brought up in a faith family and my upbringing was we were outward look-ing to other people around us in the neighbourhood. So from my parents I got this example of always seeing myself I guess I was already in that frame of mind, wanting to help people. And so since I have been in faith myself and then the [X group] opening gave me an opportunity to put that into practice that love I felt for people and being with people and just enjoying other people's lives.

Giving something back to the community

Motivation can also stem from a feeling of indebtedness to a community. Research findings suggest this is often related to a personal experience that being part of a group had helped them to surmount, either in relation to a turn to faith, through community support mechanisms, or invariably both. Examples of personal experi-ences that people cited as significant included overcoming drug addiction, getting out of homelessness, dealing with the change of going to university or coming to terms with bereavement. Motivations in this case were related to expressing com-munity solidarity, though not explicitly on a faith basis, by responding to local needs for support, for example, by providing leisure activities and training for young peo-ple. Such activities were often targeted within a neighbourhood spatial area which happened to coincide with an ethnic or religious group. Research indicated that deci-sions to volunteer in this context were made with a view to support those with whom they felt they had solidarity. In choosing to act, the individual was able to reinforce their own sense of solidarity with the group. As one Jewish volunteer suggested:

> I think also in terms of why as Jewish people might choose to do something, there is a very strong sense say with the Darfur campaigning at the moment and campaigning on Zimbabwe, that comes from a very strong sense of if we are to take lessons from our own experience during the holocaust and persecution, then one of those lessons has to be speaking up on behalf of other people. . . . So I think there are certain kinds of campaigns where it is very much informed by our collective Jewish experience and the lessons that we have taken from that as well.

Motivations associated with solidarity and a desire to give back to the community among individuals of FBOs may or may not be associated with religious belief or life. They can also imply a certain kind of instrumentalism, for example, through gaining group respect and/or a sense of belonging.

'Getting on': acting out of self or organizational interest

The availability of free time, for example, through retirement, wanting to add voluntary experience to a curriculum vitae, or gain particular skills that might help in a future career was also seen as a motivation for some. As one Muslim focus group participant commented:

> One of the reasons, again being slightly selfish, to get involved was because I knew it would give me good experience in terms of confidence and in terms of being able to speak to young people. Because I was thinking of pursuing a teaching career anyway and I did need some sort of boost and some sort of experience on my C.V. as well as just the skills anyway to talk to young people. I was involved with the show which really, really helped me do that, especially when young kids were ringing in, speaking to you, getting you involved in competitions, just wanting to talk or whatever. It was really, really useful.

The importance of these factors appears to be related to the position in the life cycle of the individual. According to an Evangelical Christian focus group participant:

> At that particular time we had just retired and we had time to do it so it's a different part of our life and met some of our needs. And hopefully we were grabbed by the vision that here is Jesus actually doing his business of getting out there amongst the people rather than people coming to Jesus.

Young volunteers in particular often highlighted self-interest motivations, perhaps due to their inability to access careers through other means. In this case, volunteering was more likely to be short term, though it could develop into a longer-term rationale based on other motivations explored above.

Resource-based and goal-orientated motives can also be identified within FBOs and through representatives engaged in governing bodies and public partnerships. Partnership working with statutory partners can, for example, help FBOs secure additional resources through public funding and/or political influence. This may assist FBOs and volunteers to ensure community needs and broader social action goals are better met. As one member of Christian faith, involved in building a Church community centre, explained:

> You just end up getting in contact with local authorities because they are the people working on the ground. So it's being as a sort of practitioner in communities that I have had to relate to the local authorities, usually because I wanted resources for work in the community. And what that then does is gets you into their structures, and you link, if I can use that word, with the people who have got access to those resources and then you become part of the policy making thing because you have experience of working on the ground ... [so] through being a practitioner, you get to a position where you can have a say.

In this case, an interest in communities and social action helped this individual develop relationships with statutory authorities, which opened up opportunities to engage on public sector governing bodies and working groups.

Some focus group participants that volunteered through FBOs viewed self-interest motivations as inappropriate. There was a sense that other motives concerned with 'helping others' were more 'authentic' and associated with 'spiritual empowerment' and philanthropy which is closely related to tenets of faith. In other words, 'authentic volunteers' were seen to be motivated by their faith values and not interested in volunteering for the rewards of a higher community profile or for personal gain in any way. However, in spite of this view, the existence of 'instrumentalist' motivations for civic engagement by faith groups clearly exists as in other organizations. Likewise, there were others who not only recognized the existence of such motivations, but who were also able to rationalize them as a positive factor.

Seeking transformation (personal or worldly)

For some focus group participants, their initial motivation was influenced by a sense that involvement fulfilled a need for personal development, or the transformation of others:

> I really just feel in my heart that I need to give something back, and as well as that my faith plays a big part in it. I really want to help people to see that there is more to life than what they are going through, the places they are in, that there is light at the end of the tunnel. If I can touch just one person just to bring them out of it then it makes my life a lot happier, a lot more fulfilled. And I feel blessed by God for doing these things, it's an all round thing really." (Evangelical Christian)

> What you said, giving people avenues is so important I think. And I think my motivation was wow I can really feel valued as well, I think there was a 'what's in it for me' element definitely at that age, and then you get hooked and then it is only after that initial stage that you think wow why wouldn't I do this, this is so rewarding. (Jewish)

Such motivations and 'rewards' were sometimes linked to religion through, for example, 'rewards' in an afterlife or final judgment. However, differing views over this were raised, and others saw engagement as being more indirectly 'rewarded'. For some, motivations were not so much faith-related as connected to general personal growth in terms of self-worth or empowerment and/or other ideological commitments. As one member of a FBO campaigning for social change remarked:

> Speaking for myself, I am not a Catholic so I am not here for a religious reason, I am just supporting the work that the Catholic Workers are doing here. And so a number of us are of different faiths or of no faith. Although the cafe is operated by the Catholic Worker, we are all here for different reasons, and not necessarily [have] anything to do with the Catholic Church ... in that respect it is inclusive both in terms of the people who volunteer here and in terms of the people who use the cafe. (Volunteer of a faith-based charity)

Again, engagement in activities of a transformative nature was considered to be enriched through collaboration with a faith group or community. This was seen to reinforce identities and belonging, and strengthen their personal faith. As one Muslim focus group interviewee explained: people are on different 'journeys' and were able to 'learn from each other and grow'.

So far, the analysis suggests no clear distinctions or assumptions can be made between a 'faith' or 'secular' culture when looking at motivations for engagement via FBOs. While religion is an important motivating factor and support for engagement in social action and co-governance, it is by no means the only one. More 'secular', and in some cases, instrumentalist motivations also exist, for example, helping others with whom an individual feels personal solidarity, seeking to improve a c.v. and/or securing state funding or political influence in order to ensure community needs and social action objectives are better met. In some cases, a complex mix of 'faith-based' and 'secular' motivations may be present. The next section explores the interface between religious motivations, reasoning, values and language (termed spiritual capital, see Baker, 2009) and the more 'secular' policy domain as it takes place through co-governance (e.g. public funding of FBOs and faith participation in partnerships).

Spiritual capital in the public realm: an asymmetric 'burden' of translation?

It is clear that religion can be a significant factor motivating volunteering in FBOs and co-governance with statutory partners. However, what is less clear is the extent to which spiritual capital is explicit and considered acceptable within a more 'secular' policy context. According to one interviewee, communities and statutory partners have different values, dialogues and ways of understanding that don't easily translate:

> Communities are about relationships (who you get on with), they are about how you feel about the people around you, they are about feeling safe, they are about trying to understand what is going on. [They] are more meaning driven e.g. why is this happening to us? Local authorities are about 'we have got to do something about this' [and] 'how do I achieve this target'. They are much more action orientated. The ends are important, not so much the means by which they do it ... The dialogues in local authorities can sometimes be quite instrumental, about feeding the machine, and about the money that comes in, and that making sure the money is attracted, and making sure the money is spent, and making sure the outputs are right, and the outcomes are right. (Christian faith representative)

Interview evidence also suggests that religious people often feel a need to translate religious reasoning and language into more 'secular' forms within public policy debates. According to one member of the Salvation Army, faith groups can find it difficult to express religious beliefs and principles in a secularized policy context due to fear of 'sounding a bit weird' or because they themselves take them for granted. There is a need to adopt a more 'secularized' language in this context; using terms such as 'honesty, tolerance and the importance of relationships', as opposed to more instinctive Christian language of 'grace, peace, joy and love'. Other words, such as 'service' (to the community) are important within the Bahá'í tradition. In some cases, words may not be directly translatable into English and can have several English understandings (e.g. seva in Hinduism and Sikhism).

This led to concerns about what is 'lost in translation'. Another Christian faith representative on an LSP stated:

> I don't think you can have a huge faith input. And what I mean by that is the values and principles we feel as important from a Christian perspective, not evangelism. It's quite difficult to say that in the Board meeting unless you use very careful language ... I can say what I think is right about social justice and so on, but I am not quite so strong as saying well it actually links back to a faith statement. But I am learning.

This appears to support Habermas's (2006) notion of an asymmetrical burden on faith groups to translate. As the above interviewee explained:

> People either want me to turn that [the value social justice] into something very practical, which might be increasing access to information and services so that they [migrant workers] can have equal access. There is not a commitment in that [partnership] group to say we will campaign for, publically, the group of people that are discriminated against ... Civil servants can handle systems which increase public awareness, for example, pushing out leaflets. It's much more difficult for some organisations to hoist up a flag called social justice ... so I have had to change my language a bit.

Even where effective translation takes place, debates around morality can sometimes challenge policy makers and practitioners because they bring to the surface values that are submerged for political reasons (e.g. the redistributive aspects of some government policy), or because they involve a direct challenge to public policy norms (from equal opportunities to short-term target-driven funding) (Lowndes and Chapman, 2007). For some partners, challenge is viewed positively:

> I think this is a good challenge. If there is a benefit to some of these in terms of partnership working more broadly in the involvement, it's to have that challenge ... Whilst we all think that we are previously doing things well, you really don't know unless you are subject to that challenge where somebody is saying, but why is that going on or can't we do it this way. I don't think our structures help develop challenge, because to be perfectly honest, that is where we meet in the public eye and the private ones have a completely different feel. If you went along to the partnership board you would think this is two hours of my life which has been awfully interesting but what has it achieved in terms of really challenging, because no one can really say in those meetings. Probably the faith representatives can in a way, but nobody as a councillor or council leader can say we are wasting money here and we should do it differently. They are not going to say that. In a private forum there can be that level of challenge. (Council Leader and member of a Local Strategic Partnership)

There may also be concerns among statutory partners in relation to proselytizing and over certain attitudes and principles associated with religion, for example, in relation to sexual orientation. These may give rise to challenges over the legitimacy of faith representation and anxieties by statutory partners over funding FBOs. In some cases, there may even be hostility towards FBOs. According to one interviewee, a Pentacostal bishop,

... there are some people, as I was saying earlier, who don't believe that faith groups should be part of the public debate. And so, of course, that aggressive secular or aggressive, sometimes even agnostic, but aggressive atheist streak is there [although he went on to argue that] ... I think that is minor because most people now recognise, actually faith plays an important part in our lives ... I don't think there are huge numbers of people who think that they must actively resist people of faith participating in the public square.

At the same time, there are concerns among faith groups that public funding regimes and pressures can lead some FBOs to behave in a more secular way; that is, to drift away from, downplay or compromise on faith-based beliefs, commitments, language and values because they are under-resourced, required to meet funding targets and conditions and/or face anxiety about not securing funding due to their religious connections.

It seems reasonable to suppose that greater policy clarity, guidance and understanding over the role, significance and place of religious beliefs, practices, values and language in the public domain may help overcome some of these tensions alongside other measures (for example, training and improved faith/secular literacy around values, language, beliefs and practices). There are indications that policy debates and action are beginning to take place along these lines. The Commission for Integration and Cohesion has recommended that clear guidelines be provided to statutory authorities enabling them to award public service contracts to faith groups without fearing it will lead to proselytizing or pressure on service users to accept religious beliefs (Commission on Integration and Cohesion, 2007: 132). The previous Labour government also announced a three-year package of support aimed at building capacity around community cohesion in its Face to Face and Side by Side strategy (CLG, 2008: 10–11). This included funding to help build the capacity of Regional Faith Forums, the development of guidance material to local authorities and sharing of effective practice.

The previous Labour government was also committed to a programme of faith literacy in the public sector (CLG, 2008: 43). This is important in improving understanding of religious and faith-based organizational diversity, among other things. Baker (2009: 120) suggests faith literacy should facilitate a move beyond functionalist levels of discourse, around 'what to do at a civic function and how to get funding', to one that aids the uncovering of values and visions of those engaged in the public domain. This, he suggests (2009: 120), 'will involve a commitment to a more profound type of literacy involving deep listening to language that expresses core values and visions, and a commitment to the exploitation of the many points of connection and overlap'. Faithworks, a Christian organization seeking to promote unity and partnership within and between faiths and secular authorities, also argues that better understanding by government of the motivational nature of faith and the different roles faith groups play in communities is needed (Duncan and Madeiros, 2007). Yet, improved literacy should not just be a requirement of state and wider civil society actors. As a Christian faith representative stated:

I think, you know, the whole idea of religious literacy, which I think is a much flaunted idea, is a two way process. I mean I think it is a reasonable criticism by policy makers in government that religious people ought to learn their world as well . . . It is a bit of an arrogant position that faith communities say you've got to listen to us, but actually we don't learn the language that that needs to be expressed in. And I think what you really need is a dialogue, and you need translators who can translate the language of both bodies because both of them have quite interesting dialogue going on within themselves.

In other words, state–faith relations would also benefit from better understanding by FBOs and citizens about how the state works, its language, structures and agendas. Together, this suggests that secular agencies and partners need to be open to learning and understanding distinctive faith-based organizational needs, interests, language and ways of operating, and FBOs need to become better at articulating to secular agencies 'what they are about, who they are, what they stand for and how they behave' (member of a Christian faith-based charity).

Conclusion

This chapter has argued that no clear distinctions or assumptions can be made between a 'faith' or 'secular' culture when looking at motivations for faith-based social action and citizen engagement in the public realm. FBOs vary in the nature and degree to which they are linked to a faith tradition, the religiosity of citizens volunteering within FBOs varies and motivations for volunteering and engagement in co-governance through FBOs are informed by religious as well as non-religious rationales. The UK constitutional arrangements, with the established Church of England having a special relationship with the state, the history of dialogue and consultation between faith leaders and the state, and more recent opportunities for faith engagement in the policy process also challenges the notion of a 'secular' state in Britain. Together, this suggests the dominant view within the academic and policy literature regarding a clash between competing rationalities of a more secular and instrumental state on the one hand, and more spiritual and religious 'faith sector' on the other, risks seeing individuals and organizations in a one-dimensional way, as being psychologically or culturally determined as 'secular' or 'of faith'. It may also lead to incorrect assumptions being made about motives, beliefs and actions. The evidence presented here suggests that the picture is much more complex. A labelling of 'faith' or 'secular' organizations and citizens can obscure overlapping boundaries, beliefs and identities between the two, which in turn can offer scope for better understanding and effective translation between faith-based and more 'secular' cultures.

While difficulties in translation can and do emerge between faith communities and statutory partners, they can be overcome where efforts are made by FBOs, citizens and statutory partners to better understand each other and where they work together on the basis of shared interests and goals. Even so, the evidence presented here suggests that the onus for translation can often fall on FBOs and faith representatives to translate religious motivations, values and language into more 'secularized' forms. This appears to fit Rawls's conception that religious motivations for acting should be justified by 'public reasons' as he defines them.

Such notions are, however, criticized by those who argue that this 'occludes people's most basic reasons for acting' and 'inhibits the formation of a genuinely common life with others because we are never able to respond to and engage with their primary concerns and self-understanding' (Bretherton, 2010, 51). Bretherton points out that Rawls's account prevents real dialogue and encounters by limiting efforts to converse with others on their own terms, which in turn can result in ignorance concerning the real reasons for action. This appears to resonate with perceptions around the lack of understanding of faith-based organizations and motivations by statutory partners and suggests a need for continued debate and dialogue on motivations, reasoning and language, whether faith-based or otherwise. This needs to stretch deeper than a mere organizational labelling of FBOs to reflect what is often a more complex mix of faith or non-faith based individuals, motivations and processes.

Enhanced understanding is likely to be ever more important in the context of the new coalition government in the United Kingdom. Public sector cutbacks, an emphasis on the 'big society' and building stronger and more integrated communities by the new government is likely to bring new potential opportunities for faith, voluntary and charitable groups to engage with statutory partners, through shaping the meaning of the 'big society', advising on spending priorities, delivering public services and promoting social responsibility and community action. There are also challenges. FBOs, as well as other voluntary and charitable groups, are likely to find themselves facing greater competition for public funding resulting from cuts and changes in priorities. Reduced community cohesion funding via local authority area-based grants and DCLG have been announced and, while the Conservative manifesto pledges to promote and support faith, voluntary and charitable groups, it emphasizes that this should be based on their effectiveness in countering poverty and deprivation rather than on the basis of ethnicity or faith. All this suggests an even greater need for FBOs and statutory organizations to enhance their understanding of each other and find more effective ways of working in partnership.

Notes

1   In this chapter, FBOs refer to worshipping communities and voluntary and community organizations that are to some extent grounded in a faith tradition. This may be through reference to religion or associated commitments in their mission, founding history, governance or project. As Sider and Unruh (see 2005: 119–20) remind us, the degree and manner in which organizations are linked to a faith tradition can vary from what they term 'faith permeated' organizations, where connection with religious faith is evident at all levels of mission, staffing and governance, through to 'faith background' organizations, which tend to appear secular, although they may have a historical tie to a faith tradition. This distinction between FBOs and individual participation or volunteering is important as people of religion or no religion may get involved in civic engagement through FBOs and/or secular organizations alike.

2   The analysis draws on data collected between 2005 and 2010 as part of six
    research projects: (1) 'Faith, Hope and Clarity: Developing a Model of Faith
    Group Involvement in Civil Renewal' funded by the Home Office (see Lowndes
    and Chapman, 2005); (2) 'Faith and the Voluntary Sector in Urban Governance:
    Distinctive Yet Similar?' funded by De Montfort University (2007; see Chap-
    man, 2009); (3) 'Faith-Based Social Action: Literature Review and Interview
    Findings' funded by the Faith-Based Regeneration Network (2008; see Dinham
    et al., 2008); (4) 'Faith Representation in Urban Governance' funded by De
    Montfort University (2009); (5) The 'Long-Term National Evaluation of Local
    Area Agreements and Local Strategic Partnerships' funded by the Department
    for Communities and Local Government (2007–2010); and (6) Volunteering
    and Faith Communities in England, funded by Volunteering England (see
    Boeck et al., 2009). The authors wish to thank the funders and all those who
    gave up their time and shared their insights and experiences as part of the
    research. The authors would also like to thank Professor Vivien Lowndes for
    her contribution to the Home Office project and her feedback on drafts. Leila
    Hamalainen would like to thank all other members of the Volunteering Eng-
    land research team, particularly Thilo Boeck, Jennie Fleming and Roger Smith.
3   See Chapman (2009), Dinham and Lowndes (2009) and Chapman and
    Lowndes (2008) for a more detailed overview.

References

Baker, C. (2009), 'Blurred Encounters? Religious Literacy, Spiritual Capital and
    Language', in A. Dinham et al. (eds), *Faith in the Public Realm: Controversies,
    Policies and Practices*. Bristol: The Policy Press.

Baker, C., and Skinner, H. (2005), *Telling the Stories: How Churches are Contribut-
    ing to Social Capital*. Manchester: William Temple Foundation.

Berkeley, N. et al. (2006), *Faithful Representation: Faith Representatives on Local
    Public Partnerships: Summary, Key Findings and Recommendations*. London:
    Church Urban Fund.

Boeck, T. et al. (2009), *Volunteering and Faith Communities in England*. London:
    Volunteering England.

Bretherton, L. (2010), *Christianity and Contemporary Politics*. West Sussex: Wiley/
    Blackwell.

Chapman, R. (2009), 'Faith and the Voluntary Sector in Urban Governance:
    Distinctive Yet Similar?' in A. Dinham et al. (eds), *Faith in the Public Realm:
    Controversies, Policies and Practices*. Bristol: Policy Press.

Chapman, R., and Lowndes, V. (2008), 'Faith in Governance: The Potential and
    Pitfalls of Involving Faith Groups in Urban Governance', *Planning, Practice and
    Research* 23 (1), 57–75.

Commission on Integration and Cohesion (2007), *Our Shared Future*. Wetherby:
    Author.

Communities and Local Government (CLG) (2008), *Face to Face and Side by Side:
    A Framework for Partnership in our Multi Faith Society*. London, DCLG.

—. (2009), *Long Term Evaluation of Local Area Agreements and Local Strategic Partnerships: Report on the 2008 Survey of All English Local Strategic Partnerships*. London: Department of Communities and Local Government.

Davie, G. (1994), *Religion in Britain Since 1945: Believing without Belonging.* Oxford: Blackwell Publishers.

Dinham, A., and Lowndes, V. (2008), 'Religion, Resources and Representation: Three Narratives of Faith Engagement in British Urban Governance', *Urban Affairs Review* 43 (6), 817–45.

—. (2009), 'Faith and the Public Realm', in A. Dinham et al. (eds), *Faith in the Public Realm: Controversies, Policies and Practices*. Bristol: Policy Press.

Dinham, A. et al. (2008), *Faith-Based Social Action: Scale and Scope*. London: Faith-Based Regeneration Network.

Duncan, M., and Madeiros, J. (2007), *The Integration and Cohesion Agenda: A Faithworks Perspective*. London: Faithworks.

Farnell et al. (2003), '*Faith*' in Urban Regeneration: Engaging Faith Communities in Urban Regeneration*. Bristol: The Policy Press.

—. (2006), *'Faith' in Rural Communities: Contributions of Social Capital to Community Vibrancy*. Warwickshire: ACORA Publishing.

Furbey, R. (2007), 'Faith, Social Capital and Social Cohesion', in V. Jochum, B. Pratten and K. Wilding (eds), *Faith and Voluntary Action: An Overview of Current Evidence and Debates*. London: NCVO.

Furbey, R. et al. (2006), *Faith as Social Capital: Connecting or Dividing?* Bristol: Policy Press and Joseph Rowntree Foundation.

Grieve, J. et al. (2007), *Faith in the Community: The Contribution of Faith-Based Organisations to Rural Voluntary Action*. London: NCVO.

Habermas, J. (2006), 'Religion in the Public Sphere', *European Journal of Philosophy* 14 (1), 1–25.

Home Office (2004), *Working Together: Co-operation between Government and Faith Communities*. London: Stationary Office.

Lowndes, V., and Chapman, R. (2005), *Faith, Hope and Clarity: Developing a Model of Faith Group Involvement in Civil Renewal,* Main Report. Leicester: De Montfort University.

—. (2007), 'Faith, Hope and Clarity: Faith Groups and Civil Renewal', in T. Brannan, P. John and G. Stoker (eds), *Re-Energizing Citizenship: Strategies for Civil Renewal,* Hampshire: Palgrave Macmillan.

Lukka, P.. and Locke, M. (2000), 'Faith, Voluntary Action and Social Policy: A Review of Research, Voluntary Action', *Voluntary Action* 3, 24–41.

Lukka, P. et al. (2003), *Faith and Voluntary Action: Community, Values and Resources*. London: Institute for Volunteering Research.

National Council for Voluntary Organisations (NCVO) (2007), *Faith and Voluntary Action: An Overview of Current Evidence and Debates*. London: NCVO.

Northwest Regional Development Agency (NWRDA) (2003), *Faith in England's Northwest: The Contribution made by Faith Communities to Civil Society in the Region.* Warrington: Northwest Development Agency.

Ravat, R. (2004), *Embracing the Present, Planning the Future: Social Action by the Faith Communities of Leicester.* Bury St Edmunds: St Edmundsbury Borough Council Printing Services.

Reith, T. (2003), *Releasing the Resources of the Faith Sector: A Faithworks Report.* London: Faithworks.

Sider, R., and Unruh, H. (2004), 'Typology of Religious Characteristics of Social Service and Educational Organisations and Programs', *Nonprofit and Voluntary Sector Quarterly* 33 (1), 109–34.

Smith, G. (2004), 'Faith in the Community and Communities of Faith? Government Rhetoric and Religious Identity in Urban Britain', *Journal of Contemporary Religion* 19 (2), 185–204.

Taylor, M., and Warburton, D. (2003), 'Legitimacy and the Role of UK Third Sector Organizations in the Policy Process', *Voluntas: International Journal of Voluntary and Nonprofit Organizations* 14 (3), 330–32.

Weller et al. (2007), *Religions in the UK 2007–2010.* Derby: University of Derby Multi-Faith Centre.

Wolfe, A. (1998), 'What is Altruism?', in W. Powell and E. Clemens (eds), *Private Action and the Public Good* New Haven, CT: Yale University Press.

Part IV

Theological and Secular Interpretations

12 Exploring the Postsecular State: The Case of Amsterdam

Nynke de Witte

Introduction

After a period in which religion was largely absent from public and political debates in the Netherlands, there has been renewed interest in the place of religion in the public sphere (Van den Donk, Jonkers, Kronjee and Plum, 2006). Van Bijsterveld (2008: 116–17) in this context observes a radical turn from 'faith in the myth of secularization' towards a 'hyper sensitivity for religion'. The presence of non-Western religious communities and the 'moral panic' surrounding Islam specifically has re-opened discussions on the relationship between the state and religion (Kennedy and Valenta, 2006: 342–45).

Between the seventeenth century and the beginning of the twentieth century, the Netherlands transformed from a relatively tolerant polity dominated by the Calvinist Church into a 'pillarised' society, in which Protestants, Catholics, as well as Socialists and Liberals, were institutionalized in the political system (Lijphart, 1975). Pillarization came under pressure from strong secularization since the 1960s, which brought about the finalization of the separation of state and church in the new constitution of 1983. The new constitution makes no reference to any church anymore and grants religious and non-religious beliefs equal freedom. Although it ended legal financial relations between the state and organized religions, this did not mean that religious institutions or religious activities could no longer be subsidized. Such financial support, however, has become largely dependent on the willingness of local authorities as a consequence of decentralization (Knippenberg, 2006).

While state–religion relations are often studied at the level of nation–states, in practice, claims from religious communities are often dealt with by local authorities who are, due to decentralization, responsible for a wide range of policies. In an attempt to shed light on the meaning of the postsecular city from the perspective of the local state, this chapter will discuss Amsterdam's recent policies and practices concerning subsidizing religious and faith-based organizations. The chapter is divided into four sections. Section one briefly reviews the role of the state in theoretical discussions on the emergence of postsecular societies. It introduces Dalferth's conceptualization of postsecular states, which will be used as an ideal type to evaluate Amsterdam's recent policy practices of state–religion cooperation. The second section presents the vision of state–religion relations as it was recently defended by the Board of Mayor and Alderman in Amsterdam. Section three discusses Amsterdam's recent (financial) support for religious communities and faith-based organizations in different policy areas. The last section concludes with an assessment of Amsterdam's (postsecular) vision and policy practices, and draws some conclusions about postsecular state–religion relations.[1]

Postsecular society and postsecular state

If a postsecular society refers to a society that has to 'adjust itself to the continued existence of religious communities in an increasingly secularized environment' (Habermas, 2008), what role does the state play in such readjustment? According to Dalferth, it is not so much society at large becoming postsecular, but the state. Accordingly Dalferth (2009: 21) describes postsecular societies as:

> those societies in which states no longer define themselves as secular. Hence the real locus for the use of the term 'post-secular' is not at the level of society at large or of individual life but at the level of the state or the political sphere or system.

The idea that modern societies require a secular state is often taken for granted. Bader (2007: 17) notes that 'Liberal, democratic, republican, socialist, feminist or otherwise "progressive" political parties share the assumption that modern states are "secular" states that require a strict constitutional, legal, administrative, political and cultural separation of state from organized religions'. While secularism emerged in response to the confessional wars waged in Europe in the sixteenth and seventeenth centuries, its continued relevance has become contested. While some scholars have redefined secularism within specific national contexts (Modood, 2008; Bhargava 2008), others have rejected secularism all together as a necessary condition for liberal democratic states (Bader, 2007). Bader (2007: 98) remarks: 'only in opposition to old and new religious threats by fundamentalists, intending to replace state indifference or state autonomy with a theocratic regime, does the insistence on the secular character of law and the state make sense'.

This chapter examines how local authorities in Amsterdam have recently defined their position on state–religion relations and dealt in practice with religious groups and faith-based organizations. To explore Amsterdam as a possible postsecular city, the ideal types of states presented by Dalferth (2009) provide a helpful starting point. Based on the political history of the West, Dalferth distinguishes between religious, tolerant, secular and postsecular types of states. While religious states prescribe to citizens which religion to practice, tolerant states tolerate citizens to practise any religion without necessarily treating them equal. Secular states do treat citizens equally regardless of their religious or non-religious convictions and do not support or oppose any particular religion or non-religion.

Secular states (as opposed to anti-religious states that prescribe atheism or ban particular religions) leave it to their citizens to choose between religious or non-religious ways of life, they stop themselves by law from interfering with the religious or non-religious orientations and practices of their citizens, and they take explicitly and in a legally binding way a neutral stance toward all questions of religion. (Dalferth, 2009: 16)

As guardian of the secular public sphere, the state defines itself as neutral vis-à-vis religion and non-religion, by 'restricting itself by law to pass or accept any pro- or antireligious law' (Dalferth, 2009: 18). A postsecular state, on the other hand, is neither self-declared religious nor secular. It does not prescribe or privilege a certain religion or non-religion, but neither does it claim an explicit neutral stance vis-à-vis questions of religion or non-religion.

A post-secular state is indifferent to questions of religion or non-religion, and not merely neutral: There may be many religions and non-religions in society, but the state does not bother to define its relations to them in a particular way. (Dalferth, 2009: 19)

For a postsecular state, Dalferth argues, there is simply no need to reject the identification with religion or claim neutrality with respect to religion or non-religion. Rather than being a society with a renewed interest in spiritual life, the crux of a postsecular society, according to Dalferth, is that questions of religion have become irrelevant for the self-understanding of states.

The state, when defining its relations to society at large or to particular spheres of society, no longer privileges religion from other spheres by insisting on being "neutral" or "secular" as regards religion ... If there is religion, it is a fact of life. But it is nothing that requires society at large, or any social sub-sphere, to take a particular positive, or negative, or neutral stance to it. (Dalferth, 2009: 19–20)

While Dalferth draws conclusions from these changes in Western societies for Christian theology, this chapter will examine the applicability of his conception of postsecular states for recent discussions on and practices of state–religion cooperation in Amsterdam.

Amsterdam's postsecular turn?

Although Amsterdam has been described as an 'unchurchly municipality' (*onkerkelijke gemeente*) (Knippenberg, 1992: 1) and 'capital of secularity' (Martin, 2005: 54), in the last decades rapid de-churching has been combined with religious persistence and the arrival of new religions and spiritualities.[2] In this context, Van der Rooden (2007: 1) writes that religion and secularization have 'developed in tandem' in Amsterdam in the last one century and a half. Results from a small survey in 2000 (Municipality of Amsterdam, 2001) indicate that 41 per cent of the population regards him/herself affiliated with a religion, religious or other life conviction; 17 per cent with Christianity (5 per cent Protestant, 10 per cent Roman Catholic), 14 per cent with Islam, 1 per cent with Judaism, 3 per cent unknown, 9 per cent other and 56 per cent is not affiliated (Municipality of Amsterdam, 2001).[3] What makes Amsterdam an interesting case by which to explore the postsecular city, however, is not so much the continued relevance of religion in a secularized society, but recent discussions on state–religion relations.

The public presence of new faith groups in the city have generated new discussions on the legitimate role and place of religion in the public domain. In a lecture on the separation of church and state in 2004, the mayor of Amsterdam, Job Cohen, concluded that:

> Religion 'works' for its believers. Now migration from one country to another has become a normal affair, religion can also work like that in our cities, especially when other bonding structures fail. And then we are better off to recognize than deny this. . . . The true dynamic power of religion can only be understood if we understand that religions offer believers a perspective for a just or more just society. . . . The search for a more just society should be a point where believers and secularists can reach to each other's hands. (free translation of Cohen 2004)

As a prominent member of the Social Democrat Party and self-declared non-believer, Cohen is an interesting example of someone advocating a postsecular position.[4] In 2006, after his party had acquired many Muslim votes in the city, he argued that the time had come for Social Democrats to stop seeing religion as something out of date or threatening, but instead see it as a potentially valuable form of social engagement (Cohen, 2006). His lecture, titled 'Social Democracy and Religion, Reversed Break-Through' referred to the breakthrough that Christians had made in the past, when they started aligning themselves with non-Christians to strive for social democracy (see also Borgman, 2006: 332). While Cohen has made various pleas for state cooperation with religious and faith-based organizations, he has also stressed the importance of a secular state as a precondition to provide space to a plurality of lifestyles, convictions of life and religions in the public sphere (Cohen, 2009).

Cohen's views on religion and the financial support for some religious organizations in Amsterdam in particular have not been free from criticism, especially by those who favour a strict separation between church and state.[5] In response to political controversies surrounding (indirect) financial support for religious organizations in the city, in 2008, the Amsterdam Board of Mayor and Alderman prepared a policy memorandum on their interpretation of the separation of church and state (Municipality of Amsterdam, 2008). It provides a vision and framework of how the Board wishes to deal with cases that involve a religious or philosophical (*levensbeschouwelijke*) component.

The paper builds on the Dutch tradition of state–religion relations, and highlights four principles that have determined these relations: the separation of church and state, freedom of religion, equality and neutrality of the government. The policy memorandum concludes that the separation of church and state – defined as the institutional and substantive autonomy of state from church and church from state – does not prohibit relations with and (financial) support for (non-religious) activities of organizations with a religious or philosophical foundation. To specify the criteria for providing financial support to organizations with a religious foundation, it elaborates on different interpretations of the principle of neutrality, distinguishing between exclusive, inclusive or compensating neutrality (Municipality of Amsterdam, 2008: 7–9).[6]

While exclusive neutrality is compared to the French concept of *laïcité* which excludes religion from the 'religiously neutral' public sphere, inclusive neutrality gives equal and proportional room and support to the expressions and practices of religions and convictions of life by individuals and groups in the public sphere. Different from the inclusive neutrality practised during times of pillarization, however, inclusive neutrality is interpreted by the Amsterdam authorities mainly in terms of non-discrimination. Consequently, financial support for (the activities of) mosque associations or (migrant) churches, for instance, are deemed possible when this serves the city's policy goals, does not privilege one religious group over another, and treats similar activities of non-religious groups equally (Municipality of Amsterdam, 2008: 8–9). Compensating neutrality, finally, refers to a situation in which the government favours certain religions or life convictions over others in the context of historical or structural inequality or social disadvantages of certain religious groups. The aim of this support is to provide the preconditions for equal participation of all religious groups in society (Municipality of Amsterdam, 2008: 8–9).

In the memorandum the Board rejects exclusive neutrality, which is deemed in conflict with the constitution and Dutch tradition of state–religion relations; the Board embraces inclusive neutrality, and under special circumstances, compensating neutrality. It argues for 'contextual decision making' to decide which type of neutrality is most appropriate to use in which circumstances. The memorandum also makes explicit that it wants to give Islam a similar position as other religions and life convictions. When the policy memorandum was discussed in the Amsterdam municipal council, most critique was focused on the concept of compensating neutrality, which was criticized for privileging certain religious groups. All parties voted in favour of making inclusive neutrality a starting point for local policies (City Council Amsterdam, 2008).[7]

How does this vision of state–religion relations correspond with Dalferth's description of postsecular states? On the one hand, the fact that a vision of state–religion relations is required does not match the description of Dalferth's postsecular state that is indifferent towards questions of religion. The same is true for the emphasis on state neutrality. On the other hand, and in accordance with Dalferth's idea of a postsecular state, the Amsterdam authorities do not specify a singular position on state–religion relations. Instead, the Board justifies different possible relations, ranging from inclusive and compensating neutrality. The interpretation of inclusive neutrality – as non-discrimination – is in line with the indifferent attitude of a postsecular state towards the religious or non-religious identity of its citizens and organizations. Compensating neutrality, on the other hand, indicates that the state refrains from being explicitly neutral with respect to religious matters, by justifying support for certain religious groups. The latter position is not based on the fact that the state identifies with particular religious groups (as in a religious state), but informed by the need to compensate for situations of inequity or disadvantage.

Policy practices of state–religion cooperation

Integration policy is highlighted in the memorandum as one of the areas in which the city hall actively implements inclusive and compensating neutrality: by supporting the establishment of new houses of worship to guarantee religious freedom, while also making use of the religious infrastructure in the city for specific policy goals. The policy memorandum also mentions recent cooperation with religious organizations in the context of anti-radicalization policies and long-standing cooperation with faith-based social service organizations (Municipality of Amsterdam, 2008: 11–13). The next subsections review practices of state–religion cooperation in these different policy areas, in order to scrutinize Amsterdam as a postsecular state.

Support for new houses of worship

While in the last decades many traditional churches in the city have been demolished or were given a new function (e.g. housing, office space, recreation facility), new houses of worship have been established as well, mostly by immigrant communities. The local government has been involved in this process in various ways, most importantly by making (or denying) space for religious facilities in urban plans and by providing (or denying) financial support to initiatives for new worship places. As will be demonstrated below, the actual support given to new houses of worship and reasons for doing so have changed.

Between 1976 and 1984, the city hall was responsible for the implementation of two national subsidy schemes that became available for the establishment of houses of worship for Islamic guest workers in the Netherlands (Landman, 1992: 278–82). The reasons for these schemes were twofold: to guarantee effective religious freedom and to compensate Islamic immigrants for historical disadvantage compared to Christian groups that had benefited from subsidies in the past, most recently through the Church Construction Act (*Wet Premie Kerkenbouw*) between 1962 and 1975 (Rath et al., 2001). As this subsidy scheme only applied to Muslims that had been recruited as guest workers, and not to Suriname Muslims, the Amsterdam government decided in 1982 to provide a subsidy also to the foundation of Welfare for Muslims (connected to the *World Islam Mission*) to build a mosque (called *Taibah*) in the *Bijlmermeer,* in the South-East district. The subsidy was motivated by the lack of available religious facilities in the area, and the exclusion of the organization from the national subsidy scheme (City Council Amsterdam, 1990).

After the constitutional changes in 1983, national state subsidies for the purpose of building mosques or other houses of worship were no longer available, and the Amsterdam municipal council decided to no longer directly subsidize new religious facilities. However, it did establish a special working group in 1984 to give advice on how to improve the housing situation of non-Christian/Jewish houses of worship that had been established in the city (City Council Amsterdam, 1990). It resulted in a regulation allowing credit guarantees for religious groups without sufficient financial means, and direct financial support for houses of worship that were forced to move out in the context of urban renewal. Financed by the budget for local minorities policy (as integration policy was called at that time), the regulation aimed to overcome the disadvantage that existed for ethnic minorities to practise their beliefs, thereby providing another example of compensating neutrality. The regulation, which lasted until 1990, supported building and rebuilding costs of various mosques and Hindu temples (City Council Amsterdam, 1990).

Since 1991 the regulation of places of worship has become mainly a responsibility of city districts.[8] Two large projects have become emblematic for state–religion cooperation on houses of worship in Amsterdam: the multi-church/community centres *De Kandelaar* and *De Westermoskee*. Government support for both projects is mentioned in the policy memorandum on the separation of church and state as examples of compensating neutrality. As will be argued below, the reasons for supporting both projects were informed not only by the idea of compensation, but also by specific political interests.

The idea behind the establishment of *De Kandelaar* in the *Bijlmermeer* evolved as a response to an untenable situation of various Evangelical, Pentecostal and Charismatic Churches established by migrants from Ghana and other (West) African countries. Because suitable locations and financial resources were lacking, many of these so-called 'migrant churches' had established places of worship in garages underneath high-rise apartment buildings.[9] When some of these apartments were demolished in the 1990s, in the context of a large-scale urban regeneration plan (Den Uyl, 2008), several churches found themselves without a place of worship. Some of them joined forces and made plans to build a church centre together. After years of making claims at the city district, in 1997, the city district started a plan together with 15 migrant churches and the housing corporation Rochdale to build three multi-church centres (*kerkverzamelgebouwen*) in the neighbourhood.

In 2007, one of the buildings, The Candle (*De Kandelaar*), was realized. Because the migrant churches did not have enough financial resources to own the building or become the sole renters, the project had transformed from a multi-church centre into a multifunctional community centre, including not only five church halls providing a place of worship to 15 churches, but also meeting rooms for self-organizations, office space, apartments, a restaurant and a crèche (Van der Meulen, 2009: 168–70). The local housing corporation that owns the building rents the church halls to The Candle foundation, representing five Ghanaian churches, who in turn, sub-rent the church halls to an additional nine churches in the area.

Making use of European funds for urban development projects and co-finance from the city hall and city district for urban renewal, the local authorities facilitated the building of *De Kandelaar* by providing a project manager, town planners and subsidies. While the district president used a discourse of compensating neutrality after the publication of the policy memorandum on the separation of church and state (City district South-East, 2008), other arguments for supporting the project have been put forward as well. Goossen (2006: 119, 124) remarks that the city district became more willing to provide (financial) support for the realization of places of worship for migrants, when churches started to stress their social role in the neighbourhood. In 2005, the city district indeed argued that support for the project was justified on the grounds that migrant churches provided assistance to vulnerable groups and assisted in the integration of newcomers. Van der Meulen (2009) further suggests that 'black–white tensions' in the neighbourhood were important in understanding the shift in the district authorities' attitude towards solving location problems of migrant churches. Only after African pastors publicly contested the (financial) support of the city district for the relocation of a white congregation in the area did the city district become involved in accommodating African churches as well. That the city district is not primarily concerned with the historical or structural inequality of migrant churches could also explain why many churches in the neighbourhood are still without suitable places of worship.

While The Candle is often hailed as a success story of state–religion cooperation in Amsterdam, support for building the *Westermoskee* in the De Baarsjes district has become an example of failed cooperation. In this district, the Turkish mosque association *Aya Sofia* of the Milli Görüş movement[10] has been involved in negotiations with the district authorities and city hall to build a new mosque for over a decade (Sunier, 2006). After years of legal conflict, in 2000, the new city district president and the director of the umbrella organization of Milli Görüş in the north of the Netherlands reached a compromise, which included plans for housing as well as a mosque on the plot owned by the mosque association. While housing corporation *Het Oosten* would be responsible for developing housing units and parking facilities, the investment fund of Milli Görüş, Manderen, would assume financial responsibility for the building of the mosque. The mosque would be built in the 'Amsterdam school' style and given a Dutch name, *De Westermoskee* (Westermosque), named after the neighbouring church *Westerkerk* (Westerchurch). The latter reflected the fact that the mosque association had become open towards Dutch society and was at the forefront of defining 'Dutch' Islam (Sunier, 2006: 22).

In order to help the association meet the financial requirement for building the mosque, the different parties agreed on a scheme by which the city hall would buy the plot from Manderen and make the mosque association a long-lease tenant. Moreover, the municipality bought the plot for a higher price than the market value, thereby providing the mosque association with indirect financial support in the form of a loan. What seemed to have the potential of becoming a success of state–religion cooperation ended in a deadlock, when conflict arose over the ground-deal (*gronddeal*), both within the municipal council and within the Milli Görüş movement (see also City district De Baarsjes, 2008). Internal disagreement within the movement caused changes in the leadership of Milli Görüş in 2006. The involvement of the European headquarters of Milli Görüş in Cologne – known for having more conservative views – in the appointment of the new leadership, raised concerns on the part of the district authorities and the housing corporation. It was feared that the mosque association would no longer be able to follow its 'liberal' and 'pro-integration' approach. In order to ensure such an approach and the mosque's independence from the German headquarters, an agreement document 'Working on the future' was signed by the new parties involved. However, internal conflict within the movement in combination with growing suspicion on the part of the local authorities and the housing corporation has blocked further progress on the mosque project (City district De Baarsjes, 2008).

In the policy memorandum, the ground deal is justified by both inclusive and compensating neutrality. Because this instrument is used by urban planners to facilitate certain spatial developments, it is argued that there is no reason for not applying it for facilitating the building of places of worship. The policy memorandum mentions that between 1967 and 2007, similar ground deals were made in ten cases, including churches, temples and mosques (Municipality of Amsterdam, 2008: 11–12). The fact that the municipality gave Manderen a relatively high ground price, however, was justified by their wish to facilitate the building of the mosque for reasons of compensating neutrality. The example of *De Westermoskee* also illustrates that compensating neutrality in this case was clearly linked to a political preference for liberal Islam.

The voting against compensating neutrality in the city council indicates that government support for new houses of worship on the basis of compensating neutrality alone has become questionable. Rather than compensating neutrality, the authorities seem in favour of inclusive neutrality. Such an approach can also be found in a policy document of the Planning Department from 2004, which advised city districts to take religious needs for space into account in urban renewal plans. Although this does indicate a shift from exclusive to inclusive neutrality in spatial planning policies, it is the social role of religious institutions for newcomers that is put forward as justification to reserve space for religious facilities, rather than concerns about guaranteeing religious freedom or compensation. Other recommendations include the re-usage of existing religious buildings, creating multi-church buildings and locating larger religious communities – whose members are spread over the city – in urban business districts (Municipality of Amsterdam, 2004). Unlike the vision of compensating neutrality advocated in the 1970s and 1980s, the policy document communicates a vision of inclusive neutrality understood as non-discrimination: claims for houses of worship are treated as 'social provisions' or 'public attracting services'.[11]

Support for Islamic organizations in the context of integration and anti-radicalization policy

In the policy memorandum on the separation of church and state, special reference is made to the policy paper 'Belonging and Participation' to illustrate how inclusive neutrality is applied in integration policies. The paper states that the government intends to support organizations that stimulate integration (which is defined in terms of participation and belonging), irrespective of their secular, religious, ethnic or mixed basis (Municipality of Amsterdam, 2003: 10). Although cooperation with religious organizations in the context of integration policy is not new, the reasons for doing so have changed over time. Government cooperation with Islamic organizations in the context of integration policies suggests insight into these changes.

In the 1980s, Islamic organizations of Turks, Moroccans and Surinamese were seen as important partners in the implementation of the Local Minorities Policy that was aimed at the emancipation of ethnic minorities. Due to the alleged separation of church and state, structural financial support was only given to secular self-organizations of ethnic minorities; however, religious organizations were encouraged to set up independent sociocultural associations, in order to become eligible to apply for subsidies. Moreover, mosque associations were also included in the Moroccan and Turkish advisory boards (Vermeulen, 2005: 80; Maussen, 2006: 91). When national integration policy in the 1990s shifted from a focus on the emancipation of ethnic minorities towards the integration and participation of individual migrants, the Amsterdam government abolished structural (but not project) subsidies to ethnic minority organizations in 1994 (Maussen, 2006: 91). The advisory boards for ethnic minorities were abolished in 2002 and replaced by a diversity advisory board in 2004.

A new vision on integration was presented in 1999, in the policy document 'The Power of a Diverse City' (Municipality of Amsterdam, 1999), which conceptualized the strength of Amsterdam society as the sum of the individuals who lived in the city. Moreover, culture and religion were presented in this report as components of individual lifestyles that belong to the private sphere, rather than being constitutive of groups (Maussen, 2006: 67–78, 91). The target groups of the new diversity were no longer ethnic minorities, but people of foreign descent, women, disabled persons and homosexuals. This new vision on integration is continued in the previously mentioned policy paper 'Belonging and Participation' (Municipality of Amsterdam, 2003) and in the policy paper 'Perspectives and opportunities: Amsterdam's integration policy in the context of the program "We Amsterdammers"' (Municipality of Amsterdam, 2005a). Instead of the emancipation of minorities, the participation and belonging of all people in Amsterdam has become the main objective of integration policy. Paradoxically, this new approach has provided Islamic organizations with new funding opportunities, as the government now claims to be indifferent towards the religious and non-religious identity of civil society organizations that contribute to the city's integration agenda. Special interest has been given to the informal care and social capital within Islamic communities.[12]

Security concerns have also influenced cooperation with Islamic organizations. Islamic fundamentalism has become an important issue on the city's security agenda since the murder of filmmaker and columnist Theo van Gogh in November 2004. Not long afterward, the city hall presented an action plan titled 'We the people of Amsterdam' (Municipality of Amsterdam, 2005a) aimed at combating terrorism, preventing radicalization and mobilizing positive forces in society. Cooperation with local mosques has been regarded as instrumental for the restoration of social cohesion. In addition to subsidies for numerous inter-religious dialogue projects, an initiative for an Islamic cultural centre was subsidized as well, which became the subject of political controversy because of the alleged violation of the separation of state and church principle, and the motive of the city hall to stimulate the development of 'Western' and 'European Islam' (City Council Amsterdam, 2006). Most controversial, however, has been the financial support for mosque associations willing to cooperate in combating Islamic radicalization.

The Amsterdam authorities did not adopt an anti-Islam discourse, which had become dominant at the national level since the turn of the millennium. Rather, they tried to cooperate with Islamic organizations in various ways. The policy paper 'Amsterdam against radicalization' can be interpreted as arguing that while religious organizations in the context of integration policy are considered as 'voluntary organizations' that can receive subsidies for certain projects, in the context of anti-radicalization policy they become 'partners' of the government (Municipality of Amsterdam, 2007: 30). Such a partnership has been sought, because a religious discourse was deemed necessary in the fight against Islamic radicalization. In the city district Old-West, community workers tried to get a working relationship with members of an orthodox mosque, and in the Baarsjes district, the authorities drafted a 'protocol to prevent extremism' together with three mosque associations (Maussen, 2006: 101, 105). The city hall recently subsidized a large project to prevent Islamic radicalization among Moroccan youth, involving several mosques in the city.[13] The policy memorandum on the separation of church and state seems to present such forms of state–religion cooperation as examples of inclusive neutrality. But rather than state indifference towards the religious identity of mosque organizations, the government showed explicit interest in mosque associations, because of their specific religious discourse.

Support for faith-based social service organizations

In spite of the long-standing cooperation with faith-based social service organizations in the city, subsidy policies involving faith-based organizations have recently become the subject of critique. Historically, faith-based organizations have played an important role in the provision of social services in the city. Before the development of the welfare state, church-related organizations, such as the *Protestantse Diaconie, Lutherse Diaconie* and the *Roomsch Catholijk Oude Armen Kantoor* were largely responsible for the care and social control of 'their' poor in the city and owned and managed hospitals, homes for elderly, orphanages, and so on. With the development of the welfare state in the second part of the twentieth century, the central state took over most of the financial responsibilities for social security, while leaving the provision of many services in the hands of non-profit (including faith-based) organizations (Burger and Veldheer, 2001: 225). Following the framework of equal financing of public and faith-based schools, this type of inclusive neutrality based on the principle of *subsidiarity* (the term used by the Roman Catholic Church) or sovereignty (the term used by the Reformed Church) was also applied to the welfare sector.

Since the 1960s, secularization has diminished the power of the confessional pillars. At the same time, increasing dependence on decreasing amounts of public funding since the late 1970s stimulated the merging and fusion of many formerly pillarized welfare organizations into professional semi-public organizations (Burger and Veldheer, 2001: 226; Meijs 2007: 51). Moreover, as the government's focus shifted from intermediary social service organizations towards clients, many organizations transformed from having a pillarized to a functional structure (Burger and Dekker, 2001: 71). Since the 1980s, the central government has largely withdrawn from the social sector, by decentralizing responsibilities and privatizing service delivery. As a result, both profit and non-profit service providers compete for government contracts and clients in the welfare market (Burger and Dekker, 2001: 227). The recent Social Support Act (House of Representatives, 2004–2005) that came into effect in January 2007 is the latest step in this process. It has made social and care services the responsibility of local authorities, who are encouraged to support informal care and volunteer work in order to reduce peoples' dependence on public welfare provisions, while ensuring public service delivery by private parties.

Nowadays faith-based organizations are mainly involved in service delivery to the most vulnerable groups in society, such as homeless people, drug addicts, undocumented migrants or ex-convicts. While most faith-based organizations in Amsterdam operate on a relatively small scale, some have gained a large market share in certain niches of service delivery. The Goodwill Centre of the Salvation Army in Amsterdam, for instance, is a big player in the field of accommodation and shelter for the most vulnerable groups. It manages various working units operating in Amsterdam, including shelters for the homeless, accommodation for women, centres for young delinquents, homecare, youth welfare work and employment training. It relies almost 100 per cent on government funding, and is involved in public tendering in the field of domestic care, while in other areas it is granted subsidies to develop projects. It meets regularly with the local authorities and other (secular and faith-based) organizations providing similar support services in a Council for Social Relief (*Platform Opvang Amsterdam*). Although the Goodwill Centre claims not to engage in direct proselytizing, and many employees are not members of the Salvation Army, all employees are required to subscribe to the mission statement of the Army, which includes the importance of proselytizing in relation to relief for the poor.[14]

Government support for faith-based social service organizations only became a subject to critique after the organization Youth for Christ (YfC) won a public tender in 2009 to implement public youth work in the Baarsjes district, an area with a large concentration of Muslim youth. It had won the competition due to its professional working methods and relatively low salaries.[15] Even though the responsible alderman (and district president) emphasized that an agreement had been made that the organization would not engage in proselytizing, the contract was heavily criticized in the district council. City councillors argued that an organization with the mission 'to bring youth into contact with Jesus Christ' would not be able to conduct 'neutral' youth work. Concerns were mostly related to the possible exclusion of youngsters of different faiths, the attitude of youth workers towards issues such as homosexuality and the discriminatory hiring practices of the organization (City district council De Baarsjes, 2008; City district council

De Baarsjes, 2009). As a consequence of these political discussions, the district president stepped down, and a new round of negotiations between the city district and the organization resulted in concessions to hire non-Christian personnel and the creation of a separate foundation and website.

In the discussions with the city council on the policy memorandum on the separation of church and state, the mayor compared the financial support for YfC with the long-standing support of the city hall for the work of the Salvation Army. The spokeswoman of the GreenLeft Party did not agree with this comparison, as she regarded youth work as a kind of childrearing support aimed at the 'general public', while services of the Salvation Army are focused on a 'specific group'. Moreover, the latter services are also provided by others, while YfC had acquired a monopoly on the implementation of public youth work in the district. Like her colleagues in the Baarsjes district, she opposed YfC conducting public youth work, because 'youth work should be neutral and Youth for Christ does its work from the desire to bring youth in contact with Jesus Christ' (City Council Amsterdam, 2008: 23).

Another faith-based organization that became a subject of criticism is *Tot Heil des Volks* (For the Salvation of the People), which received public money for their ministry to prostitutes (called *Het Scharlaken Koord* or Scarlet Cord). Like YfC and the Salvation Army, the organization makes use of faith criteria in hiring personnel. After questions about the neutrality of the organization in the city council in September 2009 (City Council Amsterdam, 2009a), the responsible alderman gave an assurance that the actual service provision would be conducted on a 'neutral' basis, but also made it clear that the hiring policy was largely up to the organization. She also stressed that there are other (including public) organizations providing similar services to prostitutes. Nevertheless, in November 2009, a motion from the Liberal Party was accepted (without the vote from the Christian Democrats) stating that the city hall will not give contracts to organizations that discriminate against certain groups in their employment policy (City Council Amsterdam, 2009b).

Although this decision seems in conflict with the Law for Equal Treatment which exempts faith-based organizations from the scope of anti-discrimination law in hiring policies concerning personnel in executive positions, it does indicate a shift from inclusive to exclusive neutrality in the field of social policies.[16] Paradoxically, the recent Social Support Act seems to provide new opportunities for churches and mosques to receive project subsidies for their social activities (Dautzenberg and Westerlaak, 2007). However, in actuality, cooperation with and support for social activities of churches is limited and also fragmented: while some city districts actively cooperate with and finance churches for their social work, others refrain from doing so.[17]

Conclusion

If a postsecular state is understood to be a state that is neither self-declared religious nor secular, the Netherlands provides an interesting case to study its meaning in practice. The 1983 constitution is neither self-declared religious nor secular, and grants religious and other life convictions equal treatment and freedom. From a historical perspective, however, it would be inadequate to call the constitution postsecular, because it did not replace a self-declared secular state and law, but developed out of a system of religious pillarization. While in the era of pillarization the equal treatment of organized religions in the public sphere informed state–religion relations, the separation of state and church in 1983, in combination with an increasingly heterogeneous religious landscape and a withdrawing state, have paved the way for more differentiated and localized forms of state–religion relations. This is exemplified by the discussions and policy practices in Amsterdam, which were reviewed in this chapter to shed light on the postsecular city.

Amsterdam's policies and practices were evaluated against Dalferth's conceptualization of postsecular states, which are claimed to be neither secular nor religious. Being largely indifferent towards questions of religion and non-religion, such states, according to Dalferth, no longer define their relations to organized religions in a particular way. This implies that they neither privilege a certain religion or non-religion, nor do they claim to be strictly neutral. It has been argued that the pledge for both inclusive and compensating neutrality by the Amsterdam Board of Mayor and Alderman in 2008 has striking similarities with Dalferth's description of a postsecular state. While the principle of inclusive neutrality exemplifies the indifferent attitude of the Amsterdam authorities towards the religious identity of citizens and organizations, the principle of compensating neutrality indicates that the city hall is willing to refrain from being explicitly neutral towards religious matters.

In policy practice, however, the Amsterdam authorities have followed divergent and contradictory approaches to dealing with religious groups and faith-based organizations. While compensating neutrality was implemented in the 1980s and 1990s by (sporadically) providing financial support to new places of worship in the city, there are indications that this phase has come to an end. Recent indications to take applications for religious spaces into account on an even-handed basis with claims for other 'social provisions' or 'public attracting services' indicate that non-discrimination is the preferred policy approach. Within the context of integration policies, mosque associations were in the 1980s and 1990s largely excluded from subsidies, although they were included in advisory boards of ethnic minorities. The new 'diversity' approach, however, follows inclusive neutrality or non-discrimination. At the same time, however, security concerns have made the local authorities anything but indifferent to questions of Islam, thereby indicating the limits of postsecular indifference. In the area of welfare policies, finally, funding to faith-based social service organizations has recently been criticized, thereby indicating a possible shift from inclusive to exclusive neutrality.

If the Amsterdam case tells us anything about postsecular states, it is the unpredictability of state–religion relations. This is not surprising though, as postsecular states determine their support for religious and faith-based organizations not on the basis of a fixed position vis-à-vis religion, but on the basis of specific policy interests. As these interests change over time, so does state support for and cooperation with religious and faith-based organizations. No longer, therefore, in a postsecular state does it make sense to talk of models of state–religion relations. This does not mean, however, that questions of religion are irrelevant for postsecular states. While postsecular states might be indifferent towards questions of religion in terms of their self-definition, they cannot be indifferent towards the public role of religion in society. Amsterdam's policy practices demonstrate that while the government actively supports religious groups and faith-based organizations that contribute to policy goals, it also takes action against undesirable public manifestations of religion. Future state–religion relations will therefore largely depend on local authorities' interpretations of the societal value or harm of religious and faith-based organizations, rather than on predetermined principles of separation between state and church or state neutrality.

Notes

1 The chapter largely draws on data collected between September 2008 and December 2009 for the seventh framework FACIT project on Faith-Based Organisations and Social Exclusion in European Cities.

2 There are strong indicators of fast secularization especially among the traditional Dutch churches. While Roman Catholic and Protestant denominations around 1900 were still responsible for some 70 per cent of the population of the city, in 1984, its number has decreased to less than 40 per cent (Municipality of Amsterdam, 2001).

3 The category of other includes humanism, Buddhism, Hinduism, anthroposophy and New Age.

4 Job Cohen was mayor of Amsterdam from 15 January 2001 to 12 March 2010, when he became party leader of the Social Democrat Party.

5 For an overview of the different viewpoints that are present in national public debates on this issue, see Harchaoui 2008.

6 This conceptualization of state neutrality is copied from Van der Burg (2006).

7 All parties supported a motion from the Social Democrats, Liberals and Christian Democrats, proposing to make only inclusive neutrality a starting point for policy, not compensating neutrality.

8 Amsterdam is subdivided into 15 city districts (*stadsdelen*), a system implemented in the 1980s to make decision making more efficient and bring government closer to the people. While the city hall (mayor, aldermen and municipal Council) is responsible for the overall policies of the city, the city districts have power over affairs that concern their district. The current 15 city districts will be reduced to seven in 2010.

9 The term 'migrant church' is contested, especially by some pastors working in the neighbourhood, who prefer to use the term 'international church' in order to do right to the variety of backgrounds of their members. In addition, they argue, their members are first and foremost Christians, not migrants.

10 Milli Görüş is an Islamic social and political movement in Turkey (not committed to the official state religion), with several branches in Europe and European headquarters in Cologne. Since 1997, Milli Görüş has two regional

umbrella organizations in the Netherlands, one in the north and one in the south of the country.

11   In the document, it can be read that in development plans (*bestemmingsplan-nen*), existing religious buildings are often regarded as 'societal provisions' (*maatschappelijke voorziening*), while in structural plan (*structuurplan*), religious provisions are included within the category of 'public attracting services' (Municipality of Amsterdam, 2004).

12   This interest is demonstrated by a research conducted for the city hall in 2004 on the social role of mosques in the city (Driessen, Van der Werf and Boulal, 2004) and a conference organized in 2005 titled 'The mosque as connecting link', exploring cooperation between mosque organizations, city districts and welfare organizations.

13   The project was initiated by the national umbrella organization of Moroccan mosques (UMMON), the Council of Moroccan mosques in Amsterdam and Surroundings (RvM) and the Amsterdam Centre for Foreigners (ACB).

14   Interview with Koos Koelewijn, policymaker at the Goodwill Centre on 24 June 2009.

15   Interview with Roel Boogaard, region manager of YfC Amsterdam and Rotterdam on 3 July 2009.

16   In accordance with a special clause in the General Equal Treatment Law specific to faith-based organizations, the Commission for Equal Treatment judged in 1996 and 1997 that the Salvation Army had the right to select personnel on the basis of their convictions.

17   In a conference organized by the Amsterdam Council for Life Convictions and Religions in June 2009 to discuss the policy memorandum on the separation of church and state, the local authorities were criticized on two issues: the lack of recognition and support for social work of churches in the city and the divergent approaches of city districts towards cooperation with churches.

References

Bader, V. (2007), *Democracy or Secularism? Associational Governance of Religious Diversity*. Amsterdam: Amsterdam University Press.

Bhargava, R. (2008), 'Political Secularism: Why It Is Needed and What Can be Learnt from Its Indian Version', in G. B. Levey and T. Modood (eds), *Secularism, Religion, and Multicultural Citizenship*. Cambridge: Cambridge University Press.

Borgman, E. (2006), 'De onlosmakelijke verbondenheid van religie en publiek domein: pleidooi voor een "omgekeerde doorbraak"', in W. B. H. J. van de Donk et al. (eds), *Geloven in het publieke domein: Verkenningen van een dubbele transformatie*. Amsterdam: Amsterdam University Press / Wetenschappelijke Raad voor het Regeringsbeleid.

Burger, A., and Dekker, P. (2001), *The Nonprofit Sector in the Netherlands*. Den Haag, The Netherlands: Social and Cultural Planning Office.

Burger, A., and Veldheer, V. (2001), 'The Growth of the Nonprofit Sector in the Netherlands', *Nonprofit and Voluntary Sector Quarterly* 30 (2), 221–46.

City Council Amsterdam (1990), 'Evaluatierapportage over de subsidieregeling voor religieuze voorzieningen voor etnische minderheden', Gemeenteblad, nr. 438,retrievedfromhttp://biodata.asp4all.nl/centralestad/1990/BGB2000000432/BGB2000000432.pdf (accessed on 1 December 2009).

City Council Amsterdam (2006), 'Raadsnotulen 29 November 2006', Gemeenteblad, Afd. 2 (13 December 2006), retrieved from http://biodata.asp4all.nl/andreas/2006/09012f978023a93a/09012f978023a93a.pdf (accessed on 1 December 2009).

City Council Amsterdam (2008), 'Raadsnotulen 30 October 2008', Gemeenteblad, Afd. 2 (14 November 2008), retrieved from http://biodata.asp4all.nl/andreas/20 08/09012f9780505f0d/09012f9780505f0d.pdf (accessed on 1 December 2009).

City Council Amsterdam (2009a), 'Raadsnotulen 9 September 2009', Gemeenteblad, Afd. 2 (23 September 2009), retrieved from http://biodata.asp4all.nl/and reas/2008/09012f9780505f0d/09012f9780505f0d.pdf (accessed on 6 December 2009).

City Council Amsterdam (2009b), 'Raadsnotulen 18 November 2009', Integrale Uitzending, available at: http://amsterdam.notubiz.nl/popup.php?i=popupNotucastDemand&type=2&preVergId=1748#agendaItem736539 (accessed on 6 December 2009).

City district De Baarsjes (2008), *Dossier Westermoskee*. Amsterdam: Gemeente Amsterdam, retrieved from www.baarsjes.nl/algemene_onderdelen/nieuws_website/nieuws_website_2008/03_maart/het_dossier (accessed on 1 December 2009).

City district council De Baarsjes (2008), 'Raadsvergadering 28 October 2008 (concept)', retrieved from http://debaarsjes.raadsinformatie.nl/cgi-bin/showdoc.cgi/action=view/id=81942/type=pdf/conceptverslag_raadsvergadering_28_oktober.pdf (accessed on 1 December 2009).

City district council De Baarsjes (2009), 'Raadsvergadering 27 January 2009 (concept)', retrieved from http://debaarsjes.raadsinformatie.nl/cgi-bin/ showdoc.cgi/action=view/id=89686/type=pdf/Conceptverslag_raadsvergadering_27_januari.pdf (Aaccessed on 1 December 2009).

City district South-East (2005), 'SEO Themabijeenkomst De positie van de kerken in Zuidoost', 21 March 2005, retrieved from www.zuidoost.amsterdam.nl/zuidoost_werkt_aan/sociaal_economische/sociaal-_economisch/artikelen/seo_themabijeenkomst?ActItmIdt (accessed on 1 December, 2009).

City district South-East (2008), 'De week van Elvira Sweets (49)', 5 December 2008, retrieved from www.zuidoost.amsterdam.nl/maak_kennis_met_de/dagelijks_bestuur/de_week_van_elvira/archief/2008/de_week_van_elvira_2d (accessed on 1 December 2009).

Cohen, J. (2004), 'Scheiding van kerk en staat in the 21e eeuw', Willem van Oranjelezing at Delft, 1 June 2004, www.dmo.amsterdam.nl/@5768/pagina/ (accessed on 12 November 2009).

—. (2006), 'Sociaal-democratie en religie. De omgekeerde doorbraak', *Socialisme & Democratie* 63 (7/8), 49–53.

—. (2009), 'Van der Grinten Lezing', Radboud Universiteit Nijmegen, 3 June 2009,http://amsterdam.nl/algemene_onderdelen/indexen/wethouderpagina's/burgemeester/toespraken/@198891/van_der_grinten/ (accessed on 12 November 2009).

Dalferth, I. U. (2010), 'Post-secular Society: Christianity and the Dialectics of the Secular', *Journal of the American Academy of Religion* 78 (2), 317–45.

Dautzenberg, M., and Westerlaak, M. van (2007), *Kerken en moskeeën onder de WMO: Een verkennend onderzoek naar kansen en bedreigingen.* Amsterdam: DSP-Groep.

Den Uyl, M. (2008), 'Solving Problems – or Merely Shifting them Elsewhere? Contradictions in Urban Renewal in the Bijlmermeer, Amsterdam', *Global Built Environment Review* 6 (3), 15–33.

Driessen, D., van der Werf, M. and Boulal, A. (2004), *Laat het van twee kanten komen: eindrapportage van een (quick scan) van de maatschappelijke rol van moskeeën in Amsterdam.* Amsterdam: Nieuwe Maan Communicatie Adviesgroep.

Goossen, K. (2006), 'Op weg naar kerkverzamelgebouwen voor migrantenkerken, Migrantenkerken en politieke en civiele participatie', in H. Euser, K. Goossen, M. de Vries, and S. Wartena (eds), *Migranten in Mokum, De betekenis van migrantenkerken voor de stad Amsterdam.* Amsterdam: VU.

Habermas, J. (2008), 'Notes on a Postsecular Society', www.signandsight.com/features/1714.html (accessed on 1 December 2009).

Harchaoui, S. (2008), 'Overheid en religieuze organisaties', paper written for the Workshops Staatsrechtconferentie 2008, University of Amsterdam, www.jur.uva.nl/staatsrechtconferentie/object.cfm/05ABE7FB-1321-B0BE-683B1D97866C4EA6 (accessed on 1 December 2009).

House of Representatives (2004–2005), *Nieuwe regels betreffende maatschappelijke ondersteuning (Wet maatschappelijke ondersteuning).* Tweede Kamer, vergaderjaar 2004–2005, 30131, nr.3.

Kennedy, J., and Valenta, M. (2006), 'Religious Pluralism and the Dutch State: Reflections on the Future of Article 23', in W. B. H. J. van de Donk et al. (eds), *Geloven in het publieke domein: Verkenningen van een dubbele transformatie.* Amsterdam: Amsterdam University Press/Wetenschappelijke Raad voor het Regeringsbeleid.

Knippenberg, H. (1992), *De religieuze kaart van Nederland.* Assen: Van Gorcum.

—. (2006), 'The Changing Relationship between State and Church/Religion in the Netherlands', *GeoJournal* 67, 317–30.

Landman, N. (1992), *Van Mat tot Minaret, De institutionalisering van de islam in Nederland.* Amsterdam: VU.

Lijphart, A. (1975), *The Politics of Accommodation: Pluralism and Democracy in the Netherlands.* Berkeley: University of California Press.

Martin, D. (2005), *On Secularization: Towards a Revised General Theory.* Aldershot: Ashgate.

Maussen, M. (2006), *Ruimte voor de islam? Stedelijk beleid, voorzieningen, organisaties.* Apeldoorn/Antwerpen: Het Spinhuis.

Meijs, L. C. P. M. (2007), 'Torn Between Two Sectors: Government or Business?', *The International Journal of Volunteer Administration* 24 (3), 50–53.

Modood, T. (2008), 'Muslims, Religious Equality and Secularism', in G. B. Levey and T. Modood (eds), *Secularism, Religion, and Multicultural Citizenship*. Cambridge: Cambridge University Press.

Municipality of Amsterdam (1999), *De kracht van de diverse stad. Uitgangspunten van het diversiteitsbeleid van de gemeente Amsterdam*. Bestuursdienst, Gemeenteblad, nr. 675, http://biodata.asp4all.nl/centralestad/1999/BGB1000007445/BGB1000007445.pdf (accessed on 1 December 2009).

Municipality of Amsterdam (2001), 'Geloven in Amsterdam', J. van Steenhoven, Dienst Onderzoek and Statistiek. Factsheet no. 5, June 2001, http://www.os.amsterdam.nl/pdf/2006_ob_religie_5.pdf (accessed on 21 May 2009).

Municipality of Amsterdam (2003), *Erbij horen en meedoen. Notitie inzake uitgangspunten voor integratiebeleid in de gemeente Amsterdam*. J. Helmers, Bestuursdienst, Gemeenteblad, nr. 214, http://biodata.asp4all.nl/centralestad/2003/1742/1742.pdf (accessed on 1 December, 2009).

Municipality of Amsterdam (2004), *Vestigingsbeleid voor religieuze instellingen in Amsterdam. Gemeente Amsterdam*. Dienst Ruimtelijke Ordening, retrieved from http://www.dro.amsterdam.nl/aspx/download.aspx?nocache=true&file=/contents/pages/97133/vestigingsbeleid_religieuze1.pdf (accessed on 1 December, 2009).

Municipality of Amsterdam (2005a), *Actieplan 'Wij Amsterdammers'*. Bestuursdienst, http://amsterdam.nl/aspx/download.aspx?file=/contents/pages/5117/actieplanwijamsterdammers.pdf (accessed on 1 December 2009).

Municipality of Amsterdam (2005b), *Perspectief en Kansen, Amsterdams' integratiebeleid tegen de achtergrond van het programma Wij Amsterdammers*. Dienst Maatschappelijke Ontwikkeling, http://biodata.asp4all.nl/andreas/2006/09012f97801bb438/09012f97801bb438.pdf (accessed on 1 December 2009).

Municipality of Amsterdam (2007), *Amsterdam tegen radicalisering*. PAS, IHH and COT, http://biodata.asp4all.nl/andreas/2007/09012f9780383bf2/09012f9780383bf2.pdf (accessed on 1 December 2009).

Municipality of Amsterdam (2008), *Notitie Scheiding van kerk en staat*. Burgemeester and Wethouders, http://amsterdam.nl/algemene_onderdelen/indexen/wethouderpagina's/burgemeester/dossiers/@133851/scheiding_van_kerk/ (accessed on 1 December 2009).

Rooden, P. Van (2007), 'Godsdienst en Secularisatie in Amsterdam' 'Vallás és szekularizáció Amszterdamban', *Budapesti Negyed* 2007), www.xs4all.nl/~pvrooden/Peter/publicaties/2007b.pdf (accessed on 1 December 2009).

Sunier, T. (2006), 'The Western Mosque: Space in Physical Place', *ISIM Review* 18, 22–23.

Van Bijsterveld, S. (2008), *Overheid en godsdienst, Herijking van een onderlinge relatie*. Nijmegen: Wolf Legal Publishers.

Van den Donk, W. B. H. J., A. P. Jonkers, G. J. Kronjee and R. J. J. M. Plum (eds) (2006), *Geloven in het publieke domein: Verkenningen van een dubbele transformatie*. Amsterdam: Amsterdam University Press/Wetenschappelijke Raad voor het Regeringsbeleid.

Van der Burg, W. (2006), *Over hoofddoekjes, zwarte kousen en de seculiere samenleving. De noodzaak van een inclusieve democratie en een theologie der voorlopigheid*. Kampen: Theologische Universiteit van de Protestantse Kerk in Nederland.

Van der Meulen, M. (2009), 'The Continuing Importance of the Local. African Churches and the Search for Worship Space in Amsterdam', *African Diaspora* 2, 159–81.

Vermeulen, F. (2006), *The Immigrant Organising Process. Turkish Organisations in Amsterdam and Berlin and Surinamese Organisations in Amsterdam, 1960–2000*. Amsterdam: Amsterdam University Press.

13 On Christianity as Truly Public

Angus Paddison

Introduction

It is obvious why people of goodwill and intention should care about cities and all
who live in them. Who, after all, could look upon the relentless sprawl of shanty
dwellings in cities like Johannesburg or São Paulo and not despair? Who could not
dare to dream that there might be another way to regenerate British cities other
than erecting yet more banal shopping centres – the cathedrals of our age – and
designer apartments, the latter seemingly arranged to ensure that we remain strangers to one another? Who could not support the re-imagination of the way our
cities are arranged and planned, so that they might be places of encounter and
inspiration? Unless we wish to commit the unpardonable folly of supposing that
people of late modernity are devoid of any good, both the church and theologians
should encourage all who seek to improve the experience of those who dwell in
cities. Nevertheless, such co-operative sentiments should not be allowed to obscure
a series of key questions. Why should the church and, more particularly, theologians
care about cities? What risks lie within the church's participation in so-called public
projects? What is the church's distinctive politics which it can offer to city dwellers?
Answers to these questions, I submit, will not be adequately generated from the
perspective of *political* theology but from a resolutely *theological* politics, a resolve
to view politics through the church's faith and practices. Theological politics
re-orders our imaginations precisely because it looks to the life of Jesus and the life
of the church and 'understands the politics of the world, and relates to it, in the light
of this new politics' (Rasmusson, 1995: 188). As such, theological politics thinks
not just politically about theology, but theologically about politics and so allows a
different type of politics to be seen in the midst of the cities in which we live.

This chapter is therefore an attempt to reason theologically in our so-called
postsecular context about the city and the political encounters that such cities
allow for and make possible. Key interlocutors will be those with work associated
with postliberal and 'Radical Orthodox' theologians like Stanley Hauerwas
and John Milbank. Uniting the various interlocutors is a robust emphasis on the
political identity of the church.

Theology and the city

Why should we reason *theologically* about cities? Implicit in this question is the suggestion that theologians would have strayed off their proper territory if caught speculating on something as worldly as cities and their theological significance. Is it not a theologian's office to ruminate on how many angels can dance on the head of a pin or, alternatively, to reserve their attention to the harmless realms of the inner soul? There is much to be said in response to this policing of theology's boundaries. Three reasons in particular can be highlighted as to why theologians might wish to join Ash Amin in building 'the good city' (Amin, 2006).

First, theology is properly interested in all things; there are few disciplines in the modern university that theology cannot make a contribution to or learn from. Theologians are interdisciplinary creatures by nature, not out of some rootless dilettantism, but precisely because theology is anchored to a non-negotiable *positum* – God as the source of all things, the one through whom all things that exist have their meaning and purpose. As such, theologians in the modern university have no option but to trespass onto numerous adjoining fields of study for theology 'in making the horribly immodest claim that it is, in some way, about all things . . . has no particular subject matter, but rather attempts to say something about everything in relation to God' (Oliver, 2008: 20). Theologians are interested in cities because, like everything else around us, their role within the economy of salvation must be discerned.

Second, a theologian's commitment to this world is only an echo of God's non-negotiable, overwhelming relationship with the world as revealed in the unfolding of the triune life. God, becoming incarnate in Jesus Christ and dwelling among us and in the world (John 1.14), accordingly invests places with sacramental significance, as bearing the possibility of revealing the divine. The gospel *is* a God who, in taking on flesh, raising his Son from the dead and ascending, has irrevocably bound together the things of this world with the world above (Eph. 1.10). Christianity as a deeply material religion therefore is 'not an abstraction – in our living as Christians we continually work with and in the world, and the world works with and in us' (Ward, 2003: 463). We must not, Graham Ward goes on, play out the body/soul dualism which has bedevilled Christianity in the way we relate church and city (Ward, 2003: 469–70). Matter and spirit must not be viewed as existing in some zero-sum game – throughout the Old and New Testaments, God uses what is material to convey the divine while still retaining its material quality. In a manner that echoes God's purposes for the material, how we order our cities can either convey dark or hopeful visions of what it is to be a human – theologians have a responsibility to interrogate what views of the human are embodied in the city. 'Cities are in fact moral agents' (Wolterstorff, 1983: 128) and need to be read as such. How we live in and relate to the world around us is a question, the answer to which bears sacramental possibilities, that is it can lead us to the *ends* of our human life. Christian theologians will want to join Ash Amin in asking what makes a good city (Amin, 2006). The radical difference between what Amin says and theopolitical reflection on the city is the insistence that looking to Christ is only a way of being *more* worldly, *more* realistic. '[T]here is no real Christian existence outside the reality of the world, and no real worldliness outside the reality of the world', Dietrich Bonhoeffer vigorously states (Bonhoeffer, 2009: 61).

There is a third reason why theologians, *as theologians*, should concern themselves with the city. Cities, as wholly human projects, are magnets for a dizzying array of cultures, ethnic backgrounds and creeds, and so embody in themselves the central political challenge of our time: what it is to live in a space 'that is shared by others, with whom we have to negotiate, whose concerns we have to ponder and interact with' (Williams, 2005: 15). Given the limitations of mainstream political answers to this challenge, unless the church wants to find itself 'placed' by the hegemonic secular reach of the modern nation–state, a nation–state whose tentacles now extend into civil society (Bell, 2004), it is vital that the church contribute to meeting the challenge of 'how to simultaneously foster social cohesion and respect diversity' (Bretherton, 2006: 376). This is part of the task of theological politics.

These three explanations for why theologians should reflect on the good city are intertwined with one another. The task of relating all things to God is a permanent rebuke to the modern conceit that politics – and therefore the city – can be autonomous from theological scrutiny. The task of thinking theologically is not separate from the task of thinking politically. But if we are to say that everything is 'theological' and related in some way to God (as claimed above), then this is a claim that should restrain our desire to politicize everything (Long and Fox with York, 2007: 207). Hence, this chapter prioritizes theological politics ahead of political theology as a constant reminder of the determinative role of theological considerations. Equipping ourselves with the insights of theological politics, I turn now to critique the intellectual home of much thinking on the church and the city – 'public theology'.[1] In the section that follows, I shall expose the connections between 'public theology' and secularism. In the subsequent section of this chapter, I shall undertake the more positive task of thinking through what the political presence of the church in city looks like from the perspective of theological politics. The challenge for those who do not wish to join in the confession is whether our cities have the capacity to accommodate the strange difference that is the church.

Public theology and secularism

Evidence often presented of our postsecular times is the manner in which religion is being openly courted by politicians as a potential partner in policy delivery and community projects. How should the church respond to this new attention? The church's precise answer to this question will be determined by the extent to which it appreciates its own life and worship as already political, and so *of the essence* for how it engages with other modes of social organization. And with an eye on thinking about cities theologically, a church attentive to its own life as political will raise some searching questions on the limitations of 'public theology', the school from which much theological work on the city emanates (e.g. Graham and Lowe, 2009).

Equally, pronouncements from members of the British government on the role of faith groups in society speak in terms congenial to 'public theology': many government initiatives to incorporate faith groups are the secular reflection of the commitments of 'public theology'. As I shall argue, this recent courting of religion should be seen less as a postsecular move but more as a new twist in the story that is secularism, the project required by liberal democracy which advocates a neutral state among religious differences, and in the process ends up re-shaping, indeed deforming religion itself. The task of theological politics and, more importantly, the church, is to remain alert to how so-called neutrality is thick with a liberal view of religion and its circumscribed place within society.

What kinds of moral activity are gathered under the term 'public theology?' One contributor to recent Christian thinking on the church and the city defines 'public theology' as 'the sharing of insights, concerns and good practice . . . for the sake of public (or common) goods' (Baker, 2009a: 68). Implicit in theological politics is the notion that 'public theology' risks an uncritical alliance with those powers of modernity that would dictate to the church what it must deem 'private' (therefore harmless) and what it must deem to be 'public' (fit for airing in the public square). The irony is that 'public theology', although motivated by a clear desire to de-privatize Christianity, finds itself still bound by the confines and logic of secularism.

The problematic assumptions of 'public theology' are given away in its very name, a name which from the outset yields to the prejudice that theology is an essentially private discourse that has to be translated if it is to be heard in the public square (Long, 2001: 72). 'Public theology' assumes, or at best does not challenge, the assumption that faith is a series of private, religious commitments (should that be choices?) and then privileges the politics of the state and civil society as the public for which theology has to change its register if it is to have relevance. The public in sight in 'public theology' is not the church, but the state or society, a space which is understood by those within it as basically autonomous.[1] From the outset, worldviews functionally atheistic are privileged (Schindler, 1994). Given the opening convictions of this essay – that theology is interested in all things as they relate to God – theological politics is likely to be allergic to any suggestion that faith is a private discourse waiting to be positioned within a more comprehensive, more public setting. Neither can we rest content with the platitude that churches should get involved practically now and worry about theory later. Ontologies *do* matter. A purely immanent account of who we are and the nature of society is not a matter of abstract theory, but plays itself out in the way we live together and the cities we construct (Smith, 2004: 232). The regeneration of our cities is a theological question all the way down in the same way that the erection of one more 'destination' shopping centre is a theological statement.

In the assumption that civil society is basically intelligible on its own terms – without reference to Christian interpretative lenses – what is lost sight of is the richness of 'a Christian depiction of reality' (Rasmusson, 2005: 108). The setting provided by 'public theology' is one in which the church is required to adjust to universal understandings of civil society or the state, putting to one side any notion that the Christian faith and its practices might hold an interpretative leverage over these powers. Implicitly at work in this attenuated role for the church is a certain view of ethics and how ethical behaviour is sustained. For public theology is a means of subordinating theological questions to ethics, ethics being deemed to be universal and independent from any particular context. This is either a massively optimistic or misguided stance to adopt, for all ethics requires a context and a history to render action intelligible.[2] As an optimistic stance, 'public theology' is ill-equipped to navigate the ways in which, devoid of the church as the decisive context, the 'state or the market' will step in and 'provide[s] the intelligibility for our actions' (Long, 2001: 84).[3] Christians may think that we can act morally independent of 'historically contingent communities' (Hauerwas, 2003: 17), yet we will only find that we are being formed by political and cultural forces other than the church. Given that Christian ethics is – if it is to retain integrity – human behaviour responsive to God's act in Christ and the life of the church, then the Christian is likely to be wary of any attempt to make these material realities innocuous. In its bid to be heard 'public theology' short-circuits the question of how (note *not* whether) the church is to engage with *other* political formations such as the market, the nation–state and civil society.

Theological politics points out that much work that gathers under the umbrella term political theology also represent forms of 'public theology', and so equally risk making the church and its distinctive interpretative contribution irrelevant. Too much political theology assumes that the church must associate itself with the politics monopolized by the secular state which exhibits a model of interaction dominated by the management of competing wills. Yet deference to the state's monopolization of what is political and public will ultimately only render the church *less* political and *less* public. As Reinhard Hütter warns, a

'political theology' that attempts to 'politicize' the church can only ... deepen the church's irrelevance and undermine the church's public (political) nature by submitting and recon-ditioning the church according to the *saeculum's* understanding of itself as the ultimate and normative public. (Hütter, 2004: 32)

Public theology may be a bid for religion to be heard once more in the public square – but it will not be long before people work out that there are others who can say better what the church is only echoing. Once the church is in this decline towards irrelevance, the only role left for faith is to motivate or inspire public action in the name of the nation's interests. If this subordination of religion to the nation–state project sounds overdrawn, we need only appeal to a press release issued by the Home Office in June 2001 reporting how David Blunkett, the then Home Secretary, spoke of 'the Government's commitment to "strengthening the part faith communities play in promoting the values which bind us together as a nation"' (Blunkett, 2001). So, too, John Denham, Communities and Local Government secretary, said in November 2009:

We need to build our national identity together – through shared experience and explora-tion. Through a strong shared set of values. Through our ability to handle issues where we disagree with respect and without conflict. And faith communities together have a vital role to play here. (Denham, 2009)

Observers have been quick to point out that at work in the government's eagerness to embrace faith groups is a fundamentally secular understanding of religion (Smith, 2004: 198). In this outlook:

> [r]eligion is a universal essence detachable from particular ecclesial practices, and as such can provide the motivation necessary for all citizens of whatever creed to regard the nation-state as their primary community, and thus produce peaceful consensus. (Cavanaugh, 2002: 82)

This quote from William Cavanaugh clearly resonates with the statements of the two UK Cabinet ministers above. Note also how heavy is the emphasis in these government statements on religion as representing a set of 'values' which have to be translated or we might say, in line with the mercantilist strains of the word, cashed in for policies (the language of values shall be returned to below). In a speech to the Christian Socialist Movement in 2001, one concern of which was what he called 'the critical issue of translating values into policies', Tony Blair spoke of how:

> [o]ur major faith traditions . . . play a fundamental role in supporting and propagating values which bind us together as a nation . . . [l]ooking outwards to the needs of others, beyond your own immediate members, is a prime expression of your beliefs and values. And in carrying out this mission you have developed some of the most effective voluntary and community organisations in the country. (Blair, 2001)

Should the church not be flattered by this new attention to the church's life and faith? Moreover, is the government's willingness to engage with faith groups not evidence of the postsecular times in which we find ourselves? From the perspective of theological politics, the church should be wary of such government initiatives, for even, perhaps especially, with this new attention we are still within the logic of secularism. Here, in line with figures like Talal Asad and Charles Taylor, 'secularism' as a modern project which seeks to re-locate religion is distinguished from either the range of meanings covered by the term 'secular' (a pre-modern Christian term) or the much-debated social process of 'secularization', a term also used in pre-modern Christianity (Asad, 1999: 185–86). In the logic of secularism:

> [t]o say that a society is secular does not mean that "religion" is banished from its politics, law, and forms of association. Rather, religion is admitted into these domains on the condition that it take particular forms; when it departs from these forms it confronts a set of regulatory barriers'. (Mahmood, 2001: 226)

Secularism is marked not necessarily by the attempt to deny people's multiple affiliations and identities, but by positing the state as a transcendent unifier of all people. Religion is ordered to the task of being a citizen (Taylor, 1998: 44). The risk for the state is that religion often bears within it the capacity to destabilize this compact. Note how often the galvanizing of the nation and its common identity is spoken of in the passages we have quoted from the UK politicians – no coincidence given how closely involved the nation–state project and secularism are.

Moreover, the state in its supposed neutral treatment towards religion ends up presenting a certain view of religion and what it is, reminding us that even the most benign versions of secularism end up reshaping the form religion 'takes, the subjectivities it endorses, and the epistemological claims it can make' (Mahmood, 2006: 326). So, even in the midst of friendly speeches from government ministers on the role of FBOs, confined as they are within the logic of secularism, what for Christianity is peculiar to it – its worship, its Scripture, its divine constitution – are displaced, and our attention is instead directed towards the universal principles that the church as a faith group can serve (Mahmood, 2006: 341). People of faith are talked of, but only ultimately as individuals. The church as a political body is not highlighted. Key here is the language of individuals and their freely chosen 'values', but invisible here is any notion of the church as a body. 'Faith' is spoken of in connection with the social activism it can inspire, in place of any emphasis on the church as a body whose life is itself a political answer to the nature of what is good and true and makes for human flourishing (Smith, 2009: 108).

In this setting, freedom of religion represents an alluring temptation – it is an arrangement by which religion may contribute to so-called public debates but only with certain conditions. There is much to be gained from the freedom of religion – yet to accept unquestioningly the state's stance of religious neutrality (bound as it is to freedom of religion) is to miss an opportunity to discern how this very stance, as a theological stance, impacts upon our understandings of both who we are as humans and religion and its limits (Long, 1991: 280). 'Liberalism allows apparent total diversity of choice; at the same time it is really a formal conspiracy to ensure that no choice can ever be significantly effective' (Milbank, 2008: 28). Just as 'public theology' subordinates the church as a people to a body deemed more comprehensive and more determinative, so freedom of religion *places* religion. Once again, we need to tread carefully here – the object of such talk is not the overthrow of the clear benefits of liberalism, of which freedom from coercion is undoubtedly one, but the reinvigoration of a people, the church, capable of *negotiating* the imperial reach of liberalism and nation–states (Hauerwas, 1992: 18–19).

From within the logic of the secularism at work in recent courting of FBOs, the church is one voluntary sector among others in which adherents ally themselves to subjectively held 'beliefs'. The social imaginary that is modern secularity shifts religion into the realms of what is felt (Asad, 1993: 39–41; Taylor, 2004), and so clears the way for a secular space ruled by the esteemed ways of knowing the world provided by economics, science and sociology. Recall the use of the word 'values' by all three politicians above. In the context of modern secularism, 'values' lack any ontological force and are optional extras to economics, science, social science *inter alia* as autonomous ways of knowing the world. The problem with prioritizing talk of 'values' is that such talk impedes the ends striven for by the self-same Christians who also adopt such language,[4] keeping us entangled in the very political arrangements from which release is sought. [T]alking about "values"', Eugene McCarraher asserts in a review of Jim Wallis's manifesto on civil theology, *God's Politics*, 'is a way of *not* talking about *practices*, whose discussion mandates attention to the very quotidian and inescapably carnal ways we make love, raise children, and work in the office' (McCarraher, 2005). Values are what is left when the church's convictions and practices have lost their vital relationship *within* the context of a community whose life has teleological direction, leaving us with a religion that is mere 'motivation' or 'inspiration'. Talk of values makes sense within a political context where society is an amalgam of free, and so competing, wills who give 'value' to that which they choose. To emphasize, 'values' is a word which has come to make sense and seem obvious only in a wider cultural and intellectual context, despite the tendency there is to hide this tradition in the shade.[5] Values, representing a competing tradition, divert attention from the assumption that Christian practices are inseparable from the context of a worshipping community whose collective life has a direction more decisive than sheer preference (Long and Fox with York, 2007: 60). More importantly, something as ontologically flimsy as a value, whose most decisive location is in the individual's volition, is limited in its power to interpret and re-shape our world (McCarraher, 2007). Talk of values reinforces the tendency of 'public theology' to work with the 'givens' of contemporary politics, rather than to re-order and re-interpret these givens in the light of the Christian narrative.

'Public theology', as evinced by academics, church leaders and politicians, is, this chapter is advancing, contained within the reach of secularism and its definition of religion.[6] When religion is seen as something freely chosen by individuals and so essentially private, it has to be translated into public worth. Yet, as Talal Asad asserts, there are some testing questions to ask of this 'translation' mode of understanding religion: 'If religious symbols are understood, on the analogy with words, as vehicles for meaning, can such meanings be established independently of the forms of life in which they are used?' (Asad, 1993: 53). Is the meaning of Christian talk of justice not rendered by the thickness of the Christian narrative and the church's life, destabilizing any imagined split between private belief and public behaviour?

Appeal can be made here to the work of the prolific American theological ethicist, Stanley Hauerwas. For Hauerwas, when a Christian speaks of justice or love, these are *realities* that can only be filled out by specific attention to the gospel – attempts to render them intelligible by appeal to external criteria might be palatable to certain forms of liberal political orders, but will naturally end up presenting a distinctly flaccid version of the gospel unable to help Christians see how their convictions have the capacity to re-shape the 'real' world presented to them. Justice finds its content and meaning from within the narrative (Scripture, which tells the story both of God and the people of God) in which the church is inscribed and is now extending. '[D]escriptions do not come given but rather are determined by practices that require articulation in whole ways of life' (Hauerwas, 2000: 48). More specifically, what Christians think about virtues (note not 'values') such as justice is not something acquired separately from the formation of worship. (After all, if we could know what Christians think about justice without worshipping, the obvious question is – why worship?) It is by insisting that Christian convictions are inseparable from their social embodiment that we can prevent the privatization of the Christian faith (Hauerwas, 1995: 210). Accordingly, Hauerwas would be wary of the church's glib participation in a social activism which was functionally atheistic and where 'thick' Christian convictions were rendered invisible and simply not put to use. This is the lure of 'public theology' – in a bid for effectiveness, the church aligns itself to pre-determined notions of 'justice', 'pluralism' or 'tolerance'. The problem is that the particular convictions and practices the church is asked to shed or reserve to the 'private' in order to participate in the public sphere are precisely the resources needed to interrogate and criticize models of justice and pluralism framed (self-consciously or otherwise) in the shadow of the market or bureaucratic nation–state.

We need therefore to work towards a situation where 'public theology' is as much an oxymoron as saying 'female women' – theology by its very nature is public, just as the church's life is already an answer to the question of whether the church should be political. 'The church is a politics, to ask it to be involved in politics is to ask to adopt an alien first premise' (Long and Fox with York, 2007: 97). What then is the church's political contribution to the city?

Sketching a theological politics

The church's primary political contribution to the city is to be a *witness*. The church is a sign of the new kingdom that has broken into the world, a pointer to the new possibilities for human life together. The decisive political contribution of the church to the city lies therefore 'in the witness which it has to give to it and to all human societies in the form of the order of its own upbuilding and constitution' (Barth, 2004: 721). Through its life, the church witnesses to other 'possibilities, not merely in heaven but on earth, not merely one day but already' (Barth, 2004: 721). What more may we say about the political shape of this witness? Some notes in response to this question can be sketched with the help of, among others, the Mennonite theologian, John Howard Yoder.

The church is a worshipping community. It is perhaps not surprising that in the speeches and statements of ministers on the role of FBOs, the *public worship* of the church is sidelined. 'Public theology' can also seem to allot worship little more than a motivational role (e.g. Baker, 2009b: 111–12). This is less surprising if we recall that worship, by re-narrating our world, is 'the communal cultivation of an alternative construction of society' (Yoder, 1984: 43). To be sure, care needs to be exercised here – that worship cultivates a counter-cultural outlook is not the reason for, but it is the result of, the church's worship. Thus, Nathan Kerr criticizes the instrumentalization of worship in the hands of Stanley Hauerwas and John Howard Yoder who both see value in the counter-cultural value of worship (Kerr, 2009: 172). Worship is not the 'reason' for anything else, be it either the cultivation of social or economic justice or anti-liberal insights – it is itself political and ethical (Wannenwetsch, 2004: 57).

Worship is the *primary* political act of the church because it is the church's loving, faithful participation in that which the church holds to be true and good, the pursuit of the good being the central political task. Thus, John Howard Yoder insists that practices like baptism, sharing the Eucharist and forgiveness are political signs of the new community, a witness lodged within this world. '[T]he church by her way of being represents the promise of another world, which is not somewhere else but which is to come here' (Yoder, 1984: 91). As a witness, the church is not set apart from the world in which it lives – it is a witness to the world, but also a witness *in* the world.

Witnessing to a politics which makes the gospel strange, once again, the church is not to be chaplain to the powers of the day but rather through its own life is to make known the new community that God has made possible in the life of the church (Milbank, 1990: 381). 'The church is called to be now what the world is called to be ultimately' (Yoder, 1984: 91). The church as witness is not beguiled by notions of seizing the levers of history or adopting a 'socially responsible' position. As we have suggested, churches that think they must be responsible to the needs of the nation risk sanctifying reigning orders and the way they invite us to think. Ordered to a realization that it is the church's office 'to be not in charge', the church in the city is faithful before it is effective (Yoder, 2003: 168–80). Why does the church as witness prioritize faithfulness before effectiveness? Simply because the church's moral action is coordinated to the cross and resurrection, and so the church need not worry about taking a grip on history and leading it in the right direction for faithful action is always somehow 'a reflection of a victory already won' (Yoder, 1997: 195).

A church that is *in* the world yet 'not in charge' of the world and faithful before it is effective is, in Yoder's terms, a church true to its exilic status. Exiles are bound to the world in which they find themselves – the diasporic church, that is, the church 'sent' out, recognizes that there is 'no *ecclesia* apart from our being bound by the Spirit to *this* world' (Kerr, 2009: 190, emphasis in original). It is no coincidence that it is in the context of the exile that Israel is told (in a verse that Yoder rotates much of his thought around) that they must seek, 'the welfare of the city ... and pray to the LORD on its behalf, for in its welfare you will find your welfare' (Jer. 29.7). This mention of prayer is not incidental. For praying is one of the marks of the church, what Graham Ward has boldly labelled 'the most political act any Christian can engage in' through which we offer up 'the whole world we are caught up in' (Ward, 2009: 281). Praying is political because it is a habitual outworking of the conviction that God is involved in the transformation of this world and that our resources alone will not be sufficient. Samuel Wells, a theologian with considerable experience of urban regeneration projects, points to prayer as a key contribution to building the good city:

> Church meetings start with a prayer; regeneration meetings never do. For church regulars saying a prayer at the start of a meeting may have become a habit given scant considera- tion. But at a regeneration meeting, sensing something curiously missing which one has elsewhere taken for granted, one becomes slowly aware that this gathering is taking upon

itself an enormous task … Habits of thankfulness and asking for help come easily to those used to prayer…. This is perhaps the least threatening, most humble contribution of the Christian – to find words to articulate common need. (Wells, 2003: 25)

Conclusion

We end where we began. The church should of course work with all those who seek the good of the cities in which we live. Yet terms like 'the good' or 'the public' cannot escape theological scrutiny. Theological politics is a polite, if persistent, reminder that if everything is theological, then there will be no theology-free space where social scientists or economists might retreat. In the context of a political culture that attempts to hide the depths of our disagreements, this calls for some radical political re-arrangements. For what we will need most when church and society reasons together about 'the meaning of the good life' is 'a public culture hospitable to the disagreements that will inevitably arise' (Sandel, 2009: 261). If the church can play its part in creating such a political culture, then that will be contribution enough to whatever we might mean by 'the public'.

Notes

1   Of course, public theologians do not suppose that the state or civil society is a God-free space, but many of their interlocutors do, and public theologians do not do enough work on interrogating the different metaphysical assumptions at work here.

2   So Alasdair MacIntyre: '[e]very action is the bearer and expression of more or less theory-laden beliefs and concepts; every piece of theorizing and every expression of belief is a political and moral action' (2007: 61).

3   The reluctance to see how ethics is a timeful and so embedded of a practice is common to many forms of liberalism that prioritize an individual devoid of any ties who enters freely into association with other individuals. Yet there is no action from anywhere.

4   The language of 'values' was echoed positively by Bob Fyffe, general secretary of Churches Together in Britain and Ireland, in response to John Denham's speech for Inter-Faith week. See http://www.ctbi.org.uk/420 (accessed 29/11/2009).

5   So Long and Fox, with York: 'the argument that theology is about values has itself become a tradition that beckons us to respond. To respond to this tradition, however, requires a self-deception. It requires that we respond to a tradition that denies itself as a tradition under the false assumption that the moral life is nothing more than the values we choose for ourselves based on the congruity of our own interest with our own reasons' (2007: 62).

6   The link between the imagined division between what is properly public and what is private and the emergence of 'religious studies' as a discrete discipline in modernity is well brought out in Oliver 2008.

References

Amin, A. (2006), 'The Good City', *Urban Studies* 43, 1009–23.

Asad, T. (1993), *Genealogies of Religion: Discipline and Reasons of Power in Christianity and Islam*. Baltimore: The Johns Hopkins University Press.

—. (1999), 'Religion, Nation-State, Secularism', in P. van der Veer and L. Hartmut (eds), *Nation and Religion: Perspectives on Europe and Asia*. Princeton: Princeton University Press.

Baker, C. (2009a), *The Hybrid Church in the City: Third Space Thinking* (2nd edn). London: SCM.

—(2009b), 'Blurred Encounters? Religious Literacy, Spiritual Capital and Language', in A. Dinham, R. Furbey and V. Lowndes (eds), *Faith in the Public Realm: Controversies, Policies and Practices*. Bristol: Policy Press.

Barth, K. (2004), *Church Dogmatics* IV/2, trans. G.W. Bromiley. London: T&T Clark International.

Bell, D. M. Jr. (2004), 'State and Civil Society', in P. Scott and W. T. Cavanaugh (eds), *The Blackwell Companion to Political Theology*. Oxford: Blackwell.

Blair, T. (2001), 'PM Speech to the Christian Socialist Movement', 29 March 2001, www.number10.gov.uk/Page3243 (accessed 26 November 2009).

Blunkett, D. (2001), 'Partnership with Faith Communities Vital to Civil Renewal'. Home Office Press Release, 19 June 2001, www.gov-news.org/gov/uk/news/partnership_with_faith_communities_vital/10327.html (accessed 26 November 2009).

Bonhoeffer, D. (2009), *Ethics*, Ilse Tödt et al. (trans). Minneapolis: Fortress.

Bretherton, L. (2006), 'A New Establishment? Theological Politics and the Emerging Shape of Church-State Relations', *Political Theology* 7 (2006), 371–92.

Cavanaugh, W. T. (2002), *Theopolitical Imagination: Discovering the Liturgy as a Political Act in an Age of Global Consumerism*. London: T&T Clark.

Denham, J. (2009), 'Speech for Inter Faith Week', 12 November 2009, www.communities.gov.uk/speeches/corporate/interfaithweek2009. (accessed 27 November 2009).

Graham, E., and Lowe, S. (2009), *What Makes A Good City? Public Theology and the Urban Church*. London: DLT.

Hauerwas, S. (1992), *Against the Nations: War and Survival in a Liberal Society*. Notre Dame: University of Notre Dame Press.

—. (1995), *In Good Company: The Church as Polis*. Notre Dame: University of Notre Dame Press.

—. (2000), *A Better Hope: Resources for a Church Confronting Capitalism, Democracy, and Postmodernity*. Grand Rapids: Brazos.

—. (2003), *The Peaceable Kingdom: A Primer in Christian Ethics* (2nd edn). London: SCM.

Hütter, R. (2004), *Bound to Be Free: Evangelical Catholic Engagements in Ecclesiology, Ethics, and Ecumenism*. Grand Rapids, MI: Eerdmans.

Kerr, N. (2009), *Christ, History and Apocalyptic: The Politics of Christian Mission*. Eugene, OR: Cascade.

Long, D. S. (2001), *The Goodness of God: Theology, Church, and Social Order.* Grand Rapids, MI: Brazos.

Long, D. S., and N. R. Fox with T. York (2007), *Calculated Futures: Theology, Ethics, and Economics.* Baylor, TX: Baylor University Press.

MacIntyre, A. (2007), *After Virtue* (3rd edn). London: Duckworth.

Mahmood, S. (2001), 'Feminist Theory, Embodiment, and the Docile Agent: Some Reflections on Egyptian Islamic Revival', *Cultural Anthropology* 16, 202–36.

—. (2006), 'Secularism, Hermeneutics, and Empire: The Politics of Islamic Reformation', *Political Culture* 18, 323–47.

McCarraher, E. (2005), 'The Revolution Begins in the Pews', *Books and Culture*, May 2005. www.christianitytoday.com/bc/2005/mayjun/11.26.html (accessed 24 November 2009).

—. (2007), 'Britney Spears and the Downward Arc of Empire: An Interview with Eugene McCarraher', *The Other Journal,* Fall 2007. http://theotherjournal.com/article.php?id=287 (accessed 24 November 2009).

Milbank, J. (1990), *Theology and Social Theory: Beyond Secular Reason.* Oxford: Blackwell.

Milbank, J. (2008), 'The Gift of Ruling: Secularization and Political Authority', in J. K. A. Smith (ed.), *After Modernity? Secularity, Globalization and the Re-enchantment of the World.* Waco, TX: Baylor University Press.

Oliver, S. (2008), 'What Can Theology Offer to Religious Studies?', in M. Warrier and S. Oliver (eds), *Theology and Religious Studies: An Exploration of Disciplinary Boundaries.* London: T&T Clark.

Ramusson, A. (1995), *The Church as Polis: From Political Theology to Theological Politics as Exemplified by Jürgen Moltmann and Stanley Hauerwas.* Notre Dame: University of Notre Dame Press.

—. (2005), 'The Politics of Diaspora: The Post-Christendom Theologies of Karl Barth and John Howard Yoder', in L. G. Jones, R. Hütter and C. R. Velloso Ewell (eds), *God, Truth and Witness: Engaging Stanley Hauerwas.* Grand Rapids, MI: Brazos.

Sandel, M. J. (2009), *Justice: What's the Right Thing to Do?* London: Allen Lane.

Schindler, D. L. (1994), 'Religious Freedom, Truth, and American Liberalism: Another Look at John Courtney Murray', *Communio* 21, 696–741.

Smith, G. (1998), 'Faith in Community and Communities of Faith? Government Rhetoric and Religious Identity in Urban Britain', *Journal of Contemporary Religion* 19, 185–204.

Smith, J. K. A. (2004), *Introducing Radical Orthodoxy: Mapping a Post-secular Theology.* Grand Rapids: Baker Academic.

—. (2009), *The Devil Reads Derrida and Other Essays on the University, the Church, Politics, and the Arts.* Grand Rapids, MI: Eerdmans.

Taylor, C. (2004), *Modern Social Imaginaries.* Durham, NC: Duke University Press.

—. (1998), 'Modes of Secularism', in R. Bhargava (ed.), *Secularism and its Critics.* Dehli: Oxford University Press.

Taylor, C., and Ward, G. (2009), *The Politics of Discipleship: Becoming Postmaterial Citizens.* Grand Rapids, MI: Baker Academic.

Wannenwetsch, B. (2004), *Political Worship*, trans. Margaret Kohl. Oxford: Oxford University Press.

Ward, G. (2003), 'Why is the City So Important for Christian Theology?', *Cross Currents* 52, 462–73.

Wells, S. (2003), *Community-Led Regeneration and the Local Church*. Cambridge: Grove Books.

Williams, R. (2005), 'Urbanization, the Christian Church and the human project', in Andrew Walker (ed.), *Spirituality in the City*. London: SPCK.

Wolterstorff, N. (1983), *Until Justice and Peace Embrace*. Grand Rapids. MI: Eerdmans.

Yoder, J H. (1984), *The Priestly Kingdom: Social Ethics as Gospel*. Notre Dame: University of Notre Dame Press.

—. (1997), *For the Nations: Essays Evangelical and Public*. Grand Rapids, MI: Eerdmans.

—. (2003), *The Jewish-Christian Schism Revisited*, M. G. Cartwright and P. Ochs (eds). London: SCM.

14 Emerging Postsecular Rapprochement in the Contemporary City

Paul Cloke

A postsecular landscape?

My interest in the postsecular has been sparked by practical involvement in two particular spheres of social action over the last decade or so.[1] First, as a researcher and a volunteer, I became involved with the homelessness 'scene' in the UK city of Bristol, where on-street homelessness was a visible reminder of the plight of people who had for various reasons fallen through the welfare safety net. As I became more aware of the subterranean landscapes of homelessness in the city, it became apparent that a wide range of non-statutory services had been established to offer care, support and basic living provision to those for whom statutory support was insufficient or inappropriate. A number of hostels were available: some, such as those run by the Salvation Army and the Cyrenians, were well-known facets of the local landscape, while others were hidden away, offering secluded service to those who feared the repercussions of domestic violence. A night shelter had been established in memory of a local homeless man and provided last-ditch shelter for those men and women with emergency accommodation needs. Several soup runs provided sustenance to rough sleepers, and a number of drop-ins provided meals and advice during the day. These services are narrated elsewhere (see Cloke, May and Johnsen, 2010), but their presence and significance – repeated in different cities throughout the United Kingdom – opened up a picture for me of an important impulse of care in the contemporary city.

Many of these facilities had been established by faith-based (mostly Christian) organizations, as an expression of a theo-ethical response to an obvious social problem in the city. Others, however, were run by charitable organizations with no particular expression of faith. Some organizations (notably the Salvation Army) were characterized by a long-term historical presence in the area. Others were more recent responses to the contemporary issues of the city. In almost all cases, there was a mixing of different faith, religious, political and ideological motivations among organizers' staff and volunteers. At the night shelter, for example, church groups, students groups and a range of other volunteers worked together, united by the ethical desire to do something practical for homeless people and, if necessary, holding back potential moral and political differences in the process. This willingness to work together *with* different people *for* different people was a key characteristic of the service landscape. Faith groups welcomed co-workers with no religious persuasion, and vice versa, in a rapprochement of ethical praxis forged out of the necessity to provide a response to the needs of homeless people in the city.

Involvement in local fair-trade activities in the city presented a similar amalgam of theological, ethical and political interests. Having been engaged in research on fair trade, and being married to a Traidcraft activist, I caught glimpses of the complex networks of protest, social movements and encouragement of alternative consumption that constitute the local manifestation of fair trade. Here, there is again a strong theo-ethical prompt among faith-based groups to recognize fair trade as a device for practising ethics of care and global responsibility. Within church networks, for example, there are often fair trade evangelists who play a significant role in stirring conscience and shaping buying power such that this form of ethical consumption can become *de rigeur* (see Cloke, Barnett et al., 2010). However, faith-based fair trade activists are usually also part of a wider network of activism that can operate at citywide levels (Malpass et al., 2007) or in other institutional contexts such as schools (Pykett et al., 2010). Here again, there is a significant example of rapprochement between different groups of people, motivated by faith and no faith, but finding it possible to work together on a particular ethical issue despite the probability that political and moral stances on other issues could prove problematic unless kept very much in the background.

These two personal examples may seem parochial, but they seem to point to a willingness on the part of differently motivated people to work together on particular issues. And this coalition of Christian and non-Christian is also working across other religious boundaries. Jane Wills's (2004) account of the broad-based community alliance, *London Citizens*, highlights the capacity of a multi-faith and no-faith collaboration to campaign for a living wage or for employment rights for foreign-born workers. The scale and significance of these various kinds of non-statutory organizations in the contemporary city demands attention, not only because of their importance as voices of protest and service providers, but also because they demonstrate a rapprochement between groups previously thought to be separated by a powerful secular/religious divide. Such rapprochement seems to challenge a view of the world that insists on a secular public sphere and consigns religion to the private. In short, it provides strong grounded evidence of a wider societal trend, which has increasingly come to be labelled as *postsecularism*.

Klaus Eder's (2006) account of postsecular modernity reminds us of the paradox that the supposedly secular societies of Europe are now becoming increasingly subject to religious discourse. As has been recognized elsewhere (e.g. see Davie, 2007) he argues that secularization has by no means brought about the disappearance of religion: religion did not disappear, it simply disappeared from the public sphere. According to Eder, then, secularization merely "hushed up" religion, relegating it to quiet private spaces where it could not be heard in wider societal debates. In the European context, he suggests, churches have become intensely private spaces where people go to show their faith as a group, meaning that less people are pursuing their religion publicly or demonstrating their religion in the streets of the city. There is a contrast here with the United States (Berger et al., 2008) where religion has remained more public not only because of a wide array of denominational options, but also because the economic interests represented by churches and churchgoers have coincided with a strong set of political interests and have thus retained a place in public debate despite the wider trends towards secularization. Religion in the United States has thus been far harder to "hush up" than has been the case in Europe. Nevertheless, in Eder's view, religion in Europe has found its voice again and has become confident enough to emerge again in the public sphere, although the religious voice is not a concerted institutional voice but rather a multifaceted, often individualized or small-scale contribution to public affairs. This idea of the re-emergence of the religious – Eder sees it as a return to the presecular phase – as ground-level contribution to public life, echoes strongly the localized evidence of faith-based rapprochement in issues relating to home-lessness and fair trade.

The idea of postsecularism has by now, of course, reached an over-easy purchase in philosophical and sociological reviews of contemporary times. Charles Taylor (2007) has charted the resurgence of religion as a complex and adaptive network of symbolism, ritual and narrative capable both of delivering meaning and purpose to life and of embracing the creative possibilities of being human. For Taylor, the postsecular involves a rebuttal of secularist bias, a rejection of the fractured mentality of the secular age in favour of a return to a more sacred and enchanting world buttressed by belief in the possibilities of transcendence. A more tempered approach has been outlined by Jurgen Habermas (2010) who outlines three overlapping phenomena, the convergence of which has led to the *impression* of a worldwide resurgence of religion. First, he argues that orthodox and con-servative groups within established religious organizations are on the advance throughout the world – and this includes Hinduism and Buddhism as well as the monotheistic religions. These advances are at their most dynamic in the decentral-ized networks of Islam in sub-Saharan Africa and Pentecostalism in Latin America. Secondly, the most rapidly growing religious movements tend to be radicalized by fundamentalist adherence to rigid moral values and literal understandings of scriptures. Thirdly, the potential for innate violence over religious causes has been clearly displayed in the practices and outcomes of Islamic terrorism. For Haber-mas, then, any conception of the postsecular should have at its heart a set of processes in which public consciousness is adjusting to the continued existence of religious communities in an increasingly secularized societal setting. Postsecular society, then, is wrapped up in a change of public consciousness formed in the context of this religious expansion and mobility, fundamentalist radicalization and the instrumentalization of the potential for religious violence.

Habermas offers an analysis of three elements of this change in public conscious-ness. First, European citizens are all too well aware of the presence of intrusive fundamentalist religious movements in their spheres of influence; an awareness that inevitably undermines any secularist dogma about the disappearance of religion. Secondly, religion is visibly gaining influence in national and local public spheres both as a community of interpretation (Schussler Fiorenza, 1992) – attaining influential purchase over public opinion on moral and ethical issues – and in some cases (as in the UK examples used above), as a community of service and care, sometimes contracted by governments to carry out welfare tasks (see Cloke, Williams and Thomas, 2009). Thirdly, public consciousness is inevitably affected by immigration and asylum seeking, raising issues of how immigrant cultures can be integrated into postcolonial societies, and how tolerant coexistence can be achieved by different religious communities. These factors pose a normative question about how to participate in a postsecular society. As Habermas asks:

> How should we see ourselves as members of a post-secular society and what must we reciprocally expect from one another in order to ensure that in firmly entrenched nation states, social relations remain civil despite the growth of a plurality of cultures and religious world views? (2008, 7)

In answer to his own question, Habermas distinguishes between 'secular' – the indifferent stance of an unbelieving person who relates agnostically to religious validity claims – and 'secularist' – the polemic negative response to religious doctrine and action. Secularists, in his view, may be incompatible with a postsecular balance between shared citizenship and respect for cultural difference; whereas secular citizens are more able to discover, even in religious utterances, various semantic meanings and personal intuitions that cross over more easily into their secular discourses.

The recognition of emerging postsecular rapprochement in the contemporary city can surely learn much from these debates. From Klaus Eder, we can seek to learn more about how the hushed-up voice of religion has been released back into the public sector, in order to make a ground-level contribution to public life. What is it within faith-motivated communities that is leading to a re-emphasis of praxis rather than dogma, and to what degree is such praxis constrained by a perceived need to work within faith boundaries rather than in wider and potentially more risky partnerships? From Jurgen Habermas, we can seek to learn more about how critiques of secularization reflect distinctions, for example, between secular and secularist, and about the degree to which mutualities are appearing between religious and secular discourses that permit broad-based alliances and a willingness to focus on ethical sympathies, even if that means setting moral differences aside. What is it, then, within the emerging critique of secular society that lays an appropriate foundation for postsecular rapprochement? In the remainder of this chapter, I begin to trace two currents that lie at the heart of emergent spaces of postsecular alliance in the city: the philosophical and political move beyond secularism, with attendant changes to public consciousness in areas of identity and difference; and the spiritual move towards religious praxis, with attendant possibilities for discursive crossover between faith-motivated and secular parties.

Moving beyond secularism?

Debates over the nature and shortcomings of the era of secularism reflect many of the observations in Eder's and Habermas's conception of the postsecular. It is clear that part of the context of such debates is a strong secularist protest against any raising of the public profile of religion. A moral panic (Gray, 2008) has arisen around the trial of religion by bestsellers, as authors such as Dawkins (2006), Dennett (2006) and Hitchens (2007) have sought to demonize religion as the source of many of the world's evils. However, there has also been a wider and more critical debate about the achievements and outcomes of secularism which has begun to draw in some secular (if not secularist) opinion into explorations of different socio-political futures. For example, in a philosophical exploration of postsecularism, Philip Blond (1998) notes three main characteristics that are relevant to a desire to move beyond the secular era. First, there has been a tendency for secular society to exclude a public role for religious moderates, thus allowing religion to fall into the hands of fundamentalist extremists who have the capacity to ostracize and condemn 'other' groups in a religious politics that Hedges (2006) labels as a dangerous form of fascism. Here, we should recognize that there are significant differences, for example, between the politics inspired by religion in the United Kingdom (although Blond himself has been associated with Conservative politics in Britain) and the more extreme right-wing fundamentalism in the United States, but the assertion that the rise of fundamentalism has been afforded by societal secularization is an interesting one. Secondly, secularism has inspired a public consciousness that the kinds of progress achieved by modernistic science can be replicated in areas of politics, ethics and welfare. However, such a consciousness has quite quickly eroded, as political themes of individual self-interest and market hegemony have diminished the welfare state and led to what John Milbank has called 'a debased democratic politics' (2006: 338). Thirdly, secularism has soon been accompanied by a lack of hope and a cynical pessimism about finding new ways to relate differently to one another and to the environment in which we live. Society has become increasingly acquisitive, individualized, polarized and vulnerable to 'market failure'. There is now a dreary acceptance that how we live is regulated by the market-state's ability to shape how we govern ourselves, leading to a public consciousness that people don't believe in anything anymore, and that they can't change things or make a difference. In this period of 'post-political pessimism' (Eagleton, 2009), people seem to have lost the capacity to participate, to be inspired or to be enchanted. Clearly these are unacceptable generalizations, but a key point here is that secularism's emphasis on the visible and eschewing of the possibilities of the invisible has erased from much of the public consciousness any sense in which individuals and their worlds might be transformed.

In this context, it is interesting to note that some leading contributors to debates around the future of materialist socialism have been attracted to ideas drawn from religion and faith as prompts to the pursuit of justice and hope in contemporary society. It is as though the search for hopeful futures beyond post-political pessimism is finding new crossover discourses from writings and events reflecting faith and belief, albeit in fragmented rather than overarching narratives. John Milbank has observed how several key thinkers have begun to invoke theological ideas in order to narrate alternative futures:

> Derrida sustains the openness of signs and the absoluteness of the ethical command by recourse to … negative theology; Deleuze sustains the possibility of a deterritorialisation of matter and meaning in terms of a Spinozistic virtual absolute; Badiou sustains the possibility of a revolutionary event in terms of the one historical event of the arrival of the very logic of the event as such, which is none other than Pauline grace; Zizek sustains the possibility of a revolutionary love beyond desire by reference to the historical emergence of the ultimate sublime object, which reconciles us to the void constituted only through a rift in the void. This sublime object is Christ. (Milbank, 2005: 398)

Milbank is not arguing here that contemporary Left-leaning philosophers are undergoing some kind of religious epiphany, but there is a pointer to some crossover discourses relating to theo-ethics of grace, love and hope that offer a desirable excess beyond the material logic and rationale of the secular era. In particular, these religious discourses offer scope to go beyond current engagements with otherness that tend to be governed by a societal lens of moral detachment and ethical indifference, meaning that solidarity with others rests on their apparent status of victims rather than as part of creative celebration and aspiration. Theo-ethical discourses of loving others, however, involves recognition that these others personify the image of God, and that interrelations with them involve 'the mutual recognition of our positive realizations and capacities' (Milbank, 2005: 399). Religious discourses, then, eschew a simple celebration of alterity, and point to an equality with difference, and this narrative can be traced in two different ways in the development of postsecular rapprochements in the city. First, following Derrida (1996) the appeal of these crossover discourses involves a deconstructive grasp of religious narratives that departs radically from the specificity of particular religious movements and organizations, and recognizes lines of flight in postmodern, nomadic forms. Secondly, following Zizek (2001) and Badiou (2001), there is a closer link between Christian religion and an idealist materialism that refuses to collapse into a triumphant celebration of that ideal. In both cases, there is scope for rapprochement in the form of bringing love, hope and charity into praxis, such as in the issues of homelessness and fair trade, as discussed above.

It can therefore be argued that the philosophical and political critique of secularization has prompted both a secularist defence and a series of crossover discourses that potentially represent the common ground on which faith-based and non-faith activity can be allied. This is the *discursive arena* of postsecularism, and it is evident not only in philosophical and political critique, but also in imaginary texts of the age. For example, John McClure (2007) demonstrates in contemporary American fiction a close interest in postsecular re-enchantment and resurgence of religion that can be explained neither by secularist narratives nor by the classic representations of religion itself. Indeed, McClure endorses postsecularism as a kind of third way in which partial faiths and beliefs provide a desirable alternative to the excesses of secularist and religious ideologies. What we know less about is how the postsecularism of the discursive arena interacts with *arenas of postsecular praxis*. It is surely too simplistic to envisage praxis as an inevitable outcome of discourse – a putting into practice of philosophical critique (see McLennan, 2007). Indeed, it seems just as likely that the discursive arena of postsecularism has been constructed as a rationale and legitimation for already existing postsecular activity. We can envisage, therefore, that the interrelations between arenas of discourse and praxis are complex and multidirectional.

The main context in which emergent postsecular praxis has been understood to date is that of a political landscape dominated by neoliberalism, understood not as a series of top-down edicts, but rather as being constituted through a set of every-day 'techniques' (Larner, 2003). These techniques suggest a series of apparently mundane processes and practices that create and recreate neoliberal spaces and subjects at a range of different scales. One such area of technique has been to open up welfare services to participation by non-statutory groups. What were previously state-provided services have been increasingly contracted out or excised from the realm of public activity, and opportunities have arisen for third-sector and private-sector organizations to engage in co-governance in order to fill the gap. As Luke Bretherton has noted:

> The distinctive character of the move to co-governance lies in the development of a broad repertoire of delivery mechanisms that seek to combine the diverse knowledge and resources of stakeholders in the business, public and charity or 'third' sectors in order to address a specific issue. Faith groups are a key constituency that governments are seeking to enlist in addressing these issues as they are seen as repositories of the kinds of cultural, moral and social resources vital for effecting change. (Bretherton, 2010: 34)

As Bretherton acknowledges, faith-based organizations have become an important facet of co-governance in the United Kingdom – an importance that is often interpreted as an instrumental usefulness because they bring a number of key attributes to the table. Dinham and Lowndes (2009) list three such attributes: faith groups bring with them a repository of resources, including buildings, finance and volunteers; they can play a potentially important role in developing community cohesion, especially where interfaith networks provide bonding and bridging social capital in hard-to-reach areas; and they are useful in extending forms of participative governance by helping to add diversity to community representation, especially in multicultural areas.

It would be all too easy to regard this particular emergence of faith-based participation in public affairs in terms of what Peck and Tickell (2002) have termed 'little platoons . . . in the service of neo-liberal goals' (390). This critique is particularly strong in situations where faith-based organizations are seemingly drawn into welfare tasks in such a way as to suggest an abrogation of state responsibility. For example, the recent suggestion in the United Kingdom that the government is considering plans to distribute to unemployed people food vouchers redeemable at food banks across the country run by a Christian charity (The Trussell Trust) seems to represent such an abrogation (see Lewis, 2010). However as Williams et al.

(forthcoming) have argued, faith-based organizations may represent more than mere puppets of governance. Using a framework suggested by Ling (2000) and developed by May et al. (2005), the influence of faith groups beyond sheer instrumentalism can be identified in a number of domains of action: they offer a rationale for partnership on the basis of particular strengths, such as local awareness, expertise and creativity; they are inherently being accepted as an appropriate technology of governance, fit for the task of serving the marginalized; and they represent a series of appropriate subjectivities, notably suggesting good citizenship linked to charity, volunteering and active community participation. Moreover, the involvement of faith-based organizations in the rationales, technologies and subjectivities of neoliberal governance in the city seems likely to have had some inevitable impact on the shaping of 'appropriate conduct' in the city. For example, a recent account of homelessness in British cities (Cloke, May and Johnsen, 2010) suggests that U.S.-inspired narratives of revanchism, positioning homeless people as being swept up by the revengeful and profit-motivated acts of regulation and surveillance by property developers and city centre managers, need to be augmented by narratives of care, reflecting the provision of non-statutory services for homeless people. Faith-based organizations have been prominent in the establishment and performance of these landscapes of care, and are thus in some ways working to resist revanchism by modelling alternative conduct in the city.

It is important not to exaggerate the impact of this emergent role for faith-based organizations, not least because a range of other third-sector organizations have also played influential roles in the conduct and subjectivities of the city over this period. Indeed the boundary between faith-based organizations and other third-sector groups has become rather porous – a potential signal of the postsecular nature of some of these activities. Thus, the involvement of faith-based organizations in welfare provision has sometimes involved partnerships and contractual relationships that have necessitated a dilution or a 'hushing up' of the faith bases on which the organizations are founded. Indeed, there is significant evidence that some faith-based organizations have opted to become more professionally secular so as to secure a better relationship with both funders and clients (see Cloke et al., 2009). Even among those organizations which have clearly remained faith based, there has been a bifurcation into 'insider' and 'outsider' strategies (May et al., 2006). Insider organizations will accept state funding, with attendant strings attached, and may in so doing have to suppress some of the faith-motivated bases of their participation, although faith motivation often remains a strong element of how care and welfare are brought performatively into being in the operations of these organizations (see Conradson, 2003). Outsider organizations will often rely on charitable donations and volunteer labour to undertake work outside of state funding. These 'shoestring' operations can often be dismissed as amateur participants in the service and welfare infrastructure, but this positioning permits organizations more easily to escape the grip of neoliberal technologies and subjectivities, and thereby to hold onto a more explicit faith-based *raison d'etre* for their activities.

Here, then, there is some evidence of a meeting place between the *discursive* and *praxis* arenas of the postsecular; a swirl of moving-beyond-secularism in the ideological and political landscapes of the city, as faith-based and materialist narratives converge into emergent spaces of postsecular denouement. The emergence is not new per se; it notably draws in the work of an organization such as the Salvation Army which has a long-standing presence in urban service landscapes. However, new political ideas are bringing about what Connolly (1999: 185) has described as an 'overt metaphysical/religious pluralism' in public life, resulting in a 'positive engagement out of the multicultural plurality of contemporary life'. Contrary to some representations of postsecularism, this emergence does not seem to have been founded on a general return to hegemonic religious values, but rather reflects an acceptance of a plurality of religious and metaphysical perspectives in these public discourses. These postsecular rapprochements, therefore, seem to reflect a shift in the public 'secularist self-understanding' (de Vries, 2006) rather than any wholesale transformation of the secular state or the public role of religion. There is still much to be known about the conditions under which this change to secularist self-understanding is occurring. In particular, little is understood about the technologies and practices of translation which permit reflexive critiques of the secular age to interact with an openness on the part of secular organizations and people to go along with the crossover narratives that bring them into contact with, and sometimes into partnership with, faith-based groups. However, what is clear is that these conditions of postsecular possibility have opened up new spaces of opportunity for faith groups to bring their own brands of salt, light and fragrance out into the public arena, giving emphasis to praxis rather than dogma, and breaking out from being hushed up in the public sphere. Part of this opportunity seems to rest on an embrace of the demands of a postsecular faith ethics that places virtue in a new and positive relation to difference, suggesting faith action that takes the form of service and *caritas* without strings, rather than public activity that is principally geared towards conversion-oriented evangelism. It is to this shift in theo-ethics that the chapter now turns.

Moving towards faith praxis

In this section, I illustrate the theme of faith praxis through a Christian lens. Clearly the multicultural nature of the contemporary city means that any discussion of the public positioning of faith should take account of a range of different religions and a multitude of different potential shifts towards more plural theo-ethics of otherness as equality with difference in society. However, my focus here stems from research and personal experience with Christian faith groups, and a desire to understand what changes have been necessary to reconfigure Christian faith into the possibility of postsecular rapprochement. First, it is important to note that Christian faith groups recognize their position in wider societal terms. Thus, Frost notes that as a socio-political reality 'Christendom has been in decline for the last 250 years' (2006: 3) while Murray (2004) insists that the United Kingdom is currently in an age of 'post-Christendom'. This recognition that society has moved beyond Christian hegemony raises important questions about the ways in which the practice of faith in post-Christendom is changing in such a way as to contribute to emerging postsecular possibilities for rapprochement. Here I want to suggest that two trajectories – the recognition of possibilities in the invisible nature of faith and the increasing importance of praxis as a way of discovering faith ethics – are significant in understanding the role of Christian faith as an emergent public dynamic.

Part of the critique of the secular era involved recognition of its blindness towards the non-material and non-rational. Although Christian theology has been founded on aspects of the invisible spiritual, one element of the changing practice of theology in post-Christendom has been the speaking into the wider search for the possibilities of what is *invisible* rather than visible in contemporary society. Thus, there has been an increased emphasis on a faith, spirituality and religion that offer a reality beyond the visible – what Caputo (2001) calls a "hyper-real" – offering a resource and attendant narratives that in many ways eluded the rather more general and narrow-minded formulation of what was possible within secular modernity. In some respects, this reflects an invocation of post-structural theologies; Caputo argues that this hyper-real is difficult to encounter in faith which reflects what he describes as the all-knowing, God-substituting certainties of fundamentalist religion. Instead he points to the kind of faith that is a passionate not-knowing; an embrace of endless translatability between God and love, beauty, truth and justice in which faith is integrally connected with the transformability of our lives and the possibilities of a transformed future. In this depiction, faith becomes an enactment – a leap of love – into this hyper-reality; an unhinging of human powers and a drawing on invisible powers that allows faith to be 'left hanging on a prayer for the impossible' (Caputo, 2001: 136).

By this account, religious faith offers narratives which reflect the hyper-real as a portal to invisible powers and to a hope in the seemingly impossible. Such narratives chime well with the critique of the secular age, reflecting a new interest in spiritual landscapes (Dewsbury and Cloke 2009) and in the possibilities for a new sense of the sacred within the emergent postsecular, found, according to Caputo (2006), in the 'anarchic effects produced by re-sacralizing the settled secular order, disturbing and disordering the disenchanted world, producing an anarchic chasmos of odd brilliant disturbances, of gifts that spring up like magic in the midst of scrambled economies' (291). For Caputo, evidence of these leaps of love into the hyper-real can be found precisely in the involvement of faith-motivated people in serving socially marginalized people. These acts of love are in many senses impossible – how can helping to provide shelter for a few people solve problems of homelessness; how can promoting consumption of fair trade goods impact on world poverty – yet by being willing to countenance the impossible, these religious people are led to spill out their passion into situations of social, economic or political need. In the process, however, they can themselves become impossible people, capable of confusing themselves and their purposes with the person and purpose of God, and thereby sometimes compromising the freedoms of people who disagree with them. Religion can easily end up being at odds with itself, especially when leaps into the hyper-real are informed by very different theological and denominational platforms.

The second trait of an emergent public role for Christian faith is the increasing importance of *praxis* within the faith networks concerned. It is not only secularists who have grown weary of the bumper-sticker theologies and quick-fix certainties of Christian religious fundamentalism. Many people within Christian faith networks have found that an increased interest in the invisible has led to a commitment to the possibilities of ethical practice (Oakley, 2005). As Hutter (1997) suggests, many Christian faith groups are recognizing in a new way that biblical theology is inaccessible without a core horizon of practices that make sense of that theology and of the church more generally. In other words, many Christians are being encouraged to discover the meaning of their faith *as they practice it* in a triumvirate relationship between God, self and community, rather than as part of a more enclosed and cerebral relationship between God and self.

This emphasis on praxis has a number of different dimensions. First, their increasing significance has been attributed to *ethics* in the practice of faith. Clearly it is not possible to delineate *a* theo-ethics – a clear and accepted pathway from scriptural precepts to a contemporary ethics of praxis (Cloke, 2010). At the extreme, the application of different Christian theology has been problematic and regressive: over-rigid foundationalism has resulted in tyrannical and dangerous fundamentalism, while over-enthusiastic postmodernism has led to an uncompromising relativism. However, it is possible to detect a form of Christian virtue ethics emanating from a mix of tradition and immanence (see Wright, 2010), and a consequent valorization in faith networks of virtuous action both as an aspiration and as a practical goal. Milbank suggests that 'the Christian mythos is able to rescue virtue from deconstruction into violent agnostic difference' (Milbank, 2006: 380), and ethical praxis allows virtue to be positioned in a rather different, and more positive, relation to difference than has been the case hitherto in the secular era. In this way, charity can be reproduced as love and friendship, and caring can involve a creative giving and relating based upon a wish to serve rather than to proselytize (see Coles, 1997). Milbank summarizes this positioning in terms of a 'counter-ethics' of duty and virtue:

> Christian belief belongs to Christian practice and sustains its affirmations about God and creation only by repeating and enacting a metanarrative about how God speaks in the world in order to redeem it. In enacting this metanarrative, one elaborates a distinctive practice – a counter-ethics embodying a social ontology, an account of duty and virtue. (Milbank, 2006: 429)

Some of the key practices of emergent postsecular rapprochement in the contemporary city have been characterized by an enactment of these counter-ethics by faith groups seeking to enable virtue to be reconciled with difference.

A third trait of this more public role for Christian religion is the ability to inculcate *hope*, by providing narratives about the injustices and calamitous orthodoxies of the current order. In theological terms, previous tendencies to separate out eschatological and political elements of hope, and in some quarters to demonize any form of "social gospel" as unacceptably liberal and anti-evangelical, have been replaced at least in part by a move to conjoin the eschatological, the ethical and the political (Wright, 2007). As a consequence, faith groups have been heavily involved in political protest, particularly at the national level, on behalf of particular marginalized groups such as asylum seekers, impoverished children and people with debt problems (Cloke, Williams and Thomas, 2009). Hope discourses are very much part of the crossover narratives which can fuel postsecular partnership, and the hope vested in the subversive power of spiritual belief has been an emergent force in the circulation of hope discourses. Such discourses point to the possibility of the prophetic (Brueggemann, 1986; 2001) which nurtures, nourishes and evokes a consciousness and perception which is different from that of the dominant culture. They also emphasize the possibility of recognizing and engaging with spiritual interiority (Wink, 1984, 1986, 1992) – that is, diagnosing the powers inherent in the current order in terms of the spiritual inside as well as the material manifestations of the exterior (see Cloke, forthcoming). Finally, they recognize the possibility of alternative discernment; a grasp of the inner spiritual nature of the political, economic and cultural institutions of the day can lead to a rise in alternate consciousness, perception and emotion, and can enable ruptures in the seemingly hegemonic spaces of the current order, producing new lines of flight and potentially new spaces of hope. Together, these possibilities can provide narratives which help to illuminate current practices and spaces, and enable the release of new politics and poetics of postsecular resistance in the contemporary city.

I am not suggesting here any kind of totalizing transformation of religion in the United Kingdom resulting in a homogeneous positioning of faith groups in urban landscapes of postsecularism. Expressions of church, and of spiritual network, take a multitude of different forms, some of which remain doggedly traditional in their personal and private expressions of faith, while others remain wedded to an evangelical framework that resists what are sometimes regarded as 'unequally yoked' partnerships with other religions or secular concerns. There is a wide variety of faith practice in the contemporary city, much of which would not recognize, let alone deploy, narratives involving the possibilities of the hyper-real, ethical praxis or prophetic psycho-geographies, let alone Caputo's re-sacralizing of the settled order through an anarchic chaosmos of brilliant disturbance. Accordingly, any idea that the discursive and praxis arenas of postsecularism are interacting energetically in the contemporary Christian church would be a crass overstatement. It needs to be emphasized that not all faith groups are tuned into ethics of receptive generosity and unconditional service, and indeed that some such groups may reflect a continuing pursuit of controlling power over marginalized people.

What I am suggesting, however, is that there *is* an emerging current of faith-motivated activity that is able to contribute to emerging postsecular rapprochement. This current takes many forms. First, it can be seen in the activities of some large urban churches in *mainstream denominations*, in which the call to perform Christian faith in the community is both preached and practised. In these cases, there will typically be one or more 'devices' (Barnett et al., 2005) through which the meaning of being a Christian in the community is explored. In this way, faith-motivated people become involved in serving homeless people, visiting prisoners, supporting new immigrants and asylum seekers and the like, and in so doing become involved in wider projects (such as night shelters, drop-ins and soup runs in the context of homelessness – see Cloke, May and Johnsen 2010) that can exhibit postsecular characteristics. Interestingly, such participation often seems to be prompted by an application of key scriptural narratives (e.g. Matthew, ch. 15 [NIV]): 'I was a stranger and you invited me in, I needed clothes and you clothed me, I was sick and you looked after me, I was in prison and you came to visit me') that carry a particular significance in terms of the targeted recognition of the need for action in the city. Secondly, there are a range of *new expressions of church* that eschew traditional denominations and seek to embody a radically transformative theology of social engagement based on habitual social praxis. These range from the so-called 'emerging churches' (Gibbs and Bolger, 2006) to more incarnational approaches, involving the establishment of intentional Christian communities in socially marginalized areas of the city (Thomas, 2011). Thirdly, there are *faith movements beyond the church,* ranging from neo-anarchistic local movements seeking to find communal ways of living out prophetic and hope-filled praxis (see, e.g., Claiborne, 2006), to different forms of new monasticism (Wilson-Hartgrove, 2008). Emerging out of these very different contexts, it is possible to see various forms of radical faith praxis that chime well with the concerns of more secular radical politics, claiming similar ethical ground but working out of different expressions of motivation. Here, then, is the potential for a significant contribution to wider postsecular rapprochement, as the urgency of praxis allows a broader coming together of ethical values and devices through which to serve that can to some extent blur the public/private boundaries of religion and secular action. In this way, faith praxis has begun to move out into mainstream activity in such a way as to be welcomed into what was previously assumed to be secular space.

Conclusion

This chapter has identified two currents from which the swirl of postsecular rapprochement seems to be emerging in the contemporary city. First, there appear to be elements of the reflexive critique of the secular era that are enabling an appropriate foundation for a changing public consciousness about the role and positionality of religion. Not only are theological and theo-ethical references apparent in this reflexive arena, but there is a parallel political move to create space for faith-based organizations in the governance of welfare services. These elements are not directly linked causally – the niches for faith-based activity seem to stem more from neoliberal traits than from a radical political rethink of secularist society – but they are connected through crossovers between religion and secular society, both in terms of collaborative local activism, and via an increasing willingness to work with "crossover narratives" involving theo-ethical ideas about caritas and agape. Secondly, elements of religion seem to have accepted the importance of praxis as a defining *modus operandi* for the practice of faith. In some cases, such praxis involves collaboration with other faiths, or with secular groups with whom moral differences occur, yet these can be set aside at least temporarily for the greater good of *doing something* from a compatible ethical basis. Thus, the 'hushed-up' voice of religion is being gradually released back into the public sector.

Understanding how these currents work out differently in practice is an ongoing project, but it seems likely that postsecular practice will be shaped both by a societal-level search for new narratives of hope, partnership and action, and by local-level configurations of rapprochement. We need to know much more about how secular and faith-based organizations are variously willing to forsake previously fundamentalist and oppositional positionings in order to engage in rapprochement. It seems likely that such rapprochement may be easier to achieve in ethically defined sectors of care, welfare and justice than in more morally defined territories, although these arenas are often interrelated, suggesting that rapprochement may take emergent and fleeting rather than concrete and permanent forms. Emergent postsecular spaces and practices may therefore be most evident in traces, flows, fragrances and effectual tolerances, performed out of a mutual sense of theo-poetics rather than more structural political alignments. These theo-poetics point to a 'politics of becoming' (Connolly, 1999) in which new energies and lines of flight emerge from the power of powerlessness; the possibility of impossibility; and the translation of attributes such as peace, generosity, forgiveness, mercy and hospitality into everyday practices. It is in these ground-level performative politics of becoming that postsecular rapprochement may well continue to emerge in the contemporary city.

Note

1   This chapter is a significantly reworked and summarized version of a paper presented to the Religion, Politics and the Postsecular City conference, held at the University of Groningen in November 2008. That paper is published as: Cloke, P. (2010), 'Theo-ethics and Radical Faith-based Praxis in the Postsecular City', in A. Molendijk, J. Beaumont and C. Jedan (eds), *Exploring The Postsecular: The Religious, The Political and The Urban*. Leiden: Brill.

References

Badiou, A. (2001), *Ethics*. London: Verso.

Barnett, C., Cloke P., Clarke, N. and Malpass, A. (2005), 'Consuming Ethics: Articulating the Subjects and Spaces of Ethical Consumption', *Antipode* 37, 23–45.

Berger, P., Davie, G. and Fokas, E. (2008), *Religious America. Secular Europe?* Aldershot: Ashgate.

Blond, P. (1998), 'Introduction: Theology before Philosophy', in Blond, P. (ed.), *Postsecular Philosophy: Between Philosophy and Theology*. London: Routledge.

Bretherton, L. (2010), *Christianity and Contemporary Politics*. Chichester: Wiley-Blackwell.

Brueggemann, W. (1986), *Hopeful Imagination*. Philadelphia: Fortress Press.

—. (2001), *The Prophetic Imagination* (2nd edn). Minneapolis: Fortress Press.

Caputo, J. (2001), *On Religion*. London: Routledge.

—. (2006), *The Weakness of God: A Theology of the Event*. Bloomington: Indiana University Press.

Claiborne, S. (2006). *The Irresistible Revolution*. Grand Rapids MI: Zondervan.

Cloke, P. (forthcoming), Malum et bonum: emerging geographies of evil. *Cultural Geographies*.

Cloke, P., Williams, A. and Thomas, S. (2009), *Faith-based Organisations and Social Exclusion in European Cities (FACIT): UK National Report*. Exeter: University of Exeter School of Geography.

Cloke, P., May, J. and Johnsen, S. (2010), *Swept Up Lives?* Oxford: Blackwell.

Cloke, P., Barnett, C., Clarke, N. and Malpass, A. (2011), 'Faith in Ethical Consumption', in Thomas, L. (ed.) *Consumerism and Sustainability: Paradise Lost?* Basingstoke: Palgrave Macmillan.Coles, R. (1997), *Rethinking Generosity: Critical Theory and the Politics of Caritas*. Ithaca, NY: Cornell University Press.

Connolly, W. (1999), *Why I Am Not a Secularlist*. Minneapolis: University of Minnesota Press.

Conradson, D. (2003), 'Doing Organisational Space: Practices of Voluntary Welfare in the City. *Environment and Planning A* 35, 1975–1992.

Davie, G. (2007), *The Sociology of Religion*. London: Sage.

Dawkins, R. (2006), *The God Delusion*. London: Bantam Press.

De Vries, H. (2006), 'Introduction: Before, Around and Beyond the Theologico-political', in H. De Vries and L. Sullivan, L. (eds) *Political Theologies: Public Religions in a Post-Secular World*. Bronx, NY: University of Fordham Press.

Dennett, D. (2006), *Breaking the Spell: Religion as a Natural Phenomenon*. Harmondsworth: Penguin.

Derrida, J. (1996), *The Gift of Death: Religion and Postmodernism*. Chicago: Chicago University Press.

Dewsbury, J. D., and Cloke, P. (2009), 'Spiritual Landscapes: Existence, Performance and Immanence', *Social and Cultural Geography* 10, 695–711.

Dinham, A., and Lowndes, V. (2009), 'Faith and the Public Realm', in Dinham, A., Furbey, R. and Lowndes, V. (eds), *Faith In The Public Realm: Controversies, Policies and Practices*, Bristol: Policy Press.

Eagleton, T. (2009), *Reason, Faith, Revolution: Reflections on the God Debate*. New Haven, CT: Yale University Press.

Eder, K. (2006), 'Post-secularism: A Return to the Public Sphere', *Eurozine*, 17 August.

Frost M. (2006), *Exiles: Living Missionally in a Post-Christian Culture*. Peabody, MA: Hendrickson.

Gibbs, E., and Bolger, R. (2006), *Emergent Churches: Creating Christian Community in Postmodern Cultures*. London: SPCK.

Gray, J. (2008) 'The Atheist Delusion', *The Guardian* (15 March), 4–6.

Habermas, J. (2008), 'Notes on a Post-secular Society', *Signandsight.com*, 18 June, 1–23.

—. (2010), *An Awareness of What is Missing: Faith and Reason in a Post-secular Age.* Cambridge: Polity Press.

Hedges, C. (2006), *American Fascists.* New York: Free Press.

Herriot, P. (2008), *Religious Fundamentalism.* London: Routledge.

Hitchens, D. (2007), *God Is Not Great.* London: Atlantic Books.

Hutter, R. (1997), *Suffering Divine Things: Theology as Church Practice.* Grand Rapids, MI: Eerdmans.

Larner, W. (2003), 'Neoliberalism?' *Environment and Planning D: Society and Space* 21, 509–12.

Lewis, P. (2010), 'Ministers Consider Scheme to Hand Out Food Vouchers to Unemployed', *The Guardian,* 3 July 2010, 4.

Ling, T. (2000), 'Unpacking Partnership: The Case of Health Care', in D. Clarke, S. Gewirtz and E. McLaughlin (eds), *New Managerialism, New Welfare?* London: Sage.

Malpass, A., Cloke P., Barnett C. and Clarke C. (2007), 'Fairtrade Urbanism? The Politics of Place Beyond Place in the Bristol Fairtrade City Campaign', *International Journal of Urban and Regional Research* 31, 633–46.

May, J., Cloke, P. and Johnsen, S. (2005), 'Re-phasing Neo-liberalism: New Labour and Britain's Crisis of Street Homelessness', *Antipode* 37, 703–30.

—. (2006), 'Shelter at the Margins: New Labour and the Changing State of Emergency Accommodation for Single Homeless People in Britain', *Policy and Politics* 34, 711–30.

McLennan, G. (2007), 'Towards Postsecular Sociology?' *Sociology* 41, 857–70.

McLure, J. (2007), *Partial Faiths: Postsecular Fiction in the Age of Pynchon and Morrison.* Athens, GA: University of Georgia Press.

Milbank, J. (2005), 'Materialism and Transcendence', in C. Davis, J. Milbank and S. Zizek (eds), *Theology and the Political: New Debates.* Durham, NC: Duke University Press.

—. (2006), *Theology and Social Theory* (2nd edn). Oxford: Blackwell.

Murray, B. (2004), *Post-Christendom: Church and Mission in a Strange New World.* Carlisle: Paternoster.

Oakley, M. (2005), 'Reclaiming Faith', in A. Walker (ed.), *Spirituality in the City.* London: SPCK.

Peck, J., and Tickell, A. (2002), 'Neoliberalising space', *Antipode,* 34, 380–404.

Pykett, J., Cloke, P., Barnett, C., Clarke, N. and Malpass, A. (2010), 'Learning to be Global Citizens', *Environment and Planning D: Society and Space* 28, 487–508.

Schussler Fiorenza, F. (1992), 'The Church as a Community of Interpretation', in D. Browning and F. Schussler Fiorenza (eds), *Habermas, Modernity and Public Theology.* New York: Crossroad, New York.

Taylor, C. (2007), *A Secular Age.* Cambridge, MA: Belknap Press.

Thomas S. (2011, forthcoming), 'Incarnational Faith', in J. Beaumont, P. Cloke and J. Vranken (eds), *Faith, Welfare and Exclusion in European Cities.* Bristol: Policy Press.

Williams, A. Cloke, P. and Thomas, S. (forthcoming), 'Contesting co-option: faith-based organisations , social exclusion and neoliberal urban governance'.

Wills, J. (2004), 'Campaigning for Low Paid Workers: The East London Communities Organisation (TELCO) Living Wage Campaign', in W. Brown, G. Healy, E. Heery and P. Taylor (eds), *The Future of Worker Representation.* Oxford: Oxford University Press.

Wilson-Hartgrove, J. (2008), *New Monasticism: What It Has to Say to Today's Church.* Ada, MI: Brazos Press.

Wink, W. (1984), *Naming the Powers.* Minneapolis: Fortress Press.

—. (1986), *Unmasking the Powers.* Minneapolis: Fortress Press.

—. (1992), *Engaging the Powers.* Minneapolis: Fortress Press.

Wright, T. (2007), *Surprised By Hope.* London: SPCK.

—. (2010), *Virtue Reborn.* London: SPCK.

Zizek, S. (2001), *The Fragile Absolute.* London: Routledge.

Afterword: Postsecular Cities

Christopher Baker and Justin Beaumont

The time has come to review our interdisciplinary journey towards the postsecular city. Do any thematic areas of commonality emerge, or any areas of consensus as to analysis or practical engagement? Or are the different voices that speak into the postsecular city simply too distinctive and fragmentary for any sense of an overall or coherent picture to emerge? Indeed, following David Ley's cautionary note sounded in the Preface to this volume, is the very concept of the postsecular the right one by which to analyse the reconfiguring relationship between the religious and the urban as we approach the end of the first decade of the twenty-first century?

In this concluding chapter, we reflect therefore on what has emerged in the course of this volume and what we have discovered about the nature of postsecular space. This reflection will then allow us to assess the strengths and weaknesses of the concept of the postsecular city itself. We conclude by identifying some areas of future research that we see as taking the areas of debate and discovery further.

What is the nature of postsecular urban space?

During the course of this volume, it has been possible to discern three lenses by which to reflect upon the nature of the postsecular city: as a liminal space, as a formal or informal laboratory space and as an arena in which pedagogical and ethical transformation can take place. In the analysis of these spaces we make use of some of Ed Soja's work as shaping frameworks – in particular his categories of Postmetropolis and the real and imagined city. Although (as we point out), Soja has chosen not to use the presence of urban religion as a factor in the shaping of his theories, we see a potential crossover of his thinking with several of the debates that have emerged in the course of this volume.

The postsecular city as liminal space

The journey from the familiar to the unfamiliar

The postsecular city might well be conceived as part of a wider liminal space in which we, as urban citizens collectively, embark upon a journey from one threshold to the next. In terms of Western experience, we have now largely left behind the fixed 'security' of the industrial town or city, with its carefully demarcated zones based on class and status: the workers in the terrace housing (often verging on slums) closest to the factories; the foremen with their slightly larger housing; the middle management with their bay windows and gardens; and the factory owners in their villas on the hills, breathing in the clean air and with the pleasant views over the rolling landscape. Of course, as Engels (2008/1892) pointed out as early as the 1840s with regard to this new form of spatial arrangement, at least in the Manchester of the time, the growing inequalities enshrined in the modern industrial metropolis, founded on the principles of rationality, efficiency and technological advance, made it a 'hypocritical' city (1892: 47). It allowed the middle and upper class (or the bourgeoisie), cocooned in their safe and pleasant enclaves, and shielded by the facades of shops and businesses on the main routes into the industrial areas, to rarely witness, and therefore conveniently forget, the horrors of the modern capitalist system. But at least, despite the often squalid conditions in which the working class lived, one could derive a great sense of strength and pride from knowing that one belonged to a collective. And there was a sense of security to be derived from the knowledge that one was an integral part of a dense tapestry of social connections and cultural norms that had evolved around specific 'urban village' locations with their own strong sense of identity. See, for example, Anthony Rea's anthology (1988) of first-hand accounts of the experiences of Manchester's Italian community in the industrial suburb of Ancoats (or Little Italy as it was dubbed) in the late eighteenth and early nineteenth centuries.

Of course, a steady erosion of these social connections has occurred since the 1950s and 1960s with the decanting of the urban poor into new towns and peripheral housing estates in the name of modernist planning efficiency. This spatial disruption to communities was compounded by the inexorable process of de-industrialization in the West during the 1970s and 1980s. By the early 1990s, a new urban form was beginning to emerge, with the appearance of the post-industrial city, synonymous with the postmodern city of glass and iconic/ironic design, predicated on the virtues of hypermobility, experience (or affect – see Thrift 2008), innovation, information, knowledge transfer, and consumption. British theologian Graham Ward, in a coruscating critique of the 'postmodern cities of desire' points to the shifting rootlessness of the contemporary urban environment in which apparent transparency only serves to occlude the dynamics of power and makes it difficult (in contrast to the old industrial city) to know where one is placed – indeed, how one should place oneself.

In ambitious city halls around the world, in our electronic global age, the image they wish to impress upon the city is of a city comparable to Oz, or some eternal city of glass and halogen uplighting. The contemporary successful city is measured to how close it can approximate to the clean and radiant cities, cities without shadows – transparent, controlled, reliable, efficient, culturally interesting and diverse . . . Contemporary cities encapsulate the [following] analysis . . . That democracy is fashioned around a void, a space left empty with the disappearance of the king, a space that the sovereignty of the people can not fill because 'the people' is too ambiguous and nebulous a figure to occupy that space. . . . there is no focus for the city's power other than its own brand. (Ward, 2009: 216)

Postsecular cities and the fourth urban revolution

So all of us have been disorientated by the shift from the industrial to the post-industrial city – we have entered a liminal space and not yet passed through to reach a firm threshold on the other side. In this sense, we are reminded of Ed Soja's work on the Postmetropolis (2000) – the new and still emerging urban form that is arising out of the demise of the industrial, modern city.

In this speculative but interesting theory, Soja develops the idea that the geo-history of urbanization has passed through three phases, or revolutions, over the course of the past 11,000 years. The first he claims took place in the upland regions of Southwest Asia and led to 'the initial urban-based invention of full-scale agriculture'. The second revolution emerges some five millennia later from the alluvial lowlands of the Fertile Crescent and represents 'the formulation of the city–state and the city-based empire'. The third emerges after another gap of five millennia or so within the emerging Industrial Revolution of Western Europe, and forms 'the foundation of a specifically urban-industrial capitalism'. Finally (and after a period of mere 150 years or so), Soja raises the question of whether, after a period of 'intensive urban restructuring' since the 1970s we are passing into the fourth urban revolution – what he characterizes as his Postmetropolis (Soja, 2000: xv).

We are aware of the tendency of meta-theorists such as Soja to present urban trends in very definitive terms. Nevertheless we consider that certain elements of Soja's analytical framework, which he begins to unpack in terms of his discussion (after Sandercock) on notions of Cosmopolis (2000: 189–229) have a resonance in postsecular space. Thus, with reference to the work of postcolonial theorists such as Arjun Appadurai, Benedict Anderson, Gayatri Spivak, Homi Bhabha and drawing on his earlier work (1996) on the contribution of feminist and womanist geographers and theorists (such as bell hooks, Gillian Rose and Kirsten Ross), Soja talks about the importance of the creation spaces of reterritorialization. If deterritorialization involves 'the breaking down of the Fordist worlds of production . . . and the long-standing political and discursive hegemony of the nation–state' (2000: 212), then reterritorialization 'is the critical response to globalization and post-Fordist restructuring'. It involves 'generating new efforts by individuals and collectivities, cities and regions . . . as a means of resisting and/ or adapting to the contemporary condition' (2000: 212). It is in these acts of reterritorialization that 'the most progressive social movements in the future are likely to be found', and where, in echoes of Homi Bhabha's work, the Third Space is to be found, that 'enables other positions to emerge and sets up new structures of authority, new political initiatives' (2000: 211).

Towards the end of his book *Postmetropolis*, Soja sees hope, or at least 'new beginnings' (2000: 409) in 'innovative forms of urban confederalism', which include closer collaboration between local and regional governance bodies and include coalitions of 'NGOs . . . Labour Unions, philanthropic institutions, more progressive regional councils and religious organizations, and other active units of civil society' (2000: 410). So it is that Soja's ideas concerning spatial justice (a theme more fully developed in later work – 2010) based on emerging ideas of hybridity, moments of encounter, mutual learning and diversity have a resonance with what we have discovered in postsecular urban space.

Frictionless and frictioned spaces

Soja characterizes Postmetropolis as an increasingly random and sprawling ecology in which is contained a whole series of spatially proximate but culturally and economically distanced 'spaces' within an increasingly disconnected 'mosaic'. These spaces can be labelled (after Jameson, 1991) as either frictionless or deeply frictioned.

The *frictionless* spaces of time–space compression are for Soja the milieu of technology (e.g. universities and business parks) and consumption (shopping malls and exurban leisure hubs) and the gated urban sprawl of the edge cities or city centres where the creative or supercreative class (Florida, 2002) of entrepreneurs, designers and innovators live. It is also the increasingly immiserated space where the management class seek to keep a toe hold in the real estate havens of the neo-urbanist suburbs in the face of mounting costs, working longer hours and increased commuting (Soja, 2000: 262–3)

The spaces of *friction* are what Soja (after Davis, 1990) calls the 'fractal' cities, the hyper-ghettoes or anti-ghettoes (Wacquant, 2008) – those spaces of inner-urban decay and conflict where the poor (or drone or excluded class) are trapped in vicious cycles of economic decline, worsening public housing stock and growing criminalization. Into these indigenous poor communities without the skills to compete in the global capital market comes the global migrant, (the Other) from a different culture, religion and language, and who is seen as a competitor for jobs, housing and other public services. The Other is also seen as a threat to cultural identity and homogeneity, especially (but not restricted to them) by those white descendants of original working class communities (see Elaine Graham and Andrew Davey's chapter in this volume). These then are the spaces of friction and bifurcation, but which are increasingly disconnected and free-floating in the amorphous form of the Postmetropolis.

The religious dimensions of postmetropolis

It is worth speculating as to how Soja might now rewrite his geohistory of the past 11,000 years in the light of early twenty-first-century urban experience. On the basis of the evidence gathered so far in this volume, he would now have to include the emergence of the postsecular city as a major contour of his Postmetropolis.

As we have already intimated, a large omission (in retrospect) is the lack of any sustained religious critique and discussion as part of a mapping of the Postmetropolis by Soja. If there had been this dimension, then Soja would have been far more attuned to the religious dimension of *frictioned* space in which the lived urban environment is a battleground for cultural and ideological control. For example, in this volume we have seen how religion and religious identity has profoundly affected the way people view and contest urban space, in, for example, Jerusalem (Tovi Fenster), and in the East End of London (John Eade).

But had Soja also been aware of the spiritual and religious reenchantment taking place in Postmetropolis, then he could have seen how religion is also not only mutating into, but contributing to, *frictionless* space by astutely mimicking the urban design and flows of product and communication created by neoliberal global capitalism. So for example, mega-churches in cities such as Singapore and Sydney effortlessly embed themselves into the leisure event/shopping mall nexus of the postmodern global city (as described for this volume by Robbie Goh). He would also have been aware of the 'spiritual' reappropriation of the concept of the land as 'landscape' (as a commodity held in trust for the benefit of both human and non-human actors) which is becoming increasingly significant in urban and community development projects. So for example the contested battle to preserve the sacred value of land around both public planning and university-based development schemes (as described by Leonie Sandercock and Maged Senbel) reflects the often hidden story of how spirituality becomes part of localized resistance against the appropriation of space for profit by the fluid ubiquity of global investment strategies. Within our understanding of the postsecular city as a liminal space we have seen how both frictionless and frictioned spaces have been created by the persistent, mutating and re-emerging presence of religion and spirituality in our contemporary urban form.

The only problem with defining postsecular space as a liminal space, part of the Postmetropolis landscape, is that no one has chosen to undertake this journey voluntarily. No one has chosen to enter this liminal space in order to undertake a rite of passage and emerge from the journey transformed into something else. Indeed a fundamental tension lies at the heart of this volume. It is the tension between Soja's Postmetropolis and its potential religion, liminality, fluidity, hybridity, interaction, moments of encounter, exchange, learning and reconciliation of difference, with wider concerns of metanarratives within social science about the postsecular. This collection heralds in our mind the beginning of an important debate about not just the future of urban studies (geography, planning, sociology etc.) but also how we reconcile the Other, difference, politics of identity with a grand scheme of integration under conditions of rampant global neoliberalism. This unknown journey has shaken everyone out of their preferred comfort zone, where all they had to do was deal with perceived realities from the unshakeable certainty of their preferred world view (either religious or secular). And because there is no specific reason for choosing to enter the postsecular city (it has happened around us so to speak) there is no clear sense of what the finished product will look like – how will we know when we have arrived?

Well of course, the answer is we won't. As Leonie Sandercock says of *Cosmopolis*, (the postcolonial city of diversity and plurality) '. . . [it is] my imagined Utopia, a construction site of the mind, a city/ region in which there is a genuine connection with, and respect and space for, the cultural Other' (Sandercock, 1998: 125). However, as Sandercock points out, the crucial difference between her 'imagined' utopia and the physical, technocratic utopias envisaged by the modernist planners of the twentieth century is that 'it can never be realised, but must always be in the making' (Sandercock, 1998: 163). We think that these references to a 'construction site of the mind' and a city/society 'always in the making' could also double as an apt description of the postsecular city as well. It grasps the essential fluidity and unknowability of the project, as well as those dimensions that aspire to more utopian planning and governance. This is a theme we will explore in more detail in relation to the idea of the real and imagined city.

The postsecular city as laboratory

The reference to Sandercock's view of *Cosmopolis* as 'always in the making – a [perpetual] construction site of the mind' also resonates with ideas of experimentation. The idea of experiment leads us (more positively perhaps) to conceive of the postsecular city as a form of laboratory in which urban social actors from all disciplines and perspectives see the new blurring of space between religious and secularizing forces as not something to be feared, but as something to be embraced. These social actors come to see the postsecular city, in its perpetual liminality, as a space for risk taking and experimentation (see Anni Greve's chapter for an historical elaboration of this theme). They see it as an opportunity to learn new practices and develop new identities that are broadly successful and functional in shaping and defining a new urban space. Part of the conditions for this laboratory type setting have been created by government, and its social policy and welfare agenda of encouraging faiths to be more directly involved in the delivery of public services (such as social care and education) and experiments in multi-level governance. This dimension has been explored in the chapters offering discussion and debate on the current state of play between faith-based organizations and secular urban government in Europe with regard to contributions to public life and policy (see Nynke de Witte and Greg Ashworth's chapters in this volume).

The ambiguous, verging on the controversial, dimensions of this relationship between government and faith have been well rehearsed by ourselves and others (Molendijk et al., 2010; Baker, 2009; Beaumont 2004, 2008a, 2008b). Is the appeal by the state/market to faith groups to become key political players (under the guise of a narrative of declining stocks of social capital in materialistically sated and neoliberal political economies), a cynical ploy to co-opt their predisposition to provide help and succour for narrow political and economic ends? Or does the postsecular society offer a genuine loosening of praxis and discourse such that faith groups can offer an authentic counter-narrative and alternative to out-worn technologies of volunteering, welfare and community development? Or is the reality somewhere in between? That the postsecular city is primarily a pragmatic environment rather than an ideological one, and that both religious and non-religious partners are mature enough to recognize that the complexity and entrenched nature of the common problems facing urban societies (poverty, inequality, environmental degradation, terrorism, environmental threat etc.) are beyond the skill and resources of either to meet on their own. Do we therefore face a genuine recognition of the need for a constructive debate, sharing ideas and resources within a symbiotic or synchronistic dialogue that talks at the level of meta-ethical and metaphysical outcomes, as well as material and short-term considerations?

To be sure we are raising more questions here than posing answers. But there is at any rate certainly evidence that the postsecular city is creating new spaces of *rapprochement* between religious and non-religious social actors (see Paul Cloke's chapter) which have the flavour of informal experimentation, rather than the more formalized schemes dictated and brought into being by government policy and funding. However, it is also equally the case that the apparently more open and dynamic ethos of the postsecular city still refuses to address deep-seated issues of exclusion and control – the postfeminist, postsecular city for example, has done little to create more public and free spaces for women to participate in and enjoy the city, and for women of faith in particular (a case persuasively argued in this volume by Clara Greed).

Either way, what cannot be denied is that major policy initiatives in the United Kingdom (and their equivalents in most other European States) such as the Third Way, and now the Big Society, see religion as a vital component (or ingredient) in the successful recipe for the good city (cf. Amin, 2006). Secular governments' experimentation with religion sees no sign of abating in the near future.

The postsecular city as space of ethical transformation – in search of the real *and* imagined city

A strong undercurrent running through this volume has been how the emergence of the postsecular city has precipitated a return to the discourse on values, virtues and ethics. Since the publication of Alasdair Macintyre's rallying thesis in his book *After Virtue* which called into question the sustainable basis of social interaction located purely within an Enlightenment materialist utilitarianism, many commentators and philosophers appear to agree that much has been lost by a denuded and immanentist language. This language denies ontological debates into the nature and persistence of Evil (for example) a proper rigour and depth (see Gregor McLennan's chapter for an overview of these debates). However, an even more significant undercurrent has been how the reemergence of the 'virtue' debate has opened up the possibility of the rapprochement between religious and non-religious social actors hinted at earlier. This move towards rapprochement has opened up the possibility of not only creating new spaces of praxis but, more crucially perhaps, new spaces of dialogue. In Chapter 2 of this volume, under the terms of a 'dialectical understanding of cultural secularization' (Habermas, 2006), we noted the importance of allowing religiously inspired discourse to enter the public square. Because this discourse is connected to a transcendent rather than immanent plane or plateau (a lá Deleuze, 1987) it prefers to speak of the possibility of change and transformation that is both personal and communal, both material and immaterial. In this religiously derived discourse, we find the language of sin, repentance, forgiveness, grace – and in some expressions – judgement. To enter this new public space, in which this discourse is now said to be valid, is to be prepared to be cognitively and emotionally, as well as ethically, changed (irrespective of religious or secular orientation) or at least altered in some way. This expresses powerfully the pedagogical potential of the postsecular public space, which if allowed to develop in mature and mutually inclusive ways, is likely to generate a more sustainable Big Society than that which is currently the case within UK government thinking (see Rachael Chapman and Leila Hamaleinen's chapter on the important struggles that lie ahead in this respect).

Much of the pedagogical and ethical drive described above, as generated by the postsecular city, is figuratively and suggestively pre-empted in the search for what Soja has called the real *and* imagined city (emphasis ours). This category of Soja's thinking about the future of the city derives from his prior work on the Thirdspace (1996) (which in some ways brings us back full circle to the idea of the postsecular city as liminal space) and which is heavily influenced by the work of Henri Lefebvre. Lefebvre in his ground-breaking book *The Production of Space* (1991) was keen to enrich the hegemony of modernist linear philosophy and Marxist dialectical thought (which favoured historical and social analyses) by giving a proper priority to the spatial, thus creating a three-dimensional framework for social critical analysis. Lefebvre referred to this triangulation of the historical, the social and the spatial as a triple dialectic. Via this triple dialectic, Lefebvre devises a three-fold typology of space:

1. Perceived space (*espace percu*) is the materialized, socially produced space that is directly sensible and open to accurate empirical measurement and description. In other words it is Spatial Practice. Under Soja's rebranding of Lefebvre's triple dialect (what Soja calls trialectics) this is the First Space.
2. Conceived space (*espace concu*) is the conceptualised space of sociology – the space of scientists, planners, urbanists, technocratic subdividers. It is therefore also related to the production of space because of the order and design that creators of this space impose – it is space that is created by the control of knowledge, signs and codes. These representations of space are Soja's Second Space.
3. Lefebvre's Third Space is lived space (*espace vecu*) which encompasses the previous two because it represents the 'clandestine or hidden side of social life'. This category of analysis attempts (unlike *espace percu*) to emphasize the 'partial unknoweability, the mystery and secretiveness, the non-verbal subliminity of space of representations'. This is space as it is directly lived and deciphered by artists, writers and philosophers, rather than analysed by social scientists. This deciphering is subversive but also creative in the sense that it overlays physical space with symbolic representations. By combining the power of both *the real and the imagined,* these lived spaces of representation are thus creative counter spaces – spaces of resistance to the dominant order of controlled and signed space – and they usually emerge from the periphery and the margin. As Soja himself comments, 'with its radical openness and its teeming imagery, this third space of Lefebvre closely approximates what I am defining as Thirdspace.' (Soja, 1996: 66–8) (italics ours)

Despite the rather abstract nature of Lefebvre's neo-Marxist spatial analysis, we believe that religious individuals and groups will largely warm to the following elements of Soja's Thirdspace reformulation of it. First, there is the broad commitment to pursue urban justice and encourage the transformation of spatialities into more just and inclusive spaces of production and representation. The various lines of critical enquiry on and ethico-political engagement for social and spatial justice strike a chord here. Slogans such as the right to the city and the just city have much to gain from a broadening of the conceptual and practical apparatus to include secular, humanist and faith groups in their analyses. Second a potential for a shared ethical commitment to ideas of 'the commons' or the common good (see Amin, 2006). Finally, Soja's concept of the 'real *and* the imagined city' is deeply attractive to religious groups in particular, because it allows them to engage at two levels simultaneously.

On the first level, engagement with the 'real' city reflects their proactive concern with the local communities in which they live. As has been related in several of our chapter contributions, faith groups are a vital component of active social care and even political mobilization within the urban spaces they inhabit. And in many cases, they are the only institutions capable of engaging with the most marginalized and disenfranchised sectors of the population.

However the idea of the 'imagined city', with Lefebvre's and Soja's explicit references to a better alternative society that lies both within and beyond the present urban order, will resonate with the deeply held theological visions of change and transformation held by several religious groups. Indeed this volume has been an attempt to create an equal interaction between theology and critical urban geography and social science on an equal footing, not privileging the one over the other, but creating an environment in which mutual learning and recognition can perhaps take place. This series of visions, for example, reflected in utopian scenarios within the Christian tradition, of the City of God, prepared as a bride, coming down out of heaven, presents a powerful vision of the city which is both physically beautiful (as an environment) but also morally beautiful – as a space of openness, tolerance and justice in which the nations of the world can gather and live in peace, and suffering and even death will be no more. As the book of Revelation describes it:

> Then the angel showed me the river of the water of life, bright as crystal, flowing from the throne of God and of the Lamb, through the middle of the street of the city. On either side of the river is the tree of life with its twelve kinds of fruit, producing its fruit each month; and the leaves of the tree are for the healing of the nations. (Book of Revelation 22: 1–2)

These spiritually imagined visions of the perfect city/urban society including those from the Hebrew prophetic traditions (see Micah ch. 4 vv.1–4; Zechariah ch. 14 vv. 16–19 and Isaiah ch. 56 vv. 1–8) provide a powerful source of motivation and energy for engagement of faith groups within urban contexts. It is part of the 'spiritual' capital that creates the ethical and affectual impulse for the practical contributions faith groups are often prepared to make to the well-being of the wider communities in which they live (see Baker, 2009 for a full discussion of the concept of religious and spiritual capital).

The postsecular city as concept – strengths and limitations

So far we have suggested three 'lenses' or 'co-ordinating spatial perspectives' through which we might analyse the postsecular city that have emerged directly from the chapter contributions for this volume: the liminal, the laboratory and the rediscovery of ethical principles. However, in each of these categories we have acknowledged the ambivalence of these perspectives. In so many ways, new and exciting spaces and places (both physical, ethical and spiritual) have been opened up. It is as though religion has replaced class in the postsecular city as the liberative hermeneutic ('religious citizens of the world unite') for a brighter future. And yet in other ways, fault lines associated with religious identity have also been exacerbated and strengthened, deeply dividing communities and creating unease bordering on fear and suspicion for many living in the city. It is now time to briefly review whether the concept of the postsecular city is the most appropriate tool by which to analyse the reconfiguring relationship between the religious and the urban described within this volume.

The concept of the postsecular city is probably most effective as a synonym for describing the extraordinarily persistent and innovatively mutating presence of religion in postmodern, late capitalist cities in the West. As David Ley has pointed out in his Preface, even in the secular cities of the West, religion never went away – churches and mission centres have continued to minister to the suburbs and the inner-urban areas from the early nineteenth century to the present, despite their official removal by the State from the technologies of European social welfare after the Second World War. Meanwhile, the first British mosque in the United Kingdom was founded in Liverpool by the English convert, William Abdullah Quiliam in 1889. And of course, for many new mega-cities and city regions in the South, religion never disappeared either, but is continuing to have, via its role as a medium for renewed nationalism as well as a catalyst for neoliberal economic development (see Robbie Goh's chapter for this volume), an even stronger presence in urban spaces in these regions. As Anni Greve has reminded us, the Weberian narrative of the decline of (public) religion from the late medieval to the modern period is a deceptively simplistic one. Religion has been present and active in the both the Western and the Eastern city in the past four or five hundred years, but is now very much to the fore in our postmodern times in ways that are both new and unfamiliar as well as ways that are traditional and familiar.

The generic strength of the postsecular city concept therefore is that it has encouraged such a wide variety of disciplines (but especially human geography, sociology of religion, political philosophy and theology) to re-examine the traditional interaction between urbanism and religion in the early twenty-first century. As a concept it usefully covers not just the spatial, but also the political and cultural dynamics of our contemporary cities, shaped by the processes of globalization and postcolonialism. The concept of the postsecular city has identified and given a new parameter to this liminal and laboratory-type space in which new discourses and collaborative praxis concerning the nature and telos of the twenty-first century city can be debated and examined.

It is however the generic inclusivity of this concept (albeit from Western, post-Enlightenment roots) that is also the source of its limitations. In order to move the debate on, we firmly believe that the concept of the postsecular city needs to be broken down into a series of discrete and contextually specific areas, which are nevertheless linked because they all shed light on the evolving relationship between religion and urban spatialities. We are aware of at least seven areas for future international research and analysis that would fit the criteria of these connected but discrete enquiries into the nature of the postsecular city. These areas are as yet a speculative, rather than an exhaustive list:

1. The global rise in Pentecostalism and its decisive shift towards social justice, civil society and community development paradigms of urban engagement often in preference to their more traditional individually focused prosperity gospel approach. In many places they are replacing older, established Christian churches as the preferred partner for social welfare and public service provision.
2. The role of religious identity in providing a vehicle for local communal politics in contested urban spaces of diversity and scarce resource (e.g. Mumbai or Jerusalem), but also as moral framework for providing the search for reconciliation.
3. The role of spirituality and religion in the search for the immaterial (prompted in part by fear of natural or urban catastrophe, e.g. acts of mass terrorism, or economic insecurity) which is now global in scope (see especially in Western Europe, post-Soviet and Anzac nations, China, India, North America).
4. The deployment of religion in narratives of nation-building and the remoralizing of societies in the face of economic crisis and downturn, social disruption and mass migration.
5. The role of religion in diasporic home-making and identity-formation for those immigrating to other continents in search of work and a new life, or displaced by global catastrophe.
6. The role of religions in social justice narratives and the common search for the Good City (i.e. examples of religious and secular rapprochement and partnership) and in particular the role of religions in general and radical faith based praxis more specifically in the quest for the right to the city and the just city.
7. The role of religion in embodying and thus endorsing certain types of political economy within global cities (e.g. the Sharia-inflected Islamic neo-liberal capitalism of Arabic Gulf States, such as Dubai and Abu Dhabi, in comparison to other Islamic political economies).

It may well be that overlapping themes and experiences from these discrete areas of enquiry into the postsecular will emerge in the future. It is also reasonably clear to us that a concept derived from Western, post-Enlightenment debates about the so-called crisis in secularism and modernism, and innovatively applied to the analysis of the urban is likely to be an important marker for new debate but ultimately an inadequate and somewhat unsophisticated tool by which to map and analyse the persistent and mutating influence between religion and twenty-first-century cities across the world as a whole. Future research and theorization might therefore need to shift from the study of postsecular cities per se to the postsecular analysis of cities. Such a shift would suggest that the postsecular is not only a lens for reinterpreting cities and their diversities, it becomes a methodological and theoretical challenge for new ways of seeing what until now we have been looking at but not really SEEING. Those secularly inflected tools and methods that have up to now attempted to map our diverse and plural cities (postcolonial theory, multicultural theory, equalities and human rights theory) now perhaps seem too 'behind the curve' to really map and analyse what is really going on in our increasingly urbanised world. Do we now not also need an analytical tool or framework called the postsecular? We are in effect, waking up to the realities of the twenty-first-century diverse, liminal, fluid, dangerous, beautiful, exciting, divided and religiously imbued city of global neoliberalism.

We believe that our volume, and the *Exploring the Postsecular: the religious the political and urban* (Molendijk et al., 2010) that precedes it, when taken together, herald a new beginning. The time is nigh for serious retheorization of cities that combines the power of political economy with religion in the analysis of global neoliberal urbanism and its radical and just alternatives.

References

Amin, A. (2006), 'The Good City', *Urban Studies* 43 (5–6), 1009–23.

Baker, C. (2009), 'Blurred Encounters? Religious Literacy, spiritual capital and language', in A. Dinham et al. (eds), *Faith in the Public Realm: Controversies, Policies and Practices*. Bristol: Policy Press.

Beaumont, J. R. (2004), 'Workfare, Associationism and the "Underclass" in the United States: Contrasting Faith-based Action on Urban Poverty in a Liberal Welfare Regime', in H. Noordegraaf and R. Volz (eds), *European Churches Confronting Poverty: Social Action against Social Exclusion*. Bochum: SWI Verlag.

—. (2008a). 'Introduction: Faith-based Organizations and Urban Social Issues', *Urban Studies* 45 (10), 2011–17.

—. (2008b), 'Faith Action on Urban Social Issues', *Urban Studies* 45 (10), 2019–34.

Davis, M. (1990), *City of Quartz: Excavating the Future of Los Angeles*. London: Verso.

Deleuze, G., and Guattari, F. (1987), *A Thousand Plateaus*. London: Continuum.

Engels, F. (2008), *The Condition of the Working Class in England in 1844*. New York: Cosimo (a facsimile of the 1892 English edition).

Florida, R. (2002), *The Rise of the Creative Class and How It's Tranforming Work, Leisure, Community and Everyday Life*. New York: Basic Books.

Habermas, J. (2006). 'Religion in the Public Sphere', *European Journal of Philosophy* 14, 1–25.

Jameson, F. (1991), *Postmodernism or the Cultural Logic of Late Capitalism.* London: Verso.

Lefebvre, H. (1991), *The Production of Space.* Oxford: Blackwell.

MacIntyre, A. (1981), *After Virtue: A Study in Moral Theology.* Notre Dame, IN: Notre Dame University Press.

Molendijk, A. L., Beaumont, J. and Jedan, C. (eds) (2010), *Exploring the Postsecular: The Religious, the Political and the Urban.* Leiden: Brill.

Rea, A. (1988), *Manchester's Little Italy.* Manchester: Neil Richardson Publications.

Sandercock, L. (1998), *Towards Cosmopolis: Planning for Multicultural Cities.* Chichester: John Wiley.

Soja, E. (1996), *Thirdspace: Journeys to Los Angeles and Other Real-and-Imagined Places.* Oxford: Blackwell.

—. (2000), *Postmetropolis: Critical Studies of Cities and Regions.* Oxford: Blackwell.

—. (2010), *Seeking Spatial Justice.* Minneapolis: University of Minnesota Press.

Wacquant, L. (2008), *Urban Outcasts: A Comparative Sociology of Advanced Marginality.* Cambridge: Polity Press.

Ward, G. (2009), *The Politics of Discipleship: Becoming Postmaterial Citizens.* London: SCM Press.

General Index

Index of Names

10449949R0

Made in the USA
Lexington, KY
25 July 2011